Retailing in the 21st Century

Manfred Krafft • Murali K. Mantrala
Editors

Retailing in the 21st Century

Current and Future Trends

Second Edition

 Springer

Editors

Professor Dr. Manfred Krafft
Universität Münster
Institute of Marketing
Am Stadtgraben 13-15
48143 Münster
Germany
mkrafft@uni-muenster.de

Professor Murali K. Mantrala, PhD
University of Missouri - Columbia
College of Business
438 Cornell Hall
Columbia, MO 65211
USA
mantralam@missouri.edu

ISBN 978-3-540-72001-0   e-ISBN 978-3-540-72003-4
DOI 10.1007/978-3-540-72003-4
Springer Heidelberg Dordrecht London New York

Library of Congress Control Number: 2009942782

Cover design: WMXDesign GmbH, Germany

Printed on acid-free paper

Springer is part of Springer Science+Business Media (www.springer.com)

Foreword to the Second Edition

Eckhard Cordes

Chief Executive Officer of METRO Group

The world of retailing continues to change rapidly. Major changes since the publication of the first edition of this book include (1) the takeoff of RFID-based technology, (2) the world's growing recognition of environmental and climate change problems, and (3) the retailing revolutions in emerging markets, especially in Eastern Europe, China and India. METRO Group has continued to take a leadership role in all these areas.

Specifically, in collaboration with its partners under the METRO Group Future Store Initiative, METRO Group opened in 2008 a new and larger "Future Store" demonstrating the use of advanced retailing technologies. In 2007, METRO Group completed a major step in the nation-wide operational rollout of the Radio Frequency Identification (RFID) technology to 180 Metro Cash & Carry and Real stores in Germany as well as to the central warehouses of METRO Group Logistics. Since then merchandise deliveries at these locations can be recorded automatically. The remaining locations will be converted during this year. This is the largest operational rollout of this technology in the European retail sector.

Next, long before global concerns about environmental and climate change became front-page news, METRO Group had been following deliberate *greener retailing* policies for several years. The central element of these activities is the continuous optimization of the Group's energy management. Already in late 2004, the Energy and Technology Department of METRO Group Asset Management started to systematically identify energy saving opportunities within the Group, e.g., the use of the latest solar technology in Metro Cash & Carry stores in Vietnam. Store locations with an exceptionally high energy consumption and expense are subject to local assessment analyses. This has led to significant energy rehabilitation measures at different locations. For example, changes in the venting system at the Metro Cash & Carry location Walzmühle Ludwigshafen in Germany drastically reduced the local energy consumption and brought down carbon dioxide emissions by about 800 tons per year. More recently, after several positive pilot studies, plans for a Group-wide changeover from conventional coolants to environmentally sound alternatives are underway. Improved logistics models are also guaranteeing more energy-efficient, less polluting, as well as lower-cost distribution of merchandise to 2,200 locations operated by the METRO Group. Consequently, METRO Group was the first German retail company to publish its carbon footprint in 2008.

Lastly, internationalization remains an important thrust of METRO Group's strategy. Recently, the METRO Group opened its first Metro Cash & Carry wholesale center in the Pakistan metropolis of Lahore. Thus, the company is now represented in a total of 32 countries – with Metro Cash & Carry alone running operations in 29 countries. The METRO Group today is the most international retail and wholesale company in the world and is strongly committed to being an economic stronghold and change agent in important emerging markets. In this vein I am pleased to see the second edition of the book including a new chapter on the growth of modern retail formats in India, where Metro Cash & Carry has a significant presence.

To improve contemporary retailing's public image, enhance the knowledge of its practitioners, and stimulate further retailing research, there is a great need for a reader that combines basic information as well as an overlook on current trends and issues in the world of trade. I believe that the second edition of *Retailing in the 21st Century – Current and Future Trends* effectively meets these objectives. The first edition has sold over 3,000 copies and has been or will be translated into other languages including Russian, Ukrainian, and Korean. I am sure the second edition will do as well and reach more corners of the global retailing world.

The editors of this book have successfully brought together an impressive list of 48 authors who include industry experts and leading academic scholars from Europe, the United States, Australia, and India. In the 26 chapters of this unique book, these experts share their knowledge and insights about diverse topics ranging from retailing trends around the world to retailing strategies, marketing, operations, and human resource management. In particular, the book provides valuable information on recent developments in marketing and technology in retailing, including RFID, electronic price tags, digital advertising displays, self check-out systems, personal selling assistants, and smart kiosks. The expert authors describe how these technologies affect consumer behavior, employee behavior, and competitive behavior. They also look ahead into the near future of retailing.

I find the combination of insights from practitioners as well as from scientists one of the major strengths of this book, leading to interesting blends of practical and academic knowledge. I am especially pleased to see the addition of a new chapter on retail entrepreneurship that tells the story of Leopold Stiefel – one of the co-founders of Media Markt and Saturn and a 'master retailer' from our own Group. Overall, I believe that practitioners as well as academics will strongly benefit from this book and find it stimulating and thought-provoking. Examples of best practice in retailing and most recent findings from academic research convey interesting insights into current and future trends.

As the Chief Executive Officer of METRO Group, I am glad to see the publication of the second edition of the book *Retailing in the 21st Century: Current and Future Trends* edited by Manfred Krafft and Murali Mantrala. METRO Group helped realize the first edition of this book project and is delighted to support the second edition. This book will continue to be required reading in our internal management development programs.

Eckhard Cordes   Duesseldorf, August 2009

Chief Executive Officer of METRO Group

Acknowledgments for the Second Edition

The success of the first edition of "Retailing in the 21st century" has exceeded expectations. It was sold out very quickly, and has been adopted by retail executives and scholars around the world. This expanded second edition of the book now includes two new chapters on the role of retail entrepreneurs and on retailing in India. With regard to the first of these new chapters, we gratefully acknowledge the contribution of Leopold Stiefel, the founder of Media Markt and one of Europe's most successful retail entrepreneurs, who shared his insights with us in an extended personal interview. We are also grateful to our two new and our 44 original contributors for their inputs towards bringing out this second edition. We are also pleased with the continuing support from the METRO Group, and thank its Chief Executive Officer Eckhard Cordes for contributing the Foreword to the second edition. Last but not least, we are indebted to our publisher Springer for their continuing strong support and encouragement for this book.

Manfred Krafft
University of Muenster, Germany

Murali K. Mantrala
University of Missouri, Columbia, USA

Acknowledgments for the First Edition

Before we started on this project in late 2003, we were unaware of the huge investments of time and effort that go into editing a book. We naïvely thought that you simply ask some colleagues to cover certain topics, wait for their chapters being submitted on time, do some editing and send the whole material to the publisher. Now we know better ...! Since the authors who contributed to this book are either top executives or among the world's leading retailing academics with many demands on their time, our tight deadlines for submitting first drafts of the chapters, peer reviews of all manuscripts and final revisions of the contributions got challenged quite frequently. Throughout, however, there was remarkable enthusiasm for this project shown by all our contributors, and we are gratified by their dedication, commitment to quality and responsiveness that enabled this book of twenty-three chapters by 46 experts to be completed in fourteen months from the contributors' kick-off meeting in mid-June 2004. Our many thanks to all our contributors!

This book would have never taken off without the generous support of METRO AG and exclusive access to information about METRO Group's Future Store Initiative. It would never have been completed without the unstinting support, administrative and editorial assistance of Frederike Göhlich of University of Muenster, Thomas Hamela, Hans-Joachim Körber, Julia Merkel, Zygmunt Mierdorf, and Gerd Wolfram of METRO AG, and Martina Bihn and Irene Barrios-Kezic of Springer. Our heartfelt thanks to all these dedicated individuals!

Finally, this project consumed quite some of our leisure time that should have been devoted to our families. Though we are quite enthusiastic and proud about the final outcome of our work, we also feel sorry about neglecting them on many weekends and holidays we should have been with them. For all their patience and moral support, we dedicate this book to Anna-Kristina, Christine, Elisabeth, Ole-Michel, Surya, Vidya and Ashwini.

Manfred Krafft
University of Muenster, Germany

Murali K. Mantrala
University of Missouri, Columbia, USA

Table of Contents

Overview

Manfred Krafft[1] and Murali K. Mantrala[2]

[1] University of Muenster, Germany
[2] University of Missouri, Columbia, USA

Retailing in the new millennium stands as an exciting, complex and vital business sector in most developed as well as emerging economies. The Foreword of this book by *Eckhard Cordes*, CEO of METRO Group, highlights the rapid changes taking place today in the world of retailing. Key trends and developments such as changing customer needs and increasing interest in the shopping experience as much as products, retailer consolidation, emerging multi-channel retailing strategies, changing nature of competition within and between retailing formats, globalization and technological breakthroughs such as radio frequency identification (RFID) and personal selling assistants (PSAs), are having or will soon have a dramatic impact on the way large retailers do business in this new century. The 2nd edition of *Retailing in the 21st Century* is intended to help business leaders, analysts, policymakers, retailing executives, consultants and academics better understand these trends in retailing and their current and potential impacts, develop strategies and tactics for better performance, and identify issues and questions for further research. With twenty-five crisp and insightful chapters contributed by many of the world's leading experts in various facets of retailing, *Retailing in the 21st Century* offers in one book a compendium of state-of-the-art, cutting-edge knowledge to understand and guide successful retailing in the new millennium.

Overview of Chapters

The twenty-five chapters in the book are divided into three Parts: (I) Introduction; (II) Global, Environmental and Market Trends; (III) Trends in Retail Management. The chapters in Part I provide an overview of current trends in retailing, key drivers of retail success in national and international markets, and the role of entrepreneurship. Part II contains chapters that examine, in more depth, specific trends in different geographical regions of the world, trends in retailing technology and data environments, and market trends with respect to retail customers, channels and competitors. Part III covers trends and evolving issues in the management

M. Krafft and M.K. Mantrala (eds.), *Retailing in the 21st Century: Current and Future Trends*, 1
DOI 10.1007/978-3-540-72003-4_1, © Springer-Verlag Berlin Heidelberg 2010

of a retail firm's human resources, marketing mix, i.e., pricing, promotion and distribution, and supply chains. All chapters review and provide insights into current trends as well as offer predictions for the future. Below, we provide more details on the specific chapters in each of these three Parts.

Introduction

The Introductory section consists of three chapters which focus on the key success factors driving national and international success in retailing including the role of the entrepreneur.

Retail Success and Key Drivers

This chapter, co-authored by *Dhruv Grewal, R. Krishnan, Michael Levy*, and *Jeanne Munger*, describes broad changes currently occurring across the retail landscape, e.g., retail consolidation, and challenges facing retailers such as intensifying competitive pressures, overstoring, and savvier, value-seeking customers. Observing that in spite of these obstacles many retailers continue to succeed, the authors present a framework that identifies the key drivers of success in today's retailing environment. Specifically, they distinguish between four segments of retailers: *Innovative, Low-Price, Big Middle* and *In Trouble* retailers. The authors note that most successful retailers compete in the Big Middle which is where the largest potential base of customers reside. Success drivers of Big Middle retailers include store atmospherics, customer service, attractive merchandise selections at value prices, efficient supply chain management, and advanced technology. Looking ahead, the authors foresee further retail consolidation and success being enjoyed by those retailers who continuously provide value, are innovative, and are able to control their costs.

Retailing in a Global World: Case Study of Metro Cash & Carry

After four decades of being in the retailing business, METRO Group has become the fourth-largest retailer in the world. Currently, about 60 % of the company's revenue comes from outside Germany. The story of the growth and transformation of METRO Group from its humble beginnings in the Ruhr valley of Germany just 45 years ago to a global retailing giant is an interesting case study that is described by *Zygmunt Mierdorf, Murali K. Mantrala*, and *Manfred Krafft*. The authors review METRO Group's history and strategies and draw lessons and implications for retailers interested in international growth. In their case, they focus on Metro Cash & Carry (C&C), the most successful of METRO Group's four major sales divisions. Metro C&C is a self-service wholesaling concept that is also the most international unit, with more than 650 outlets in 29 countries.

Entrepreneurship in Retailing: Leopold Stiefel's "Big Idea" and the Growth of Media Markt and Saturn

The stories of the founders of American retail firms such as Wal-Mart, J. C. Penney, Sears and Woolworth's are well-known in the retail industry. However, little is generally known about the role, personality, and leadership style of founders of today's successful companies outside of the United States. One European company in the electronic goods retail business that has enjoyed tremendous growth and generated substantial profits in recent years is Media Markt and Saturn. The cofounder of this successful company, Leopold Stiefel, is considered to be one of the most interesting personalities in retailing in central Europe. Within 25 years, Leopold Stiefel has developed Media Markt and Saturn from a single store in Munich to one of the largest electronic goods retailers in the world, generating 19 billion USD in revenues from about 770 stores in 16 European countries. In this chapter, *Murali K. Mantrala* and *Manfred Krafft* describe Media Markt and Saturn's history, the biography of Leopold Stiefel, and his "big idea" and insights into modern retailing expressed in an extended personal interview. The authors identify key elements of Stiefel's marketing strategy driving the growth and shaping the current and future outlook for Media Markt and Saturn.

Global, Environmental, and Market Trends

Part II of this book consists of a total of eleven chapters: four chapters on Global Trends; four chapters on Environmental Trends; and three chapters on Market Trends.

Global Trends

Retail Trends in Europe

The rapid restructuring of European retailing is described in this chapter by *John Dawson*. In this process, retailing is changing from a *reactive* to a *proactive* sector in the European economy. The author considers four characteristics of this restructuring: fast growth of large firms, a more strategic approach to managerial decision taking, more complex organisational structures, and more retailer co-ordinated value chains. He examines why these changes are taking place and the implications for retailers. Dawson identifies 'experience innovation' playing a central role in how European retailers are changing the sector. He foresees future developments in European retailing being driven by continued innovation, greater retail control of branding, development of the experience innovation and customer experience management approach, and a steady exploitation of economies of scale and scope. However, the big unknown factor is the role that government will play in shaping and regulating retailing in Europe in the coming years.

Trends in U.S. Retailing

In this chapter, *Barton A. Weitz* and *Mary Brett Whitfield*, identify three important consumer trends affecting retailers in the highly competitive U.S. retail industry: (1) the size and importance of two age cohorts—*baby boomers* and *generation Y*; (2) the growing ethnic diversity; and (3) the increasing sophistication of shoppers. In response to these trends, retailers are using the classic competitive strategies of low cost and differentiation. Retailers are either developing approaches for lowering their costs (scale economies, supply chain management and technology) to provide lower prices, or tailoring and personalizing their offer to better satisfy the needs of specific market segments by providing unique merchandise and services. Within this context, Weitz and Whitfield explore specific trends in the various retail sectors: food, general merchandise, and non-store retailing. The chapter concludes with a visionary look at how technology will be used to provide customers a more intimate shopping experience in the future.

Trends in Retailing in East Asia

The author of this chapter, *Roy Larke*, describes the rapid development of retailing in East Asia in recent years. Despite a wide diversity in cultures, languages, and incomes, this region has become a magnet for international retailers due to a high population base and relatively low levels of existing competition. Some markets, notably Malaysia, Thailand, Singapore and Hong Kong, are already host to numerous international retail firms, but the largest markets of China and Japan are now just beginning to receive the attention of overseas retailers. Larke emphasizes that it is not just Western firms with Western ideas who are spreading in East Asian distribution. Japanese retailers are also highly active across the region and represent the largest presence in terms of company numbers of any single nationality currently operating in China and other parts of East Asia. Together, Western and Japanese retailers are playing a major role in changing and modernizing distribution structures and understanding their impact on local economies and consumer cultures is an important issue for future research.

Insights into the Growth of New Retail Formats in India

A revolution in modern retailing has taken place in the vast, emerging market of India over the last five years. This development has become a subject of worldwide interest. The authors of this chapter, *Piyush Kumar Sinha and Sanjay Kumar Kar*, describe this transformation in the Indian retail sector, and its growth and investment patterns. They provide insights into the variety of existing and new players in the field, and the experimentation characterizing their choices of modern retail formats. Currently, hypermarkets and supermarkets are growing very fast. Consumer dynamics in India are changing and retailers need to formulate their strategies and tactics to deliver value to the consumer. Sinha and Kar outline and offer directions for dealing with the challenges and opportunities facing retailers in India today.

Environmental Trends

Future Store Technologies and Their Impact on Grocery Retailing

Co-authored by *Kirthi Kalyanam*, *Rajiv Lal*, and *Gerd Wolfram*, this chapter provides an overview of the innovative technologies that were deployed in METRO Group's pilot 'Future Store' in Rheinberg, Germany including: personal selling assistants, digital advertising displays, electronic price tags, and radio frequency identification (RFID) technologies. The authors describe consumer and retailer use case scenarios supported by these technologies. They assess the deployment of these technologies and describe the rollout decisions taken by METRO Group. The chapter closes with an assessment of the expected impact on the future of grocery retailing. The authors predict that retailers who have the ability to integrate these technologies to launch new strategies that enhance the customer experience will be the biggest beneficiaries.

The Third Wave of Marketing Intelligence

In this chapter, *Raymond R. Burke* identifies three waves of change that have transformed marketing research in retail settings over the past 25 years. The first wave that started at the beginning of the '80s was the wide diffusion of UPC barcode scanning. The second wave that began ten years later was customer relationship management or CRM based on retailer introduction of customer loyalty cards. This chapter focuses on the third wave of marketing intelligence, called *customer experience management*, which is just getting underway. Recent innovations in the real-time tracking of customer behavior in retail stores allow marketers to measure consumer response to the in-store environment and manage the shopping process. Burke reviews the genesis of customer experience management, describes available tools for tracking shopper behavior and measuring store performance, and discusses two case studies which illustrate the use of tracking research in retail settings. The chapter concludes with a discussion of the challenges in conducting computer-based observational research and future directions.

Applications of Intelligent Technologies in Retail Marketing

Most large retailers today have made efforts to create data warehouses that combine the massive databases formed by barcode and/or RFID systems together with the data coming from typically disparate on-line transaction processing (OLTP) systems (e.g., finance, inventory, and sales) at a single location. Smart and powerful data analyses technologies are now needed to extract knowledge from these data warehouses as well as support decision-making in today's increasingly complex retailing operations environments. Such data analyses tools are termed 'intelligent' if they are *adaptive*, i.e., react to and learn from changes in inputs from their environment. This chapter by *Vadlamani Ravi, Kalyan Raman*, and *Murali K. Mantrala* describes several intelligent technologies such as *fuzzy logic systems*, *neural networks analyses* and *soft computing*, their advantages relative to traditional statistical methods, and their recent and potential applications in retail marketing.

New Automated Checkout Systems

In this chapter, *Thorsten Litfin* and *Gerd Wolfram* describe new automated self checkout systems that enable shoppers to scan, bag and pay for their purchases with very little or no help from store personnel. Although this technology has existed for more than a decade, it is still in the early stage of the diffusion process. The authors discuss the potential benefits of automated self check out systems for retailers, e.g., lower costs and greater flexibility, as well as for customers such as shorter queues, a faster checkout process, more privacy and greater control of their purchasing. However, customer's acceptance of such systems is crucial for their success. The authors describe primary research based on a conceptual model of customer acceptance that was conducted at METRO Group's Future Store to learn more about the prospects for self checkout systems and differences between users and non-users of such systems. Based on the findings of this study and other empirical research, the authors offer directions on how vendors of these systems and retailers can encourage greater customer acceptance of these systems in the future.

Market Trends

Understanding Retail Customers

Retail customer behavior is the focus of this chapter by *Mark Uncles*. The chapter begins with a retrospective assessment of our understanding of retail customers, paying particular attention to patterns of consumer choice. Based on this assessment, the author concludes that considerable advances have been made in the analysis and understanding of what customers buy, how much they buy, at what price, and so forth. Nonetheless, there remain many unresolved issues and understanding these is becoming harder because the customer landscape is changing, indeed a *buyer-centric* revolution is taking place in retailing, under the influence of four forces of change: the rise of technologically-savvy customers, the spreading fad and fashion-consciousness of retail customers, the growing importance of experiential shopping, and increasing consumer assertiveness. Uncles discusses how these forces of change are having an impact on consumer choices and presenting new challenges for retail analysts.

Future Trends of Multi-channel Retailing

Retailers find themselves in an increasingly complex environment shaped by the rise of new competing channels and store formats on the one hand, and, on the other hand, consumers who demonstrate multi-channel shopping behavior and needs structure. In this chapter, *Peter Sonneck* and *Sören Ott* describe these two trends and the challenges they pose for individual retailers endeavouring to interpret consumers' multi-channel shopping process and satisfy their individual needs and requirements. The authors propose a framework to perform such analyses and offer guidelines for how retailers can react to multi-channel shopping behaviour and develop their related strategies. The authors conclude that the future belongs to multi-channel rather than single-channel retail organizations, particularly those that offer a network of channels, rather than a 'parallel configuration,' and store formats that are transparent to consumers.

Retail Competition

This chapter by *Edward J. Fox* and *Raj Sethuraman* focuses on key trends and evolving issues in the two types of prevailing competition —*within-* and *between-format*—among packaged goods retailers, e.g., grocery stores and mass merchandisers. The authors organize their discussion around four key dimensions of retail competition: *price, variety, assortment*, and *store location*. They note that there is a trend of increasing between-format competition as all retailers extend their product offerings to provide one-stop shopping convenience for their customers. On the other hand, since consumers want more locational convenience with limited assortments, retailers respond with smaller store formats (e.g., dollar stores, Wal-Mart Neighborhood Markets). International expansion, consolidation within formats, and multi-channel retailing are discussed as the major within-format competition trends. Finally, both between- and within-type competition are affected by the trend of retailers moving off the mall to standalone or strip center locations.

Trends in Retail Management

Part III of this book consists of a total of eleven chapters that cover People, Product Assortments, Pricing, Distribution, Promotions, Marketing Communications, and Supply Chain Management.

People

New Challenges in Retail Human Resource Management

This chapter, written by *Julia Merkel, Paul Jackson* and *Doreén Pick*, describes the critical role of Human Resource Management (HRM) in the formulation and execution of business strategies of international retailers. Rapid changes in retailing business necessitate new concepts and solutions in HRM. The authors give an overview of these changes, which include both external developments, e.g., changes in consumer behavior, selling formats and the competitive landscape, and internal changes such as those related to corporate governance and information technologies, and the new challenges they pose for HR managers of international retailers. The authors emphasize that it is HR managers' responsibility to ensure that the organization's business strategy adapts to cultural differences of diverse countries as well prepare a diverse workforce for the future world of retailing business. The chapters outline a series of steps to be taken by HRM of retailers to meet these goals.

Product

Retail Assortment: More ≠ Better

Retailers have assumed that larger product assortments better meet consumer needs. Thus, the number of products offered within retail categories has escalated in recent years despite higher inventory costs and greater risk of out-of-stocks. In this chapter, *Susan M. Broniarczyk* and *Wayne D. Hoyer* review recent research that questions this conventional wisdom and show that more product assortment does not necessarily lead to a better shopping experience for the consumer. The authors focus on four questions: 1) How do consumers perceive assortment?; 2) How should assortments be organized?; 3) How do marketing mix variables interact with assortment?; and 4) How does assortment affect consumer choice? The authors' review of research indicates that through selective reduction and proper organization, retailers can shrink the number of products offered without lowering consumer perceptions of assortment. Moreover, shoppers seem more satisfied with their shopping experience and more likely to make a purchase from smaller product assortments. Thus, having an *optimal* rather than simply large assortment is critical for retailers. New technology such as RFID tags is expected to facilitate such assortment management.

Out-of-Stock Situations: Reactions, Antecedents, Management Solutions, and a Future Perspective

Out-of-stocks (OOS) remain an issue of concern for many retailers as they can have strong negative consequences for them, including lost sales opportunities and consumer complaints. In this chapter, *Peter C. Verhoef* and *Laurens M. Sloot* review findings from empirical studies of consumer reactions towards OOS situations, the antecedents of these reactions and management solutions to reduce OOS. Surveys indicate that the most prevalent consumer reactions to OOS are brand switching and postponement of the purchase. Important antecedents of these reactions relate mainly to the brand and the product, such as brand equity. The authors also discuss new developments such as the adoption of RFID technology and automated store ordering systems and their likely impact on OOS in the future. They predict that the use of these new technologies will substantially reduce OOS in the coming years.

Pricing

Recent Trends and Emerging Practices in Retailer Pricing

Ruth N. Bolton, Venkatesh Shankar and *Detra Y. Montoya* identify and examine the impact of four major retailing trends, namely, retail consolidation, changing manufacturer practices, advances in technology, and the emergence of e-tailing, on retailer pricing practices. In this new retailing environment, there is a renewed emphasis on profitable pricing strategies. Specifically, the authors' analysis of successful pricing strategies suggests a movement toward customized pricing which they examine in depth utilizing a six-step pricing architecture. The authors anticipate that in the future, there will be movement away from heavy trade allowances, increased customization to local conditions, greater pricing flexibility, and more multi-channel consistency of retailer pricing.

Retail Pricing – Higher Profits Through Improved Pricing Processes

In this chapter, *Hermann Simon, Andreas von der Gathen* and *Philip W. Daus* identify three major drivers of profit: price, volume and costs. Despite the enormous impact of price on profits, and the huge potential for improvement in the area of pricing, retailers have paid very little attention so far to the optimization of pricing *processes*. Prices are still set on the basis of intuition and subjective judgment rather than being developed in a systematic manner, leading to reduced margins and lower profitability. To tap new profit potential, retailers should establish superior pricing processes. This article gives an overview of key elements of pricing processes and develops a five-step scheme for implementing improved pricing processes, beginning with the formulation of strategic guidelines and ending with how to establish a control and monitoring system for pricing.

Distribution (Place)

Current Status and Future Evolution of Retail Formats

In this chapter, *Dieter Ahlert, Markus Blut* and *Heiner Evanschitzky* survey the current retail landscape of G8 countries. The authors observe that each national economy has its own retail structure and there is variation in the development and significance of retail formats across countries. Further, retailers who dominate selected formats in their domestic market have been quite successful in transferring these same formats to other countries. The authors also note that there is potential in specific underdeveloped retail markets for the introduction of particular retail formats by national or international retailers. Thus, this comparative analysis of the current status of the retail landscape in various G8 countries offers insights into how retailing in these countries will evolve in the future.

Electronic Retailing

It has frequently been emphasized that there are several unique benefits and limitations offered by an electronic channel as compared to store and catalog channels. In his chapter on electronic retailing, *Barton A. Weitz* discusses the classes of merchandise and services being sold through the electronic channel today and likely to be sold in the future, the retailers who are best positioned to successfully sell merchandise and services through an electronic channel, the growth of multi-channel retailers and the issues they face, and specific opportunities and problems involved in selling through an electronic channel, such as personalization, privacy, pricing, and fulfillment. The chapter also offers some projections of the worldwide growth of electronic retail sales in the future.

Operations, Promotion, and Marketing Communications

Supply Chain Management in a Promotional Environment

Grocery retailer supply chains in Europe are characterized by high promotion intensity. For example, promotions of selected items such as diapers from Procter & Gamble are frequently used to drive store traffic to gain market share and visibility. This chapter by *Arnd Huchzermeier* and *Ananth V. Iyer* focuses on supply chain management issues associated with products frequently on promotion. The authors emphasize the need for an accurate forecast of the demand impact of such promotions and its role in affecting orders and inventories. Their approach accounts for demand forecasting, coordination issues with suppliers and the management of logistics to the store. This problem is complicated by the consumer choice of package size and purchase quantity in a competitive environment. The chapter includes a state-of-the-art review of the relevant literature and a discussion of current research insights on the benefit of manufacturer-retailer collaboration in such an environment.

Sales Promotions

The chapter by *Karen Gedenk, Scott A. Neslin* and *Kusum L. Ailawadi* aims at two objectives. First, the authors take a look at what is known about the effectiveness of retailer promotions so far. Retailers have been using sales promotions like temporary price reductions, coupons, displays, and feature advertising for a long time and a lot of research has been done on their effects. Gedenk, Neslin and Ailawadi review which promotion instruments retailers may use, which effects these promotions may have on sales and profits, and what is known about the strength of these effects. Second, the authors look at the opportunities for sales promotions that arise from new technologies like loyalty cards, personal shopping assistants, electronic shelf labels, and electronic advertising displays. First, these technologies allow retailers to give consumers more targeted information on promotions at the point-of-purchase. For example, consumers may be alerted to a promotion for detergent, when their shopping cart is close to the detergent aisle. Second, retailers may use the technologies to target not information, but the promotion itself. For example, loyalty card data can be used to target coupons at specific consumers. Third, the new technologies may be used to enhance cross-selling. The authors review the new technologies available, as well as the opportunities arising from them for more effective retail promotions in the future.

Understanding Customer Loyalty Programs

Loyalty programs (LPs) have become an extremely prevalent marketing tool across a large number of industries. In particular in retailing, LPs are in many cases a critical part of the entire offering. Despite the prevalence of LPs, there are still many open questions regarding their efficiency and effectiveness. *Werner J. Reinartz* addresses this aspect in his chapter by generating structured insights around the strategic management of LPs. First, his chapter gives a descriptive overview with respect to the different types and design characteristics of LPs. Following this overview, the chapter discusses the specific possible roles that LPs play as a marketing instrument, that is, "What are the various managerial objectives of introducing a LP?". Finally, the chapter summarizes the findings from recent academic research around LPs, addressing the question of why different LPs have been more or less successful in reaching their objective. The chapter concludes with a summary and an outlook on future LP issues.

Integrated Marketing Communications in Retailing

The key challenge for retailers in the near future is to build strong brands by orchestrating new in-store technologies that facilitate real-time communication (e.g., RFID, wireless sensors, ubiquitous and mobile computing, personal shopping assistant or "smart carts") with the usual out-of-store branding communications to customers (e.g., print advertisement). To accomplish this goal, retailers will find the concept of Integrated Marketing Communications (IMC) relevant for designing profitable marketing strategies. In this chapter *Kalyan Raman* and *Prasad A. Naik* review the genesis and definition of IMC, present the standard multimedia model of communications, and elucidate the emerging results from the IMC model that reveal how retailers should act *differently* when determining the communications budget amount and its allocation in the presence of synergies. In addition, the authors discuss the effects of uncertainty on the profitability of IMC programs. Finally, the authors extend the IMC framework to futuristic retailing and identify new research avenues.

PART I:

Introduction

Retail Success and Key Drivers

Dhruv Grewal[1], Ram Krishnan[2], Michael Levy[3], and Jeanne Munger[4]

[1] Babson College, Babson Park, USA
[2] University of Miami, Coral Gables, Florida, USA
[3] Babson College, Babson Park, USA
[4] University of Southern Maine, School of Business, Portland, USA

Retail Success and Key Drivers

The global retail landscape is changing in some dramatic ways. Retail sales are currently improving. At the same time, competitiveness of both the U.S. retail and global marketplace is escalating. Whereas category dominant retailers were once the store of choice for a variety of products, chains like Wal-Mart, Carrefour, METRO Group, Tesco and Target have taken over in most categories ranging from toys to jewelry. As the world's leading retailer, Wal-Mart has a formidable history of providing greater value to consumers than its competitors, in part due to its innovative supply chain management. French-based Carrefour, the world's second largest retailer, operates five different formats in 30 countries (but not in the United States).[1] Based in Germany, METRO Group is ranked fourth in global sales after Wal-Mart, Carrefour, and Tesco, and it operates four different types of retail formats in 32 countries (Table 1).

Costco is the sixth largest retailer in the U.S. and the ninth largest in the world.[2] It has developed a unique retailing strategy that has allowed it to outperform other warehouse club stores such as Sam's Club. A critical component of their strategy is value-based pricing. They generally do not markup merchandise more than 14%, compared to most supermarkets and department stores who markup products 25 and 50%, respectively. They also create a lot of excitement by offering limited assortments of prestigious merchandise, such as Waterford Crystal, Polo/Ralph Lauren apparel, and fine diamonds. Their total assortment is about 4,000 stock keeping units (SKU), compared to about 150,000 SKU in a typical Wal-Mart store.

---

[1] "2006 Global Powers of Retailing," *Stores,* January 2006, pg. 16.
[2] Fink, Jim. "The Best Blue Chip for 2007: Costco," *The Motley Fool,* November 9, 2006.

M. Krafft and M.K. Mantrala (eds.), *Retailing in the 21st Century: Current and Future Trends,*   15
DOI 10.1007/978-3-540-72003-4_2, © Springer-Verlag Berlin Heidelberg 2010

Table 1. Top 10 Global Retailers

Company	Origin	Sales in 2007 in € (billion, net)	employees	Rank 2007	Rank 2005	Rank 1996
Wal-Mart Stores, Inc	US	270.88	2,000,000	1	1	1
Carrefour SA*	France	82.15	490,042	2	2	8
Tesco plc	UK	67.98	440,000	3	5	18
METRO Group	Germany	64.34	280,000	4	4	4
Home Depot, Inc.	US	55.94	300,000	5	3	24
CVS Caremark Corp.	US	55.81	190,000	6	–	–
The Kroger co.	US	50.75	323,000	7	6	13
Schwarz Group	Germany	49.60	260,000	8	10	33
Costco Wholesale Corp.	US	47.78	127,000	9	7	12
Target Corp.	US	45.79	366,000	10	–	–

inclusive Joint Venture

(Source: METRO Group)

This highly edited assortment creates a sense of urgency for their customers – buy it now or it will be gone tomorrow. While a typical grocery store might carry ten brands of ketchup in three different sizes, Costco will carry only one SKU. It has also taken a very proactive orientation towards its employees, and compensates them generously. Although Costco's innovative approach has proved to be successful, they continue to look for new ways to offer exciting products, prices, and retailing experiences.[3]

Significant consolidation by big players such as the acquisition of May Department Stores by Federated Department Stores, expansion of existing retailers into new geographic areas and into new channels, forward integration by manufacturers, and dramatic improvements in productivity are all shaping this increasingly competitive industry. This leads to more over storing – a disproportional increase in the number of retailers in relation to the growth in the population – in more and more markets. In this environment, customer retention is becoming difficult as shoppers become savvier, willing to shop at a wide variety of stores and across a broad range of retailing formats (see, e.g., Weitz, Whitfield, Ott in this book). Indeed, a number of market pressures are forcing retailers to consider how to provide customers with greater perceived value than competitors.

The global business environment has not been kind to retailers since 9/11. The confluence of a number of factors adds to their challenges: deflation, high unemployment, lower consumer confidence, accounting irregularities, terrorism,

---

[3] Matthew Boyle, "Why Costco is So Addictive," *Fortune*, October 25, 2006.

war in Iraq, ethnic violence in many parts of the world, higher oil prices, and a drop in tourism. Retailers are responding to these challenges in a variety of ways. Some are rising to the challenges and entrepreneurially launching new formats, while others are remaining competitive by driving down costs using sophisticated communication and information systems to manage their businesses. For example, at the 12,105 Seven Eleven stores in Japan, each customer's market basket is scanned. These data are sent via satellite and the Internet to corporate headquarters. Headquarters then aggregates the data by region, product, and time, and make that information available to all stores and suppliers by the following morning. Orders for fast food and fresh food items are placed three times a day, magazines once a day, and processed food items three times a week. Because of the stores' limited size, deliveries are made 10 times a day.[4] Those retailers who do not respond quickly in appropriate ways find themselves floundering and being forced to take a deep hard look at their businesses, at times taking refuge behind bankruptcy protection.

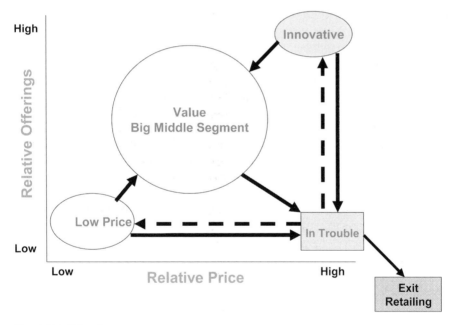

Fig. 1. Retail Landscape

(Source: Levy, Grewal, Peterson and Connolly (2005))

---

[4] Hau L. Lee and Seungjin Whang, "Demand Chain Excellence: A Tale of Two Retailers," *Supply Chain Management Review,* March 1, 2001, p. 40.

Retailers facing these challenges must understand the key drivers of retail success in order to remain viable. Building on our research and review of the various characteristics of the retail industry, we present an overview of the retail landscape framework and describe strategic levers that retailers must consider as they deliver value to their customers.

Retailing is indeed a dynamic enterprise, and we propose a model to describe some of the more successful retail strategies that have emerged in the last few decades (See Figure 1).[5] This model describes the evolution of retail strategy based on two dimensions: relative price, which is depicted on the horizontal axis, and relative offerings, depicted on the vertical axis. Retailers typically fall in one of four segments: Innovative, Big-Middle, Low-Price and In-Trouble. Retailers occupying the Innovative segment direct their strategies toward quality-conscious markets seeking premium offerings; Low-Price retailers appeal to price-conscious segments; the Big Middle retailers thrive because of their value offerings, and the In-Trouble retailers are those who are unable to deliver high levels of value relative to their competitors. We will now briefly examine each of these.

Innovative Segment

Driven by intense competition and choosy consumers, retailers like Trader Joe's have adopted innovative retail formats to increase the value of the shopping experience. Trader Joe's, the specialty grocery chain, goes beyond offering quality and variety. It carefully manages the customer experience so customers have fun—with a friendly and helpful staff, unique product selection, a sense of discovery from finding something new on the shelf, and tasty samples. Customers who enjoy the experience will inevitably buy something they hadn't originally intended to. The intent is to design a unique shopping experience that integrates the consumer into the process to create a lasting, pleasant memory, and ultimately a loyal customer. Providing consumers with a stimulating experience and a sense of trial before the purchase, and leaving a strong positive impression is the primary goal of these retailers.

Other retailers, such as Neiman Marcus, Nordstrom, Saks Fifth Avenue and many small designer boutiques are also enjoying robust sales. They have a loyal following where customers enjoy the experience of shopping. This also appeals to foreign tourists who are taking advantage of the weak U.S. dollar. High-end stores in particular are the direct beneficiaries of this trend.

---

[5] This section draws from: Levy, Michael, Dhruv Grewal, Robert A. Peterson and Bob Connolly (2005), "The Concept of the "Big Middle"," *Journal of Retailing, 81 (2), 83-88.*

Low-Price Segment

So called "extreme value" retailers like Dollar General, Family Dollar, and 99 Cents Only Stores are typical examples of retailers in this segment. Extreme value retailers are general merchandise discount stores that are found in either lower-income urban or rural areas and are much smaller than traditional discount stores. They compete by offering good value primarily through their low prices. Whereas the "extreme value" retailers are adding stylish private brand collections and some luxury goods like frozen shrimp to their assortment, low prices remain the center-piece of their strategy. Double-digit growth of "extreme value" retailers shows that stocking fast-turnaround items in 8,000 to 10,000 square foot stores is a good business model. Moreover, they appeal to today's time-starved consumers because they are easy to shop, being small stores primarily located in easy-access strip shopping centers. Even though the average dollar store transaction is only $9, the average margin of 32% outpaces convenience stores (29%), drug stores (27%) supermarkets (31%), discounters (24%) and warehouse clubs (11%) by keeping prices in check and offering brand and product mixes valued by customers.[6] Lower operating costs contribute to higher dollar store profitability. The double-digit growth of dollar store-type operations has certainly been an eye opener for major players, like Target, Albertsons, and Kroger who are opening dollar aisles in their stores to compete with dollar stores.

Save-A-Lot, a wholly owned subsidiary of the grocery retailer SUPERVALU, is an extreme value retailer that offers food at prices as much as 40 percent lower than those of conventional supermarkets. Although Save-A-Lot, which has in-creased its selling space by about 10 percent per year, operates more than 1,200 stores across the U.S., analysts believe that number could easily double or triple in just a few more years. Behind Wal-Mart Supercenters, it is the fastest growing retail chain in the United States. Save-A-Lot also is starting to roll out "combo" stores that sell both groceries and fixed-price general merchandise. Save-A-Lot combines the pricing power and efficiency of a Wal-Mart Supercenter with the small-store environment of a convenience store. Save-A-Lot carries about 1,250 items, but only the best selling brands in each category. Its limited assortment strategy allows the company to sell products quickly and avoid getting stuck with excess inventory that eats into its profit margins.

The Big Middle Segment

Wal-Mart, Kohl's, Lowe's, and Best Buy are typical examples of retailers in the Big Middle. Since the Big Middle is the source of the largest potential base of customers, it is where most successful retailers want to compete in the long-term,

---

[6] "A Concept that Makes Sense," *MMR Annual Report*, MMR, Vol. 21, No. 8, Business and Industry, Gale Group, Inc., May 3, 2004, p. 125.

although it is possible to be successful in the short-term using a different approach. In fact, many of the retailers now in the Big Middle have gotten there by way of initially providing either an innovative offering or low price or both, thus providing superior value to customers. For example, Ann Taylor began by offering innovative products that provided customers with high levels of value through superior benefits, whereas Target had its start by providing customers with high levels of value through low prices for good quality goods by means of its operational excellence. Others, like Lowe's home improvement stores, were innovative in terms of their assortment and category dominant format, while also offering value through its ability to build partnerships with suppliers.

Big Middle retailers have succeeded in leveraging their innovative or low-price position to transform their niche appeal to the mass market. They own an entirely different position in the marketplace by offering innovative merchandise assortments in terms of depth and breadth at reasonable prices. Clearly, they have successfully transformed themselves from being perceived as the innovative leaders or the low-price leaders into a hybrid of the two that appeals to a much larger customer base. They reposition themselves by transforming their image as either offering simply innovative merchandise or low price to being retailers that provide great value in a broader array of merchandise.

Wal-Mart has recently faltered in their expansion strategy. They have, for instance, underestimated the power of labor to influence local municipalities to enact "store size" laws, minimum wage laws, and health care benefits. They are also facing a number of lawsuits. Wal-Mart has responded in part by modifying their assortment, such as offering low price prescription drugs, and expanded banking services. It has also finally realized its "one size fits all" mentality doesn't actually fit all. As a result, they are customizing assortments to cater to urban areas, and geographical and ethnic idiosyncrasies.

Once retailers move into the Big Middle, they cannot expect to rest on their laurels, or they will get "in trouble" and potentially be forced to exit retailing altogether. The Big Middle is a very competitive and profitable space. Other retailers are constantly vying for consumers' attention and a place in the Big Middle. Simply being in the Big Middle is not sufficient for long-term viability. A case in point is conventional department stores. Once the darlings of Wall Street, they are now considered among the dinosaurs of retailing because they have not been able to sustain superior value through innovative offerings and high levels of service for the mass market.

Strategic Levers for Retail Success Through Value

Retailers who successfully compete in The Big Middle provide a compelling value proposition to the customer and are able to quickly respond to market changes. The successful ones maintain a nimble and flexible mindset and constantly monitor changes in the marketing environment. They realize that being flexible and being able to quickly adapt to changes in the marketplace are key to their survival. Examples of companies that position themselves to capitalize on market trends abound.

Consumers have become more attracted to "ethical" products which are those that are not produced by sweatshop labor and the working conditions have met high safety standards. In 2005 for instance, U.K. shoppers spent $50 billion on ethical goods and services, with a concentration on clothing. U.S. demand for ethical products is also high. An interesting derivative of "ethical" products is a program called Product Red Label, in which a group of manufacturers and retailers such as The Gap, Emporio Armani, Motorola, and Apple are producing clothing, cell phones, sunglasses and a variety of other products in sweatshop-free environments. A portion of the profits are donated to The Global Fund to Fight AIDS, Tuberculosis, and Malaria in Africa. [7]

Retailers are adjusting their business models to include philanthropic giving as part of its strategy. Instead of donating to charities separately from its retail business, retailers are now marketing its products for the purpose of giving to a charity. Retailers are realizing that being socially responsible is giving them a competitive advantage and a lifelong positive reputation in the eyes of consumers. Since philanthropic message is tied in to the product, the, retail experience becomes more uplifting and satisfying because the customers believe they are making a difference. These products are generally very successful, which makes it a win-win situation for both the retailer and the consumer. [8]

Retailers who have marketed to Generation Y since they were toddlers now believe they need to continue to follow this market as they mature. Generation Y is characterized by people in their 20s who are now completing college and starting their first jobs. Many retailers are actually abandoning portions of their teenage market to focus on this older Generation Y by opening new and different concepts. Abercrombie & Fitch, for instance started Ruehl No. 925, directed to 20-35 year olds. Not only is the pricing higher than Abercrombie & Fitch, but the retail environment is a "cross between a New York brownstone and a swanky boutique hotel". In 2004, Metropark, the fashion chain opened with a partly club, partly street boutique atmosphere. The twenty-something crowd appreciates the boutique, unique, mature atmosphere combined with the New York City club feel. [9][10]

Astute retailers can reap the benefits of responding to market trends. Demographic changes, emerging lifestyles centered on the home, and lower interest rates have buoyed the sales of home furnishings companies like Ikea, Kohl's and

[7] Stephanie Hanes, "Nice Clothes – But Are They Ethical?" *Christian Science Monitor*, October 15, 2006.

[8] Michael Barbaro, "Candles, Jeans, Lipsticks: Products With Ulterior Motives," *New York Times,* November 13, 2006.

[9] Stephanie Kang, "Chasing Generation Y," *Wall Street Journal*, September 1, 2006.

[10] Stephanie Hanes, "Nice Clothes – But Are They Ethical?" *Christian Science Monitor*, October 15, 2006.

Williams Sonoma. Retailers that traditionally did not sell furniture like Costco, Sam's Club, Wal-Mart, Target and J.C. Penney have recently expanded their furniture offerings in response to these trends. Others have been adept at pursuing underdeveloped market opportunities, for example sales to particular demographic groups. Designed to appeal to women, Lowe's has enjoyed a handsome payoff and a strong competitive position against well-entrenched retailers like Home Depot. In Germany, Generation Market, a supermarket chain, is redesigning its stores and offerings to cater to older consumers. It is predicted that one in three Germans will be 50+ by 2010.[11] The fundamental key to success lies in retailers' abilities to be nimble or flexible in organizing their offerings in response to new opportunities in the market.

Best Buy has experimented in several stores with retailing and customer service that is appealing to women. The stores have lowered its audio volume, made the aisles wider, added play areas for children and most importantly trained its sales people to communicate better with women. Some stores even have full-time personal shopping assistants to help female shoppers navigate the store. Other women who do not have any interest in electronics can recline in a massage chair while a personal shopper gets the merchandise for them.[12]

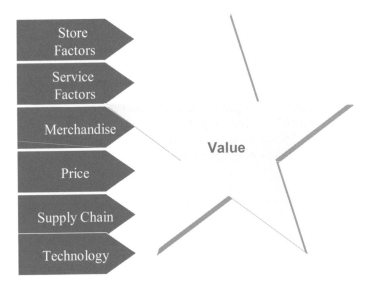

Fig. 2. Strategic Levers Impacting on Retailing Success Through Value

[11] http://abcnews.go.com/WNT/Business/story?id=2883983&page=1 – February 17, 2007-World news)

[12] Chris Serres, "Best Buy Displays a Feminine Side," *Minneapolis Star Tribune,* November 15, 2006.

Central to the ability to capitalize on new opportunities is the importance of managing elements of the offering that influence consumers' perceptions of value. Although there are many factors that affect customers' value perception, six major levers of retail success: store factors, service factors, merchandise, price, supply chain, and technology (See Figure 2), will be discussed. Other potential strategic levers, such as the role of store promotions and customer loyalty management are discussed in other chapters by Gedenk, Neslin, Ailawadi, and reinartz in this book.)

Store Factors

A key strategic value driver at the store level is developing the right combination of format and retail environmental factors. Customers often look beyond the functional benefits of a physical store to the overall experience it offers. Since much of the shopping experience is rather mundane, those retailers who can distinguish themselves with unusual and exciting store atmospherics add value to the shopping experience. Some examples of innovative retailers that are migrating to or are in the Big Middle because they excel at store factors are Crate and Barrel, Starbucks, Japan's Jomo gas stations, Bass Pro Shops Outdoor World, and American Girl.

A variety of factors influence customers' store patronage intentions, some of which are quite subtle. Environmental cues, such as design and ambience, can have a noticeable effect. Consumers' perceptions of value and their subsequent patronage are heavily influenced by their perceptions of the store's "look and feel." Music, color, scent, and crowding can also significantly impact the overall shopping experience.[13] The emotional responses that are induced by the store experience can have a pronounced impact on the amount of time and money spent in the store. Therefore, the extent to which stores offer a more pleasant shopping experience fosters a good mood, resulting in greater spending. Store atmospherics, as they impact perceptions that shopping is a fun and enjoyable experience, are an important strategic tool to manage properly for competitive advantage (see chapters by Uncles, Burke, in this book).

Service Factors

Given the time and effort that is invested by retailers to attract customers into their stores, it is amazing how so many retailers pay little attention to customer service. It is common to visit a retail store and see half-filled shopping carts abandoned by

---

[13] Baker, Julie, A. Parasuraman, Dhruv Grewal and Glenn Voss (2002), "The Influence of Multiple Store Environment Cues on Perceived Merchandise Value and Patronage Intentions," *Journal of Marketing*, 66 (April), 120-141. Spangenberg, Eric R., Ayn E. Crowley, and Pamela W. Henderson (1996), "Improving the Store Environment: Do Olfactory Cues Affect Evaluations and Behaviors?" *Journal of Marketing*, 60 (April), 67-80. Hui, Michael K. and John E.G. Bateson (1991), "Perceived Control and the Effects of Crowding and Consumer Choice on the Service Experience," *Journal of Consumer Research*, 18 (September), 174-184.

shoppers who were tired of waiting for their turn at the check-out, or to see shoppers looking for a particular item they wanted to purchase but could not find a service provider to assist them in locating the item or provide the information they need to ensure it is the right item. But those retailers who do provide great customer service distinguish themselves from their competitors, and therefore add significant value to their offering. Innovative retailers that are migrating to or are in the Big Middle because they excel at service factors are American Girl, Build-A-Bear, Trader Joe's, Best Buy, Container Store, and Lowe's.

One of the main drivers of good customer service is the convenience that a particular store provides. Retailers need to ensure that their store service personnel are well trained to provide five sources of convenience: decision convenience, being able to provide customers with appropriate information so they can make informed buying decisions; access convenience, making sure they know where merchandise is and will assist customers in finding it; transaction convenience, training to facilitate transactions such as check-out and returns; benefits convenience, helping customers understand the benefits of the products and services that will result in a more enjoyable experience; and finally post-benefit convenience, providing the training and empowerment to rectify post-purchase problems.[14] Retailers that attend to aspects of customer service can contribute to customer perceptions of value, resulting in a strong competitive position.

Merchandise

Most retailers devote a tremendous amount of time and effort to merchandise management. Retailers who excel in merchandise management do so in one of two ways. First, they can concentrate on finding unique merchandise that appeal to their target customers (for more discussion of consumers' perceptions of retailers merchandise assortment, see chapters by Broniarczyk and Hoyer in this book). Second, they can be certain that enough merchandise is where the customer wants it, when she wants it. Those who can do both, like Spain's Zara or Sweden's H&M, are even more likely to provide superior value for their customers. Innovative retailers that are migrating to or are in the Big Middle because they excel at merchandise management are Wal-Mart, Carrefour, METRO Group, Urban Outfitters, Trader Joe's, Crate and Barrel, Starbucks, American Girl, Build-A-Bear, Target, Dollar General and other "extreme value" retailers.

Generally speaking, greater product variety leads to higher sales levels, however, retailers do not have the luxury of simply adding more inventory in an era where productivity in merchandise management is essential to long-term viability. Innovative merchandise management can be both a challenge and an opportunity especially for multi-channel retailers. Some retailers, such as Staples, have taken

---

[14] See Berry, Leonard, Kathleen Seiders and Dhruv Grewal (2002), "Understanding Service Convenience," *Journal of Marketing*, 66 (July), 1-17.

slower moving SKUs out of their physical stores, but made them available either through in-store computer kiosks or over the Internet. Such a system brings value to both the retailer and their customers. Customers benefit because they can acquire items that might be unavailable otherwise. Retailers benefit by making the best use of their inventory investment.

Price

Price is a critical factor that consumers consider in ascertaining the overall value of an offering, i.e., whether or not the benefits of the exchange outweigh the sacrifices. Understanding what the customer is being asked to give up in an exchange for what they get is therefore key to the ability of the retailer to deliver superior value. Marketers should carefully determine the price of a good based on the value of what is being offered in the mind of the potential buyer. Retailers that are migrating to or are in the Big Middle because they excel at the pricing factor are Wal-Mart, Target, Carrefour, METRO Group, Trader Joe's, Zara, H&M, Kohl's, Lowe's, Dollar General and other "extreme value" retailers.

Until recently, retailers typically based their initial pricing and subsequent markdown decisions on arbitrary rules that they believed had worked well in the past.[15] Fortunately, a few specialized firms recently have developed software packages to assist retailers in making these important pricing decisions. Some of the largest retailers in the country (e.g., Home Depot, J.C. Penney) have invested millions of dollars in sophisticated pricing optimization software. The Canadian apparel retailer Northern Group Retail Ltd. started using Oracle's price optimization software and, in a test, was able to generate $60,000 of additional gross margin dollars on one stock keeping unit (SKU) by holding its outerwear at full price, though prior experience indicated that it should have reduced the cost by 30 percent.

Similarly, price and promotion optimization software developed by SAP's KhiMetrics has been implemented successfully by top retailers in the grocery, drug, electronics, specialty, and mass merchandising fields. Results from controlled field experiments demonstrated that gross margin increased five to 15 percent, depending on the retailer's margins, and the results were consistent across retail industries.

The monetary price of an offering is the only strategic lever of retail success that generates revenue. It is also one of the most conspicuous sacrifices that consumers make in the value exchange, although the real retail price should be thought of in terms of the monetary cost as well as the time and energy it takes to acquire a product. Retailers can lower the total cost of acquiring a product by either setting a low monetary price or by reducing the time and effort expended by customers.

---

[15] This section draws from, Levy, Michael, Dhruv Grewal, Praveen Kopalle and James Hess (2004), "Emerging Trends in Pricing Practice: Implications for Research," *Journal of Retailing*, 80 (30), xiii-xxi.

Supply Chain

In times of slow or no sales growth, rising expenses, and increased difficulty finding great locations, a managerial acumen toward supply chain management can generate significant profits straight to the bottom line. This involves efficiently and effectively integrating one's suppliers, manufacturers, warehouses, stores, and transportation intermediaries into a seamless value chain so that merchandise is produced and distributed in the right quantities, to the right locations, and at the right time, in order to minimize system-wide costs, while satisfying the service levels required by its customers. Retailers that are migrating to or are in the Big Middle because they excel at supply chain management are Wal-Mart, METRO Group, 7-Eleven Stores in Japan, H&M and Zara.

To illustrate the power of supply chain management for providing customer value, consider Spain's Zara, which runs about 1,500 fashionable clothing stores in 72 countries (including 41 in the United States). The chain has annual sales of over 6.8 billion Euro, an impressive number for a chain founded just almost 35 years ago. Zara produces the majority of its own clothes, and makes over 40% of its own fabric.

Zara also operates its own worldwide distribution network. Controlling the supply chain gives Zara the flexibility that its competitors can only dream about. It allows Zara to operate with virtually very little inventory build ups because its stores get deliveries twice a week, and newly supplied items rarely remain on the retail shelves for more than a week. In fact, Zara has mastered the art of quick-response (QR) inventory system with a vengeance. Zara takes only four to five weeks to design a new collection and then about a week to manufacture it. Its competitors, by comparison, need an average of six months to design a new collection, and another three weeks to manufacture it.

The company accomplishes this by adding value through an astute use of information and technology. All of its stores are electronically linked to the Company's headquarters in Spain. Store managers together with a fleet of sharp-eyed, design-savvy, trend-spotters in Zara's staff routinely prowl fashion hot-spots such as university campuses and happening night clubs. Their job is to function as company's eyes and ears, to spot the next wave. Using wireless, handheld devices, they send images back to corporate headquarters so that designers can produce blueprints for close-at-hand manufacturers to get stitching and produce garments that will be hanging in Zara stores within weeks.

In effect, Zara's designers have real-time information when deciding with the commercial team on the fabric, cut, and price-points of a new line of garments. This combination of real-time information sharing and internalized production means that Zara can work with almost no stock and still have new designs in the store twice a week. Customers love the results of this high-velocity quick-response operation – they queue up in long lines at Zara's stores on designated delivery days, a phenomenon dubbed "Zaramania" by the press.

Technology

The use of technology goes hand-in-hand with superior supply chain management. It is not surprising therefore, that the same retailers who we believe are migrating to or are in the Big Middle because they excel at supply chain management also utilize superior technology.

These successful retailers use technology throughout their supply chain. Most retailers collect sales data at the point-of-sale. It is what is done with the data after it is collected that separates superior retailers from the rest. As we noted in the Zara example, retailers can use sales data to work closely with their suppliers to plan production and inventory replenishment. Advanced systems like CPFR (collaboration, planning, forecasting, and replenishment) use the data to construct a replenishment forecast that is shared by the retailer and vendor before it is executed (see e.g., chapter by Huchzermeier, Iyer in this book).

Some retailers, notably Wal-Mart and METRO Group, are experimenting with radio-frequency-identification (RFID) technology. Wal-Mart has mandated that by 2006, all shipments to their distribution centers must have their cases and pallets fitted with RFID tags—tiny computer chips that can automatically transmit to a special scanner all of the information about a container's contents or about individual products. The prospect of affordable tags is exciting the supply chain. If every item in a store were tagged, RFID technology could be used to locate mislaid products, to deter theft, and even to offer customers personalized sales pitches through displays mounted in dressing rooms. Ultimately, tags and readers could replace bar codes and checkout labor altogether.

A retailer or consumer goods maker using RFID could cut total warehouse labor costs by nearly 3 percent, chiefly through more efficient receiving, shipping, and exception handling. More promising still are the potential effects of RFID on vendor-managed inventory systems. By exchanging the information gleaned from RFID readers over the Internet, a consumer goods maker could manage its own stock replenishment for key customers more efficiently, saving both parties 20 to 40 percent or more in inventory and out-of-stock costs.

Purchase data is also the basis for advanced CRM (customer relationship management) programs. CRM is a business philosophy and set of strategies, programs, and systems that focuses on identifying and building loyalty with a retailer's most valued customers. Loyal customers are the backbone of any successful retail enterprise because they are the most profitable. CRM programs, or loyalty programs as they are commonly called, can be as simple as a punch-card at a sandwich shop to very complex programs used by airlines and high-end specialty shops and department stores like Neiman Marcus and Harrods (see chapter by Reinartz in this book).

Retailers are experimenting with physical technologies as well. Some stores, like Staples, are utilizing in-store kiosks to help customers and store employees learn about merchandise and order items that the stores to not stock. METRO

Group's store of the Future Initiative includes self-scanning devices and innovative check-out systems enabling the customer to pay without a cashier and resulting in shorter waiting periods at the check-out (described in chapter by Kalyanam, Lal, Wolfram in this book). Customers will also carry small computers that will help them find products and receive important information.

Retailing Challenges and Trends for the Future

A number of enormous challenges face retailers in the 21st century.

Trend 1: Consolidation in the Retailing Industry

Numerous retailers are facing imminent problems since they are unable to deliver high levels of value relative to their more astute   competitors. As a consequence, significant consolidation by big retailers is likely to take place, e.g., the acquisition of Sears by Kmart and the merger of May Department Stores with Federated Stores, Inc.

Trend 2: Value Is Key

Successful retailers are developing strategies that offer customers greater value over competitors' and are sustaining them over time. To do so, they are focusing their energies on creating centers of excellence, such as connecting with their customers, being a leader in terms of the merchandise and assortment that they provide, and having excellent operations in place. Although retailers that provide value don't always do so at a low price, extreme value retailers like Dollar General are expected to continue to take share of wallet from the retailers that have traditionally appealed to lower income, treasure hunting, and otherwise value-conscious consumers.

Trend 3: Being Innovative

Retailers are more and more experimenting with their store formats. Additionally, they are effectively designing and managing the various strategic levels to enhance the overall customer shopping experience. The problem with being known as an innovative retailer is that it can only remain innovative as long as its customers believe the innovations are fresh and exciting. Recall, department stores were once thought of as being an innovative retail format. Thus, innovative retailers must continuously implement new ideas or else their customers will begin to view them as being "old hat."

Retailing in the Global World:
Case Study of Metro Cash & Carry

Zygmunt Mierdorf[1], Murali K. Mantrala[2], and Manfred Krafft[3]

[1] CIO, METRO AG, Duesseldorf, Germany
[2] University of Missouri, Columbia, USA
[3] University of Muenster, Germany

At the end of 2007, Germany's METRO Group had over 280,000 employees and an annual turnover of 66 billion Euro making it the fourth largest retailer in the world behind Wal-Mart (a turnover of 271 billion Euro), Carrefour (82 billion Euro) and Tesco (68 billion Euro). Further, nearly 60% of METRO Group's revenues came from outside Germany. The story of the growth and transformation of METRO Group from its humble beginnings in the Ruhr valley of Germany just 45 years ago to its present size and scope as a global retailing group is an interesting and important case study, particularly from the viewpoint of providing insights into successful international retailing and global expansion. In this chapter, we describe and review METRO Group's history and strategies within and outside of Germany, drawing lessons and implications for retailers interested in international growth.

The METRO Group today, whose management holding group is METRO AG in Germany, is comprised of four major sales divisions: The "Cash & Carry" (C&C) stores of the affiliated Metro and Makro companies which make this Group the worldwide leader in self-service wholesaling, the Real chain of food hypermarkets, the nonfood specialty stores chains Media Markt and Saturn which are the leading consumer electronics stores in Europe and the Galeria Kaufhof department store chain. Altogether, METRO Group now has a presence in 32 countries and its four sales divisions together have almost 2,200 locations distributed as follows: 655 Metro and Makro Cash & Carry outlets in 29 countries; 439 Real outlets in five countries; 768 Media Markt and Saturn outlets in 16 countries; 141 Kaufhof outlets in two countries.

M. Krafft and M.K. Mantrala (eds.), *Retailing in the 21st Century: Current and Future Trends,*   31
DOI 10.1007/978-3-540-72003-4_3, © Springer-Verlag Berlin Heidelberg 2010

Metro Cash & Carry History and Evolution

The Introduction of Cash & Carry Format

The history of the METRO Group began with the introduction of the fundamentally new distribution concept of *self-service wholesale*, or more simply the *"Cash & Carry"* concept, into Germany by Otto Beisheim. The first Metro Cash & Carry self-service wholesale store opened its doors in 1964 in Mülheim/Ruhr, followed shortly by a second in Essen the same year. The "Cash & Carry" principle means that the customers select their merchandize at the store, pay in cash and transport it all by themselves. Further, the Cash & Carry concept is essentially a B2B (business-to-business) wholesale format, aimed at supplying the needs of "professional customers", i.e., buyers of other organizations and institutional customers such as retailers, restaurant owners, service companies, canteens, cafeterias or hotels. The aim was to sell products of any type required by professional customers, on a permanent basis and in large quantities and formats, all at a favorable wholesale price and of a high quality. The concept required professional customers to become members before they could shop at Metro Cash & Carry stores. Membership cards were issued to customers only after they were authenticated as institutional buyers. "From professionals for professionals" was the company's motto.

Otto Beisheim's idea and concept was distinctive, timely and appealing to institutional customers as traditional home delivery wholesale at the time was unable to meet the demands of the continuously growing medium-sized businesses during this period of the post-World War II German "economic miracle". Metro Cash & Carry's first store in Mülheim had a much larger selling space (14,000 sqm) than the traditional wholesale store at that time, enabling it to offer a distinctly more comprehensive and diverse assortment, over 20,000 food items and 30,000 non-food products, under one roof. In particular, restaurant owners and food retailers among its customers benefited greatly from the large assortment of fresh food products. Also, being a "wholesaler" rather than traditional retailer, German regulations allowed Metro Cash & Carry stores to be kept open for longer hours (until 10 PM on weekdays) than traditional retailers and grocers who had to close by 6:30 PM. The longer hours were convenient for professional buyers who had more time to shop for supplies after their own business day hours were over.

Metro Cash & Carry Expansion in Germany

Metro Cash & Carry opened another three stores in Germany in 1967 and continuously extended the network in the following years. Today, at least one wholesale store can be found in every major German city. Metro Cash & Carry also does not face any major competitors in the Cash & Carry trade segment. The only other significant player in this domain is Fegro/Selgros which is still a relatively small player (but nonetheless taken very seriously by the METRO Group).

Entering New Businesses in Germany

In the mid-1980s, motivated by the goals of growth, expansion and building bigger and better stores with more personalized service in other retailing sectors, Metro Cash & Carry management acquired two big retail companies in the food sector (Massa, Meister) and a share in the Kaufhof department store chain. The latter acquisition faced resistance from anti-trust authorities in Germany until the early 1990s when consolidations in the retail industry became a trend. Subsequently, the anti-trust opposition diminished and METRO AG finally acquired Kaufhof and integrated it into their expansion effort.

In the remaining sections of this chapter, we focus on the international growth history and strategy of Metro Cash & Carry's operations.

International Expansion of Metro's Cash & Carry Business

The overall success of the Metro Cash & Carry concept is not only demonstrated by millions of satisfied customers but also by the business figures: At annual sales of over 33 billion Euro in fiscal year 2008 and a net operating profit (EBIT) of over Euro 1.3 billion Euro, this is the largest sales division of METRO Group. Interestingly, Almost 83 % of Metro Cash & Carry's growing revenues now come from outside Germany. Worldwide, in 2008, this sales division of METRO Group employed more than 110,000 people at 655 locations (a combined total selling space of 5.2 million square meters) in 29 countries. Metro Cash & Carry operates in these different countries with three store formats: Classic, Junior and Eco. With a selling space of 10,000 to 16,000 square meters, Classic is the predominant store format in Germany while the smaller formats Junior and Eco are mainly found abroad.

Strategic Objectives of Metro Cash & Carry Internationalization

A primary goal of Metro Cash & Carry's internationalization effort is to attain and maintain a leadership position in both the Western and Eastern European markets. Expansion to the US is not on the cards yet as Metro Cash & Carry sees the US market as intensely competitive with some of the world's oldest, biggest and strongest retailers operating there. Further, compared to the US, Metro Cash & Carry feels there is much greater untapped potential left in Eastern Europe and in Asia. Next, Metro Cash & Carry's international expansion strategy is to grow organically rather than via acquisitions of new retailing businesses as it earlier did in Germany. The company's experience with those previous ventures taught it that organic growth, i.e., growing from within, rather than new company acquisitions is the way to go, because organic growth allows them to keep their culture and closely adhere to their basic business concept, making it easier for employees to understand and execute the growth strategy. In particular, Metro Cash & Carry has found it is much easier to replicate its concept in other countries than by buying a new company, transferring knowledge, and managing a typically painful process of changing to Metro Cash & Carry's way of doing business. The latter usually entails significant losses of people and time. In contrast, with the right people and resources in place, Metro Cash & Carry has found organic expansion of its operations to be much more successful.

Internationalization History

Metro Cash & Carry started looking beyond its national borders quite early on. The first step was taken in 1968 through the partnership with the Dutch business group *Steenkolen Handelsvereeniging (SHV)*, which was the basis for the founding of *Makro Zelfbedieningsgroothandel*. The SHV group was very much interested in the Cash & Carry concept and had built a similar structure in the Netherlands under the name Makro Cash & Carry. Metro Cash & Carry and Makro Cash & Carry shareholder groups arrived at an arrangement under which they avoided going into head-to-head competition with the same concept in the same country and coordinated their new market entry strategies. The basic idea was that the Makro group would expand into markets where it was stronger with holding a 60% stake and Metro Cash & Carry having a 40% stake in the new venture. Similarly, Metro Cash & Carry would enter markets where it was stronger with 60% stake and Makro Cash & Carry holding 40% stake. This partnership arrangement between SHV and Metro Cash & Carry has continued essentially unchanged throughout the subsequent international expansion of the Cash & Carry concept. The arrangement has worked despite Metro Cash & Carry and Makro Cash & Carry having very different management philosophies, e.g., Metro Cash & Carry's concept management is much more centralized compared to Makro Cash & Carry's.

By 1972, Metro Cash & Carry and Makro Cash & Carry had expanded into Southern and Western Europe. Table 1 shows how Metro Cash & Carry's presence has grown internationally. As indicated in Table 1, the group operates under the name of Makro Cash & Carry in nine of these country-markets, while it is Metro Cash & Carry in the other 19 countries.

Upon examining Table 1, it is evident that Metro Cash & Carry's international expansion has proceeded in three waves: Starting in 1968 in the Netherlands, the first wave was essentially a period of expansion in Western Europe in the 1970s that included entries into Belgium, France, UK, Spain, Austria, Denmark, and Italy. The next wave of expansion took place in the 1990s, starting with Portugal, and countries around the Mediterranean Sea, namely Turkey, Greece, Morocco, progressing through Eastern European countries, Hungary, Czech Republic, Bulgaria, Poland, and Romania, and then into China in 1996. Thus, Metro Cash & Carry business expansion into Eastern Europe started long before people were talking about adding these countries into the European Union leading to its slogan: "Already operating in all places where the Euro is still to come". This speaks to Metro Cash & Carry's management's foresight, willingness and ability to take a qualified risk, and the transferability and strength of the Cash & Carry format concept to survive in

Table 1. International Activities of Metro Cash & Carry (as of: 31/12/2008)

Country	Brand	Outlets	Market Entry
Netherlands	makro Cash & Carry	17	1968
Austria	Metro Cash & Carry	12	1971
Denmark	Metro Cash & Carry	5	1971
France	Metro Cash & Carry	91	1971
Great Britain	makro Cash & Carry	33	1971
Italy	Metro Cash & Carry	48	1972
Spain	makro Cash & Carry	34	1972
Belgium	makro Cash & Carry	11	1973
Portugal	makro Cash & Carry	11	1990
Turkey	Metro Cash & Carry	13	1990
Marocco	makro Cash & Carry	8	1991
Greece	makro Cash & Carry	9	1992
Hungary	Metro Cash & Carry	13	1994
Poland	makro Cash & Carry	29	1994
China	Metro Cash & Carry	38	1996
Romania	Metro Cash & Carry	24	1996
Czech Republic	makro Cash & Carry	13	1997
Bulgaria	Metro Cash & Carry	11	1999
Slovakia	Metro Cash & Carry	5	2000
Croatia	Metro Cash & Carry	6	2001
Russia	Metro Cash & Carry	48	2001
Japan	Metro Cash & Carry	4	2002
Vietnam	Metro Cash & Carry	8	2002
India	Metro Cash & Carry	5	2003
Ukraine	Metro Cash & Carry	23	2003
Moldova	Metro Cash & Carry	3	2004
Serbia	Metro Cash & Carry	5	2005
Pakistan	makro Cash & Carry	2	2007
Total		**529**	–
Germany	Metro Cash & Carry	126	1964
Total		**655**	–

(Source: Metro C&C)

countries with a low per capita income because of its self-financing dynamic. Metro Cash & Carry in fact is the only company with a national license for their format in China giving it an important first-mover advantage. More than ten years later, Metro Cash & Carry is now operating 38 stores in the Middle Kingdom together with its Chinese partner Jinjiang; and another 40 stores are scheduled to open in the mid-term in regions where they will face no direct competition due to their pioneering advantage.

The third wave, starting in year 2000, continues Metro Cash & Carry's eastward expansion and includes entries into Slovakia, Croatia, Russia, Japan, Vietnam, India, Ukraine, Moldova and Serbia.

New Market Entry Strategy, Process, and Steps

METRO Group's entry into a new country is always spearheaded by its Cash & Carry division because of its broad experience and tried, tested, and standardized merchandising concepts that have been found to work across different countries despite their various structural, cultural and consumer differences. In these efforts, Metro Cash & Carry follows a very systematic international entry process that proceeds in several stages described below.

Step 1: *Country scoring.* A preliminary market attractiveness scoring model is applied to all countries being considered for the next foreign market entry and the most promising candidates are identified.

Step 2: *Environment and market analysis.* If a certain country appears to be a viable candidate for market entry, a preliminary study of the country's economic, political, societal and legislative environments, its market potential and competitive situation is conducted.

Step 3: *Feasibility study.* If the country-market is still rated as attractive after Step 2, a more extensive feasibility study involving on-site research of all management and operational processes required to support the venture is conducted by a team of specialists from all relevant departments of Metro Cash & Carry, such as purchasing, marketing, legal and human resource departments. Based on the results of this study, the entry decision is made and if it is a "GO" decision, the locations, sizes, types of stores are decided

Step 4: *Entry management.* The country management team selected to oversee and manage the market entry refines the outlet concept and sets the merchandising, pricing and purchasing policies. This team also looks for real estate, selects and concludes contracts with suppliers and begins the personnel recruiting process. Typically, each new Metro Cash & Carry store requires three hundred employees. The local headquarters for the outlet chain are set up on the site of the first store. Customer marketing programs are also launched at the same time. While Metro Cash & Carry endeavors to set up the stores according to a uniform basic format concept in all countries, each individual case involves numerous negotiations with local authorities as the tax and legal requirements differ markedly from country to country. Thus, a key effort of the new country management team is to understand the political environment and establish a good working relationship with local government, politicians and tax regulators.

Step 5: *Recruiting qualified local personnel.* In this critical step, Metro Cash & Carry initiates a search for local managers and staff (e.g. managing director, buying, sales and administration staff) to operate the stores according to Metro Cash & Carry standards, supported by a number of expatriates. Metro Cash & Carry strongly believes it is advantageous to have managers and staff drawn locally, who are familiar with the preferences and purchasing patterns of the local consumers and can adapt the business to the country's environment in an optimum manner. This policy of relying much more on local employees than expatriates is very different from other companies, e.g., Carrefour maintains all-French international operations. Metro Cash & Carry's approach thus contributes to the growth of the host country's labor markets, and in some countries, e.g., Poland, it took only a few years for the company to become one of the host nation's largest private employers. Until suitable local employees are recruited, however, the country management team, consisting of senior Metro Cash & Carry headquarter executives with previous international experience, runs the business on an interim basis.

Step 6: *Training.* Local recruits are trained in intensive group programs so they fully understand the Metro Cash & Carry concept and its business philosophy and culture, before taking over operations in their own country. Professionals from the core business of Metro Cash & Carry are being trained in critical business areas both at an international training campus locally in all Metro Cash & Carry countries. Metro Cash & Carry International in fact now has four training centers around the world, located in France, Germany, China and Russia with different areas of competence (e.g. the fresh food business is a competence of the training center in France). Today, Metro Cash & Carry headquarter's training team is multicultural, comprising of an international team of instructors and coaches. Metro Cash & Carry's corporate language is English. More specifically, training is aimed at developing an international spirit in the organization, while remaining true to the basic concept of the business as it was originally conceived in Germany, and empowering trainees to easily transfer Metro Cash & Carry's business concept to their home offices, in their own or another country. (For example, Metro Cash & Carry now has a lot of managers from Eastern European countries working in Western European countries.).

An illustration of Metro Cash & Carry's international market entry process is provided by its entry into Russia in November 2001 when it opened its first two wholesale stores in Moscow. The streamlined and systematic country market entry process that has evolved over the years made it possible to reduce the time required for the development from the planning stage through to the opening of the first store to as little as one year. The following summarizes the Russia entry timeline:

October 2000 – Based on the country scoring model, Russia is identified as a market with good potential for Metro Cash & Carry.

November 2000 – A preliminary investigation of the main aspects of the economic, political, commercial law conditions of the Russian market is conducted.

December 2000 – Following positive results of the preliminary study, a detailed feasibility study of the Russian market is prepared by an experienced management team that meets with and collects data from businesspeople, suppliers and politicians. Important operational issues such as purchasing, sales, marketing, law and personnel are fleshed out.

January 2001 – Based on the feasibility study, METRO Group's Executive and Supervisory Boards give the go-ahead to enter the Russian market and allocate the funds for the first two stores. (After that, any further expansion in the country will have to finance itself by way of organic growth.)

January 2001 – A search for suitable locations is initiated and two sites in Moscow are selected.

February 2001 – The customer marketing programs/acquisition process begins.

March 2001 – Upon receipt of the building permit, construction of the two Metro Cash & Carry stores begins. Meetings with the local authorities, neighbors and political decisionmakers become part of the day-to-day business.

April 2001 – Locally recruited managers are prepared for their roles in the Moscow stores at the Cash & Carry headquarters in Düsseldorf, Germany.

May 2001 – Recruitment of 800 staff for the Moscow outlet begins.

July 2001 – Metro Cash & Carry negotiates and concludes contracts with local suppliers for the Moscow stores.

September 2001 – The merchandise assortment of 15,000 items per store is developed, and details are entered into a computerized database.

November 2001 – Metro Cash & Carry in Russia is opened with support from Metro Cash & Carry Bulgaria. Such start-up assistance from sister operations already operating in similar countries is a tried and tested method for supporting Metro Cash & Carry's entry into new markets.

Key Challenges and Success Factors in International Expansion

Metro Cash & Carry has faced many challenges in its international expansion drive. Some of the key challenges are discussed below.

People: The biggest challenge has always been recruiting the right people and training them in the company's business rules and standards in order to achieve consistency in Metro Cash & Carry's offering across the globe (see chapter on Human Resource Management in this book).

Culture: Years of internationalization and expansion have taught Metro Cash & Carry that local culture plays an important role and the German way is not always the right way. Metro Cash & Carry now sees respectful treatment of and adaptation to cultural differences in shopping and consumption patterns across countries as a continuing challenge that must be appropriately addressed by its country management. For example, in Romania and Bulgaria it was found initially that customers bought everything they could possibly buy on one trip because they were not sure the same offering would be available the next day. So, for some time, Metro Cash & Carry had to engage in an education program to make customers understand that the assortment and terms offered would be the same consistently every day and customers would only have to buy what they would need on any given shopping occasion. Thus, cross-cultural training and education has now become a prerequisite for all Metro Cash & Carry managers.

Product sourcing: Catering to and satisfying local customer preferences and tastes is a hurdle to be negotiated in every new country market. Based on its early experience, Metro Cash & Carry now buys up to 90% of its food product assortments from local suppliers in the individual countries. This is especially true in fresh food and dairy product segments. For example in China, fresh food could also mean alive animals, and a retailer has to adapt and add this assortment to its structure. Assortment in the non-food segment is, however, much more standardized across Metro Cash & Carry's country markets.

Local economic development and conditions: Another ongoing challenge is adapting to differences in countries' economic conditions, e.g., adjusting pricing in the face of high inflation rates in some countries, e.g., Turkey's inflation rate was over 80% at one time, or creating a supply chain adapted to a country's supporting infrastructure (or lack thereof, e.g., India is far behind China in this respect).

So far, Metro Cash & Carry's track record suggests that it has developed the capability to successfully address and tackle the above kinds of international retailing challenges. Key factors that have enabled this success include:

(1) *Uniqueness of the Cash & Carry concept*: Metro Cash & Carry does not have a true international competitor in the modern Cash & Carry domain. The Cash & Carry concept as developed by Metro Cash & Carry is rather unique and there are no direct competitors barring a few small players in Germany itself. Further, the Cash & Carry format's "selffinancing" features allows it to adapt very well to countries with different economic climates and levels of economic development.

(2) *Transferability of the "blueprint" of the Cash & Carry concept*: Metro Cash & Carry has perfected and refined the Cash & Carry concept, over several decades and across many countries, into an easily understood and communicated business blueprint to guide managers in new countries.

(3) *Foresight and first-mover advantages*: As already mentioned, Metro Cash & Carry management has shown foresight and willingness to take some calculated risks in entering country markets in Eastern Europe, Russia, China, India, Pakistan and most recently, Kazakhstan and Egypt, well before its competition.

(4) *"Localized" merchandise assortment*: A particular feature of the distribution concept of Metro Cash & Carry is the range of goods it offers which is geared to the needs of the respective regional customer habits and local customer expectations. In fact, Metro Cash & Carry usually procures over 90 percent of its merchandise from local manufacturers and suppliers in the respective countries. In addition, the stores also offer international assortments of global brands and Metro Cash & Carry private labels sought by local customers, e.g., in Germany, Metro Cash & Carry offers numerous Turkish food products because of Germany's large minority of Turkish inhabitants.

(5) *Quality of product assortment*: Worldwide, a special feature of the Metro Cash & Carry and Makro Cash & Carry wholesale stores is the freshness of the food on offer. This is the result of efficient logistics systems, regional purchasing, and the group-wide quality assurance guarantee that the food is always absolutely fresh. Further, through its local sourcing, Metro Cash & Carry is actively supporting the local farmers, manufacturers and suppliers in developing modern cultivation, production and distribution methods. This garners it tremendous goodwill and quality supplies.

(6) *Systematic and deliberate market entry process:* As already described, the systematic research preceding entry has helped Metro Cash & Carry avoid a number of pitfalls that can overturn even an entrant with huge resources. A case in point is Wal-Mart's entry into Germany which is widely regarded as a major failure of the world's largest retailer because it attempted to convert local customers and employees to the Wal-Mart way rather than the other way around, i.e., researching how it might have to adapt to the German culture, shopping habits and behaviors.

(7) *Employing local management and human resources*: Metro Cash & Carry derives significant benefits from its policy of recruiting local managers and employees as well as the goodwill of the host country governments.

(8) *Exploiting information technology and customer database management*: The exploitation of knowledge in customer data bases fosters transparency and permits detailed understanding of customer purchase patterns, leading to optimized communications, product assortment structure, promotions (see e.g., chapter by Burke; Gedenk, Neslin, Ailawadi in this book).

(9) *Using flexible organization structure*: In its new country ventures, Metro Cash & Carry's organization structure is such that it effectively localizes all the decisions which are relevant for the business "front-end" and/or are customer-related, making them the sole responsibility of country management or even store man-

agement. These decisions include: store location, people management, product assortment, pricing, customer acquisition & management, and advertising. However, everything which relates to the "back-end" e.g., IT, logistics, accounting, buying, tends to be centralized.

(10) *Replication and learning from both success and failure*: The repetition of the same basic business model with little variation in its concept is a key strength. As one senior Metro Cash & Carry executive puts it: "We take a blue print of a concept and transfer it to another country and then multiply it. I think one of Metro Cash & Carry's success factors is the ability to multiply this format easily outside of the home country." Thus, in many respects, the most modern and best Metro Cash & Carry stores are not found in Germany but rather in Poland, Romania or Russia because they incorporate the latest concept with all improvements from previous experiences built in.

Internationalization of Other METRO Group Businesses

There is no doubt that METRO Group's global growth is led by its Metro Cash & Carry operation which allows the Group to learn very quickly how to do business in each new country, thereby providing it a solid competitive advantage and platform for the expansion of METRO Group's other retailing formats in that country. That is, Cash & Carry permits METRO Group's other businesses to hit the ground running while most of their direct international competitors in those segments have to learn how to do business in that country from scratch. Examples of exploiting the experience and equity from the Metro Cash & Carry operation in new operations include the development of Real in Romania and Russia. In each country, METRO Group has been able to exploit business synergies, government relations, purchasing economies of scale etc., to successfully grow its other lines of business after successful entry with the Cash & Carry format. More generally, another key lesson gained from the international Cash & Carry expansion experience is the value of following an organic growth strategy in which every new outlet is an outgrowth and replication of the previous one. That is, the global growth strategy of all of METRO Group's divisions like Media Markt, Saturn, etc. is to advance along the same development path. They all attempt to follow a tried and tested, easy-to-follow blueprint for the format, while allowing for some local adaptation. Thus, every Media Markt store is basically the same – whether it is located in Germany, Spain, Poland, Hungary, or Portugal.

Conclusion

Overall, Metro Cash & Carry's international experience has informed its management that the major long-run differentiatior in international retail competition is the way the retailer's people sell the business concept and manage their relations with local customers in each country-market. This includes how the retailer adapts to the local market's culture and interacts with local customers. Competitive trends suggest that customers can eventually buy the same product/s in all competing store formats. Ultimately, therefore, it is the retailer's people who will make the difference, while the back-end systems will create cost efficiencies and economies of scale. However, competitive advantages due to the latter are temporary as intelligent competitors will eventually copy successful systems. Indeed it is possible, as one Metro Cash & Carry executive puts it, that "25 years down the road we won't have our individual IT-system, but just buy it like we buy electricity or other commodities from a service provider." In addition to people, other key differentiators are the set-up of the store, marketing communications, and the retailer's brand building process. In the end, retailers have to build store loyalty among the customers to maintain their edge, e.g., make customers believe "if you want to buy a TV-set, think Media Markt. Don't think Samsung, Sony, LG or whatever. Think Media Markt or Saturn. Whatever you want, will be there." Such global brand-building along with international growth is an important goal and plank of METRO Group's competitive strategy.

In closing, based on its experience to date, the METRO Group sees tremendous potential for the Metro Cash & Carry concept and brand worldwide. Over three billion people and thus more than half of the world's population live in countries where the company is represented today. Every year, new stores are opened and new markets are tapped. The focus in the foreseeable future will remain on Eastern Europe and Asia, as demonstrated by the Ukraine and India, that are among the younger members of the Metro Cash & Carry family. Nowadays, two-thirds of all new stores opened are established in the growth regions Asia and Eastern Europe. Future expansion is expected to concentrate on China and Russia. China and India are expected to become the centers of growth over the next 5 to 20 years as many Western economies enter into economic decline. Metro Cash & Carry is convinced that future growth of its business will be in the East rather than in the West. However they have learnt that sheer growth of the top-line in the retail industry does not mean anything. It has to be profitable growth. "If you want to buy something you must understand very clearly if this can create value in your own organization. If not, better leave it." Metro Cash & Carry sees its tried and tested Cash & Carry "blueprint" combined with important customer loyalty and brand-building activities as the key to its long-term success.

References

http://www.metrogroup.de/servlet/PB/menu/1023871_12/index.html

Entrepreneurship in Retailing: Leopold Stiefel's "Big Idea" and the Growth of Media Markt and Saturn

Murali K. Mantrala[1] and Manfred Krafft[2]

[1] University of Missouri, Columbia, USA
[2] University of Muenster, Germany

Introduction

Retailing is a challenging industry to enter and be successful in. How do great retail businesses get started and grow? What are the hallmarks of a successful retail entrepreneur? Most students of retailing know the story of Sam Walton and how he founded and built up Wal-Mart to a point from which it could surge ahead to eventually become the number one retailer in the world. Many are also familiar with the stories of his predecessors, among them great American retail entrepreneurs such as Richard Sears and Alvah Roebuck, Frank Winfield Woolworth, and James Cash Penney. However, the experiences of successful contemporary retailers outside of the United States, e.g., those in Europe and Asia, are not so well known on an international scale. These retail leaders' stories and insights are worth recounting, as they offer valuable guidance to budding retail entrepreneurs and managers setting up shops around the world.

The subject of this chapter is the story of an extraordinary leader in retail entrepreneurship from Germany, namely Leopold Stiefel, co-founder and long-time Managing Partner and Chairman of the Board of Media-Saturn-Holding GmbH, Ingolstadt. Media-Saturn is a 75 % subsidiary of the METRO Group, comprised of two consumer electronics retail chains – Media Markt, which Stiefel cofounded in Munich in 1979, and Saturn-Hansa Handels GmbH, which was acquired by the Holding of the Media Markt group in 1990. Under Stiefel's management, the Media-Saturn Group became the largest European consumer electronics retailer, stretching from Russia to Portugal, with net sales of over 19 billion euros in 2008. In 2006, Leopold Stiefel decided to resign from active management. In his official announcement of this move, Hans-Joachim Körber, the then CEO of the METRO Group, noted: "Without a doubt, Mr. Stiefel ranks among the most outstanding

M. Krafft and M.K. Mantrala (eds.), *Retailing in the 21st Century: Current and Future Trends*, 43
DOI 10.1007/978-3-540-72003-4_4, © Springer-Verlag Berlin Heidelberg 2010

personalities in German industry. Leopold Stiefel is one of the fathers of this extraordinary success story (of the Media-Saturn Group). He turned the concept of a large-selling-space electronics retailer into a box office hit across Europe." In this chapter, we provide insights into how Leopold Stiefel made this happen. The chapter includes extended quotes and comments from a conversation with Mr. Stiefel in late 2006, which reveal his spirit, philosophy, leadership style, and tips for entrepreneurial success.

The Company History

Media Markt opened its first store in an industrial park in Munich in 1979 and was a success with German consumers from the first day. As the scope of their business rapidly grew, the founders realized they could not raise the funds required for further expansion on their own. Eventually, Kaufhof Holding AG acquired a majority stake (54%) in the holding of the Media Markt stores in 1988 and, shortly after that, in 1990, the Media Markt-Kaufhof group took over the independent Saturn chain of electronics stores. These developments led to the formation of Media-Saturn-Holding GmbH. However, the two brands – Media Markt and Saturn – continue to be managed independently under the umbrella of Media-Saturn-Holding GmbH.

In 1996, Media-Saturn-Holding GmbH was integrated into the METRO Group with METRO AG as the majority (70%) stakeholder. Since then, this METRO Group sales division has shown accelerating growth and has been a major contributor to METRO Group's overall growth in recent years. From 1995 to 2005 alone, sales soared fivefold, from 2.8 billion euros to 13.3 billion euros, the number of stores rose from 142 to 558, and the company's full-time workforce climbed from 8,275 to 37,230. At the end of 2006, Media-Saturn-Holding GmbH reported sales of 15.2 billion euros, a total selling space of 1.9 million square meters, over 42,100 employees, and up to 100,000 articles on stock. By the end of 2008, there were more than 540 Media Markt stores, ranging between 2,500 and 8,000 square meters in selling space, in 15 European countries, while Saturn operated more than 220 locations in 11 European countries. Currently, both chains are expanding quickly within Germany and across Europe, with market entry into China underway.

In Germany, Media Markt and Saturn together operate the densest store network in consumer electronics and electrical appliances retailing. However, they remain each other's biggest competitors. Whoever needs electronic devices typically visits both Media Markt and Saturn. Research has shown that, while more than 50% of customers switch between the two companies, few know that both chains belong to the METRO Group. From the consumers' viewpoint, Media Markt and Saturn are two separate entities, each with its own philosophy, price policy, and marketing program. Their motto, as Leopold Stiefel puts it, is *"March separately, strike jointly."*

Biography of Leopold Stiefel

Leopold Stiefel was born on 19 February 1945 in Braunau/Inn, Austria, shortly before the beginning of the post-World War II period. As the son of refugees from former Yugoslavia who eventually settled with their children in Austria, where his father found work as a laborer, Stiefel went to elementary school there, leaving in 1959. Since his family did not have the money to support him through further education, Stiefel then moved to Ingolstadt and, at the age of 14, took up vocational training as a retail salesperson with a local electronics retailer, Dreyer & Schnetzer. Subsequently, he moved to work as a sales assistant at the Bavarian electronic appliances retailer J. Fröschl in 1962. Stiefel recalls that this was when he first became motivated to start and run his own business: *"In order to achieve something, I had to fight from morning to night. However, to earn a lot of money was never the main driver. I wanted to reach a point where no-one could decide things for me any more. I wanted to take off that typical salesperson dress, with a pen in your front pocket, which you had to wear those days."* Several years later, in 1968, Stiefel started working for Erich Kellerhals at another electronic appliances retail store, FEG. Eventually, Stiefel became managing director of FEG in Ingolstadt. Then, in 1979, together with Erich and Helga Kellerhals and marketing specialist Walter Gunz, Stiefel founded the first "super-sized" Media Markt consumer electronics center in an industrial park near Munich. With a winning retail format strategy (see below) accompanied by fresh and creative advertising, the Media Markt venture proved an immediate success, which was followed by rapid expansion of the retail chain — first in Bavaria, then in other parts of Germany, and now across much of Europe.

Fig. 1. The Founders of Media Markt – Erich Kellerhals, Walter Gunz, Helga Kellerhals and Leopold Stiefel

In 2000, Walter Gunz stepped back, leaving Leopold Stiefel as managing director of both Media Markt and Saturn. In this capacity, Stiefel continued to direct the success and growth of the group. As he notes, *"I played a key role, namely by maintaining the spirit of the founders. My main contribution was to drive the enormous growth of the past 14 years, from sales of a mere 1.5 billion euros in 1992 to more than 15 billion euros today"* [2006].

In late 2006, Stiefel, who is married and has three children, resigned from his management position at Media-Saturn-Holding GmbH. His future plans include getting more actively involved in local politics in Ingolstadt, where he has a seat on the city council, and pursuing his interests in the ERC Ingolstadt ice hockey club, which is sponsored by him and plays in the German ice hockey league.

The Big Idea That Got It All Started

At the time Media Markt was founded, most electronic retailers in Germany were small shops with little variety and high prices. Products were locked up in a show-case and taken out and presented only when a customer came in. *"So how to do things better was easy to see"* says Stiefel. In a nutshell, the big idea of the Media Markt founders was to offer a large assortment of branded products in spacious shops and at consistently low prices. Stiefel summarizes *"We wanted to create a store with a trade fair atmosphere where customers can choose independently, offering large assortments of branded products, good after-sales service and good prices."* More specifically, the Media Markt founders' strategy had the following four basic elements:

(1) *One-stop shopping for consumer electronics and electrical appliances.* Right from the start, Media Markt's strategy has been to offer an extensive assortment of brand name and latest model consumer electronic goods, as well as electrical household appliances, e.g., TV sets, refrigerators, washing machines, hi-fi systems, computers, and photographic equipment under one roof. This innovative concept immediately caught on when the first Media Markt store opened, and it still works today. By sticking to this concept over the years, Media Markt has built up a large, loyal customer base.

(2) *Large, attractive superstores in attractive locations.* Media Markt stores are characterized by a strong magnetic effect. They are typically located close to cities but at a sufficient distance from downtown parking problems. Thus, they attract customers from across large areas with high purchasing power. Analyses have shown time and again that the arrival of a Media Markt store also benefits other retailers. Typically, sales of all retailers in the vicinity of Media Markt stores increase after their opening. As regards store layout, Stiefel's view is that the customer has to be immediately able to recognize and be fascinated by its distinctiveness on entering a Media Markt store: As he puts it, *"The customer must have a*

Fig. 2. A State-of-the-Art Media Markt Store in Lisbon, Portugal

"light bulb moment" when entering the store. In our case it is size, quantity of choice, and so on. We need to have that." To impress shoppers in this way, Stiefel stresses that the presentation of goods should be systematic, clear, and functional. *"If your customer is about to buy a flat screen TV, then he is about to buy a designer product. Given its cost, an adequate presentation of this merchandise is required."* Further: *"All products are readily available for demonstration at the stores. This way, the customers can test the equipment at the store and inform themselves about their use. The well-structured store layout helps to quickly find one's way through the multitude of products on offer"* (see also chapter by Broniarczyk, Hoyer in this book).

(3) *Sale of merchandise at guaranteed low prices, instead of short-term special offers, accompanied by adequate professional customer assistance and service.* Media Markt's aim is to be known not only for its broad and deep product assortments but also for its comprehensive service. Media Markt recognizes that today's customers, 80 % of whom are aged between 15 and 40, are knowledgeable and technologically savvy enough to figure out when they are being "steered" toward a sale. Therefore, sales assistants are instructed always to be available to help customers, without engaging in pushy selling efforts. More specifically, sales assistants are expected to keep their distance from shoppers, giving them the freedom to look around by themselves, and only provide information and advice to those

customers who seek help. According to Stiefel, *"The sales clerk role is not to sell but to help the customer find the right thing."* Indeed, this apparent aloofness has sometimes led critics to say that Media Markt does not offer sufficient sales assistance. Nonetheless, according to Stiefel, *"We do not want to offer unsolicited advice because this could again give the impression that we are trying to aggressively persuade customers to buy our products."* Even so, the reality today is that customers are consulting the store sales and service staff more actively as the merchandise becomes more intricate and complex. Therefore, it is essential to have knowledgeable and well-trained sales assistants who are readily available to assist the customer.

(4) *Fast and competent financing, delivery, installation, and repair services*, achieved by keeping lean hierarchies that give the employees the largest possible leeway to be proactive and creative.

How Did the Founders Know There Was a Market for Their Big Idea?

Media Markt founders did not do any formal market research at the outset, because of Stiefel's belief that: *"Market research concentrates way too much on the past rather than focusing on future."* They took the plunge based on their own observations from many years of interaction with customers in their stores, which had convinced them that consumers in Germany had a large number of unfulfilled needs. Specifically, shoppers wanted more choice, convenience, and one-stop shopping that would reduce the costs and time involved in searching for the right alternative, without being subject to aggressive salespeople. Consumers already put a high value on their leisure time back then, and they value it even more today. The founders saw that existing specialty and department stores were too small and had product assortments that were way too narrow, e.g., offering only 20 different TV screens when there were 300 on the market, forcing customers to visit several stores in their search for the best alternatives and prices. This is how the Big Idea was born. As Stiefel notes: *"If we manage to do this – providing large assortments, a brand, sales assistance when asked, and professional after-sales service combined with a reasonable price – and that is exactly what we do – then customers cannot ignore us."*

Stiefel's intuitions were supported by several ongoing experiments with assortment sizes. For example, at one point Media Markt reduced the number of laptop variants on offer in its stores from 50 to 10. However, it soon became evident that many customers found only one or two of the remaining models worth considering and would leave to search for more alternatives at other stores. *"The assortment variety was simply not enough and customers stopped buying at our stores."* Therefore, they went back to offering much broader assortments. However, offering very large assortments can overwhelm or confuse shoppers. Thus, a broad assortment strategy must be accompanied by the availability of a sufficient number of capable sales assistants to help consumers make their choice. In Stiefel's view, *"You need to make sure that there are enough sales clerks and that the customer knows that he has the freedom of choice. The customer must feel that s/he will find everything s/he needs in your store and that s/he will be helped if necessary. The sales clerk's job is not to find out which product out of a set of 300 best fits the needs of a customer. Rather, the customer should be left alone to form his/her own consideration set of 3-5 products that s/he likes, and the sales clerks should be there to provide any necessary support to the customer in making the ultimate choice."*

What Were/Are Media Markt's Key Success Factors?

Stiefel has no doubt that the key factors for successful retailing are all people related. In particular, to survive the initial days of a new venture, what matters first and foremost is the caliber and motivation of its founders. According to Stiefel, it is the founders' intrinsic spirit and values and the mood they create in the fledgling organization that will drive the growth and development of a company and form its eventual corporate culture. Trying to simply emulate another company's culture or follow prescriptions from outside does not work. From the outset, Stiefel, who has a framed motto in his office saying "Smile more than others do," deliberately turned some age-old rules upside down. For example, rather than adopting the rule: *"Trust is good, control is better"* followed by many companies in Germany at the time, Stiefel's credo is: *"Control is good, trust is better."* As he puts it, *"It is Trust that directs and makes people step up. If people are given trust they will do everything not to disappoint their clients or superiors."* As described below, this attitude led Media Markt to adopt an organizational strategy that many see as one of the key elements of its success.

Media Markt's Organizational Strategy

Since 1979, the key pillars of Stiefel's winning organizational strategy have essentially been *decentralization, cultivation of "intrapreneurs"* (or inside entrepreneurs who follow their founder's example; see Pinchot 1985, Pinchot and Pellman 1999), and *trust*. This strategy as a whole was rather different from the trend prevalent in the 1980s for larger corporations to move toward greater centralization in order to make their systems more powerful, purchase more cost effectively by pooling supply quantities, and lower logistics costs. In Stiefel's view, this trend only *"concentrated on hard facts and ignored the human factor, which thrives with decentralization and flexibility."* Further: *"We recognize that some things have to be managed centrally, e.g., financial controlling and accounting systems,*

Fig. 3. Assisting Customers in a Friendly and Unobtrusive Manner Is a Key Service at Media Markt

as well as planning, dissemination, and implementation of the overall corporate strategy and plans. However, the company's leaders must have the courage to delegate many operational decisions to local managers."

In keeping with Media Markt's decentralized business model, each store operates as a separate company. In particular, Media Markt is unusual in the ownership stake and autonomy given to its store managers (or 'managing directors') and employees. First, unlike its competitors in Germany and most other countries, Media Markt offers each of its store managers a stake of up to 10 % in the store they are in charge of. Second, each store manager is given considerable autonomy and the discretion to make decisions about their store's product assortment and stocking, pricing, advertising, staffing, and service guarantees to customers. For their product assortment and purchase decisions, the store managers can draw on Media Markt's extensive supply network and services offered by corporate headquarters to negotiate better deals with suppliers, yielding cost savings that can be passed on directly to the customers.

In implementing Stiefel's philosophy of decentralization and trust, Media Markt's approach has been to establish and communicate a few clear goals to the store managers, whose performance is monitored on just four key metrics — *total sales, total earnings, total costs, and number of employees*, while giving them the freedom to determine how to achieve their goals. Stiefel notes: *"There are no more rules to restrict decisions. I want to give all store managers in our company the opportunity to be creative on their own and act as entrepreneurs, just as I wanted to when I was a sales clerk."* Further, *"We are retailers and as such are dealing with human beings: sales staff, customers, and suppliers. Always treat people in a way you would like to be treated yourself. And always try to fulfill the wishes and goals of your employees, suppliers, and – above all – your customers. Always try to meet the needs of your customers, because they are the source of our livelihood and drive everything."*

Stiefel sees the key advantages of decentralization, intrapreneurship, and trust as:

(a) Strong employee motivation and high levels of sales and service assistance to customers

As he puts it: *"Our system fosters pride and commitment to the company and induces store managers to assume the roles of managing partners and intrapreneurs, become more educated, and care about success and the welfare of their store employees just as we (the founders) do with respect to them. The local managers feel truly empowered and are therefore much more committed to the success of their store than someone working as a corporate minion. This is highly motivating and also fun."*

(b) Store assortments tailored to the specific needs of the local customer base, market demands, and opportunities and fast response to these.

The greater flexibility that comes with a high degree of decentralization is critical for retailing success, especially as the firm expands into new markets. For example, the mindset and needs of a customer in Paris are very different from those of a customer in Moscow or one in Hamburg. The competition the company faces in various regions can also be very different. Such diverse pressures cannot be effectively dealt with under a centralized system. Decentralization gives Media Markt the ability to respond flexibly to local circumstances, consumers, and competition.

(c) Bottom-up flow of innovative ideas, which benefits the entire network

Stiefel notes that Media Markt has many corporate executives traveling throughout Europe to meet local store managers face to face and communicate headquarter strategies to them. *"But after that, you have to give the local managers the freedom to experiment with their own ideas within the framework of the overall corporate strategy. All they have to do is to keep headquarters informed of their experiments. If, for instance, Munich wants to present its TVs differently or wants to build up a whole new product range then the only thing they have to do is to let HQ know. We monitor the success of such a trial and analyze whether it has to be fine-tuned to make it work better. That is why we have a network, to pool the many ideas coming up through our decentralized system, and play them back into the company and, most importantly, to implement the ideas when opening new stores."*

Media Markt in fact requires the managers of every new store opening to try out two to four innovative ideas, whatever they may be, the only constraint being that they be consistent with the basic Media Markt concept. The innovations tested can range from a new store layout to how merchandise is presented. After one year, the corporate managers assess which innovations have been successful and then roll these out to all other stores. *"In many companies there are conflicts between head-quarter executives, who think they are the most talented, and local store managers. In our case, we encourage a culture where local managers have every opportunity to try out and validate their ideas for improving the business. If one works, central managers are ready to applaud and commend the local manager for doing a fantastic job. In fact, it is exactly for this reason that we allow our employees to hold equity in our stores."*

Media Markt's Marketing Strategy

Another major source of success for Media Markt is a clearly defined marketing strategy and execution, as described below.

Segmentation and Targeting

Media Markt is focused on serving the "Big Middle Segment" (see the chapter by Grewal et al. in this book) in their respective country markets. Stiefel feels they have to be, because: *"[W]e do not sell sufficient volume. If your business model focuses on volume, you need to serve the Big Middle Segment. If you are an one-line shop, you do not necessarily have to serve the middle. In that case you don't have to apply a low-cost strategy, either. Uniqueness and service are way more important for you. These companies serve the top 10-20% of all customers. The bottom 10% are served by discounters. In between there is a field we – as a volume selling company – try to conquer."*

Store Price Image and Pricing

Media Markt's pricing strategy emulates those of similar "category killers" or big box stores such as Home Depot or Best Buy in the US. *"Our strategy is to purchase at the lowest prices and pass this low price through to the customer. We lower prices if competition forces us to do so or if we notice that a certain product is too expensive or remains in our warehouse. But we never increase prices short term to improve our margin."* Retail margins are in fact quite low in consumer electronics retailing. For example, they are in the range of 3-5% for personal computers. Stiefel observes: *"I think we just have to accept that margins are thin. The way we generate good earnings for the METRO Group is through volume. A low margin is in a way good for us because the thinner the margin, the harder it will be for a competitor who is not as efficient as we are to survive. Thus, low margins secure our future survival as long as we are better. If margins are high, many competitors survive, and that is not what we want."*

This attitude in fact occasionally leads corporate headquarters to intervene in store-level pricing decisions, which are not standardized because of the company's decentralized structure and may therefore vary across stores as a result of local demand conditions. In particular, stores in some cities without aggressive competitors may be tempted to maintain higher prices for the same merchandise than others in locations with more intense competition, and this could provoke negative reactions from consumers or analysts comparing prices across the country. Therefore, the company's management encourages store managers everywhere to always keep prices as low as possible. *"We are decentralized, but if a store persistently exceeds a certain profit margin percentage threshold, we request the management to lower prices. Otherwise there will be competitors showing this particular store that you can operate profitably with even lower prices. Then you are the loser in this market. To regain the image is much harder than to relinquish a higher profit margin."*

Advertising Strategies

Media-Saturn Holding has its own marketing department, which operates independently of the sales departments of Media Markt and Saturn. The marketing department engages advertising agencies to create its advertising campaigns. Surveys have shown that Media Markt and Saturn's attention-grabbing, humorous, but sometimes provocative advertisements have been a big driver of its success. In Germany, Media Markt has launched some of the best-known advertisements in its market segment. The Media Markt ad slogans such as *"Lasst euch nicht verarschen"* ("Don't let them make an ass of you") and *"Ich bin doch nicht blöd"* ("I am not stupid") are legendary in Germany. The latter has also been translated into the languages of the other countries where the company operates. Stiefel firmly believes that advertising is necessary but it has to be polarizing, brash, and attention-getting. Just like his views on the impact of store appearance and layout, he is convinced that – to be effective – advertising must be memorable to consumers and generate a high level of brand recognition among them. Stiefel is less concerned about whether the ads are tasteful, as he feels there is considerable heterogeneity in people's tastes anyway. Thus, he is more interested in communicating with the bulk of the customer base in the every

Fig. 4. The Old vs. the Latest Advertising Campaign of Saturn ("Stinginess Is Cool!" vs. "We Love Technology! We Hate Expensive!")

day language they use. *"You cannot appeal to 100 % of customers. You have to try to meet the* zeitgeist *or the language of people you want to reach with your ad. Some people do not understand how we can do something like the "I'm not stupid" ad. However, most people talk like that today."*

Stiefel's views led Saturn to develop an advertising campaign around its former famous slogan "Geiz ist geil!", which translates as "Stinginess is cool!", one of the most attention-grabbing, talked about, and successful advertising campaigns in modern Germany. It is now evident that this advertising campaign was so successful because it hit the note that a large portion of Germany's society was listening for: spending increasingly less on all sorts of things, but still expecting high-quality products. Stiefel notes that some people feared this slogan would trigger a refusal to buy but he says: *'Stinginess is cool!' is the best claim our company has ever made. We are not stupid. We do not want to talk against ourselves, no! Rather, we are exactly hitting the* zeitgeist*: get the best quality for the best price."* The advertising agency that proposed this sales pitch had been rejected by the company's advertising managers, who feared that it could backfire on the company. Subsequent market research with consumers in the street appeared to confirm these fears of the advertising team. However, once he heard it, Stiefel insisted that it be adopted: *"I said to them, I want to have it because I think that this is the right claim. It is polarizing and people will discuss it. That is the way for Saturn to get out of its shadowy existence under Media Markt. Today, in my opinion, the claim has become a big success factor for Saturn – namely in people's heads. Today, if you hear 'Stinginess is cool!' everybody clicks: that's Saturn."* Stiefel concludes: *"You have to do things properly and not by half-measures. You have to be strong in advertising. You have to provoke. The only things to be careful about are not to be unethical, and not to offend ethnic groups or religious sentiments. Do not provoke violence. Do not defame any groups or religions. And as long as you follow these principles, you can be bold (in your advertising)."*

Media-Saturn Group's Two-Brand Strategy

As already noted, Media Markt and Saturn continue to operate independently as two separate consumer electronics retailer brands even though they belong to the same holding. It was Stiefel's idea to keep them separate. His strategy has been vindicated by the rapid growth and success of both chains since then. Stiefel explains his rationale as follows: *"I pushed the two-label-strategy and today I am even more proud of Saturn than of Media Markt, because it is very successful. No one expected that. The two-label strategy was introduced and realized despite much resistance from those who were not able to imagine two entities in one company. I was advised to concentrate on marketing one brand to avoid having to spend much more on advertising and promoting two separate brands. However my thoughts are never cost driven but customer driven. From the customer's perspective these are two competitors. Accordingly, I have to have the courage to let them compete and resist the temptation to integrate them, e.g., by aligning prices.*

"The customer is not stupid! You probably can trick them once, but sooner or later they will recognize that there is a coordinated strategy if they find a product range and price list that is 80% congruent. This simply does not exist in our case. Each chain has the freedom to choose the assortment and the associated prices it wishes to offer in its stores. Pursuing a two-brand strategy means that the two companies have to compete against each other. This is the only way to make both of them strong. The reason is that such competition makes player no. 3 and player no. 4 suffer more and more. Two companies materialize in the customer's mind. And that is exactly what has happened with respect to Media Markt and Saturn."

Stiefel notes that the two-brand strategy of Media-Saturn is the same as the successful strategy ultimately adopted after Volkswagen *(VW)* acquired Audi in the automobile industry. Initially, they used an integrative marketing strategy, which did not work. Eventually, the VW-Audi Group returned to a more success-ful two-brand strategy, with separate VW and Audi stores. Stiefel observes: *"These days Audi and VW compete with each other. If they offer everything they have in one store, customers have to visit BMW to have the opportunity to com-pare. If the brands are kept independent, then Audi and VW customers do not have to visit BMW if they like any car of one of the two brands. That is exactly our strategy."* In closing, Stiefel remarks: *"Psychologically, we dominate the market but in reality we do not. Our aggregated market share amounts to less than 20%. That means 80% is still covered by competition. So, why should we not try to get another piece of this 80% cake by struggling with each other? Our demolition strategy pursued by both brands will be continued. We are a holding company with two brands, and these brands should fight as though they were not affiliated. There is no alignment. This is the only way it works."*

Internationalization Strategy

Supported by Kaufhof, Media Markt's international expansion – into Europe – commenced in 1988. Since then, the Media-Saturn Group has followed a deliberate, phased international expansion strategy in European countries outside of Ger-many. Stiefel observes that the basic motivation for international expansion arose from both competitive and growth considerations. His attitude is that his companies' position in Germany would be secure only if they became strong and engaged their competitors in the surrounding countries. *"First and foremost you have to build up a company that has a right to exist for the next 10, 20, 30 years. Before being attacked (in Germany) by Dixons or anyone else, we have to be the one who is attacking. Today, if you want to play with the big guys you have to go international."* Seeing enough opportunities here, Media-Saturn's international expansion strategy has remained focused on Europe. The goal is to become the key market player in Europe before the big American retailers such as Wal-Mart and Best Buy figure out how to do business and succeed in this continent of many languages and cultures.

Starting with market entry and field surveys in neighboring France, Media Markt progressively entered Austria, Switzerland, Spain, and Poland and is now present in 15 countries. Stiefel feels that Media-Saturn has been a hit in nearly all the countries they have entered, with the companies' decentralized structure playing a major role in achieving this success in the diverse national markets and structures across Europe. In Stiefel's view, thinking "centrally" in the European market would not work. *"Europe is [...] a continent comprised of very different cultures, calling for management of and adaptation to the unique needs of each individual country."* In keeping with this view, Media Markt operates a separate head office in each country, with a management staffed by local experts from the respective country and few or no German executives, be it in Poland, Italy, Spain or Greece. Moreover, Media Markt follows the same basic philosophy of fostering intrapreneurship and trust that has worked in Germany. In Poland, for example, every store manager also holds a stake of up to 10 % in his store. Basically, Stiefel took the German structure and replicated it everywhere where this was legally possible. (In some cases, e.g., Italy, regulations did not permit employee shareholding and so Media Markt used profit-sharing bonuses.) Guided by Stiefel's vision of *"filling in all holes on the European map,"* which encompasses the market entry and expansion of the store network in every country, Media-Saturn Group's systematic European expansion continues with its recent entry into Turkey, Belgium and Luxembourg.

Key Challenges in Current and Future Growth of the Enterprise

Stiefel sees the key challenges of growth as *"maintaining the founder's spirit in the organization"* and *"finding the right balance between creativity and structure as the enterprise grows."* In Stiefel's view, transferring the entrepreneurial spirit of the founders to all the people involved is a fundamental driver of success. Thus, the real leadership skill required of a founder is not simply to start a company, but to be able to grow it to the next level while maintaining the original spirit and culture. *"That is one of the most difficult challenges an entrepreneur faces – guiding the transformation from a small, very simply managed company to a larger corporation with an extended structure and management without losing the original entrepreneurial spirit. This is a tougher challenge than any other posed by supply chain, operational, or marketing aspects of the business. There are many assistants to help with those jobs, but it is the founder's role and challenge to not lose sight of the 'creative chaos' that made the company while the organization develops larger structures, systems and controls as it gets bigger."* He goes on to say: *"You have to ask yourself: What do the employees working here want that will make them feel good while doing their work? What makes employees stay at a company for more than two or three years? Basically, they want as much freedom as possible, they want to step up, and they want to be able to make some independent decisions. So the challenge is not to kill that creative culture with system or structure."*

Somewhat counterintuitively, Stiefel's solution to these challenges is: *"Become more – not less – decentralized and give more trust as you get bigger."* To pull

PART II:

Global, Environmental, and Market Trends

Retail Trends in Europe

John Dawson

Universities of Stirling and Edinburgh, UK; ESADE, Barcelona, Spain; and UMDS
Kobe, Japan

Since the early 1990s there has been a substantial re-structuring of retailing in
Europe. Further, even greater, re-structuring is likely over the next 5 years. The
implications extend beyond Europe but they have had primary impact within
European markets. The restructuring involves not only changes in horizontal competitive relationships amongst retailers but also involves new forms of relationship
with suppliers and an extension of the activities of West European retailers into
Central Europe. The restructuring has occurred alongside substantive changes in
strategies, relationships and operations. These changes have encouraged the emergence of an alternative perspective of the role of retailing that places retailing as
the initiator of added value activities in the economy rather than in its traditionally
more passive role of building on the value being added in manufacturing. The new
role places retailing in a global framework of international store operations, international sourcing of products, international flows of management and managerial
know-how, and international retailer brands. The aim of this chapter is threefold:

- to place the re-structuring in context,

- to consider its nature, and,

- to explore how the new global framework could affect Europe over the
  next decade.

The chapter comprises five parts. First, the new role of retailing is explored. Secondly, there is consideration of what is changing in the retail sector of Europe.
Thirdly, some implications of the changes are explored. The fourth part considers
why the changes are taking place. Finally, there is consideration of the underpinning nature of innovation in the changes and exploration of how future patterns
may develop.

M. Krafft and M.K. Mantrala (eds.), *Retailing in the 21st Century: Current and Future Trends*,   63
DOI 10.1007/978-3-540-72003-4_5, © Springer-Verlag Berlin Heidelberg 2010

The New Role of Retailing

Re-structuring into a global context is the most recent stage of a half a century of change in European retailing that can be seen as comprising three major phases (Dawson 1999). The first phase occurred during the years after 1945 when the priority for the retail sector was the reconstruction of both the organisational and physical structures of retailing. There was a strong American influence in managerial developments, for example in the introduction of self-service into the food sector. A number of American firms, for example JC Penney, entered Europe. City and town centres were reconstructed across much of northern Europe and retailing was used as a catalyst for the physical re-construction of cities such as Coventry, Exeter, Cologne, Rotterdam and West Berlin as well as many smaller towns. Generally, consumers were seeking more products after the several years of scarcity and retailers provided additional floor space to meet these needs.

The development of the 'Common Market' in Western Europe and the subsequent development into a more integrated European Union marks a second phase. The retail markets across Europe started to consolidate and substantial growth of a different type occurred. Marketing became accepted as a key activity for retailers with different types of retailing being designed to satisfy different consumer needs. As market segmentation developed, so retailers explored new formats. For example, the large self-service single level superstore format, often located on the edge or out-of-town, was developed through the 1970s and early 1980s in several sectors, notably the hypermarket for general merchandise, and, superstores for food, DIY, toys, electrical goods, furniture, etc. Consumers, during this second phase, wanted different products and better quality products rather than simply more products.

The third phase, which is the period of change presently evident, is characterised by a re-structuring of retailing with new roles and functions becoming evident. The convergence of information and communication technologies, the application of new materials, and other applications of technology, such as RFID, across the value chain are enabling retailing to take on more forceful roles within the economy (Dawson 2001). Economies of scale of organisations associated with global sourcing and international operation of stores are allowing retailers to become some of the largest firms within Europe. By 2004, METRO Group, Carrefour and Tesco were amongst the largest twenty firms by market capitalisation in Germany, France and UK respectively. Retailers have become major elements in the composition of European economies.

Ranked by sales[1], Carrefour, METRO Group and Tesco are in the list of the largest ten retailers in the world (Table 1). Aldi GmbH, Schwarz Unternehmens

---

[1] Obtaining comparability of sales rankings is notoriously difficult due to different accounting definitions and different ends to financial years. This ranking converts figures to $ at average rates over the year. By using conversion rates at other times, for example year end, some difference in ranking would be present.

different consumer cultures. It was only in 1993 that Tesco began to operate stores outside the UK in a way that required a different organisational structure to be devised[2]. Table 3 shows the international expansion of Tesco over the 14 years. This network of stores now requires a very different organisation than that needed to manage only UK stores in 1993. It took 10 years 1993-2003 to open 310 stores outside the UK and in one year, 2005-6, 238 were opened with 419 planned for 2006-7. It is not only international operations that require a more complex organisational structure to the firm. International sourcing centres have to be accommodated in organisations. The outsourcing of many previously in-sourced functions also changes organisations. The diversification of retailers into financial and leisure services provides further organisational complexities.

Moves Towards Retailer Co-ordinated Value Chains. In recent years the nature of the value chain within the successful retailers has changed substantially. Retailers have become increasingly involved in co-ordinating the relationships between retailers and suppliers. Thus value is created at a variety of places in the value chain, not simply at the point of final sale to the customer. In taking costs out of the channel of distribution there is a redistribution of the locus of value generation. An example of this is in the terms of trade that exist between retailers and suppliers such that a retailer's inventory is financed by suppliers. By providing a longer number of credit days than the inventory turn of the retailer, the retailer operates with negative working capital. Table 4 illustrates the degree of negative working capital enjoyed by large European retailers.

These four changes illustrate the nature of the changes taking place in European retailing during this third and current phase of major re-structuring. They are clearly

Table 4. Key Operating Ratios of Carrefour, Sainsbury and Tesco

	Inventory value as a percentage of sales			Working capital as percentage of sales		
	2005-6	2002-3	1999-00	2005-6	2002-3	1999-00
Carrefour	8.2	8.7	13.2	−12.3	−9.6	−13.5
Sainsbury	3.6	5.3	5.3	−6.2	−6.1	−6.1
Tesco	4.0	3.9	3.4	−9.6	−8.8	−9.4
Casino	9.0	8.5	8.9	−6.3	−4.2	−8.2
METRO Group	11.2	10.7	11.2	−6.9	−1.5	−2.3

(Source: company accounts)

---

[2] Tesco entered Ireland in 1978 but withdrew in 1986. The UK organisational structure was simply extended to Ireland and this is often quoted as one of the reasons for failure of the international venture. The move into France in 1993, with withdrawal in 1997, is generally regarded as the first move in the current strategy of internationalisation.

inter-related with the focus on strategy underpinning the rapid growth of the large firms and the change in financial relationships with suppliers. The four changes are illustrative of the totality of change and other changes could be highlighted. Nonetheless the conclusion that can be drawn is that the current phase of re-structuring is resulting in an increase in the complexity of the sector, a quickening in the rate of development and a more global perspective being adopted by management.

The Implications of the Changes

There are many implications of the changes in the role and structure of the retail sector across Europe. A major implication is an increased level of governmental intervention in retailing. Four particular aspects of change give rise to governmental intervention at various levels across Europe:

The Increase in Market Concentration. With the continuing growth of already large firms and their acquisition activity, the competition agencies in individual European countries and in the European Commission have become more active in reviewing levels of market concentration. In the UK the inquiry in 2003 by the Competition Commission into the proposed acquisition of Safeway by others in the grocery sector highlighted the problems of defining the market for the purposes of measuring market concentration. In some cases competition authorities are now considering the competitive impacts of the acquisition of a single store by a large retailer when this is thought to have an effect of reducing potential competition at the local market level. Although there are many unresolved issues associated with measurement of market shares, particularly at local levels, nonetheless governments increasingly are involved in market interventions.

The Decrease in the Number of Small and Micro Firms. An aspect of long term structural change has been the decline of small firms in retailing across Europe (Eurostat 2002). This loss of small firms has become more acute in recent years such that governments have been exploring ways to provide support to smaller firms through different types of policy initiative. These include limiting the local competition from large firms by restricting the establishment of new shops, providing direct financial help to the small firms to encourage investment and training, reducing the tax burdens on small firms, encouraging co-operative behaviour amongst small firms, and providing special protection to particular sub-sectors, for example pharmacists and small firms in rural areas and in the lowest income parts of cities. Governmental intervention in the market in these cases is aimed at protecting smaller firms from the full rigour of the market.

The Change in the Balance of Competitive Power Between Retailers and Their Suppliers. An implication of the changes in retailing is the growth of channel power of retailers at the expense of their suppliers (Pilat 1997). Governments have sought to intervene in the market to regulate the behaviour of the participants in the channel. This has involved policies on the nature of the contracts between retailers and suppliers, the number of credit days allowed, the types of discount that can be used, the ability of retailers to re-sell products at below cost, etc.

The Increased International Activity of Retailers. In some European countries, notably those in central Europe that attracted large amounts of foreign direct investment into retailing after 1989, the governments have been adopting policies to limit foreign ownership of retailing. The rationale for such policies is to protect local retailers and suppliers from the business practices used by the foreign, often large, firms. Those foreign retailers that have a presence in the market, having entered early, are in effect protected from peer-group competition and so may benefit from the policies aimed at limiting them.

The extent of and types of intervention of governments in the retail markets is generally increasing in Europe. The rationale for intervention is generally to ameliorate, in some way, the consequences of the structural changes in the sector. In many cases the policies are instituted without a clear understanding by government of the nature of the causes of the structural changes that generate the 'undesirable' change but there is growing awareness of the complexity of the distributive trade in respect of the vertical relationships involved.

Why Is Retailing Changing?

The reasons for the structural adjustments in this third current phase of major change in European retailing can be presented as a process linking changes in the environment to responses by retail managers. Retailing, as an activity linking consumers to goods and services, operates in local markets. As such many of the managerial decisions are a response to both the local culture of the consumers and the local culture of consumption. Within Europe these local **cultures** are subject to considerable social, economic, political and technological changes. This dynamic cultural environment requires responses from retailers that seek success through the close matching of their operations to consumer requirements. These responses underpin the **strategies** of retailers. The strategies are executed through the **formats and formulae**[3] that the retailer creates. In creating these formats and formulae the retailer enters into **relationships** with other groups, for example suppliers, finance groups, consumers, etc. In the current context of activity in Europe all four of these attributes of the retail sector – **cultures, strategies, formats & formulae**, and **relationships** – are undergoing substantial change as they inter-act. It is the changes in these attributes that provide the reasons why retailing is changing in the ways that it is.

---

[3] The formats are the generic delivery vehicles of retailers, for example, hypermarket, department store, convenience store, mail order catalogue, vending machine, etc. The formula is the branded version of the format that is created by a particular firm. Thus, a hypermarket is the format and the Tesco Extra hypermarket, Casino hypermarket, Carrefour hypermarket, Real hypermarket are the different formulae.

Culture. The changes in consumer culture in Europe after 1989 have been considerable. The emergence of market economies in central Europe meant widespread privatisation of retailing. Perhaps of greater importance in terms of consumer culture, however, has been the increased demand for products and services from consumers in the former communist countries. Steady increases in consumer wealth after the initial periods of high inflation have meant that from the mid-1990s consumers have expected a more extensive range of price-quality combinations in the retailing. In clothing for example distinct markets in street fashion, work clothes, high fashion, discount apparel, etc emerged quickly to parallel the market structures that have been developed, more gradually, in West Europe. As these Central European countries enter fully into the European Community, in phases after May 2004, so these cultures of consumption will develop more rapidly. In many cases it is the retailers of the 1990s that have created the nature of the cultures of consumption in the Central European countries.

Across much of Western Europe consumer cultures show apparent contradictory trends of standardisation and fragmentation. The fragmentation of demand is evident in many ways with ever smaller segments of consumers having specific patterns of demand. Consumers have translated their values into demands for goods and services such that there are differing values, for example the ecologically responsive groups, vegetarian groups, designer brand groups, sport obsessed groups, etc. These are in addition to the longer established groups associated with age, educational level, income, etc. This fragmentation has been encouraged by specialist media. The fragmentation has been extended even further with consumer demands varying on a temporal dimension – by time of day or day of the week. The consumer can no longer be considered as one person but has to be viewed as many different 'people' (Ziliani 1999).

In apparent contradiction to this fragmentation is a Europeanisation of some aspects of consumer demand. With the wider and faster availability of information through satellite communication, the rapid diffusion of fashion, in clothes and music particularly, has generated European-wide patterns of demand. The movement of people through Europe particularly for leisure and tourism similarly has generated a diffusion of cultures, often in food items, with consumers in Northern Europe becoming familiar with foods from the South and vice–versa. The availability of international manufacturer brands, in electrical items, food, grocery, toys, etc. stimulates this move to 'sameness' or 'Europeanisation'. The euro-integration of consumer infrastructures is often facilitated by common technologies in the home or mobile 'close to body' technologies (mobile phones, pocket computers, hand-held games machines, etc.). The driving force for much of this integration is a combination of the aspirations European politicians and multi-national manufacturers. Many European politicians have a vision of the future as a single and more standardised European market. Multi-national manufacturers wish to exploit economies of scale by producing goods for a large market, but often consumers have a more local perspective.

	Traditional Innovation	Experience Innovation
Focus of innovation	Products and processes	Experience environments - formula and relationships
Basis of value	Products and services	Co-creation of environment with customers, retailer and suppliers
Nature of value creation	Firm creates value Supply-chain-centric fulfilment of products and services Supply push and demand pull	Value is co-created Experience environments for individuals to co-construct experiences in situations Individual-centric co-creation of value
Function of technology	Facilitator of features and functions Technology and systems integration	Facilitator of experiences Experience integration
Function of supply chain	Supports fulfilment of products and services	Experience network supports co-construction of personalised experiences

Fig. 3. The Differences Between Traditional and Experience Based Innovation (Based on Prahalad and Ramaswamy, 2003)

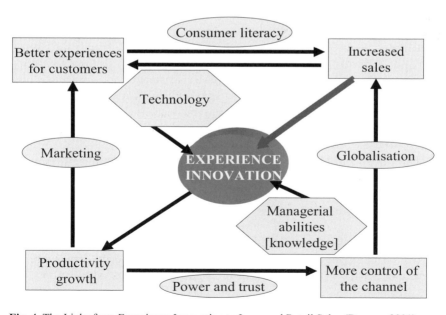

Fig. 4. The Links from Experience Innovation to Increased Retail Sales (Dawson 2001)

Thirdly, retailers in their marketing activities will look beyond the traditional issues of price and service and explore the ideas of 'experience space' and 'experience innovation'. This will mean involving consumers much more in the shopping 'experience' so that profit is co-created. The passive view of customers as agents for transactions, even sometimes for exploitation, will not be appropriate for retailers in the future. This major change in the business model, already evident in the activities of major retailers, will spread more generally through the retail sector. As the approach becomes adopted more widely it will require some major changes in managerial knowledge and adaptability. Some local retailers will find this change beyond their capability and are likely to fail. Others will respond and themselves generate new innovative ways to compete that are grounded in the local knowledge they have of consumer culture. It is these adaptive and innovative local retailers who will provide the strongest competition to the large retailers.

Fourthly, it is unlikely that the strong trend towards market concentration will be reversed and in all sectors we are likely to see increased market concentration at national, regional and local levels. The economies of scale of large firms, particularly from global sourcing, will drive price deflation, with the large retailers then focusing on increasing sales volumes to maintain their profitability. Alongside the scale economies obtained at firm level there will be economies of scope obtained at establishment level. These scope economies will also generate increases in market concentration.

Associated with these four likely changes there are two other considerations relevant to a view of retailing in Europe over the next 5 years. Several of the changes will require applications of convergent information and communication technologies to facilitate the managerial processes that will generate the change. The firms that will benefit most are those that are able to provide these facilitating technological innovations. The big unknown consideration for the future is the role that government will take in shaping and regulating retailing, directly through policies of competition and rights of establishment and indirectly through polices affecting the environment in which retailers operate. The four major trends are likely to operate irrespective of governmental intervention. The speed at which the trends will develop is what will be subject to government policies.

Acknowledgement

Work on the initial version of this chapter for the first edition took place whilst the author was in receipt of support from Ministerio de Educación y Ciencia, Madrid under award SAB2003-0246. This support is gratefully acknowledged.

These different shopping situations and motivations result in an increase in cross-shopping – a pattern of buying both premium and low-priced merchandise or patronizing expensive, status-oriented retailers and price-oriented retailers.

Retail Industry Trends

Retailers have responded to the consumer trends by (1) reducing their costs to increase value delivered, (2) targeting the needs of specific market segments and (3) beginning to offer a personalized shopping experience (Retail Forward 2003).

Cost Reduction

During the last 20 years, largely driven by the efficiencies achieved and low prices offered by Wal-Mart, U.S. retailers have focused on reducing their operating costs through (1) developing scale economies, (2) increasing supply chain efficiencies, (3) operating big box stores, (4) centralizing overhead functions and (5) beginning to adopt more analytical management techniques. This emphasis on cost reduction has increased the price differential between low service, low price retailers and higher price retailers that don't offer merchandise or customer service with meaningful differences.

Scale Economies

Many U.S. retailers have realized scale economies through aggressive internal growth and acquisition. This drive toward scale economies has greatly increased concentration in various retail sectors. For example, in 2003, the top three chains account for 30 % of drug store sales; 85 % of full-line discount store sales; and 36 % of consumer electronics store sales.

Supply Chain

Retailers are managing their supply chains more efficiently though collaboration with their vendors. They are sharing information with vendors to effectively engage in joint forecasting and planning (see, e.g., chapter by Huchzermeier and Iyer in this book). The most recent activities to further improve supply chain efficiency involve the desire to use RFID tags to track shipments.

Big Boxes

Many of the fastest growing U.S. retail sectors involve larger size stores – e.g., supercenters and category specialists – that have greater operating efficiencies.

Centralization

Retailers are also reducing costs by centralizing overhead functions. For example, department store chains such as JCPenney, Belks and Nordstrom used to have regional buyers and even store managers making merchandise assortment decisions. These retailers now have centralized buying functions and use information systems to tailor assortment to local tastes.

Analytical Methods

While many of these approaches to cost reduction (such as supply chain management) have reached a point of diminishing return for the most sophisticated U.S. retailers, a promising new era involving the use of analytical methods is just beginning. These methods are directed at getting more sales and profits out of existing stores. By using analytical tools, retailers can optimize decisions that were informally made using rules of thumb (see, e.g., chapter on applications of intelligent technologies by Ravi, Raman and Mantrala in this book).

Targeting Needs of Specific Segments

While retailers have been focusing on reducing costs and prices, retailers also are beginning to explore approaches for developing offerings directed toward the needs of specific customer segments. National retail chains have long adjusted assortments based on climate. Now retailers are adjusting store assortments and services based on more sophisticated analyses of local markets (see, e.g., Grewal et al chapter in this book).

Best Buy has developed specialized stores to focus on specific customer segments when there is significant customer-type representation in the local area. For example, stores in areas with professional high income households promote high-end entertainment systems; whereas stores in areas with busy suburban mothers dedicate more inventory to merchandise like learning software and feature softer colors, a children's technology department, a children's play area and personal shopping services.

Another trend is the rise of specialty retailers focusing on a specific segment. For example, Two Inc. targets the tween segment. Apparel assortments are fine tuned to a younger body type and special fixtures are placed at eye level for younger girls.

Another example, Chico's, with more than 300 specialty stores, sells apparel that is fashionable but clearly designed for a woman aged 35 to 55, not a teenager. Apparel is designed to flatter more mature women.

Personalizing the Shopping Experience

Retailers are just beginning to develop an understanding of what creates value for individual customers for specific shopping occasions and personalize their offerings at the point of contact. To move toward this personalization, retailers are building and analyzing customer databases that integrate information about all of the contracts the retailer has with a customer – contacts in stores (e.g., as discussed elsewhere in this book by Burke), via the Internet and with call centers .

Growth of Retail Sectors

These general trends are reflected in the growth of different retail sectors and retailers with in the sectors as discussed in the following sections.

While U.S. retail sales have grown at a modest rate paralleling the 4% to 5% growth in GDP, there are significant variations in the growth rates of different retail sectors, and firms within each sector, as shown below. For example, reflecting the attractiveness of a low cost strategy, supercenters, category specialists, warehouse clubs, and limited assortment retailers are realizing high growth while department and full line discount stores are experiencing limited growth. On the other hand, Kohl's, a department store chain, and Target, a discount store chain, are experiencing high sales growth through their distinctive offerings.

Table 1. Estimated Compounded Sales Growth 2003-2008 (%)

	Sales 2003 $ Millions	Estimated % Sales Compounded Sales Growth 2003-2008
Food Retailers		
Conventional supermarkets	455.470	2,5
Supercenters	150.995	15,0
Warehouse clubs	76.341	6,0
Convenience stores	337.000	5,0
General Merchandise Retailers		
Department stores	86.848	-1,0
Apparel and accesory specialty stores	129.790	4,4
Jewelry stores	26.848	5,8
Shoe stores	21.976	1,4
Furniture stores	52.129	4,9
Home furnishing stores	45.848	5,8
Office supply stores	24.345	3,8
Sporting goods stores	27.792	5,2
Book stores	15.180	4,5
Building material hardware, and garden supply stores	321.134	6,2
Consumer electronics and appliance stores	95.380	5,7
Drug stores	163.929	6,9
Full line discount stores	131.013	1,0
Food and General merchandise extreme value	39.585	6,2
Nonstore retailers		
Nonstore retailing	123.419	9,2
E-commerce	54.900	26,8

(Sources: U.S. Department of Commerce, company reports, National Association of Convenience Stores and Retail Forward, Inc.)

Trends in U.S. Food Retailers

The food retailing landscape is changing dramatically (Retail Forward 2004a). Twenty years ago, consumers purchased food primarily at conventional supermarkets. As shown below, nearly four out of 10 shoppers report doing most of their food shopping somewhere other than a conventional supermarket. The fastest growing segment of the food retail market are low cost, low price formats – supercenters, warehouse clubs and limited assortment supermarkets. However, traditional supermarkets and convenience stores are responding by differentiating their offering.

Table 2. Food Shopping Formats

	Format Where Most Food Shopping Is Done	Average Annual Real Sales Growth 1998-2003
Conventional supermarkets	61 %	1 %
Supercenters	19 %	23 %
Limited assortment supermarkets	6 %	N.A.
Warehouse clubs	4 %	10 %
Others including convenience stores	10 %	Varies

(Source: Retail Forward ShopperScape™, U.S. Department of Commerce, company reports, and Retail Forward, Inc.)

Supermarkets

While conventional supermarkets still sell a majority of food merchandise in the U.S., they are under substantial competitive pressure. Everyone wants a piece of the food pie. Supercenters are rapidly attracting conventional supermarket customers with their broader assortments of general merchandise at attractive prices. Full-line discount chains like Target and dollar stores are increasing the amount of space devoted to consumables. Convenience stores are also selling more fresh merchandise.

Even though supermarket chains have reduced their operating costs through consolidation, category management and better supply chain management, the format continues to have higher operating costs than supercenters. To compete successfully against intrusions by other food retail formats, conventional supermarkets are differentiating their offering by (1) emphasizing fresh perishables, (2) targeting health conscious and ethnic consumer segments, (3) providing a better in-store experience and (4) offering more private label brands.

Fresh Perishables

Fresh merchandise categories, including dairy, bakery, meats, fish, produce and coffee bars, are differentiators and profit generators for conventional supermarkets. Conventional supermarkets are building on this strength by devoting more space to fresh merchandise.

Another example of emphasizing "fresh" is offering meal-solutions for time-pressured consumers. At Wegmans (an upstate NY-based supermarket chain), customers can eat lunch overlooking the European-style Market Cafe or buy prepared meals to take home. Chefs in monogrammed white jackets and tall pleated paper hats staff the separate pizza, deli and fresh-baked bread stations. Along one wall, Caesar salads are made to order. At another station, customers have a choice of Alfredo, marinara or vodka sauce on the hot pasta. Folks who keep kosher have their own area for, perhaps, meat-stuffed cabbage and potato pancakes or a Waldorf salad.

Targeting Specific Segments

Targeting wellness oriented baby boomers, conventional supermarkets are offering more natural, organic, low-fat, low-sugar and low-salt merchandise for the growing segment of consumers who are health-conscious or have dietary restrictions. Sales at Whole Foods and Wild Oats, two national supermarket chains that focus on natural/organic food, are growing at 20 % per year.

Conventional supermarkets are also adjusting their merchandise mix to attract more ethnic shoppers. Hispanics are more likely to prepare meals from scratch, spend more on groceries, prefer stores with bilingual staff and signage and place importance on fresh food. To address these specific needs, President Supermarkets in Little Havana in Miami creates an appealing an environment for Hispanics playing merengue or mariachi music plays over the store's audio system , not Moody Blues or Neil Diamond; offering unique produce such as "Haitian mangoes", "fresh cassavas" and "Jamaican yellow yams"; and employing Cuban, Mexican, Haitian, Colombian and Peruvian grocery clerks.

Shopping Experience

Creating an enjoyable shopping experience through store ambiance and customer service is a key approach that supermarket chains are using to differentiate themselves from low-cost, low-price competitors. Supermarkets are increasingly incorporating "food as theatre" concepts such as open-air market designs, cooking classes, demos, and food tasting.

Private Labels

Private labels provide an opportunity for conventional supermarkets to increase profit margins and differentiate their assortment. Presently private labels account for only 15 % to 20 % of supermarket sales, far less than their penetration in Europe.

Supercenters

Supercenters, stores that combine a supermarket with a full line discount store, are the fastest-growing store-based retail sector in the United States. While supercenters are the fastest growing segment in food retailing, they face challenges in finding locations for new stores. In the United States, there has been a backlash to large retail stores particularly, Wal-Mart stores. These opposing sentiments are based on the views that big box stores drive local retailers out of business, offer low wages and nonunion jobs, have unfair labor practices, threaten U.S. workers because they buy imported merchandise, and cause excessive automobile and delivery truck traffic.

Limited Assortment Supermarkets

Another fast growing U.S. retail segment is limited assortment supermarkets. The two largest chains in the United States are Sav-A-Lot and Aldi. While conventional supermarkets typically carry 20,000 SKUs, limited assortment stores carry about 1,000 SKUs. Stores are designed to maximize efficiency and reduce costs. For example, merchandise is shipped in cartons that can serve as displays so that no unloading is needed. Some costly services such as free bags and paying with credit cards are not provided. Stores are typically located in second- or third-tier shopping centers with low rents. While these stores target low-income consumers, they are beginning to appeal to value-conscious, middle-income consumers.

Warehouse Clubs

Warehouse clubs are also experiencing good growth. Costco differentiates itself by offering unique upscale merchandise not available elsewhere at low prices. For example, Costco began selling fine art priced from $450 to $15,000 on its Web site. Sam's Club focuses more on small businesses, providing relevant products and services such as group health insurance. Wholesale members typically represent less than 30 % of the customer base but account for more than 70 % of sales.

Convenience Stores

Convenience stores in the United States are facing increased competition from other formats. Convenience store sales are affected by gasoline prices – increasing during periods of rising gasoline prices. But the dependency on gasoline sales is a problem because gasoline sales have low margins. In addition, supercenter and supermarket chains are attempting to increase customer store visits by offering gasoline and tying gasoline sales into their frequent shopper programs. Drug stores and full line discount stores are setting up easily accessed areas of their stores with convenience store-type merchandise.

In response to these competitive pressures, convenience stores are taking steps to decrease their dependency on gasoline sales, tailoring assortments to local markets and making their stores even more convenient to shop. To get gasoline customers to spend more on other merchandise and services, convenience stores are offering more fresh food and healthy fast food that appeal to today's on-the-go consumers, especially women and young adults. Finally convenience stores are also adding new services such as financial service kiosks that give customers the opportunity to cash checks, pay bills, and buy prepaid telephone minutes, theatre tickets and gift cards.

Convenience stores are exploring the use of technology to increase shopping convenience. For example, Sheetz, a Pennsylvania-based convenience store chain, has self-service food ordering kiosks at its gasoline pumps. Customers can order a custom-made sandwich while filling their tank and pick it up in the store when they finish.

Trends in U.S. General Merchandise Retailers

Department Sores

Traditionally, department stores attracted customers by offering a pleasing ambience, attentive service and a wide variety of merchandise under one roof. They sold softgoods (apparel and bedding) and hard goods (appliances, furniture and consumer electronics). But now most department stores focus almost exclusively on softgoods.

Department store chains can be categorized into three tiers. The first tier includes upscale, high fashion chains with exclusive designer merchandise and excellent customer service such as Neiman Marcus, Bloomingdale's (part of Federated Department Stores), and Saks Fifth Avenue (part of Saks). The second tier of department stores retailers is comprised of companies such as Macy's (also part of Federated Department Stores), May Company, and Dillard's. Retailers in this tier sell more modestly priced merchandise with less customer service. The value-oriented, third tier – dominated by Sears, JCPenney, and Kohl's – caters to more price-conscious consumers. The retail chains in the first tier have established a clearly differentiated position and are producing strong financial results. Chains in the second tier have yet to define a clear positioning and differentiation, while the value-oriented tier is facing significant competitive challenges from discount stores, particularly Target.

Even though third tier department stores are facing intense competition, Kohl's has been growing rapidly. Kohl's formula for success is offering shopping convenience for time-pressured, "soccer moms" interested in buying national brand apparel and soft home merchandise at reasonable prices. It sells national brands typically available in department stores and has exclusive sub-brand arrangements with some national brands sold at second tier department stores such as Estee Lauder cosmetics and Laura Ashley home textile and bedroom accessories.

But the key to Kohl's success is convenience. Its stores are located in suburban neighborhood centers and they are easy to shop. The stores are smaller (80,000 square feet) than traditional, mall-based department stores and are on one floor. The aisles and fixture spacings are wider than the typical department store so that customers can easily navigate the store pushing a shopping cart or baby stroller. Rather than having POS terminal at each department, the stores have centralized cash wraps (checkout stations) near the store entrances so that customers can select merchandise from different areas of the store and pay for it all at once when they are ready to leave.

Since Kohl's does not carry designer brands that require "store within a store" displays, merchandise is grouped by type of item rather than brand. It avoids the cluttered look by positioning display racks in amphitheater style, making all the merchandise visible. Colors are displayed from light to dark, a pattern that is most appealing to the eye. And unlike most stores, which try to straighten up merchandise all day, Kohl's keeps presentations sharp with a daily 2 p.m. "recovery period," when everyone in the store – from secretaries to store managers – are called upon to straighten up displays. Night crews do something similar. The total effect is to allow sales clerks to concentrate solely on customers.

Consumers feel that department stores are not as convenient as discount stores because they are located in large regional malls rather than local neighborhoods. Customer service has diminished due to cut backs in labor costs. Department stores have not been as successful as discount stores and food retailers in reducing costs by working with their vendors to establish just-in-time inventory systems, so prices are relatively high.

The performance of department stores is linked to the strengths of the brands they sell – brands such as Liz Claibourne, Tommy Hilfiger, Ralph Lauren and Estee Lauder. In light of the decline in department store patronage, many of these brands historically sold exclusively through department are pursing other growth opportunities. For example, Estee Lauder, a supplier of various cosmetic brands to first and second tier department stores, has developed three exclusive private label cosmetics lines for Kohl's. Levi Strauss created the Levi Straus Signature line for Wal-Mart and other discount stores (Marineau 2004).

Strategies

To deal with their eroding market share, department stores are (1) attempting to increase the amount of exclusive merchandise they sell, (2) undertaking marketing campaigns to develop strong images for their stores and brands and (3) building better relationships with their key customers (Retail Forward 2004b). To differentiate their merchandise offering and strengthen their image, department stores are aggressively seeking exclusive arrangements with nationally recognized brands. For example, Macy's negotiated with Tommy Hilfiger to launch its new H line exclusively with supporting advertising featuring Iman and David Bowie. JCPenney became the exclusive retailer for Bisou Bisou, a contemporary apparel brand that was previously sold through better specialty stores and upscale department stores.

In addition, department stores are placing more emphasis on developing their own private label brands. For example, Macy's has been very successful in developing a strong image for its private label brands such as INC (women's clothing) and Tools of the Trade (housewares).

In recent years, department stores' discount sales events have increased dramatically to the point that consumers have been trained to wait for the sale than buy at full price. Department stores are now shifting their marketing activities from promotional sales to brand building activities involving television advertising and specialty publications such as Saks Fifth Avenue's *S* magazine.

Finally, department stores are using technology and information systems to improve customer service in a cost effective manner. To improve customer service, wireless devices are being used on the selling floor to provide sales associates with customer and merchandise information. Department stores are collecting and analyzing information to identify their best customers and target promotions to these customers.

Full Line Discount Stores

Since Wal-Mart alone accounts for more than 58 % of full line discount store retail sales, the most significant trend in this retail sector is Wal-Mart's conversion of discount stores to supercenters (Retail Forward 2004c). In 2008, Wal-Mart operated more than 2,400 supercenters and less than 1,000 traditional discount stores. With their full supermarket offer, supercenters attract shoppers more frequently. The conventional discount stores also face intense competition from discount specialty stores that focus on a single category of merchandise, such as Old Navy, Best Buy, Bed, Bath & Beyond, Sports Authority and Lowe's.

While Wal-Mart is converting its full line discount stores, Target, one of the most successful retailers in terms of sales growth and profitability, is still growing its discount store base. Target's success is based on offering fashionable merchandise at low prices in a pleasant shopping environment. Target has developed an image of "cheap chic" by teaming with designers such as Michael Graves, Isaac Mizrahi and Giannulli Mossimo to produce inexpensive and exclusive fashionable merchandise.

Specialty Apparel and Accessories Stores

Specialty stores' success is based on offering assortments edited for a narrowly defined target market (Retail Forward 2003b). For example, Hot Topics focuses on selling licensed, music-inspired apparel to teenagers in mall-based stores. Its sales associates know what's new on the radio, in record stores, concert tours and pop culture. Its licensing, design and sourcing processes are designed so that it can move hot rock stars' fashions and logos from the concert stage to store shelves in 90 days.

Because specialty retailers focus on specific market segments, they are vulnerable to shifts in consumer tastes and preferences. Apparel and footwear specialty retailers are capturing less of the consumer's total spending because consumers are spending more on necessities involving health and home as well as "everyday" luxuries such as concert tickets and eating out.

Drug Stores

Drug stores, particularly the national chains, are experiencing sustained sales growth because the aging population requires more prescription drugs. Although the profit margins for prescription pharmaceuticals are higher than for other drug store merchandise, these margins are shrinking due to government health care policies, pharmaceutical benefit management services and public outcry about lower drug prices in other countries, especially Canada (Retail Forward 2004d).

Drugstores are also being squeezed by considerable competition from pharmacies in discount stores and supermarkets, as well as from prescription mail-order retailers. Wal-Mart is the third-largest pharmacy operator in the United States (behind Walgreens and CVS). In response, the major drug store chains are building larger stand-alone stores offering a wider assortment of merchandise, more frequently purchased food items and the convenience of drive-through windows for picking up prescriptions. To build customer loyalty, the chains are also changing the role of their pharmacists from pill dispensers to health care information providers, performing tasks such as explaining how to use a nebulizer.

Drug store retailers are using systems to allow pharmacists time to provide personalized service. For example, at Walgreens, customers can order prescription refills via the phone. They are automatically called when the prescription is ready. Based on the time they plan to pick up the prescription, a computer system automatically schedules the workload in the pharmacy. The systems also monitor the frequency of refilling prescriptions so the pharmacist can make phone calls or send e-mails to ensure patient drug compliance.

Category Specialist

Category specialists continue to flourish and expand the format to new categories such as musical instruments (Guitar Center) and outdoor activities (Bass Pro Shop and REI). By offering a complete assortment in a category at low prices, these chains can "kill" a category of merchandise for other retailers and thus are frequently called category killers. For example, Bass Pro Shop has 25 stores that are highly interactive and entertaining, catering to consumers who like to participate in

fabrication, cleaning instructions, and so forth. Finally she selects and purchases the dress with one click.

Using information displayed on her PDA, Joan, the sales associate helping Judy, suggests a handbag and scarf that would complement the dress. These accessories are displayed on the image of Judy in the dress. Judy decides to buy the scarf but not the handbag. Finally, Judy is told about the minor alterations needed to make the dress a perfect fit. She can check the retailer's Web site to find out when the alterations are completed and then indicate whether she wants the dress delivered to her home or if she will pick it up at the store.

As Judy passes through the cosmetics department on the way to her car, she sees an appealing new lipstick shade displayed on a digital sign – a message triggered by the chip on her credit card. She purchases the lipstick and a 3-ounce bottle of her favorite perfume and walks out of the store. The store systems sense her departure, and the merchandise she has selected is automatically charged to her account through the use of RFID.

References

DSN Retailing Today (2004), Dollar Formats Continue Food Expansion, DSN Retailing Today, July 19, 2004, p. 10.

Marineau, Phillip, Fitting In: In Bow to Retailer's New Clout, Levi Strauss Makes Alterations, The Wall Street Journal, June 17, 2004, p. A1.

Retail Forward (2003a). Twenty Trends for 2010: Retailing in an Age of Uncertainty. Columbus, OH: Retail Forward, April 2003, p. 8.

Retail Forward (2003b) Growth Strategies for Specialty Apparel Retailers. Columbus, OH: Retail Forward, August 2003.

Retail Forward (2004a). Industry Outlook: Food Channel. Columbus, OH: Retail Forward, February 2004.

Retail Forward (2004b) Industry Outlook: Department Stores. Columbus, OH: Retail Forward, February 2004.

Retail Forward (2004c) Industry Outlook: Mass Channel. Columbus, OH: Retail Forward, April 2004.

Retail Forward (2004d) Industry Outlook: Drug Channel. Columbus, OH: Retail Forward, August 2004.

Retail Forward (2004e) Industry Outlook: Multi-channel Retailing: Benchmarks and Practices. Columbus, OH: Retail Forward, May 2004.

Trends in Retailing in East Asia

Roy Larke

ESADE School of Business, Barcelona, Spain and UMDS Kobe, Japan

Introduction: The East Asian Retail Market

East Asia is a region currently undergoing rapid retail development. There is little mystery in this. It is by far the most densely populated region of the world, and, with some important exceptions, remains largely undeveloped in terms of modern retailing. This latter fact is changing as the world's leading grocery retailers, notably Carrefour, METRO Group, Tesco, and Wal-Mart, expand in the region, emphasizing East Asian markets as a major pillar of their global strategies. In addition, and although almost unrecognized in the Western press and academic literature, equally large retailers from Japan are also aggressively building market share in all of the key markets in the region.

Such factors make East Asia one of the most interesting regions in the world in terms of how retailing will develop over the next few years. At the same time, East Asia is not a homogenous entity. It does not have a common language, culture, religion or even a single race. There are wide disparities between countries in terms of economic development and standards of living. The geography of the region ranges from desert to jungle and from snowbound winters in northern Japan to constant 30 degree temperatures in Singapore and Indonesia. It is by no means a single market. In contrast, Europe, which is also a large and diverse market, is still more uniform.

For these reasons, it is inappropriate to attempt to analyze East Asia as a single market. At the same time, the development of retailing in the region shares two important characteristics. First, local, domestic retail markets remain relatively unsophisticated, and second, there are very few large, multinational retailers that originate from Asia. Both of these characteristics are now in transition. As East Asian markets grow, so too does the retail industry, and this has attracted a significant number of international firms most of which originate from advanced economies. These companies are already dominant in a number of East Asian retail markets and their impact on the development of retailing locally is considerable. There have been few studies concerning such impact, but the accelerated development of local retail markets as a result of foreign retailer entry is impossible to deny (Davies 2000).

M. Krafft and M.K. Mantrala (eds.), *Retailing in the 21st Century: Current and Future Trends*,   101
DOI 10.1007/978-3-540-72003-4_7, © Springer-Verlag Berlin Heidelberg 2010

Economic Background

The region of East Asia is so diverse that most major international bodies do not define it in any convenient way. Asia is an area of 50 million square kilometers and 4 billion people when considered in its broadest definition including India, Pakistan, and countries in the centre of the Asian continent. As East Asia and South East Asia are the areas where much of the retail development activity is currently taking place this chapter concentrates on this part of the region (see Table 1). Even then, East Asia alone covers 15.6 million square kilometers and is home to 2.067 billion people.

Table 1 shows the basic demographics for this region. It consists of some 16 countries in total and the diversity in the region is obvious. China alone accounts for more than 60 % of both the total population and land area. While, in contrast, a number of countries are relatively small, and population densities are high.

Table 1. Demographic Data for Region of East Asia

Country	Area	Population	Population Density	GDP per Capita
	sq km	in millions in 2007	per sq km	in US$ 2007
Cambodia	181,040	14,4	80	540
Indonesia	1,919,440	225,6	118	1650
Japan	377,853	127,8	338	37670
Laos	236,800	5,9	25	580
Malaysia	329,750	26,5	80	6540
Mongolia	1,565,000	2,6	2	1290
North Korea	120,540	23,8	197	–
PR of China	9,596,960	1320	138	2360
Philippines	300,000	87,9	293	1620
PRC Hong Kong	1,092	6,9	6319	31610
PRC Macau	25	0,5	20000	14020
Republic of China	35,980	22,9	636	17930
Singapore	693	4,6	6638	32470
South Korea	98,480	48,5	492	19690
Thailand	514,000	63,8	124	3400
Vietnam	329,560	85,1	258	790
Total	15,607,213	2066,8	132	5216

(Source: World Bank 2007)

In terms of GDP per capita, the variation is large, running from Japan, the second richest country in the world with an average GDP per head of $37,670 in 2003, to just $540 per head in Cambodia. Three countries have GDP per head below $1,000, and all of these have received little international retail development to date, but ten of the remaining 11 countries are subject to considerable interest from international retail conglomerates. They represent some of the most internationalized retail markets in the world.

Retailing data is scarce for East Asia, and what does exist concentrates on the largest countries and those seen as having the greatest potential for retail development. Until the mid 1990s, only Japan, Hong Kong, and Singapore had advanced retail markets. Today, however, South Korea, Malaysia, Taiwan and Thailand have joined these three countries, and in each case the large overseas retailers have been a major factor in the development of the retail industry.

China, with its population of more than 1 billion people, is almost a region itself. While the country lags a long way behind in terms of GDP per capita, the size of the market and the potential it represents has drawn a number of international retail companies there. At the same time, the Chinese market remains one of future potential rather than significant current return. Many overseas retailers operate there, but consumer incomes remain low and only primary and secondary cities are important consumer markets. China is, therefore, a long-term proposition for most companies.

Until recently, Japan was also a market that had received relatively less attention from international retailers. On the surface, Japan's advanced economy and large domestic retail market makes it unattractive to outsiders due to high costs in competing with existing domestic firms. Entry into other East Asian markets is seen as more cost effective. But Japan's market remains highly fragmented. This finally led to the entry of Carrefour in 2000, with Wal-Mart, METRO Group, and Tesco following shortly afterwards.

Consequently, the Chinese and Japanese retail markets almost warrant their own chapters. In terms of retail development activity, China is currently the most active market in the world, and as government restrictions on cross-regional retail activity were finally lifted under WTO rules in 2004, this activity is becoming more intense. Japan, after undergoing more than 10 years of slow economic growth and industrial restructuring, is finally emerging as a modern retail market. International penetration remains low, but the situation is changing. Better Japanese retailers are internationalizing and competing directly with Western firms across the East Asian region and particularly in China. The influence and impact of Japanese market entry is at least as strong as that of non-Asian retailers.

There are two key trends across the region as a whole. First, the size of markets in East Asia are attracting increasing numbers of international retailers. China is the most recent example but international retail development in Thailand, South Korea, Taiwan, Malaysia, and Singapore are already at a far more advanced stage. Other countries such as Vietnam, Indonesia, and the Philippines are also high on the watch lists of international retail firms. Secondly, the modernization of the

Japanese retail and distribution industries means that better companies are now multi-regional players in their own right. As discussed below, Japanese firms already have a large presence in East Asia and are now quickly catching up with Carrefour and Wal-Mart in China. This trend is set to continue and strengthen.

Retailing in East Asia

Table 2 offers a useful summary of retailing in the region. It clearly shows the contrast between different countries in terms of the market size and the varying degrees of development. Euromonitor (2002) surveyed 52 relatively advanced countries to produce these data and the rankings refer to this sample.

While Japan is the largest market by a factor of almost three, China's estimated retail sales of US$390 billion are also significant, and ranked third in the world by Euromonitor. South Korea is the only other market in the region that currently comes close to the US$100 billion mark, and ranks relatively low as the twelfth largest market in the world.

If we look at these figures in percentage terms (Figure 1), Japan alone accounts for 58.7 % of the total retail market in East Asia, and more than 82 % of total retail sales in East Asia come from Japan and China alone.

Japan also has the second richest market in the world in terms of retail sales per capita at around $7,489 per person in 2002. In contrast, however, China's per capita retail sales in the same year were only $304, ranking forty-eighth in the

Table 2. Retailing in East Asia: Summary Data

	Retail Sales		Sales per capita		Sales per store	
	US$ mill	World Rank	US$	World Rank	US$	World Rank
China	390,303.0	3	304.5	48	19,238.9	52
Hong Kong (PRC)	24,568.8	33	3,476.0	17	432,534.1	18
Indonesia	31,219.1	27	147.0	51	144,084.6	30
Japan	950,996.0	2	7,489.1	2	778,188.4	13
Malaysia	12,350.5	45	546.6	37	80,860.7	40
Philippines	29,871.8	29	386.3	45	220,069.5	24
Singapore	9,685.7	48	2,943.0	19	539,954.3	16
South Korea	87,089.5	12	1,830.3	25	120,290.4	35
Taiwan	39,728.4	23	1,776.0	27	341,300.5	22
Thailand	26,972.5	32	436.9	42	75,456.0	42
Vietnam	16,171.8	39	199.5	50	21,836.1	50

(Source: compiled from Euromonitor 2002)

world and the third lowest even in East Asia with only Indonesia and Vietnam poorer. Furthermore, retail sales per store were the lowest in China compared to any country in the Euromonitor sample at only $19,238, indicating the huge number of very small stores in the country. In contrast, Japan, which also has a relatively large number of small stores for such an advanced economy, had sales per store of $778,188, ranking thirteenth in the world. This was closely followed by Singapore at $539,954 per store, and Hong Kong at $432,534 per store. Taiwanese retailing is also fairly advanced with stores averaging sales of $341,300.

Of course, these figures do not convey the detail of the market. As mentioned above, even China alone should not be considered a single homogenous market any more than East Asia as a whole is. The bulk of the Chinese population is concentrated on the eastern seaboard and around a small number of cities including Shanghai and Beijing. The low sales per capita and per store are more an indication of the vastness of the country rather than the low potential of the market.

On the other hand, the figures relating to Japan do clearly indicate an advanced and extremely rich market, making the low penetration of overseas retailers all the more surprising. Carrefour only entered the market in 2000 (and announced its exit in 2005), and was followed by Wal-Mart in 2002, and METRO Group and Tesco in 2003. Japan has maintained an image of complexity and low reward that is no longer applicable, and this has meant that many of the retailers that have aggressively entered the rest of Asia are only just beginning to consider the Japanese market.

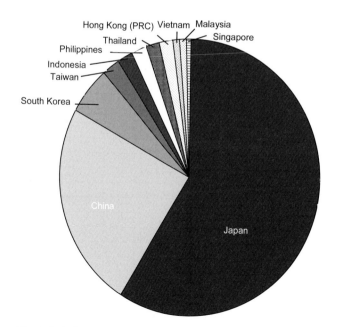

Fig. 1. Relative Retail Market Sizes in East Asia

(Source: data adapted from Euromonitor, 2002)

Despite the difficulties of obtaining comparable cross-regional data, the prospects and potential of the market in East Asia are clear. For retailers considering entry into these individual country markets there is a trade off between the difficulty and cost of entry with the actual market potential. In some cases, notably Hong Kong and Singapore, the small size of the overall market encourages only minor interest to outside entrants despite the fairly sophisticated nature and relatively rich consumers. Such markets are of interest to higher margin, niche retailers such as apparel chains, but are of far less interest to mass-merchandise retailers.

Then there are a number of countries where the market is only marginal in terms of its wealth, despite the fairly large populations and reasonable ease of entry. These include Vietnam, Philippines, and Indonesia. In each case, several international retailers have established themselves, but none of these markets is yet viewed as having enough potential to attract significant overseas interest.

The exceptions to this are Thailand and Malaysia. While fairly small, they have proved relatively open markets and have seen both Western and Japanese firms find some success there. Tesco is currently the leading retailer in Thailand with both Carrefour and Aeon also prominent. Malaysia is led by Aeon, with both Carrefour and Tesco also building their presence there.

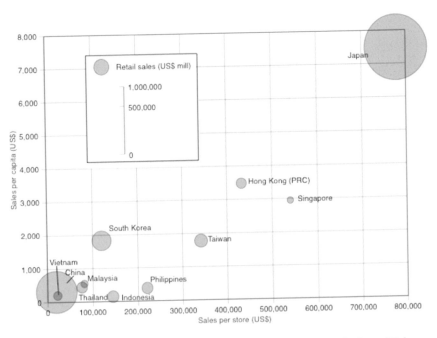

Fig. 2. East Asia: Relative Market Positions by Retail Sales, Sales per Capita and Sales per Store

(Source: data compiled from Euromonitor, 2002)

This leaves China, Taiwan, South Korea and Japan as the leading markets in the region. All four countries have seen massive retail development during the last 10 years and all four will be the focus of internationalization in the near future. With their overwhelming size and potential, China and Japan again stand somewhat separate. Japan is the only modern retail system in the region with its own advanced domestic retail companies. China is seen by most as the single highest potential market in the world, ahead of India largely due to far easier entry requirements and, surprisingly, lower bureaucratic barriers.

Internationalization of Retail Markets in Asia

The penetration of retail companies from advanced nations into markets within East Asia can be considered high. At the same time, the number of international retail companies with a significant presence in East Asia is low with the same firms appearing again and again as leaders within various East Asian markets. Table 3 provides a summary of the situation and an indication of the extent of internationalization in East Asian markets.

In the majority of countries in East Asia, the largest retailer is still a domestic company. At the time of writing, however, the Philippines is the only country with no clear overseas presence in the market, and Japan is the only other country that does not have at least one majority owned overseas retailer ranking among its leading 10 retail firms for 2003. In Japan's case, the largest overseas company is Toys R Us Japan.

In all of the other nine East Asian markets, overseas retailers rank very highly indeed. Carrefour, Dairy Farm, Aeon, Wal-Mart, and Tesco are major players in multiple markets throughout the region. Carrefour is clearly the most advanced of these, being the largest overseas retailer in four of the markets in which it operates. Equally, Dairy Farm is the leading retailer in Malaysia and Singapore, as well as being number two in its own domestic market of Hong Kong.

Even these general figures indicate the degree of interest that markets within East Asia are generating and the relative ease that large international retailers have had in establishing themselves. Furthermore, retail development in most of East Asia is still at a fairly early stage in the majority of nations. China, for example, while being seen as perhaps the world's most important market in terms of its overall future potential, only entered the WTO in 2002 and has still to fully remove regulatory restrictions on retail activity. The size of the Chinese market alone is such that international retailers are prepared to invest massive resources in developing their presence there despite the difficulties and the long-term nature of the investment required (see, e.g., description of METRO Group's expansion in East Asia by Mierdorf, Mantrala and Krafft elsewhere in this book.).

The next decade will see further expansion of international retail interests in the East Asia region. There is not a single country that can be said to be fully mature

Table 3. Sales for Largest Retail Company and Largest Non-domestic Retail Company by Country, 2003

Largest Domestic Retailer			Largest Foreign Retailer			No. of C10 oveseas retailers
		Sales 2003			Sales 2003	
Country	Rank	US$ mill	Company	Rank	US$ mill	
China	1	3,534.0	Carrefour	3	2,425.0	2
Hong Kong	1	1,899.0	Aeon	3	390.7	2
Indonesia	1	652.1	Carrefour	3	390.9	1
Japan	1	28,644.7	Toys R Us	55	1,539.9	0
Malaysia	3	297.4	Dairy Farm	1	487.0	4
Philippines	1	1,123.0	–	–	–	2
South Korea	1	6,238.0	Carrefour	8	1,347.0	2
Singapore	2	793.1	Dairy Farm	1	914.4	6
Taiwan	1	2,292.3	Carrefour	2	1,477.4	2
Thailand	2	957.1	Tesco	1	1,366.0	5
Vietnam	1	63.4	Shiseido	5	43.9	1

Note: Foreign retailer is largest identifiable majority owned non-domestic retail company (Source: compiled from Euromonitor 2002)

as a retail market. This includes the Japanese market where retailing is continuing its rapid modernization and where, even here, overseas retailers are adding a significant impact to changing the overall retail environment (Larke 2003). Elsewhere, room for further expansion and market consolidation is tremendous with only the demographically small markets of Hong Kong and Singapore being close to saturation (Davies 2000). We will see development both in terms of international retailers and new, modern domestic companies in all of China, Malaysia, South Korea, Thailand, and Taiwan. Indonesia, the Philippines, and Vietnam are likely to follow.

Eastern or Western?

The view that entry of overseas firms is detrimental to traditional distribution systems is a common one. For example, some argue that overseas entry is responsible for the breakdown of traditional distribution systems in Japan (Takayama 2001), and the same view is heard in Korea (Choi 2003) and Taiwan. At the same time, the degree of international expansion by Japanese retailers has been largely overlooked.

In truth, Western firms have very little penetration in the Japanese market. The largest non-Japanese retailer in 2003 by sales was Toys R Us, but even this was only the 55th largest chain with roughly 0.14% of the total retail market. Even

Wal-Mart's recent partial acquisition of Seiyu gave it control of only 0.8% of retail sales in 2003.

In contrast, Japanese retailers that make the move overseas are lauded as heroes by domestic commentators and generate huge public interest (Mukoyama 2003). In 1996, Mukoyama (1996) found almost 300 stores operated by Japanese firms outside Japan but even this did not include investment companies and other non-retail companies operating retailing elsewhere. Significantly, more than 83% of the stores found in the study were based in Asia, and two thirds had opened after 1990 (Table 4).

Table 4. International Spread of Japanese Retailers, Circa 1996

	Stores	% of Total	Year of Entry			
			1960s	1970s	1980s	1990s
By Store Format						
Specialty Stores	135	46.2	0	3	25	107
Department Stores	81	27.7	1	14	30	36
Supermarkets	76	26.0	0	3	24	49
Total	**292**	**100.0**	**1**	**20**	**79**	**192**
By Region and Country						
Asia	243	83.2				
Hong Kong	82	28.1	1	3	25	53
Taiwan	51	17.5	0	0	6	45
China	35	12.0	0	0	2	33
Singapore	30	10.3	0	2	11	17
Thailand	18	6.2	0	0	7	11
Malaysia	17	5.8	0	0	8	9
Macao	4	1.4				
Indonesia	3	1.0				
Brunei	1	0.3				
Australia	2	0.7				
Europe	25	8.6				
UK	10	3.4				
France	8	2.7				
Spain	2	0.7		No data reported		
Germany	2	0.7				
Netherlands	1	0.3				
Austria	1	0.3				
Italy	1	0.3				
North America	24	8.2				
USA	22	7.5				
Canada	1	0.3				
Costa Rica	1	0.3				
Total	292	100.0				

Based on content analysis of newspaper reports
(Source: compiled from Mukoyama 1996: 75 – 81)

Japanese retailers have the same competitive characteristics as retailers from Europe and North America and have been making similar inroads into the rest of East Asia. A second study in 2000 continued this trend (Kawabata 2000, Table 5). In the period between 1995 and 1999, Japanese retail companies opened 22 department stores and 130 supermarkets overseas. Among these, however, only two were opened outside Asia. Clearly, it was not just Westerners expanding into Asian markets.

In Kawabata's study it was suggested that once a Japanese firm opened a store overseas, little additional investment or market development took place. It appears that many companies viewed stores overseas merely as cash-generating operations, with profits being quickly repatriated back to Japan. There were few cases of Japanese retailers becoming part of local East Asian markets, preferring instead to target Japanese tourists. Many of these stores closed after a short period.

By the turn of the century, however, Japanese trading companies were increasingly involved in retail development overseas. As Table 6 illustrates, the largest

Table 5. Stores Opened and Closed by Japanese Retailers by Region, 1995 – 1999

	Department Stores			Supermarkets		
	Total 1955 – 99	Stores Opened	Stores Closed	Total 1955 – 99	Stores Opened	Stores Closed
Asia	87	21	15	252	129	103
China	7	2	2	66	59	43
Hong Kong	12	1	7	20	6	9
Taiwan	23	10		99	40	24
Singapore	19	2	2	14	4	6
Thailand	9		2	23	12	8
Malaysia	14	4	2	24	6	8
Indonesia	3	2		2	1	2
Others	0			4	1	3
Europe	23	0	7	1	0	1
UK	4		2	1		1
France	8		3			
Italy	2		1			
Germany	4					
Spain	4		1			
Austria	1					
Americas	12		2	19	1	14
Australia	3	1		0	0	
Other	0			8		2
Total	125	22	24	280	130	120

(Source: compiled from Kawabata 2000: pp. 70 – 75)

trading houses (or *sogo shosha*), along with a small number of other consumer goods wholesalers, have significant interests throughout Asia. These are mostly manufacturing companies but also include trading, procurement, logistics, and consulting businesses, all of which provide support for retail development.

In Japan, trading houses control the majority of imported brand licenses. As master licensees, they facilitate production and distribution through subsidiaries and intermediaries within the Japanese market. Similarly, in recent years the same trading houses have begun to act as facilitators for Japanese companies, from all industrial sectors, when entering markets in Asia. They provide financial, logistics, and local knowledge support, and in some cases also organize license businesses. Similarly, there are numerous cases of trading houses becoming involved more directly in retailing. For example, Itochu owns and operates 70% of the Paul Smith operation in Hong Kong, is a major supplier to department stores, supermarkets, and convenience stores in Taiwan and Singapore, and is a major textile and apparel manufacturer throughout the region for both local sale and for import into Japan (Shukan Toyo Keizai 2003).

With such support, Japanese retail penetration in East Asia is considerable. There were 97 separate, retailer-operated companies in Asia, of which 72 are store or mail order operations (see Table 7). These are concentrated in China and Hong Kong, with 12 in Singapore – a country where the Japanese retail presence is immediately visible in through the Isetan and Takashimaya stores there. More recent data suggests that there was considerable growth to 2005, particularly in China.

Table 6. Number of Companies Operated by Country in East Asia for Major Japanese Trading Houses, 2002 – 03

Trading Co.	Taiwan	China	South Korea	Thailand	Malaysia	Indonesia	Singapore	Hong Kong	Vietnam	Philipines	Others	Total Companies
Itochu Shoji	7	62	2	16	2	16	9	18	2	3	6	143
Sumikin Bussan		19	1	4		1	1	3	1			30
Sumitomo Shoji	8	37	1	25	12	26	15	8	7	7	7	153
Marubeni	4	42	1	11	4	11	7	9	1	8	3	101
Mitsui Bussan	4	27	2	25	8	13	14	20	2	1	5	121
Mitsubishi Shoji	6	30	2	34	6	11	5	14	5	9	5	127
Yagi Tsusho		3							1			4
Totals	29	220	9	115	32	78	51	73	18	28	26	679

(Source: Toyo Keizai 2003: pp. 1190 – 1334)

Table 7. Japanese Retail Companies with Operations in East Asia, 2003

Retailers	Taiwan	China	South Korea	Thailand	Malaysia	Indonesia	Singapore	Hong Kong	Vietnam	Philippines	Others	Total Countries
Aoyama Shoji	1	1										2
Akachan Honpo		2						2				4
Aeon	1	2		2	2							7
Ito-Yokado		2										2
Isetan	1	3		1	1		1	1				8
Cabin	1	2					1					4
Seiyu		1					2	2				5
Senshukai		1	.	1				1				3
Takasho		2										2
Daiei		4								1		5
Daiki		2										2
Takashimaya	2			1				1				4
Tokyu Department Store				1								1
Tokyo Megane	1			1	1			1				4
Nissen		1						2				3
Nisshin Shoji					1		1					2
Parco							3					3
Hasegawa		1					2		3		1	7
Fast Retailing		2										2
Family Mart	1			1	1							3
Lawson		1										1
Best Denki					1		1	1				3
Belluna								2				2
Mycal		1						1				2
Mikimoto		1						1				2
Ministop				1						1		2
Paris Miki	1	1		1	1		1	1				6
Mitsukoshi	1							2				3
Meitetsu Pare											2	2
Ryohin Keikaku								1				1
Total companies	10	30	2	9	7	0	12	19	3	2	3	97

(Source: Toyo Keizai 2003: pp. 1334 – 1348)

Ito-Yokado and Lawson have both been active in store expansion, and a number of specialty chains, such as Comme Ca, Narumiya, Daiso Sangyo, and others have begun to open stores across the region.

Japanese companies are no stronger than other international competitors, but the degree of penetration is much larger than previously recorded, and this penetration is easily keeping pace with Western firms. Equally, the local view that Japanese firms are somehow less influential compared to other overseas entrants appears totally unfounded. The only Japanese retailers with the ambition and ability to operate overseas are the largest and most sophisticated firms. They are eminently capable of success in the rest of Asia and may even possess certain competitive advantages based on better cultural understanding as they originate from Asia themselves.

Japanese Activity in China

Table 8 lists 21 retail companies established by Japanese firms in China. Due to ownership and operating restrictions, several Japanese firms operate multiple companies in the country. This development has been going on for some time, with Isetan establishing businesses in Shanghai and Tientsin as long ago as 1993, but there was an upsurge in activity from 2000 onwards. Ito-Yokado, while establishing its Changdu operation in 1998, only opened its first store in 2000. Lawson, opened its first store in 1996, but had fewer than 50 stores until 2002. Now it has close to 200 and is expanding at a rate of 100 stores a year in the Shanghai area alone.

In China, Japanese retailers remain smaller than Carrefour, Wal-Mart, METRO Group, and Auchan for example, but they are expanding fast. While Chinese consumers are not at all similar to Japanese in many ways, retailers insist that the Chinese has relatively close consumer culture (Shukan Toyo Keizai 2003). Another key catalyst is the strong link between Japanese manufacturers and retailers operating within the market, and the use of Japanese consultants, and logistics and transport firms when setting up in the country.

Available sales figures shown in Table 8 remain small, with the largest, Ito-Yokado, generating only about ¥25 billion in sales, or about the same as one large Japanese store. Carrefour is eight times larger, with Wal-Mart and METRO Group already three times larger. Unlike Carrefour, which has spread stores in many locations in China, Ito-Yokado is concentrating on Beijing and particularly on rapid store development up to the 2008 Olympics. In addition to the first Seven-Eleven, Ito-Yokado also introduced its supermarket subsidiary, York Benimaru, in 2004. With these three store formats, Ito-Yokado will pursue the same local market saturation strategy it has employed with great success in Japan.

Even for Japanese firms, there are still many pitfalls to avoid in the Chinese market. Retailers complain bitterly about the "old fashioned" and "opaque" nature of Chinese business practices, notably the use of long payment periods and large,

Table 8. Japanese Firms Operating in China, Mid-2004

Japanese Retailer	Share-holing %	Loca-tion	Retail sector	Entry date Yr.Mth	Sales ¥bn	End sales period Yr.Mth	Net Profit ¥mn	Stores	Employees
Isetan	63.0	Shanghai	Department store	1993.01	2.76	2002.12	-45.0	1	172
Isetan	75.0	Tientsin	Department store	1993.01	4.12	2002.12	34.0	1	447
Isetan	80.0	Shanghai	Department store	1997.03	5.48	2002.12	197.0	1	311
Ito-Yokado	51.0	Changdu	GMS	1997.11	9.00	2003.12	20.0	2	1,028
Ito-Yokado	36.8	Beijing	GMS	1998.04	16.00	2003.12	32.0	3	1,399
Aeon	65.0		SC	1995.10				5	2,144
Aeon	60.0	Tsingtao	SC	1996.03	75.00	–	P	2	896
Seiyu	42.0	Beijing	SC	1996.06	1.60	2003.12	OK	1	546
Daiei	95.0	Tientsin	Supermarket	1995.05	3.60	2002.12	–	12	1,000
Heiwado	75.0		SC	1998.11	7.60	2003.12	55.0	1	1,134
Lawson	49.0	Shanghai	CVS	1996.02	3.39	2003.12	L	153	149
Komeri	70.0	Luta	Home center	1996.03	2.23	2002.12	L	2	29
Itokin	100.0	Shanghai	Women's apparel	1997.07					
Itokin	97.0	Tsingtao	Women's apparel	1995.12					
Itokin	100.0	Luta	Women's apparel	1993.10		1 flagship per company, 67 concessions, 66 franchise stores			
Itokin	95.0	Tientsin	Women's apparel	1997.00					216
Aigan	45.0	Beijing	Eye wear	1994.10	0.26	–	–	8	90
Paris Miki	100.0	Shanghai	Eye wear	1993.08				89	133
Paris Miki	48.0	Shanghai	Eye wear	2000.10	1.41	–	P		
Aoyama Shoji	54.0	Shanghai	Men's wear	1994.09	0.18	2002.12	L	3	369
Fast Retailing	71.4		Apparel retail	2002.09	0.56	2003.06	– 680.0	6	–

Key: – : not available, P: profitable, L: loss making, OK: undisclosed by acceptable
Note: Net profit is after tax except for Ito-Yokado which is EBIT.
(Source: Shukan Toyo Keizai 2003: p. 57)

volume buying rebates. Interestingly, these are precisely the same practices so bemoaned by overseas retailers and distributors entering Japan in the 1970s and 1980s (Czinkota and Kotabe 1993).

Three Stages of Expansion in Asia

The operation of Japanese retail firms overseas has passed through three distinct phases. The first was one of department store expansion motivated by increased numbers of Japanese tourists going overseas. The preference of Japanese consumers to shop at Japanese retailers even when outside Japan was an important trend in the late 1980s and early 1990s, but is now waning. As a result, only a few Japanese department stores still operate outside the domestic market.

The second phase was a brief hiatus during the worst of the Japanese economic slowdown in the second half of the 1990s.

The third and current phase is a new and rapid expansion overseas, again in line with improved business confidence in Japan itself. This phase was described in detail in this chapter.

Japanese firms have primarily aimed at East Asia and are now increasingly concentrated on China alone. The key to the current phase is the establishment and strength of logistics and supplier firms in the same East Asian region. Japanese manufacturers have developed a solid base in East Asia to produce consumer products for the Japanese market, and now retailers are in a unique position to employ services offered by fellow Japanese logistics and transport companies and, most importantly, by the powerful and knowledgeable trading houses.

Except in Malaysia, where Aeon is the largest retailer by sales, no single Japanese retailer is prominent in the main markets of East Asia, but the overall number of Japanese firms is significant. With various sources placing the number of separate retail companies already operating in China alone between 20 and 40, and with at least 97 overseas retail operations established by some 30 firms across the East Asian region, Japanese firms are prominent and well ahead of any one Western country. Quite correctly, managers in Japan emphasize the cultural proximity of their business systems and their ability to supply consumer needs in other Asian markets. The current expansion is ongoing, and Japanese retailers are set to further expand in China and the rest of Asia.

Conclusion

East Asia is today the most rapidly developing retail market in the world. With its large population and densely populated markets, along with strong population growth and rapidly modernizing industrial economies, it has been a focus of attention for the world's leading retail businesses for the past 10 years. Even so, the level of development within the region varies greatly, from advanced economies such as Japan and Singapore, to agriculturally based economies such as Vietnam and the Philippines.

Overall, all retail markets in the region have become important targets for international retail firms. Hong Kong and Singapore are already developed to the point of saturation due to their small size. Thailand, Malaysia, Taiwan and South Korea all have proved fairly easy markets to enter, and with comparatively small markets overall, have also received the greatest level of development. Much of this development has been clearly led by overseas retailers entering the market from outside. In some cases, for example Aeon in Malaysia and Thailand, this development occurred over a long period, but with the entry of all of the leading Western international retailers, retail development has become much more rapid in these four countries.

Most important of all, however, is the situation in Japan and China which are respectively the second and third largest retail markets in the world. Japan has remained difficult to enter, but this is now changing as more overseas firms disprove long held myths. China has been host to international retail firms for longer than Japan, but political restrictions meant that the pace of development has remained slow and is only now able to increase as regulations are dismantled.

The overall picture in East Asia, therefore, is one of a race just about to begin. The main competitors are established and well positioned, but we are still at an early stage. In some countries, the significance of outside influence is only just being understood, and the possibility of government intervention to reduce the impact of outside firms on domestic markets looms large. Such cases have already arisen in Thailand, Malaysia, and Japan. Moreover, a much greater response from domestic retail competitors can be expected in the near future. This is particularly true in China where domestic companies have laboured under the same restrictions as foreign firms and will benefit from the same changes to regulations in coming years. Local retailers are now undergoing significant development as a result.

There is a serious need for more extensive work on distribution in East Asia and particularly in relation to the impact of development by overseas firms. As the region advances economically and consumers become more affluent, overseas firms would say they are accelerating the pace of modernization and providing the best retail options to consumers. Others would argue that this is happening at the expense of local business and that there is a worrying level of global standardization occurring with the breakdown of local consumer culture and business systems (Choi 2003; Mukoyama 2003).

The overwhelming importance of China has skewed research to date, even though China, along with Japan, is an anomaly among East Asian markets. Research on China is, on the whole, applicable only to China. In addition, as China is actually one of the least advanced nations in terms of retailing, the situation there remains speculative with future possibilities unconfirmed and numerous intervening factors both economic and political likely to have a major influence on the future development of the market. The same is true in Japan and, to some extent, in each of the other 11 main East Asian nations. It is impossible, therefore, to consider the region as a single whole.

Undoubtedly the main focus of attention will remain on China, both in terms of practical development of retail systems and academic interest. This is a pity, however, as there is still much to be learned from countries like Thailand, Malaysia, South Korea, and Taiwan, that have developed so much in the past 10 years. It is to be hoped that this gap in the literature will not become wider.

References

Choi, S. C. (2003). Moves into the Korean market by global retailers and the response of local retailers: Lesson for the Japanese retailing sector? Internationalization of Retail-ing in Asia. J. A. Dawson, M. Mukoyama, S. C. Choi and R. Larke, RoutledgeCurzon: 35-48.

Czinkota, M. R. and M. Kotabe (1993). The Japanese Distribution System. Chicago and Cambridge, Probus Publishing Company.

Davies, K. (2000). The Asian economic recession and retail change: the implications for retailer strategies in Asia. The International Review of Retail, Distribution and Consumer Research 10(4): 335.

Euromonitor (2002). World Retail Rankings. Special Report.

Kawabata, M. (2000). Kourigyo no kaigai shinshutsu to senryaku (The expansion and strategy of retailers overseas). Tokyo, Shinhyoron.

Larke, R. (2003). International retailing in Japan. Internationalization of retailing in Asia. J. A. Dawson, M. Mukoyama, S. C. Choi and R. Larke. London, RoutledgeCurzon: 6-34.

Mukoyama, M. (2003). Conclusion: the direction of future research on internationalization of retailing. Internationalization of Retailing in Asia. J. A. Dawson, M. Mukoyama, S. C. Choi and R. Larke. London, RoutledgeCurzon.: 210-4.

Shukan Toyo Keizai (2003). Gaikoku shinshutsu kigyo soran (Directory of companies expanding overseas). Tokyo, Toyo Keizai Shuppan.

Takayama, K. (2001). (The impact and reaction within the Japanese distribution industry to the overseas expansion of Western retailers). Ryutsu to Shisutemu 109: 3-11.

World Bank (2004) World Bank Group, East Asia & Pacific Data Profile. http://devdata.worldbank.org/external/CPProfile.asp, 2004.

plus-size individuals), Collection i (home furnishings), Depot (books & music), and E-Zone (Consumer electronics). It has also developed another new format in the form of the Wholesale Club to sell to the segment of consumers who purchase in bulk and look out for discounts and offers. Similarly, the LandMark group operates multiple formats such as hypermarket (Max), department store (Lifestyle), Shoemart, and Funcity[3] (Table 2). Such experimentation and identification of an appropriate format for the local conditions would separate the winners from the losers in India. It may lead a retailer to use hybrid formats to cater to different needs-based segments of the customer population.

Malls

Mall development is phenomenal in India. They are spreading fast and entering the second-tier and third-tier cities in India. Corporate houses such as ITC, TATA, Godrej, and the Sriram Group are also making steady progress in bringing malls to the rural market. Large malls provide ample space for leisure and entertainment. Some states, e.g., Punjab, have lifted entertainment tax on multiplexes until 2009. This has attracted mall developers such as PVR, Waves, Adlab, and Fun Republic. During the 1990s, 1 million square feet of mall space was added every year in India. Since then, the pace has picked up substantially, and in 2003 alone, 10 million square feet were added. About 150 million square feet of new mall space is expected to be built in the country in the next 3-5 years. Major cities would account for about 70 % of this space: Mumbai (203 % increase to 15 million square feet), Delhi (up 527 % to 23.2 million square feet), Bangalore (a rise of 128 % to 4.1 million square feet), Hyderabad (up 163 % to 1 million square feet), and Pune (up 188 % to 23.2 million square feet) are witnessing the boom. In 2005, a state such as Punjab had only a single mall with a gross leasable area (GLA) of 0.12 million square feet, but it is now expected to have 37 malls operating with GLA of 15.2 million square feet by 2009. Ludhiana, a city in the state of Punjab, is leading the way, with 11 malls occupying 5 million square feet (IMAGES & CII, 2006). The success of these malls would be determined by innovations, the right tenant mix, effective mall management, and provision of ample parking space.

Department Stores

A department store offers an extensive assortment (width and depth) of goods and services that are organized into separate departments for the purpose of efficient buying, assortment, promotion, and, above all, ease of shopping for the consumer.

---

[3] Family entertainment center offering excellent opportunity for children to learn and have fun.

A format of this kind provides the greatest selection of any general merchandise and very often serves as the anchor store in a shopping mall or shopping center. In India, there are fewer department stores than stores with other retail formats, such as supermarkets and discount stores. Shoppers' Stop, with 19 stores in 10 different cities in India, was the first department store chain in the early 1990s (Table 3). The stores have a strong focus on lifestyle retailing and are divided into five main departments, such as apparel, accessories, home décor, gift ideas, and other services. The chain's stores attract more than 12 million visitors every year, with a conversion rate (visitors to buyers) of 38 %. By 2008, Shoppers' Stop plans to have a network of 39 stores with retail space of 2,502,747 square feet. Westside, a primarily private label department store, intends to open 18 more stores in 2008, to take its network to about 30 stores. Another operator, Lifestyle India, began operations with its first store in Chennai in 1999. It operates in five cities with more than ten stores.

Hypermarkets

Hypermarkets have emerged as the biggest crowd pullers in India. They offer the most extensive merchandise mix, with product and brand choices under one roof, and create superior value owing to lower prices. Offering product categories ranging from Fresh produce and FMCG products to Electronics, Value apparel, Houseware, Do it yourself (DIY), and Outdoor products, the hypermarkets are very popular in India. Currently there are around 90 hypermarkets in the country. The number of players operating hypermarket formats is increasing day by day. Pantaloon Retail India Limited (Table 4) has the largest network of 74 Big Bazaars across India. Star India, a TATA venture, has experimented with one store in Ahmedabad and would like to open another 25 stores in the next 2 years. In early 2006, the K. Raheja Corp. (C.L. Raheja Group) introduced Hypercity, which became the country's largest hypermarket at 118,000 square feet. It carries a product range that includes Foods, Homeware, Home Entertainment, Hi-Tech, Appliances, Furniture, Sports, Toys, and Clothing. It has plans to open 55 hypermarkets by 2015. On 15 August 2007, Reliance Retail opened the first of its 'Reliance Mart' hypermarkets in Ahmedabad, with a floor space of 165,000 square feet. According to the *Hindu Business Line* of 1 September 2007, 30 such stores are planned to be operating at the end of the year.

As the market expands, and the country is in a mood to accept changes, hypermarkets are meeting with an overwhelming response from consumers. Hypermarket success depends critically on pricing, with the right product mix on offer at the right price and in the right place. Ideally, a 40 : 60 mix of food to non-food would yield a blended gross margin of around 18-19 %. Hypermarkets have to use an efficient sourcing and merchandising process to bring down the cost of operations. They also need to continuously reduce inefficiencies in the supply chain and pass on a part of that benefit to consumers. Lastly, private label or store brands are being used by these stores extensively for improving the margins.

Supermarkets

Unlike in the West, supermarkets are not yet very prominent in India. Supermarkets concentrate largely on selling food-related products and are considerably smaller than hypermarkets. Their value proposition is also different from that of the hypermarkets. The supermarkets focus on specific product categories and offer relatively good assortments. They do not play the price game, but have to depend on convenience and service to attract consumers. However, in India, convenience and service are also offered by numerous provision stores and 'sweetshops.' Fresh vegetables and fruits are sold on the pavements and in open markets. Thus, consumers have not yet made supermarkets the preferred format for buying in this category. They prefer to buy either from the local mobile vegetable sellers or from the nearest vegetable market.

Subhikhsa, Food World, Food Bazaar, Nilgiri, Reliance, TrueMart, and More are the leading supermarket operators (Table 5). Reliance opened a special chain of fruit and vegetable stores with 11 stores in Hyderabad in November 2006, and within a year it opened about 390 Reliance Fresh outlets across 11 states of India. As the eastern part of the country is showing strong resistance to opening of Reliance Fresh outlets, the retailer is focusing on the western part of India.

A typical supermarket chain such as Food Bazaar operates in major cities in India with floor space ranging from 6,000 square feet to 16,000 square feet and selling both food and non-food items. The non-food items contribute about 25% of total sales. The chain has an average of 7,000 stock keeping units (SKUs) and over 50,000 articles. Fresh produce is comprised of fruits and vegetables, which are sold loose through the concessionaire arrangement. Private labels are found in several categories, especially the commodities. For example in the utensil cleaner category, private label gives the highest margin of about 25% and commands a share of 50% in the store. These stores also offer such services as flour mills, fresh juice counters, fresh milk and dairy products, vegetable chopping and packing, salads, sandwiches, and prepared soup.

Convenience Stores

A convenience store offers location advantage for the shoppers and provides them with ease of shopping and customized service. It charges average to above average prices, depending on the product category, and carries a moderate number of SKUs. Normally it remains open for long hours and shoppers use it for buying fill-in merchandise and emergency purchases. In India, convenience stores occupied

23,000 square meters of retail space with sales of about US $ 26.95 million in 2005 and are expected to occupy 85,000 square meters of selling space by 2010 (Table 6). During the same period, sales are expected to reach US $ 105.43 million and the number of outlets is likely to grow from 510 to 2,500 (Table 7). Twenty Four Seven, a new format of convenience store in Delhi offers a portfolio of 3,500 SKUs of branded fast-moving consumer goods and another 3,500 SKUs of prescription and over-the-counter drugs besides 300 private label products across food, focusing on staples such as pulses and rice. The promoter of this format, the Modi group, plans to set up 500 convenience stores in Delhi and Mumbai by 2007-08.

Discounters

The absence of strong discounters in India has several reasons. Unlike most Western countries, Indian retailers are mainly small stores and do not have much bargaining power with manufacturers in order to negotiate terms. Owing to low economies of scale, retailers are unable to offer significant discounts on their own. Consequently, the presence of discounters is much smaller than that of supermarkets. According to the Euromonitor (2006) report, in India there are 410 discount stores with 63,000 square meters of selling space and by 2010 that figure is going to be 555 discount retail outlets, with 85,000 square meters of selling space (Table 8). Subhiksha, the Chennai-based discount retail chain, has spread nationally. According to industry sources, the retail chain is expected to reach 2,000 stores with 3.25 million square feet of retail space by 2008-09. This format is more common among apparel and shoe retailers. Loot, Promart, Koutons, and Country Cotton are some of the other leading discounters. Some retailers, such as Alpha in Mumbai, are also experimenting in offering electronic appliances and other consumer durable products. Most cities also have shop clusters that sell at lower prices; however, unlike the discounters, they deal in unbranded merchandise.

Branded Stores

The major apparel brands in India are Madura Garments, Zodiac, Raymond's, Colour Plus, and Arvind Mills. Some of the branded apparel stores prominent in India are Madura Garments (140 stores), Weekender (75 stores), Benetton (150 stores), Grasim (110 exclusive showrooms), Wills Lifestyle (40 stores), Lee (59 stores), Newport (500 stores), Wrangler (37 stores), John Players (80 stores), and Raymond. Raymond, with 260 shops, deals in fabrics, apparel, and accessories. In addition, its distribution network includes 20 exclusive Park Avenue and Parx stores and 1,000 multi-brand outlets. These specialty stores sell the well-known brands, such as Park Avenue, Parx, Manzoni, and Be. Park Avenue is an up-market brand, while Parx and Manzoni are targeted at the casual wear and the premium ranges, respectively. 'Be' is a brand specifically of women's wear. Similarly, BK Birla's Century Textile plans to increase its number of outlets from 60 currently to 100 by next year. Almost all major international brands are present in India through franchise arrangements.

There is no major Indian retailer in the sports and footwear category. Reebok (85 stores) is the market leader here in India, and there is no clear-cut runner-up. In fact, this segment is dominated mainly by foreign labels – Levi's, Lee Cooper, United Colors of Benetton, Lacoste, Adidas (76 stores), Nike (62 stores), and Woodland (58 stores). Indian labels are few and far between – Proline is the best-known Indian brand, and the other brands are more local in nature. The only other Indian retailer that is making any sort of impact is Wills Sports, with 29 stores across different cities in India. Bata has the largest chain of shoe stores.

Category Killers

The category killer concept originated in the U.S. owing to an abundance of cheap land and the dominant car culture. A category killer is a kind of discount specialty store that offers less variety but a wide assortment of merchandise in the category that is handled. By offering a wide assortment in a category at comparatively low prices, category specialists are able to 'kill' that specific category of merchandise for other retailers. Generally, such retailers use a self-service approach. They use their buying power to negotiate low prices, excellent terms, and assured supply when items are scarce. In India, this kind of retail store is not prevalent at this time. However, there is scope for such a format. In India, Mega-Mart is one sort of category killer; it sells apparel products.

'Dollar' Stores

Dollar stores have their roots in America's homey five-and-dimes, the general stores that offered a range of products at low prices. Modern dollar-store retailers are running more sophisticated operations, however, leveraging their growing buying power to strike special deals with vendors and continuously striving for unique advantages in terms of both convenience and price. Some chains sell all their goods at US $ 1 or less. Others offer selected items at higher prices. Most sell a combination of paper products, health and beauty supplies, cleaning products, paper and stationery, household goods, toys, food and, sometimes, clothing. Both private-label and brand-name goods fill the shelves. The US-based My Dollarstore started operations in Mumbai through master franchise arrangements with Sankalp Retail Value. The store opened with a floor space of about 4,000 square feet in the Nirmal Lifestyle Mall in Mumbai. By January 2007 there were 42 My Dollar-stores in major cities across India. In 2006, these stores attracted 4.5 million shoppers. In the larger cities, My Dollarstore outlets generated average footfalls of 600 per day and the retailer generated more than US $ 10 million in sales (Wall Street Journal, January 23, 2007). In September 2005, the Mallz99 chain of dollar stores also started operations in Delhi, with a plan to open 200 stores in India by 2009. The store offers over 1,000 imported products, which are each priced at INR 99 (about US $ 2). To keep the store attractive for shoppers, new products are added on a weekly basis.

Cash & Carry

This format operates essentially in the B2B context. Metro Cash & Carry opened its first cash & carry outlet in Bangalore in 2003. The retailer now has two outlets in Bangalore and one in Hyderabad; it plans to open one each in Mumbai and Kolkata. It has a membership of over 100,000 in Bangalore and over 80,000 in Hyderabad, and its main customers are hoteliers and restaurateurs (including bars), small food traders and retailers, and small business establishments. Future Group started its cash & carry operation called the Big Bazaar Club in Ahmedabad in early 2007. This retailer targets not only business customers but also large families that do bulk purchasing. Wal-Mart also has plans to set up Sam's Club stores in India within a couple of years.

Retail Development in Rural India

Chennai-based market research firm Francis Kanoi estimates the size of the rural market at US $ 24,600 million annually. During the survey in 2002, the firm took account of four categories – FMCG, durables, agri-inputs, and two- and four-wheelers – as the basis of their estimation. Rural incomes are also growing steadily. NCAER data shows that while the number of middle-class households (with annual income between US $ 900 and US $ 4,300) is 16.4 million in urban India, the corresponding figure in the rural areas is 15.6 million (Kaushik, 2004). This rural market is largely untapped, and there is a huge opportunity for new-format retailers. Among the leading corporate houses that have entered it, DCM's Hariyali Bazaar was the first. Now this company has 22 stores. ITC's Choupal Sagar, HLL's project Shakthi, and Mahamaza are some of the models being tried out. At this juncture, there is no conclusive evidence available to indicate the winning rural retail formats. However, corporate forays into rural retail are expected to bring more experimentation and innovation in terms of retail format. Godrej Adhaar, the rural retail initiative of Godrej Agrovet Ltd, operates a chain of 18 stores providing a host of services to farmers and their families and is planning to set up at least 1,000 stores across rural India in the next 5 years. Apart from Godrej Adhar and Chaupal Sagar, other formats operating successfully in the rural area are M & M Shubh Labh stores, Escorts rural stores, Tata Kisan Sansar, and Warna-bazaar, Maharashtra.

Internet Retailing

The importance of internet retailing is growing all over the world. Some internet retailers, such as e-Bay and rediff.com, are providing vendors with a platform to sell their products online, but do not take responsibility for delivering the product to the buyer. They provide only virtual shopping space to the vendors. On the other hand, online retailers such as amazon.com and walmart.com maintain their own warehouses to stock products and do take responsibility for delivering prod-ucts to the buyers. In the US, many of the brick & mortar stores are entering online retailing, as they have the physical infrastructure that can be used to capture additional consumer 'share of wallet'; examples are Target, Sears, and Kmart.

In India, during the period 2001-06, internet retailing grew at a compounded annual growth rate (CAGR) of 37.2%, and it is projected to continue growing at a CAGR of 40% until 2010 (Euromonitor, 2007). In 2005, LG Ezbuy was one of the major internet retailers in value terms, with a 23% share. Other major players in terms of value share are Times Internet (indiatimes.com), Yahoo Web services (yahoo.com), India Online (Rediff.com), Fab mall, and Sify.com. Fab mall online store offers about 3 million SKUs, attracts about 10,000 visitors per day and, on average, ships over 20,000 orders per month (Euromonitor, 2006). Fab mall sells groceries in addition to jewelry, electronics, books, movies, music, and gifts. e-Bay also has a strong presence. The Future group has entered this segment with futurebazaar.com. According to New Delhi Television Limited in May 2007, it was then making a profit of US $ 20,000 per day with 0.35 million hits.

Challenges Ahead

Rents

Rents are a challenge for retailers, as the cost of acquiring retail space in India is increasing. A study by Knight Frank India indicated that rentals in established malls in top metropolitan areas have jumped by 20-30% in the last 6 months. Generally, retailers work out a rent-to-revenue ratio with developers at which they feel they can sustain their business. Normally, this figure varies from 4% for a hypermarket (in this case rent will constitute 4% of revenues) through 10% for a department store to nearly 20% for very niche retailers. However, at a monthly rate of US $ 4 per square foot, a department store might have to make US $ 40 per square foot per month just to break even (Daftari and Sharma, 2006). In such a scenario the reality of retail business could change and increasing rents could pose the greatest threat to the profits of retailers in India.

Foreign Direct Investment

Many global retailers are now interested in investing in the Indian market. For the last 3 years, India has held the top slot in the annual Global Retail Development Index (GRDI), a study of retail investment attractiveness among 30 emerging markets conducted by the management consulting firm A.T. Kearney. However, foreign direct investment (FDI) in retail remains a politically sensitive issue. The major concern has been that the small independent retailers are not well-equipped to combat the threat that would be posed by the global retail firms. Many argue that FDI in multi-brand retail stores such as Wal-Mart and Tesco would force the small *Kirana* (mom & pop) stores out of business. However, organized retailers feel positive about FDI in the retail sector in the near future. Retail contributed about 10 % to the national GDP in 2005, and this was expected to increase over the next decade. According to an estimate of PricewaterhouseCoopers, the Indian retail market will attract an investment of US $ 412 billion by 2011, mainly in hyper markets and supermarkets. FDI in retail is being supported for the purposes of (1) retail consolidation and increase in the share of the organized retail sector; (2) generation of more employment opportunity in retail and allied activities; (3) increased supply chain efficiency, which would lead to lower prices, and superior product quality for consumers; (4) enhanced opportunity for domestic firms to join hands with global retail players, to bring in technical know-how and global practices; (5) giving shoppers an international shopping experience in terms of store ambience and shopping environment.

Political Environment

Multiparty coalition governments have become increasingly common in India. Therefore, decision making is not simple. For example, the decision to allow FDI in retail initially looked straightforward but became complicated as a result of the political circumstances. Such decisions are largely influenced by the political sentiments of the constituencies of the various political parties. Until a single party forms a government at the Center, there are likely to be delays in making such important and critical policy decisions.

Regulatory Challenges

There are some regulatory issues that international players may find difficult to tackle, and some issues are common to both the domestic and the foreign players. For example, the Land and Property laws specify that only Indians have the right to own land and property in India, and this may act as an inhibiting factor for foreign retailers. The tax structure is also not favorable to foreign players. According to industry sources, the corporate tax rate for domestic companies is 36.59%, whereas it is 41.82% for foreign companies. Currently the labor laws are slanted more toward protecting the jobs of store workers, which is contrary to the requirement of running modern formats. Amendments to store operation timing and labor laws would help both foreign and domestic retailers. In order to encourage global retailers to come to operate in India, the government may need to amend some laws and regulations.

Technology

Technology is going to play a major role in retail developments in India. Currently, most retailers operate almost everything manually. In a country where almost 97% of retailing is in the hands of small independent retailers, it can be expected that retailers are going to have some operational inefficiency. Most of the organized, or more highly developed, retailers are using available and affordable technology to capture consumer information. Modern retailers are using scanner data to adapt to customer buying behavior. Technology helps them to take better decisions in some critical areas such as new product introduction, suitable product offerings, quicker ordering, and assortment planning. Retailers use shoppers' loyalty data to design customized promotional offerings for different sets of customers. Although Indian retailers have adopted technology to some extent, the use of information is very minimal. There is a long way to go before many retailers in India come close to reaching the level of information use already prevalent among retailers in the developed markets. Some retailers, such as Shoppers' Stop, have used technology to great advantage. This retailer could be viewed as one of the best users of technology. The loyalty program of Shoppers' Stop is exemplary and matches up to those of some international retailers.

Supply Chain

Until recently, most retailers in India have invested in their front-end operations but have not invested much in back-office and supply chain operations. Thus, Indian supply chains for food products are characterized by extensive wastage and poor handling. The wastage occurs because of multiple points of manual handling, poor packaging, and lack of availability of temperature-controlled vans. The most important factor that would bring enhancement in supply chains would be greater power of some retailers relative to manufacturers. Indian Railways is planning to create the infrastructure needed to carry fresh fruits and vegetables in temperature-controlled containers from various nodal points located at railway stations in different parts of India. New entrants, such as Reliance Retail, are believed to be investing substantially in the supply chain, especially cold chains, for the provision of fresh fruits and vegetables through its Fresh stores. Many others are moving in this direction. Even such logistics companies as DHL have shown interest in bridging this gap.

Human Resources

Even though AT Kearney places India as the most attractive retail market for the second consecutive year in a row, India is lagging behind in the retail labor index, in eighth place. Owing to an explosion in the retail industry, there is an acute shortage of talent. Employee churn is very high for all players. It is very difficult to get experienced store managers to run stores. Almost all retailers are indulging in poaching. Reliance Retail is planning to employ a half a million-strong work force at various levels over the next 5 years. If we look at the human resources employed by such global retailers as Wal-Mart, Carrefour, METRO Group, Tesco, Home Depot, and Ahold, we find that Wal-Mart is the only one whose workforce exceeds half a million employees.

Looking Beyond Format

Formats are not ends in themselves. Understanding shopping dynamics is the key to success in the retail business. Retailers must understand what values shoppers are looking for and how they can deliver that desired value to the customer. However, currently most retailers in India are focusing on what they are offering and how shoppers can fit into the retailer's scheme of things. In the long-run, such strategies may not be viable. Retailers such as Sam Walton saw consumers as the source of competitive advantage. Tesco Inc. has demonstrated successfully how consumer understanding can help in redefining its business and gaining a sustainable competitive advantage. It operates five different retail formats under the same brand name with subbrands, namely Express[4] (546), Super store[5] (446), Metro[6] (160), and Extra[7] (100), to cater for consumer needs, in addition to an online store. The Group also has an additional 527 stores under the One-Stop fascia. All the formats are profitable, and each format is tailored to fulfill customer needs. It is

---

[4] Size of the store is up to 3,000 square feet and offers customers great value, quality, and fresh food close to where they live and work.

[5] Size of super store varies from 20,000 square feet to 50,000 square feet.

[6] Approximate store size is 7,000–15,000 square feet.

[7] Approximate store size is 60,000 square feet, and Extra stores offer the widest range of food and non-food lines, ranging from electrical equipment to home wares, clothing, health and beauty, and seasonal items such as garden furniture.

Table 4. Presence of Retailers Across Different Cities in India Through Hypermarket

City Name	PRIL	Reli-ance	Giant	Trent	Home Stores	Kha-dims	Hyper-city	D-Mart	Vishal	Total
Agra	1				1					2
Ahmedabad	5	1		1				1	1	9
Alwar	1									1
Ambala	1									1
Anand	1									1
Aurangabad	1									1
Bangalore	9									9
Belgaum	1									1
Bhubaneswar	2								1	3
Chennai	1									1
Coimbatore	1									1
Darjeeling	1									1
Delhi	2								1	3
Durgapur	1									1
Ghaziabad	1									1
Gurgaon	2									2
Haldia	1									1
Hubli	1									1
Hyderabad	4		1							5
Indore	1									1
Jaipur	2									2
Kanpur	1									1
Kolhapur	1									1
Kolkata	5					1			1	7
Lucknow	1				1					2
Mangalore	1									1
Meerut	1									1
Mumbai	5		1	1			1	1		9
Nagpur	2									2
Nashik	1									1
Panipath	1				1					2
Pune	4									4
Raipur	1									1
Rajkot	1									1
Sangli	1									1
Surat	1									1
Thane	2									2
Trissur	1									1
Trivandrum	1									1
Udupi	1									1
Vijayawada	1									1
Vishakapatnam	1									1
	74	1	2	2	3	1	1	2	4	90

(Source: compiled by the authors from websites and published reports up to June 2007)

Table 5. City Wise Representation of Supermarkets in India

City/Metro	Food Bazaar	Foodworld	Reliance Fresh	Haiko	SPAR	Foodland	Total
Agra	1						1
Ahmedabad	4		27				31
Ambala	1						1
Anand			1				1
Bangalore	9	28					37
Baroda			10				10
Bhubaneswar	2						2
Chennai		27					27
Coimbatore		3					3
Delhi	3						3
Durgapur	1						1
Erode		1					1
Gandhinagar			1				1
Ghaziabad	3						3
Gurgaon	1						1
Hyderabad	2	15					17
Indore	1						1
Kodai		1					1
Kolkata	6						6
Lucknow	1						1
Manglore	1						1
Mumbai	6			1	2	6	15
Mundra			1				1
Nadiad			1				1
Nagpur	1						1
Nasik	1						1
Navsari			1				1
Pondicheri		1					1
Pune	2	7					9
Rajkot	1		2				3
Salem		1					1
Sangli	1						1
Secunderabad		4					4
Surat	1		3				4
Thane	2						2
Trivandrum		1					1
Vellore		1					1
Vizag	1						1
Total	52	90	47	1	2	6	198

(Source: compiled by the authors from websites and published reports)

Fig. 1. The Personal Shopping Assistant

UPC scanners are a staple item in the retail industry. Cash register terminals have used these technologies for several decades. The development of bar codintechnology based on universal product codes (UPC) was a pre-cursor to the adoption of UPC scanners. UPC scanning technology deployed at the point of sale has had a wide-reaching effect in the retail industry. Apart from the hard benefits such as savings in labor, UPC scanning technology also provided several soft benefits. Notable among them include the ability to collect sales and marketing data such as pricing and promotion at the point of sale. These data have provided the foundation for improvements in promotional forecasting and deployment.

The PSA as deployed in the Future Store is a mobile device. Consumers walk through the store with the device affixed to their shopping cart. The PSA is equipped with wireless connectivity to ensure mobility. A radio built into the PSA transmits a wireless signal based on the 802.11 standard to an access point. An access point equipped with an antenna and connected to the regular wired network transmits the wireless signal into a wired network. Wireless access points deployed throughout the store ensure that the PSA can connect anywhere.

The basis of the wireless technology used in the PSA is the Wi-Fi standard and equipment that has enjoyed considerable amount of grassroots popularity with consumers. The typical home Wi-Fi user has broadband access provided by either a cable or a phone company. Consumers deploy a wireless router or access point to transmit the broadband signal around the home. Laptops, desktop PCs and printers connect into this wireless network.

Past deployments of wireless technology have been primarily in the backroom and for stock checking functions. Store associates use handheld wireless devices to track inventory or conduct shelf audits in stores. These traditional wireless devices are based on a specialized design incorporating hardware features that support the required functionality. To the extent that a store already has a compatible wireless network, the PSA can simply connect to the same network infrastructure.

Fig. 2. An Interactive Kiosk

The UPC scanner in the PSA leverages scanning technology used in the checkout. A recent deployment of this scanning technology has been in the form of dedicated price check terminals in discount stores such as Target and department stores such as Macy's in the U.S. market. The PSA is another such dedicated application.

The last aspect of the PSA is the approach to content. Using standard browser-based technology, the PSA can tap into much of the existing content that the retailer has already developed for their web site. Manufacturers can also provide content such as product descriptions and high quality images.

The PSA technologies extend to a web-based interactive information terminal also called a kiosk (Figure 2). Many locations in the Future Store can accommodate a kiosk. These kiosks come with additional capabilities such as the ability to print nutritional information or recipes.

As the discussion of the technology indicates, both the PSA and the interactive kiosks amalgamate technologies that have been tried and tested in other environments. The mass-market consumer is very unforgiving. The availability of tried and tested underlying technologies is crucial. This minimizes technical glitches that can contribute to consumer disappointment.

Perhaps equally important is the use of standardized consumer facing software interfaces borrowed from the web. This provides consumers with a familiar interface. Research in human factors focusing on web usability (Nielsen and Tahir 2001) argues that consumers evaluate usability based on expectations of look and feel. These expectations may form on the set of sites where they spend most of their time, e.g., many of the mainstream internet portals such as Yahoo! and MSN.

Consumer Use Scenarios

As noted in the introduction, the PSA assists the consumer on a shopping trip. In the initial deployment at the Future Store in Rheinberg, consumers who have a loyalty card can receive a PSA. PSA system recognizes them and logs them in after the consumer scans a loyalty card. This enables the interaction between the PSA and the consumer to be "personalized". The consumer can immediately retrieve a shopping list based on their previous shopping trips and stored on a central server. The PSA can provide the location of each product to the consumer and hence provide a "route map" for walking through the store. This type of feature can reduce shopping time and increase convenience. These benefits are of interest to the time-sensitive shopper.

The availability of a UPC scanner provides an additional convenience. As the consumer picks up each item in the shopping list, they can scan it with the PSA. This "scan as you go" feature has multiple benefits. It provides a "check off" against the shopping list. For promotion sensitive shoppers it confirms whether the item is on deal and the discount level from the regular price. Finally, it provides a running total of current purchases. This running total of the basket cost should appeal to shoppers in EDLP environments who are more sensitive to the basket price.

An additional set of benefits and use cases pertain to the provision of product information such as recipes. A very basic system might provide a set of recipes that a consumer can look up when they are buying a product. The scenario might evolve in the following manner: A consumer finds Pasta on promotion. This triggers an interest in making pasta for dinner and the consumer looks for a pasta recipe at the web-based terminal. The recipe indicates additional ingredients such as a particular type of pasta sauce. The consumer prints the recipe and adds the recommended type of pasta to the shopping basket. As this scenario suggests, printing capabilities can be an important feature in kiosks in these contexts.

It is easy to envision advanced capabilities that provide information that is more precise based on either the product or the consumer's preferences. For example, instead of searching for all past recipes, the consumer can scan the pasta that is on sale and ask for only recipes that explicitly match this type of product. A further refinement can make the search more personalized. For example, the consumer might be allergic to shellfish and might have indicated that in their profile. The recipe search can now exclude any recipes that incorporate shellfish.

A final and perhaps significant benefit accrues at checkout. Since the basket is pre-scanned, the actual checkout process can be very short. At the checkout, the PSA transfers the details and total amount of the shopping to the cash system. The checkout prints out the sales slip and the customer pays the amount shown.

Through this system, consumers save time because they need not take their shopping out of the trolley and place the articles on the conveyor belt (see also chapter by Litfin, Wolfram in this book).

In addition, the Extra Future Store also offers a completely novel self-checkout where the customers themselves act as cashiers. They draw their articles across a scanner and record prices. The customer then places the products in a bag, on a weighing scale. When the weight of the bag varies from the expected weight of the scanned goods, the system alerts an employee. The customer pays as usual, either cash or with EC/credit card.

The Intelligent Weighing Scale

The intelligent weighing scale, illustrated in Figure 3 is another technology introduced in the Future Store. The idea underlying the scale is straightforward. Consumes use the scale to weigh produce, obtain a price and a bar-coded label. The scale uses weighing and printing technologies that are available in scales deployed at retail checkouts.

In addition to these basic technologies, the scale has an integrated camera that recognizes the product. This feature is crucial in that it enables self-service by the consumer in a product category where products tend to be less standardized. Alternative approaches to self-service are costly. They involve prepackaging or pre-labeling many types of produce.

With respect to a consumer's shopping trip, there is interplay between the PSA and the intelligent scales. Without the intelligent scale, the automated shopping experience enabled by the PSA is not complete. The consumer would have to get produce weighed at the checkout and incur the time involved in the checkout process.

To summarize, the PSA, the web-based terminals and the intelligent weighing scales collectively enable an efficient and personalized *self-service shopping trip*

Fig. 3. Intelligent Weighing Scale

that provides some personalized assistance to the consumer. They save consumer's time and retailer's labor. The PSA also helps consumers with product information and can potentially affect the basket size by providing additional recommendations. The intelligent weighing scale works in conjunction with the PSA to complete the self-shopping experience.

Digital Advertising Displays

The Future Store tested several types of digital advertising displays. Figures 4 and 5 provide examples. The digital signs consist of flat screen displays connected to the local area network. In some cases, there is the potential to connect using wireless technologies.

Fig. 4. Digital Shelf Talker

Fig. 5. EndCap Digital Signage

Figure 4 shows an example of a digital sign placed at eye level on the shelf. In this type of deployment, the digital sign can play the role of a "shelf talker". Since the sign is not static, it has the potential to attract considerable attention from the shopper. Barcode reading capabilities are a potential enhancement. By scanning a barcode, the consumer can conduct a price check or look up information on the product.

Interactive shelf talkers might allow retailers to expand private label offerings in some product categories. National brands sell themselves without the need for extensive in-store merchandising. Private label products in certain product categories require in-store education and information. Traditionally the only approach to do this was through trained sales associates in the store – an approach that does not fit into the economics of discount food retailing. Interactive shelf talkers might allow retailers to cost-effectively merchandise and communicate the specialized benefits such as healthy ingredients or the value proposition of private labels.

Digital sign placement can also be at the end of an aisle (e.g., Figure 5). Several factors contribute to the potentially high impact of digital signs. The high resolution and bright screens make these signs distinctive. Animation and high quality graphics can also enhance the visual appeal. An end-of-aisle sign can work in conjunction with an end-cap, highlighting the products on display.

Research on promotions has documented the existence of "big bang" effects (Blattberg and Neslin 1989). A big bang effects occurs when multiple aspects of retail promotion such as a price cut, an endcap and a feature advertisement in the flyer, have an interactive effect that is greater than the sum of the parts (for more information on such effects, see chapters on retail sales promotions by Gedenk, Neslin, Ailawadi and integrated marketing communications by Raman, Naik elsewhere in this book). A digital sign on top of an endcap featuring a product that is on promotion may contribute to the big bang. On the other hand, because of their distinctiveness, they might have a strong effect all by themselves (a strong main effect).

The extent to which retailers co-ordinate the display on the digital signs with their promotional planning will depend on the relative magnitudes of the main effects and the interaction effects. An issue for manufacturers is the extent to which they should re-allocate trade promotion dollars into this type of advertising. Many aspects of digital signage have the potential to evolve. One is the nature and types of creative content in these signs. Current approaches include simple rendition of product images highlighting prices. This can evolve in a number of ways including the use of animation. Since the message can change instantly, in principle an electronic advertising sign can rotate through a large number of messages. The rotation schedule of messages is also a feature that requires additional research. Consumer attention and shopping mode (browsing versus goal-directed) when they are in the aisle might limit the number of rotations. Finally, a potential limiting feature for some of these signs is that some deployments might not be in the field of vision of shoppers. Additional research should provide insight into these issues.

Fig. 6. An Electronic Price Tag

Elecronic Price Tags

Electronic price tags (as illustrated in Figure 6) as the name indicates are replacements for current paper price tags which are placed manually and changed every so often during the course of the business.

Implementing such a technology is completely in the hands of the retailer.

Consumers have been waiting for this technology for a long time. They are tired of reaching the checkout counter and facing a surprise regarding the price they expected to pay for the item. Some estimates of price inaccuracy suggest that prices may be incorrect on 2-3 % of the items. The stores have also been waiting for this technology for three reasons: first, having the ability to display the correct price and not have any errors at the checkout counter in favor of either the stores or the consumer. Second, and more importantly, it is very frustrating for the cashier to hold up a long line while somebody has been sent to verify a price that is either not on the item or is under contention by the consumer. Finally, changing prices manually is very costly and this technology can lead to significant cost savings after the initial investment. Therefore, electronic price tags can contribute to price accuracy in stores, eliminate possible unpleasant exchanges between the consumers and store personnel, and ensure the consumer is charged the correct price. Hence, both the consumer and the stores are likely to benefit from this technology.

Another potential benefit of electronic price tags is the ability to change prices with a higher frequency. Here the literature on price discrimination comes to mind. With the ability to change prices through a stroke of a key, one can imagine prices changing frequently, and higher (lower) prices set for those willing to pay a higher (lower) price. For example, stores can potentially charge different prices for items during the morning, afternoon, and evening of each day. In addition to price, stores can also change the quality of service by time of day. Therefore, if consumers who are more affluent visit the stores in the evenings, higher prices and more staff in the evening can be an appropriate strategy for the store. Similarly, if older and less affluent consumers are likely to visit the stores in the morning, lower prices at that time may be the appropriate strategy. However, it is useful to evaluate these ideas in a broader context. Stores spend a lot of money in communicating the price image of the store. This is especially true in case of grocery stores where more than 50% of the communication effort through weekly free-standing inserts reinforces the correct price perception of the store. Thus, frequent changes to the prices in the store may undermine any effort to maintain a low price image (see also chapters by Simon, Gathen, Daus and Bolton, Shankar, Montoya in this book for more insights into effective retail pricing).

A second issue is consumer reaction to such price changes. If a beverage company's experience in Latin America is any barometer for such ideas, these ideas are likely to fail. In December 1999, the Wall Street Journal reported that the company might be considering the possibility of changing prices at its vending machine depending on the time of the day, the outside temperature, and the amount of stock in the machine. This experiment faced widespread ridicule in the press to the extent that the company had to issue a statement that it was not planning any such changes at the vending machine. Hence, it is fair to say that any use of this technology to price discriminate between consumers with higher and lower willingness to pay should take into account the social context. Consumers do pay different prices depending on when they choose to make an airline reservation and the time of travel. Similarly, the consumer is happy to pay $5 for a glass of beer on the beach, in the restaurant, or at the airport. Thus even though consumers are accustomed to paying different prices for the same good on different consumption occasions, the idea of charging different prices at different shopping occasions has to be evaluated within the context of the operating social norms.

Hence, we see the benefits of electronic price tagging technology accruing to the stores in the form of cost savings in making price changes as well as benefits from better customer service at the cashier. Consumers are also likely to be happy with electronic price tags as they would have less frequent surprises at the check-out counter.

RFID

RFID is a new technology that has the potential to revolutionize the retail industry. Just as the Universal Product Code had a big impact on the industry, RFID is the next generation of technologies in this series that has the potential to have an even bigger impact on the industry.

Radio Frequency Identification technology has been around for a while. A RFID reader can remotely identify a small transponder attached to a product and communicate that information through a computer network. A RFID system (see, e.g., Figures 7, 8, 9) therefore consists of three parts: a reader, a transponder and a computer network to process the data. RFID readers are devices that send out radio signals on a continuous basis and look for a response from one or more transponders. A computer network transmits the information from the transponder. Readers can accept responses from many transponders at any given point in time. However, given the current state of technology, the transponders need to be within a particular range of the reader to make a connection.

As of today, there are two types of transponders: active and passive. Passive transponders consist of a microchip that stores a digital code, and an antenna. When the antenna receives a radio signal from the reader, the transponder converts that radio signal into energy and then sends a digital code back to the reader. Because these transponders do not have their own source of energy and use the radio energy provided by the reader, they are limited in their ability to transmit a lot of information over long distances. The weakness in the power of the signal allows it be effective within a working range of 1-3 feet. These passive transponders cost less than a dollar – closer to 20 cents. The more expensive active transponders cost closer to 10 dollars if not more. However, these transponders use a battery as their active source of energy. They transmit more information and previously recorded information, on a continuous basis.

How revolutionary is RFID? One can imagine what life was like in the days before the UPC, the 12-digit bar code now available on every SKU that passes through the checkout counter. A portion of the code identifies the producer/manufacturer and the remainder identified the product using a standard format used by all participants in the industry. It is easy to imagine the difficulty in developing the comprehensive understanding that is necessary for every business decision for the retailer, the manufacturer and every one else involved in the physical distribution of the goods. While the Universal Product Code allowed firms to track the flow of goods as they were scanned, RFID adds a very different dimensionality to the nature of the data availability. In essence, it presents a current view of what goods are present at any

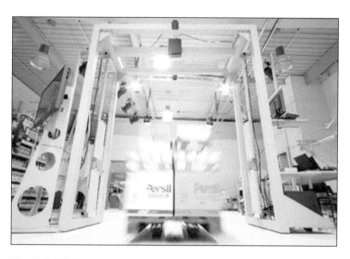

Fig. 7. RFID Gate

Fig. 8. RFID Tag

given location. In other words, goods are unlikely to get lost in any particular location. A UPC when scanned helps us conclude that the product should be in a particular location. RFID, however, helps locate the product in a warehouse or a large store. This difference is most evident in bookstores where the reference clerk knows that a particular book should be available on the rack but is unable to locate it because it has been mis-filed or not been filed. In contrast, RFID can provide the exact location of the book in the store.

Another big difference is that UPC data collection requires a scan, whereas RFID information does not. In other words, when a truck is driving into a warehouse, the transponders can communicate with the receivers without having to scan individual items. This is true even during checkout. Currently, a checkout requires scanning each item separately. This process consumes significant amount of labor and consumer patience. RFID, however, allows the consumer to checkout by passing through a doorway activated by appropriate receivers. A third salient difference is in the dimensionality of the information captured by this new technology. While the information embedded in the Universal Product Code is static, RFID captures and stores information over time that is downloaded when needed. For example, RFID can record the temperatures to which product are exposed to when transiting from the manufacturing plant all the way to the grocery store. Variations in temperature encountered in transit severely affect the taste and effectiveness of many products. Another piece of information that can be stored through this technology that would be of great benefit to the consumer is tracing the origins of the food we consume. In many countries, retailers are already using this information to differentiate their products and often find an increased consumer willingness to pay for the same.

It is easy to envisage several economic benefits accruing to producers, retailers and consumers from RFID technology. For producers, improved efficiencies and lower costs would be possible because knowing the exact location of all merchandise in the long, winding supply chain should lead to reduced inventory levels.

Conclusions and Discussion

METRO Group's Future Store offers a number of lessons. Primarily, it shows the power of testing technologies in a practical working environment as opposed to a sterile lab setting. The public interest around this unique test creates excellent visibility for the retailer and the associated partners. A second lesson from the test is regarding the availability and use of tried and tested underlying technologies. This allows them to be robust for use by end consumers. It also helps to have several enabling technologies such as web-based shopping take root.

Another set of learnings are with respect to the impact on discount retailing formats. The ability of these technologies to enhance consumer convenience and timesaving suggest that retailers can use them to attract the time-sensitive consumer. The ability to provide more personalized service might enable retailers to reach more service-oriented consumers, at the same time appealing to the price-oriented shopper. The breadth of the assortment might limit the scope of such an expansion. Technologies such as RFID will continue to lower costs and improve the efficiency of retailing. Consumers should benefit from these efficiencies. Will these technologies affect the structure of the retail industry? The answer depends largely on which sector of the retailing industry successfully deploys these technologies and the nature of the resultant shift in consumer value perceptions. As the race heats up, one thing is for sure: it will not be business as usual!

For some technologies such as self checkout and RFID, it is very likely that most retailers will adopt these technologies as they lead to reduced costs as well as enhanced customer satisfaction. Therefore, even though many retailers and their competitors will incorporate these technologies, it is unlikely to lead to a competitive advantage in the long run. However, the cost savings should lead to increased profitability for all retailers.

In terms of competition across formats, different retailers might approach these technologies differently. When a technology helps lower costs to the retailer, it is likely to be adopted by all retailers and particularly those that offer low prices as their prime value proposition. It is therefore not surprising that retailers like Wal-Mart and METRO Group are at the leading edge of experimenting with these technologies. In contrast, other implementations of these technologies that lead to an enhanced customer experience are most likely to be adopted by retailers that focus on delivering a better customer experience. This is likely to reinforce their strategic intent and provide more differentiation relative to deep discounters.

Finally yet importantly, we believe that retailers need to look beyond the benefits offered by these individual technologies on a standalone basis. They need to develop a more integrated perspective and offer solutions to consumers' sometimes-difficult store experience. Retailers that have the ability to integrate these technologies to launch new strategies to enhance the customer experience will be the biggest beneficiaries.

References

Blattberg, R. C. & S. Neslin (1989): Sales Promotion: The Long and the Short of it, Marketing Letters, 1:1, 81-97.

Hoch, Steven J., Xavier Dreze and Mary Purk (1994): EDLP, Hi-Lo, and Margin Arithmetic, Journal of Marketing, 58, (October), 16-27.

Jakob Nielsen and Marie Tahir (2001): Home Page Usability: 50 Websites Deconstructed, New Riders Press, 1st Edition.

Update: Please note, METRO Group evaluated the learnings of the Rheinberg Future Store and incorporated them in a modified Real store in Tönisvorst, near Düsseldorf, that opened in May 2008. Furthermore, the Extra sales division was sold in July 2008.

The Third Wave of Marketing Intelligence

Raymond R. Burke

Kelley School of Business, Indiana University, Bloomington, USA

Introduction

During the last 25 years, marketing research in retail settings has been transformed by technological change. The first wave of change occurred when retailers adopted point-of-sale (POS) systems with UPC barcode scanning. This provided companies with real-time data on purchase transactions and accurate estimates of product sales and market share. Retailers used this information in combination with shelf space allocation and product inventory information to measure the productivity of their stores. By modeling these data as a function of causal variables, such as product price, display activities, and feature advertising, marketers were able to assess the performance and profitability of their marketing investments (e.g., Blattberg and Neslin 1990). UPC scanning served as the foundation for syndicated research services such as A.C. Nielsen and Information Resources, and led to the development of brand and category management. Scanner data are in widespread use today and support many critical business decisions.

The second wave of change occurred when retailers started to track and analyze the purchases of individual shoppers. Some retailers, especially in the grocery industry, launched frequent shopper and customer loyalty programs to collect these data (see, e.g., chapter by Reinartz in this book). Shoppers who participate in such programs typically identify themselves with loyalty cards at the point of sale in exchange for price discounts or other incentives. Companies can also identify repeat customers by requesting their telephone numbers, capturing information from credit and debit cards, reading "cookies" stored on their computer disk drives, etc. This information is often combined with geodemographic and behavioral data from other public and private sources to create a profile and purchase history for each customer or household. These data can be used to estimate customer value and loyalty, measure individual-level response to direct mail and other targeted promotions, and conduct shopping basket analyses to identify product complementarities among other applications (Berson, Smith, Thearling 2000; Ravi, Raman, Mantrala this book). Once again, innovation led to the emergence of

M. Krafft and M.K. Mantrala (eds.), *Retailing in the 21st Century: Current and Future Trends*,   159
DOI 10.1007/978-3-540-72003-4_10, © Springer-Verlag Berlin Heidelberg 2010

new industries (data mining, data warehousing) and new practices (customer relationship management, or CRM).

Both types of data collection and analysis only became practical with the advent of the computer. With UPC scanning, the digital representation of aggregate consumer purchases, broken down by time and region, made it possible to measure the impact of temporal and geographic changes in marketing activities (e.g., product price, promotion, assortment, and advertising) on sales. With CRM, the digital representation of individual customer characteristics and purchase patterns allowed marketers to analyze shopper preferences and tailor marketing activities on a one-to-one basis. In both cases, the analyses that could be performed depended on the accuracy and detail of the representation of stimulus and response conditions.

The third wave of change is just beginning to take hold in retail stores. The technology drivers are the digital representation of the shopping environment and the real-time tracking of customers as they enter the store, walk through the aisles, and select and purchase products. Like the earlier innovations, it provides the capability to capture variations in consumer behavior over time and across people, but it adds to the mix the critical element of context. This new wave of marketing intelligence provides marketers with the tools to measure consumer response to the in-store environment and manage the shopping process. It is the foundation for *customer experience management*.

Each generation of marketing intelligence has enhanced our understanding of how marketing, customer, and environmental factors affect consumer behavior and store performance (see Table 1). In the following sections, this chapter reviews the genesis of customer experience management, describes the tools available for tracking customer behavior and measuring store performance, and discusses two case studies conducted by the author. The paper concludes with a discussion of the challenges in conducting computer-based observational research and future directions.

The Advent of Customer Experience Management

Marketers have discovered that the retail context has an impact on consumer behavior that goes beyond product assortment, pricing, and promotion issues. The shopping environment is the medium through which consumers connect with products. It affects the time consumers spend in the store, how they navigate through the aisles, and how they allocate their attention and money across departments and categories. It affects whether they notice a new product or promotion. It influences their framing of the purchase decision and their likelihood of buying complementary products. And it determines their shopping enjoyment and intention to return in the future. Manufacturers and retailers have found that it is to their mutual benefit to design shopping environments that effectively engage consumers and help to convert demand into purchase (see Burke 2005).

Table 1. The Evolution of Marketing Intelligence in Retail Settings

	Wave I	Wave II	Wave III
	Brand and category management	*Customer relationship management*	*Customer experience management*
Enabling technologies	UPC barcode scanning	Customer loyalty cards, credit/debit cards	Real-time customer tracking (RFID, GPS, video, clickstream, portable shopping devices)
Causal variables	Product assortment Shelf space Price Promotions Displays Feature advertising	*Wave I, plus:* Customer attributes (geodemographics) Purchase history Targeted promotion	*Wave II, plus:* Store layout Store atmosphere Navigational aids Product adjacencies Service levels Queues/crowding In-store events
Performance measures	Sales Market share Gross margin Sales/square foot Turn rate GMROII	Customer retention Customer loyalty Share of customer Lifetime value ROC curves	Store traffic Shopping path Aisle penetration Dwell time Product interaction Conversion rate

This new focus on the shopping process has fueled two recent trends in retailing research. The first is the increased use of observational and ethnographic research (see, e.g., Underhill 1999). Merchants have found that, by watching how customers shop in their stores, they can isolate points of friction in the shopping process and identify opportunities to improve the convenience and enjoyment of the experience. This research is usually executed by setting up one or more video cameras within the store, recording consumer shopping activity for several hours a day, and then manually coding shopper behavior at a later time. Video observation is often combined with intercept interviews to identify both how and why consumers buy.

This research provides a number of important insights. By noting the dominant pathways and directions that shoppers take through the store, retailers can position signs and displays to catch the customer's attention. By recording how long consumers spend at various locations ("dwell time"), they can identify points where shoppers will be most receptive to communication. By tracking the shopper's path through the store and monitoring which areas are shopped together, merchants can identify cross-sell opportunities. Video observation can pinpoint crowding conditions and bottlenecks in traffic flow that suggest the need to widen aisles or reposition product displays. It can be used to measure queue lengths and waiting times to flag problems with customer service. Observational research can also capture customer characteristics (age, gender, ethnicity, group composition) and shopping habits: use of shopping aids (carts, baskets, circulars, shopping lists), reading signs and packaging, taking product literature, and interacting with salespeople.

The second trend in retailing research is the increased use of computer hardware and software tools to track customer behavior in both online and conventional retail shopping environments. Unlike traditional ethnographic research, which can be very time consuming and subjective, computer tracking provides an efficient and reliable means of collecting and analyzing data on the consumer shopping process.

The first attempts at computer-based tracking used simple counters at the entrances of stores to measure incoming and outgoing traffic (Robins 1994). Various technologies have been employed for this application, including pressure-sensitive mats, infrared light beams, door-closure switches, and ceiling-mounted video cameras. These devices provide hourly traffic counts that can serve as a rudimentary measure of consumer demand or sales potential. When these counts are combined with transaction data from POS systems, retailers can calculate purchase conversion rates, a key indicator of store productivity. Store traffic and conversion information has been used for a variety of applications, including the evaluation of store promotions and sales force scheduling (Lam, Vandenbosch, Hulland, and Pearce 2001).

Over time, these counting methods have evolved into sophisticated customer tracking solutions. In online environments, detailed records of website usage behavior ("clickstreams") allow retailers to analyze the path that shoppers take through a site and assess how consumer and marketing variables affect click-through rates and purchase likelihood (see, e.g., Montgomery, Li, Srinivasan, Liechty 2004). In conventional retail stores, sophisticated RFID, GPS, and video-based customer tracking solutions have recently been developed that permit retailers to track how shoppers navigate through stores and respond to changes in the store environment (Gogoi 2005; Pereira 2005). Other methods of customer sensing, including the use of kiosks and the provision of personal shopping assistants, provide additional information on in-store customer behavior and consumer response.

Customer tracking is now in widespread use in online environments, but it has been somewhat slower to gain acceptance in conventional retail stores. This is largely due to the significant capital investment and technical complexity of installing a whole-store tracking solution. RFID, infrared, and GPS tracking systems require an infrastructure of sensors and tags to locate shoppers, carts, and hand baskets. Machine-vision-based tracking solutions require that a set of cameras be installed throughout the store. While existing security cameras may be used to collect these data, most surveillance systems do not provide adequate coverage or video fidelity. Fortunately, once a system is installed, the incremental costs for collecting and analyzing the computer tracking data are much lower than for human observation. Customers can be tracked through the entire store, 24 hours a day, 7 days a week.

Computerized tracking provides retailers with the information necessary to measure and manage the shopping process. By counting the number of customers who enter the store and walk through each aisle, department, and product category, retailers can create thermal maps showing the percentage of customers who penetrate each section of the store. If some sections are visited infrequently, this may suggest the need to provide navigational aids, reposition product displays and merchandising, run traffic-building promotions, and/or revise the store layout to improve traffic flow.

When traffic data are combined with transaction log data, retailers can calculate overall and category-specific purchase conversion rates, reflecting the store's ability to turn consumer demand into purchase. These conversion rates can be compared across product categories, time periods, and geographic regions to evaluate the store's performance and identify opportunities for improvement. If, for example, many shoppers are observed to enter a category and examine merchandise but then leave without buying, this may indicate a need to adjust the product assortment, pricing, or presentation. Because the tracking data are collected and analyzed in real time, this information can be used to dynamically adjust staffing levels, the content of digital signs, and other aspects of the shopping environment in response to momentary changes in store conditions.

Other research tools may be used in conjunction with electronic tracking to provide a more complete understanding of the shopping experience and consumer response. Customers are often interviewed after the shopping trip to gain insight into their attitudinal and emotional reactions (Donovan et al. 1994). Shoppers may also be contacted at home and asked to remember the last time they went shopping for a particular product (e.g., Kerin, Jain, Howard 1992). Consumers recall the positive and negative aspects of the shopping experience and offer suggestions for improvement.

Once the retailer has identified opportunities for improving the shopping experience using customer interviews and observational research, the next step is to make changes to the store environment and measure how shoppers respond. While it is possible to jump directly to implementation, a better approach is often to test several different concepts in the laboratory and choose the alternative that performs best. Recent innovations in computer graphics permit researchers to create highly realistic simulations of the retail shopping environment (Burke et al. 1992; Burke 1996). These simulations provide tremendous flexibility, allowing retailers to go beyond existing conventions and explore new approaches for improving the shopping experience. Like in-store tracking solutions, computer simulations can record detailed information about consumers' shopping patterns and purchasing behavior, and the results can be used to forecast future sales and profitability.

Research Applications

Two case studies are now presented to illustrate the power of customer tracking research for measuring and managing the customer shopping experience.

Measuring Retail Productivity During the Holiday Shopping Season

Retailers slash prices on popular products and spend heavily on advertising to draw consumers into their stores during the holiday season. But how do shoppers behave once inside the store? Are the legends about the customer stampedes for one-of-a-kind bargains and the last-minute shoppers on Christmas Eve really true? And how effective are stores at transforming high levels of consumer demand into purchase? For many retailers, sales during this period drive profits for the entire year.

To address these issues, Indiana University's Kelley School of Business partnered with a major consumer electronics retailer to study shopper behavior during the 2003 holiday shopping season. The research team selected two stores in the Midwest U.S. that reflected the demographics of the national population, and installed digital video recorders to capture images from four surveillance cameras positioned throughout each of the two stores.

The study observed how customers shopped during the entire holiday season – from before Thanksgiving through Christmas. The video images were analyzed using a combination of computer vision software (to count the numbers of shoppers and track their path through the store), supplemented by human judgment (to classify shoppers into demographic groups and record their use of shopping aids). The findings confirmed many of the stereotypes about holiday shoppers, but also suggested several opportunities for retailers to improve the customer experience and retail performance during the holiday season. For simplicity, the following discussion will focus on just one store, but shopping patterns were similar across both stores.

The season kicked off with "Black Friday," the day after Thanksgiving and one of the busiest shopping days of the year. Consumer shopping patterns on that day were unlike any other during the holiday season. Despite the cold, rainy weather, shoppers arrived at the store before dawn and lined up around the building waiting to buy $20 DVD players, $130 video cameras, and $200 computers. *When the doors opened at 6:00 a.m., 650 people poured into the store in the first 10 minutes. In the first hour, over 1,400 shoppers entered the store.* To put this in perspective, traffic on a typical Saturday afternoon might be in the range of 200 to 300 shoppers per hour, and numbers can approach 600 shoppers per hour on the weekend before Christmas and on Christmas Eve.

The people entering the store during those early hours were clearly destination shoppers who were anxious to buy. They traveled light, leaving kids, heavy coats, and handbags behind. Most were familiar with the store layout and walked quickly to the desired products. In some cases, they used team shopping techniques, one

allows the researcher to collect information from a representative sample of consumers, but at the expense of sample size.

An alternative approach is to use video cameras and machine-vision tools to track customer behavior. With this method, it is possible to track the path of every shopper who enters a store, and not just those who use a shopping cart or carry a special card. In practice, this requires a large number of cameras, with each camera positioned directly overhead to limit occlusions. Consequently, video tracking solutions tend to work best in smaller stores.

Another benefit of video tracking is that – with a suitable camera view – the technology can classify shoppers electronically into demographic groups (gender, age, ethnicity) based on visual appearance (Pereira 2005). If certain demographic groups have different average transaction sizes, then the retailer can weight the demographically classified traffic by these purchase rates to produce a more accurate estimate of sales potential. This technology can also be used to code the facial expressions of shoppers, capturing their emotional reactions to the in-store environment.

A second challenge in computer-based tracking concerns the digitization of the store environment. The spatial tracking information collected by video cameras or other location-sensing devices must be mapped onto the physical locations of product departments and categories, and then linked with the associated transaction data to calculate department- and category-specific penetration and purchase conversion rates. Existing store floor plans and planogram files can be used to facilitate this mapping process, but retailers must confirm that these electronic representations accurately reflect the actual store layouts. An additional level of complexity is introduced when the same products are merchandised in several locations throughout the store.

A third major issue is consumer privacy. Shoppers have expressed concern that retailers may violate their right to privacy by linking their shopping patterns to their personal identities. For example, the MIT/Cambridge Auto-ID Center conducted a series of international focus groups and one-on-one interviews which revealed that people have consistent, negative opinions about the use of RFID tags on consumer products, especially when these tags are not disabled or removed at the time of purchase (Duce 2003). To address this issue, most customer tracking studies do not attempt to identify individual shoppers, but rather focus on aggregate shopping patterns. In addition, these projects limit tracking to the in-store environment.

Conclusion

The third wave of marketing intelligence will significantly enhance the practice of retailing, allowing manufacturers and retailers to manage the shopping experience in response to the unique needs of customers and the characteristics of the shopping environment. In the future, the focus will be on measuring unfulfilled consumer demand, tracking the shopping process, measuring consumer response to changes in marketing activities, and analyzing returns and customer feedback. This information will be used to spot trends in consumer tastes, identify and address points of friction in the shopping process, and create product assortments, prices, and promotions that will attract consumer attention and stimulate purchase. Exceptional retailers have always paid close attention to customers' needs. Modern technology allows this to be done on a much larger scale and at a lower cost.

How is retailing likely to evolve in response to these innovations? From the customer's perspective, the biggest change will be the increased transparency and convenience of the retail shopping experience. Store layout, signage, and product organization will improve. Product selections will provide greater real assortment with lower levels of duplication. Consumers will be more likely to find the products they seek. The items will be in stock and offered at a fair price. Product information will help reduce consumer confusion and highlight important new benefits. New and complementary items will be featured in attractive and engaging ways. Sales associates will be available to assist shoppers when and where they need help. Checkout and returns will be quick and convenient. In general, stores will do a better job of connecting supply and demand for the benefit of both consumers and retailers.

References

Berson, Alex, Stephen J. Smith and Kurt Thearling (2000): Building Data Mining Applications for CRM, McGraw-Hill Professional Book Group.

Blattberg, Robert C., and Scott A. Neslin (1990): Sales Promotion: Concepts, Methods, and Strategies, Englewood Cliffs, NJ: Prentice Hall.

Burke, Raymond R. (1996): Virtual Shopping: Breakthrough in Marketing Research, Harvard Business Review, 74 (March-April), 120-131.

Burke, Raymond R. (2005): Retail Shoppability: A Measure of the World's Best Stores, in Future Retail Now: 40 of the World's Best Stores, The Retail Industry Leaders Association: Washington, DC.

Burke, Raymond R., Bari A. Harlam, Barbara E. Kahn and Leonard M. Lodish (1992): Comparing Dynamic Choice in Real and Computer-Simulated Environments, Journal of Consumer Research, 19 (June), 71-82.

Coleman, Calmetta Y. (2000): Eddie Bauer's Windows Add Electronics in New Customized Marketing Effort, The Wall Street Journal, November 28, Section B.

Donovan, Robert J., John R. Rossiter, Gilian Marcoolyn, and Andrew Nesdale (1994): Store Atmosphere and Purchasing Behavior, Journal of Retailing, 70 (3), 283-294.

Duce, Helen (2003): Public Policy: Understanding Public Opinion, Auto-ID Centre, Institute for Manufacturing, University of Cambridge, United Kingdom (February 1).

Gogoi, Pallavi (2005): Retailing, the High-Tech Way, BusinessWeek Online, July 6, Special Report: Retailing's New Tech.

Kerin, Roger A., Ambuj Jain, Daniel J. Howard (1992): Store Shopping Experience and Consumer Price-Quality-Value Perceptions, Journal of Retailing, 68 (4), 376-397.

Lam, Shunyin, Mark Vandenbosch, John Hulland, and Michael Pearce (2001): Evaluating Promotions in Shopping Environments: Decomposing Sales Response into Attraction, Conversion, and Spending Effects, Marketing Science, 20 (2), 194-215.

Montgomery, Alan L., Shibo Li, Kannan Srinivasan, and John C. Liechty (2004): Modeling Online Browsing and Path Analysis Using Clickstream Data, Marketing Science, 23 (4), 579-595.

Pereira, Joe (2005): Spying on the Sales Floor, The Wall Street Journal, December 21, p. B1.

Robins, Gary (1994): Retailers Explore New Applications for Customer Counting Technology, Stores (September), 43-47.

Underhill, Paco (1999): Why We Buy: The Science of Shopping, New York: Simon & Schuster.

Applications of Intelligent Technologies in Retail Marketing

Vadlamani Ravi[1], Kalyan Raman[2], and Murali K. Mantrala[3]

[1] IDRBT, Hyderabad, India
[2] Loughborough University, Leicestershire, UK
[3] University of Missouri, Columbia, USA

Introduction

Over the last two decades, various "intelligent technologies" for database analyses have significantly impacted on the design and development of new decision support systems and expert systems in diverse disciplines such as engineering, science, medicine, economics, social sciences and management. So far, however, barring a few noteworthy retailing applications reported in the academic literature, the use of intelligent technologies in retailing management practice is still quite limited. This chapter's objective is to acquaint the reader with the potential of these technologies to provide novel, effective solutions to a number of complex retail management decision problems, as well as stimulating more research and development of such solutions in practice.

The great opportunity and scope for productive use of intelligent technologies in the retailing industry today derives from the tremendous expansion in computing power and in data captured for decision-making in various domains of retailing, including inventory and supply chain management, category management, dynamic pricing, customer segmentation, market basket analysis, and retail sales forecasting. The universal adoption of barcode technologies over the last two decades has generated much of the data concerned (e.g., see chapter by Burke in this book). For example, as early as 1990, typical supermarket database sizes ranged from 1 million records for a store audit to 10 billion records for store-level scanner data (McCann and Gallagher 1990). Now, in the first decade of the 21st century, data availability is poised to explode further with the advent and adoption of RFID (radio frequency identification) technology in retailing management.

There is little doubt that RFID technology is a discontinuous innovation, with attributes that make it likely to eventually replace the older barcode technology. For example, unlike barcodes, which have to be scanned manually and read individually, RFID tags do not require line-of-sight reading and one RFID scanner can read hundreds of tags per second. Stimulated by Wal-Mart's plan for all its leading suppliers to adopt RFID technology in 2005, other large retailers, such as METRO Group in Germany, Tesco in the UK, and Carrefour SA in France, are all currently studying uses of RFID technology in areas ranging from inventory control to loss prevention. For example, an exciting aspect of the "Future Store" set up by METRO Group in Rheinberg, Germany, is the deployment of RFID for the automation of a number of retailing processes (see chapter by Kalyanam, Lal and Wolfram in this book). However, the tremendous amounts of data that even rudimentary RFID systems (i.e., read-only, serial-number, license-plate model technology) can generate are already overwhelming analysts (Schuman 2004). One major challenge is that of adapting archaic legacy systems to handle the influx of data and integrating RFID into existing retail IT systems, such as warehouse management systems, enterprise resource planning, and supply chain execution. The second challenge looming is the meaningful analysis and extraction of information from the flood of data.

An early warning that the knowledge extraction and application process may simply breakdown in the face of huge databases was sounded by McCann and Gallagher (1990). Those concerns remain true today. A recent report from analyst firm VDC (Venture Development Corp.) indicates that many large retailers are as yet "ill prepared" to handle the large volumes of data expected from RFID implementations and that indeed many have not even mastered their current barcode systems (Schuman 2004). Thus, we anticipate that barcode and RFID technology will co-exist for quite some time in the future as retailers' capabilities to extract intelligence from such voluminous data evolve.

Currently, most large retailers are engaged in efforts to create data warehouses that combine the massive databases formed by barcode and/or RFID systems with the data coming from their typically disparate online transaction processing (OLTP) systems (e.g., finance, inventory, and sales) at a single location. However, deployment of a data warehouse alone is not sufficient to guarantee retailers a good return on investment. This also requires smart technologies for "Knowledge Discovery in Databases" (KDD), which uncover meaningful patterns and rules in the data to support an organization's operational processes. Such knowledge can become an important strategic resource or source of competitive advantage for a company.

The extraction of meaningful and actionable knowledge from very large databases is termed *data mining*, a discipline that encompasses a variety of techniques, including several intelligent technologies such as *fuzzy logic systems* (Zadeh 1994) and *neural networks analysis* (Zahedi 1991) as well as traditional statistical modeling of predictive relationships between outcome and explanatory variables of interest, e.g., multiple regression analyses. However, intelligent technologies other than neural networks and machine learning can also thrive in data-poor environments. Fuzzy logic, *case-based reasoning*, and *collaborative filtering* fall in this category.

Key Characteristics of Intelligent Technologies

Technologies used for KDD are termed "intelligent" if they are *adaptive*, i.e., react to and learn from changes in inputs (i.e., the data sets) from their environment. According to Voges and Pope (2000), the hallmark of an adaptive system is that it "...[U]ndergoes a progressive modification of its population of *component structures*. The rate and direction of this modification is controlled by feedback indicating how well the structures are explaining the available data." Examples of component structures commonly used in data organization and analyses are *rule-based structures*, e.g., "if-then" rules used in marketing expert systems, *weight-based* structures used in traditional regression models and also artificial neural networks, and the *binary-coded* structures used in genetic algorithms. Intelligent technologies all involve a process whereby the basic units of the computational structure (e.g., *neurons* in artificial neural networks, *chromosomes* in genetic algorithms, *rules* in classifier systems) adapt themselves to the information contained within the data set, i.e., "self-organize" toward better solutions by following an adaptive plan (Voges and Pope 2000). In addition, intelligent technology-based decision-making systems accommodate managers' expert judgments and their experience-based subjective understanding of market forces.

The adaptive structures of intelligent technologies differ in important ways from the traditional form of mathematical and statistical structures used in classic marketing research and multivariate data analyses, e.g., variations on the general linear model such as multiple regression, multiple discriminant analysis, structural equation models, or conjoint analysis. While not "intelligent," these traditional approaches have the advantages of relative simplicity of interpretation, a well-developed literature on theory and applications, and easily mastered computer tools for practical data analysis. To achieve these advantages, however, they also have the major disadvantage of making a number of simplifying and/or restrictive assumptions and an inability to handle very complex problems with very many inputs and outputs. Intelligent technologies overcome many of these limitations and expand the range of structures considerably. For example, unlike classic statistical methods, which make specific distributional assumptions, e.g., normally distributed random disturbances, that may or may not hold in different applications, intelligent technologies are *nonparametric techniques*, i.e., they do not assume any specific statistical distributions for the data.

Retailing Applications of Intelligent Technologies

Table 1 provides a summary description of the basic idea, analytical advantages, and disadvantages of each of five classes of intelligent technologies with interesting and burgeoning retailing applications. Below we provide a brief overview and a few examples of retailing applications of these methods, to give readers a sense of their power and potential.

Table 1. Five Classes of Intelligent Technologies

Technology	Basic idea	Advantages	Disadvantages	Evolving areas of application	Future areas of application
Fuzzy logic	Models imprecision and derives human-comprehensible "if-then" rules for a fuzzy controller.	Good at embedding human experiential knowledge; low computational requirements.	Arbitrary choice of membership function skews the results.	Modeling manager's perceptions on sales; customer segmentation; predicting predict customer churn; developing quick-response reorder systems for seasonal apparel.	Fuzzy rule-based classifiers rather than fuzzy controllers find more applications when RFID use triggers more data.
Neural networks	Learn from examples using several constructs and algorithms just as a human being learns new things.	Good at function approximation, forecasting and classification tasks.	Determination of various parameters associated with training algorithms is not straightforward. Need a lot of training data and training cycles.	Forecasting retail sales and market share; segmenting customers for various purposes, such as direct marketing; modeling repeat purchase in mail-order retailing.	On-line neural networks can be used to make decisions on the fly in all these scenarios.
Soft computing	Hybridizes intelligent techniques such as fuzzy logic, neural networks, genetic algorithms, etc. in several forms to derive above stated advantages of all of them.	Amplifies advantages of the intelligent techniques while simultaneously nullifying their disadvantages.	Apparently has no disadvantages. However, does require a good amount of data, but this is not exactly a disadvantage nowadays.	Modeling apparel retail operations; competitive retail pricing and advertising; repeat purchase modeling; configuring co-operative supply chains; customer targeting in direct marketing; forecasting retail share.	Customer churn prediction; real-time problem-solving.
Case-based reasoning	Learns from examples using the *k*-nearest neighbor method, similar to human decision making.	Good when data appears as cases and when dataset is small.	Cannot be applied to large datasets; poor in generalization.	Can be used as a forecasting system for retailers in planning periodic promotions.	Again, can be used to build a forecasting system for consumer products.
Collaborative filtering	Learns from the most similar users and gives recommendations.	Can be used to generate personalized recommendations for users.	User profiles are required; when new products are launched no ratings from users are available.	Retailers can use this technique to recommend various users who like to buy things over the internet by looking into the profile of similar customers.	Though currently restricted to buying books and movie titles, it can be extended to consumer products also.

Fuzzy Logic-Based Methods and Applications

Overview

There are already many fuzzy logic-based commercial products, ranging from self-focusing cameras to computer programs for trading successfully in the financial markets. An important feature of *fuzzy logic systems* is that they model and facilitate the analyses of uncertainty caused by vagueness attributable to linguistic imprecision and ambiguities in human judgment rather than just random factors. Such uncertainty is conceptually quite different from that attributed to missing, omitted, uncontrolled, or extraneous variables in traditional econometric techniques. More specifically, fuzzy logic recognizes that objects, events, people, and phenomena in the real world cannot always be sensibly categorized into conceptually clear and unambiguous classes, as is assumed in traditional formal logic. Thus, fuzzy logic allows us to quantify concepts that do not fit into "either/or" categories but rather form *fuzzy sets*, such as the set of "tall men," "warm days," or "small crowds." These sets or concepts are fuzzy because they cannot be precisely defined.

For example, how meaningful is it to say some man is "tall" when there is no specific height at which a man becomes tall but rather a continuum of heights, ranging from short to tall? Further, the assessment lies in the eyes of the beholder. The fuzzy logic approach, however, accepts this and provides a framework to assign some rational, numerical value (that can be used by a computer) to intuitive assessments of individual elements of a fuzzy set. This is accomplished by assigning the fuzzy evaluations of conditions a value between 0 and 1.0. For example, the relationship between height and degree of "tallness" perceived by an individual can be captured by that assessor rating anybody over 6 foot as 0.9 or even 1.0 and anybody below 5 foot as 0.2 or lower. (This type of numerical evaluation is called "the degree of membership," which is the placement in the transition from 0 to 1 of conditions within a fuzzy set.) These types of assessments of fuzzy concepts provide a basis for analysis rules of the fuzzy logic method.

Objects of fuzzy logic analysis and control may include: physical control, such as machine speed, financial and economic decisions, and production improvement. In *fuzzy logic method control systems*, degree of membership is used in the following way. A measurement of speed, for example, might be found to have a degree of membership in "going too fast" of 0.8 and a degree of membership in "no change needed" of 0.4. The system program would then calculate the weighted average of between "too fast" and "no change needed" to determine feedback action to send to the input of the control system, e.g., amount of pressure on a vehicle's accelerator. That is to say that a fuzzy logic control system could be as simple as: "If the car's speed feels as if it is going too fast, relax the pressure of your foot on the accelerator." In more complex systems, controllers typically have several inputs and outputs, which may be sequenced.

To summarize, the fuzzy logic analysis and control method is, therefore:

1. Collecting one, or a large number, of assessments of conditions existing in the system to be controlled.

2. Processing all these inputs according to human-based, fuzzy "if-then" rules in combination with traditional non-fuzzy processing.

3. Averaging and weighting the resulting outputs from all the individual rules into one single output decision or signal, which informs a controlled system what to do. The output signal eventually arrived at is a precise, hard value (see e.g., Thomas Sowell, http://www.fuzzy-logic.com/Ch1.htm for a primer on fuzzy control).

Retailing Applications

Fuzzy Market Segmentation. In retailing, there are many variables of interest, such as consumer judgments about store price image, that can vary continuously from, say, *value-oriented*, e.g., Wal-Mart, to *status-oriented*, e.g., Nordstrom's. Inherently, the meanings of such linguistic labels and their measurement are vague and imprecise. Such linguistic vagueness is not fully addressed by classic marketing research scaling methodologies, but can be handled in a fuzzy analysis framework. The ability to do this has proved particularly useful in the domain of market segmentation studies, which attempt to cluster customers into groups such that individuals within groups are similar to each other and different from individuals in other groups. In practice, it is difficult to partition customers into completely nonoverlapping groups – especially on the basis of attitudinal variables and market characteristics, which are often linguistically imprecise in nature. Given such "fuzziness" in segmentation variables, standard clustering applications have not been very satisfactory. Consequently, a number of fuzzy logic-based clustering algorithms for market segmentation have been proposed over the years.

Fuzzy Control-based Quick Response (QR) Reorder Schemes for Seasonal Apparel. A cursory glance at the prerequisites for successful implementation of *Quick Response* (QR) reorder schemes for apparel retail reveals that many of these require subjective evaluation, experiential knowledge, and domain expertise. This is exactly where one can formulate several heuristic "if-then" rules that can later be used to build a powerful fuzzy controller or fuzzy inference system. For example, Hung et al. (1997) employed a fuzzy controller to develop a novel and intelligent QR reorder scheme. More specifically, Hung et al. (1997) use the fuzzy controller to specify the size of the current reorder for each SKU on a week-by-week basis beginning at the end of the first week of the selling season and ending with any week chosen by a buyer.

Fuzzy Intelligent Agents for Targeted E-Tailing. Consumers' searches for online retailer information, services, and products can be greatly facilitated by the use of linguistic descriptions and partial matching, both of which are hallmarks of fuzzy technologies. For example, Yager (2000) has demonstrated that fuzzy controller-based intelligent agents can autonomously and instantaneously personalize the display of advertisements on the basis of the viewer's characteristics.

Fuzzy Logic-based Prediction of Customer Churn (Defections). The retailing industry has become extremely competitive, and customers have become more demanding than earlier. In such a scenario, retailers need to continually discover new ways of retaining existing customers, because acquiring new customers is several times more expensive than retaining existing ones. Casabayo et al. (2004) employed a new fuzzy logic-based classification model to predict whether a customer is going to defect (switch) when a new retailer opens an outlet. In a study involving data gathered from a Spanish supermarket chain, the classifier achieved a very high accuracy of 90 % in identifying the customers who would defect. This is because churners' behavior is modeled with the help of fuzzy sets, using retailers' experiential knowledge of the behavior of potential churners and nonchurners. Such heuristic knowledge can be used to build fuzzy inference systems. Further, fuzzy systems are non-statistical in that they are insensitive to the severe imbalance in the distribution of churners and nonchurners in the data, which is typically the case.

Neural Network Methods and Applications

Overview

A neural network represents knowledge implicitly within its structure and attempts to apply inductive reasoning to process this knowledge (Zahedi, 1991). Neural networks are capable of learning, detecting, and storing databases now available for retailing management. Neural networks exploit analogies with the information-processing operations performed by human brains. Thus, a neural network is a network of massively parallel interconnected computing units called neurons, which are arranged in layers. Each neuron receives signals from other neurons and passes on a weighted combination of these signals to the next layer of neurons, generally after transforming the output signal in a nonlinear manner. The power of neural networks is intimately related to their ability to function as the fundamental logic gates that underlie all computing. That is, each of the logical operations needed to compute can be realized by connecting neurons in different ways and changing the weights between their connections. The relevance of neural networks in data-rich situations is already evident in the extensive number of applications of this technique in the financial services industry, such as the identification of good and poor credit risks in large customer populations.

In retail marketing, the central issue in many problems is predicting the behavior of customers. Neural networks provide a key tool for forecasting purposes. The forecasts are often based upon a considerable amount of available data that can be used to *train* the relevant models. The technical word "train" refers to the calibration of an intelligent system so that it can "learn" relationships and interactions in the data and thereby generate subsequent predictions. This is analogous to parameter estimation in classic statistical techniques. Training is accomplished by updating the connection weights iteratively according to a mathematical algorithm, in such a way that the error between the output of the network and the actual output given in the training data is minimized. Training generally requires considerable amounts of data, but is now quite feasible given today's large retailing databases and computer hardware and information technologies.

Retailing Applications

Retail Market Segmentation. Explosive growth in the use of loyalty schemes, personal shopping programs, scanners, cookies, and electronic data collection methods has led to the generation of an "embarrassment of riches" as far as the availability of customer data is concerned. As a direct consequence, market segmentation and target marketing have become complicated, because retailer databases are constantly becoming larger and noisier. Typically, such databases contain hundreds of variables, and it is not uncommon to find many outliers and clusters of unequal sizes. Furthermore, retailers usually use segment-specific marketing mixes. Against this backdrop, Boone and Roehm (2002) proposed using a *Hopfield-Kagmar* clustering neural network (HKNN) for segmentation purposes. The real-world dataset used for demonstration consisted of 4317 customers and six major purchase behavior variables obtained from major retailer databases.

The HKNN turned out to be less sensitive to initial guesses on centroid locations and more accurate in segmentation accuracy than the traditional hard K-means algorithm and mixture models (Boone and Roehm, 2002), for the following reasons. (i) Unlike K-means clustering, HKNN partially reassigns segment membership. Therefore, the skewing effect of an outlying customer on any segment is reduced because all customers are partially assigned to all segments. Only when the HKNN terminates does segment membership becomes unambiguous. (ii) HKNN does not require prior segment memberships to sum to one making it less sensitive to initial starting conditions (poorly specified seeds) and less likely to yield suboptimal solutions when unstructured datasets are analyzed. (iii) HKNN does not require a priori rational information (seeds) to perform well, because initially it randomly and partially assigns customers to all segments and updates segment memberships after processing each customer.

Retail Forecasting Using Neural Networks. It is clear that accurate demand forecasting is important for profitable retail operations, because a bad forecast results in either too much or too little stock, which eventually has a deleterious impact upon revenues and profitability. Agarwal and Schorling (1996) employed a neural network approach to forecast brand shares for household products and concluded that it outperformed the traditionally preferred multinomial logistic regression in terms of accuracy, for the simple reason that their model is, in essence, a massively parallel system of several logistic regression functions acting simultaneously.

Neural networks have also been successfully used in industrial forecasting. Big retailers with large market shares find industrial forecasts very useful. Traditionally, larger retailers have used time series methods and smaller retailers have relied on judgmental methods to make industrial forecasts. Better forecasts of the aggregate sales can improve the forecasts of the individual retailers, because changes in their sales levels are affected by systematic patterns. For instance, around Christmas time, most retailers' sales increase. Furthermore, models used to forecast individual store sales often include assumptions about industry-wide sales and market share. Thus, "aggregate retail sales" is used as a predictor variable in many of these models.

There are many statistical methods available for forecasting aggregate retail sales, such as Winters' exponential smoothing, Box-Jenkins' auto regressive integrated moving averages (ARIMA) model, and multiple linear regression. Neural networks offer an alternative to these methods. Alon and Sadowski (2001) have observed that the neural network solution is better able to capture dynamic nonlinear trends, seasonal patterns, and their interactions and can thereby outperform the traditional statistical models across different forecasting periods and forecasting horizons, especially when economic conditions are relatively volatile.

Modeling Repeat Purchase in Mail-order Retailing. In the mail-order response-modeling literature a critical issue is whether or not a customer will purchase during the next mailing period. Typically, the "RFM" framework that uses recency, frequency, and monetary value variables to predict repeat purchase is utilized. Viaene et al. (2001) approached this problem by applying a neural network model that isolated the most relevant RFM variables and eliminated a number of redundant or irrelevant variables without compromising its predictive power. In particular, they observed that the frequency variables dominated the recency and monetary values.

Soft Computing and Applications

Overview

The third class of technologies featuring in Table 1 is *soft computing*, which refers to the seamless integration of different, seemingly unrelated, intelligent technologies such as fuzzy logic and neural networks to exploit their synergies. This term was coined by Lotfi A. Zadeh in the early 1990s to distinguish these technologies from the conventional "hard computing" that is inspired by the mathematical methodologies of the physical sciences and focused upon precision, certainty, and rigor, leaving little room for modeling error, judgment, ambiguity, or compromise. In contrast, soft computing is driven by the idea that the gains achieved by precision and certainty are frequently not justified by their costs, whereas the inexact computation, heuristic reasoning, and subjective decision-making performed by human minds are adequate and sometimes superior for practical purposes in many contexts.

Soft computing views the human mind as a role model and builds upon a mathematical formalization of the cognitive processes that humans take for granted (Zadeh, 1994). For example, an important member of the soft computing group, namely *neuro-fuzzy* techniques, can endow products such as microwave ovens and washing machines with the capability to adapt and learn from experience and thereby determine the best settings for their tasks independently. Within the soft computing paradigm, the predominant reason for the hybridization of intelligent technologies is that they are found to be complementary rather than competitive in several aspects such as efficiency, fault and imprecision tolerance, and learning from example (Zadeh, 1994). Further, the resulting hybrid architectures tend to minimize the disadvantages of the individual technologies while exploiting their advantages.

Retailing Applications

Fuzzy Neural Network for Modeling Apparel Retail Operations. Wu et al (1995) developed a "fuzzy control neural network" (FCNN) for modeling the relationship between key inputs (e.g., product assortment and season length) and outputs (e.g., service level and lot sales) of an apparel retail operation. Here a fuzzy controller was proposed to fine-tune the selection of "learning rate," a key parameter that determines the speed and accuracy of neural network training. The model provides the retailer with a rapid, easy-to-use visual tool to aid in understanding and predicting the impact on system performance of several "what-if" scenarios such as:

- What will happen if the retail season inventory is reduced?

- What will happen if we use a poor forecast of stock-keeping unit mix and/or demand volume?

- What will be the impact if selling seasons are made shorter?

- What cost/benefits will result if reorder lead times are reduced?

The FCNN outperformed the traditional neural network in terms of speed, whereas both performed equally well in terms of accuracy.

Soft Computing-based Multi-agent Retailing Decision Support System. Aliev et al. (2000) developed a soft computing-based marketing decision support system relevant to retailing within the framework of multiple agents (decision-makers). The architecture consists of a set of contending agents that receive the same input information and generate different solutions to the full problem. These individual agents are autonomous and perform fuzzy rule-based inference. In the second stage there is a solution estimator, whose task is to estimate the expected values of the outcome of the system on the basis of the solutions provided by the contending agents. This solution estimator is a fuzzy neural network with crisp and fuzzy inputs and fuzzy weights represented as fuzzy numbers. The inputs to the fuzzy neural network consist of the current total input of the system and of the solutions produced by the

and to be integrated into the overall judgment. This subjective opinion constitutes the basis of each individual consumer's decision to accept or reject the innovation. The sum of these individual decisions produces the diffusion process and decides on the success or failure of the innovation (Rogers 2003; Albers/Litfin 2001).

The acceptance process can only be influenced successfully in the interests of the enterprise if the acceptance factors and the causal connections are known during the passage through the various phases. These connections are shown in Figure 3.

Acceptance Process

The acceptance process starts with the phase of awareness in which potential buyers get to know something about an innovation, either by chance or during the active search for a solution to an existing problem (Kollmann 1996; Clement/Litfin 1999). If the innovation is appropriate, it is integrated into the set evoked. Therefore, one precondition for acceptance of self-checkout systems is that customers know about these systems.

In the following phase of opinion formation potential buyers or potential users look for specific additional information enabling them to evaluate the innovation with respect to its ability to solve the problem. To this purpose, the perceived features of the innovation, such as relative advantage and complexity, are considered, as discussed in the next chapter. If the result of the cost-benefit analysis is positive, the trial phase of the innovation takes place. This testing reduces the risk of a wrong decision. At this point the decision is made as to whether the innovation is to be purchased and/or used in future. Only if this turns out successfully and the customers have positive experiences or form positive opinions while testing the self-checkout systems will they be prepared to use them in the future.

At the end of the process the final decision is made about whether the innovation is to be accepted or rejected. This rejection can be definitive or can be revised on the basis of new information. However, the barrier in the case of a rejection is considerably higher, since the incentives for a new assessment of self-checkouts might be relatively low because the relative advantages of this innovation over traditional checkouts may perhaps not be great for the customer.

The innovation is put into use during the implementation phase. The self-checkouts are used continuously, or customers decides when to use the new checkout systems and when the traditional checkouts. The experiences with the innovation are decisive in the final decision on whether the new systems will be permanently used and in showing up whether they have insufficiencies and whether problems encountered in handling them lead to cognitive dissonances (Festinger 1957), preventing further use.

Ideally, the innovation meets with general approval, so that it is eventually accepted. Consequently, all the measures aiming at successful acceptance of an innovation must lead not only to its adoption but also to its permanent use. Cognitive dissonances must be reduced by appropriate measures so that the decision in favor of using the innovation can be positively influenced by confirmatory information.

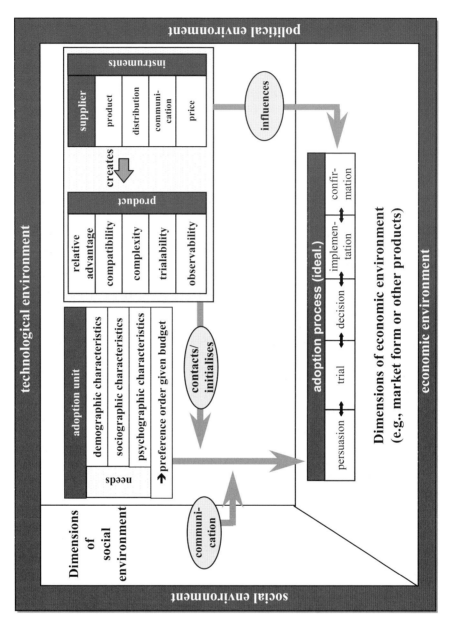

Fig. 3. The Acceptance Process
(Peters 1993)

For example, if someone sees that people regarded as not very skilled in the use of technological appliances can nonetheless use self-checkout systems successfully, this will be an incentive for previous nonusers also to try such a new system. The same applies to discussions among friends and acquaintances.

Acceptance Factors

Numerous factors influence the acceptance process and thus have a bearing on its course, duration, and outcome. We distinguish product-specific, acceptance-specific, and environmental-specific influential factors (Weiber 1992; Clement/Litfin 1999).

Product-specific factors involve elements that are mainly influenced by the innovation itself and less by the potential customers. The perceived product-specific characteristics take a predominant position as they are regarded as the decisive factors in the kind and extent of the necessary change in behavior when the innovation is accepted and used (Holak/Lehmann 1990; Tornatzky/Klein 1982). In spite of individual differences it is generally valid that the greater the relative advantage, compatibility, trialability, and observability, the greater is the likelihood and speed of acceptance (Rogers 2003). These influences are also called Rogers' criteria and are explained in Figure 4.

Shorter waiting times, protection of privacy and control of the checkout process can be some of the relative advantages of self-checkout systems. Solutions incorporating the PSA offer additional services, such as shopping lists and complementary product information. Greater anonymity and the loss of jobs may be regarded as disadvantages of the PSA. As far as the compatibility is concerned it has to be questioned whether the general use of self-service systems such as automatic telling

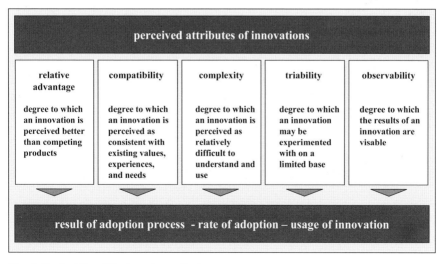

Fig. 4. Product-Specific Acceptance Factors
(Albers/Litfin 2001)

machines at the bank, ticket machines at the airport, and railway stations or self-service bottle deposit systems meets with acceptance. If there is a general negative view of self-service systems automated checkout systems can also be expected to encounter a negative response. Technical innovations are often prone to rejection because of their complexity. If the operation of a new checkout system is regarded as too complex and intuitively perceived as not understandable, this may result in high interruption rates even in the experimental phase. Furthermore, the consumers affected will not use self-checkout systems again, because they consider the amount of time and energy needed to learn how to use them to be too great. In this case they would return to traditional checkout systems. Experimenting on a limited basis has turned out to be useful when the introduction of any innovation is planned, as this minimizes the failure risk. As far as the new checkout systems are concerned, this risk could be reduced by providing users with support in the case of problems or by providing demonstrations of the function and use of such systems conducted by skilled personnel. Compared with the other Rogers' criteria, the observability of results will presumably be less significant with respect to self-checkout systems, because all that is discernible is whether or not the checkout process has worked with no problems. It is also be possible that customers will be watched by other customers while using these checkout systems and may present themselves as particularly enthusiastic about advanced technology. However, the opportunities for supermarket owners to exert any influence in this situation must be regarded as low.

Adopter-specific factors refer to the willingness of users to accept and use innovations, and they influence the search for and interpretation of information as well as the perception of product characteristics. Variables such as income, age, and preparedness to accept innovations can have a significant influence on the acceptance process (Kollmann 1996; Clement/Litfin 1998). It is often observed that younger, male consumers adopt technical innovations more rapidly. In the past they have been credited with a higher affinity to technology. For example, a customer with an increased interest in technical innovations will have developed an eye for such new technologies and will be more willing to devote time to learning its operation. Such customers are likely to accept the innovation at an earlier point in time than customers who are just not interested in technology.

In addition, environmental factors must be considered. These include factors relating to the socio-cultural, political-legal, technological, and macro-economical environment. (Rogers 2003; Weiber 1992). The general trend toward self-service in a society may also pave the way for technological innovations in supermarkets. For example, self-service bottle deposit systems have successfully established themselves in German supermarkets within a very short time. One reason for this may be that the supermarkets did not offer other alternatives. Customers who disapprove of such bottle return systems can switch over to other shops, but the extra expenditure in terms of energy and time would be out of all proportion to the sums of money involved.

All the aforementioned factors are decisive elements for the acceptance and use of innovations and have to be taken into account when introducing a self-checkout system, as it is ultimately the consumer who decides on the success or failure of this innovation.

Empirical Results on the Acceptance of New Automated Checkout Systems

According to an international study conducted by IDC, more than 90 % of retailers expect competitive advantages to accrue from the installation of self-checkout systems (Boone 2003). They believe that these self-checkout systems will, among other things, ensure improved customer service and throughput flow, as well as reducing labor costs. No retailer interviewed for this study has seen an increase in shrinkage that can be attributed to the introduction of these new checkout systems. And more than one third of these retailers agreed that loss of goods to theft has decreased since the introduction of the self-checkout systems.

This research has also shown that nearly 70 % of consumers in important countries (US, UK, Germany, Italy, and Australia) would be prepared to use these checkout systems if they were available. However, the study also indicates that American and Italian consumers would be more likely to use self-checkout systems. The share of potential users amounts to about 80 % in these countries. Almost 20 % of them would be very likely to use these new checkout systems, as against nearly 10 % in Germany. Please see Figure 5 for more detail.

An empirical study conducted in cooperation with the METRO Group Future Store Initiative examined whether self-checkout would be accepted by German consumers and which factors would influence their acceptance.[1] Personal interviews

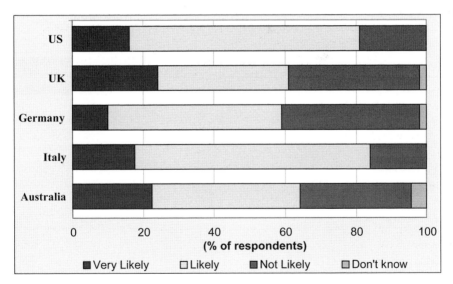

Fig. 5. Consumer Likelihood of Using Self-Checkout Systems in the Future

(Boone 2003)

---

[1] This research was conducted in cooperation with Mr. Hans-Hermann Schepers as part of the requirements for his diploma. Mr. Schepers also conducted the personal interviews.

with 398 consumers were carried out from 10 September to 2 October, 2003 in three selected supermarkets of the METRO Group in which the new self-checkout system had recently been introduced. To ensure that a sufficient quantity of users is represented in the sample, two groups of similar size were formed (user/nonuser). A random selection was made within the groups. In total, 1,089 consumers were contacted to reach the quota. There was a satisfactory response rate of 36.4%. The layout of the questionnaire is based on the adoption and acceptance theory explained in chapter 3, and the Rogers' criteria were adapted to the subject of research, i.e., the self-checkout system (Krafft/Litfin 2002). A receipt analysis was also conducted in the selected supermarkets covering the period of survey.

Receipt Analysis

The receipt analysis shows that on average nearly 10% of the customers use the self-checkout systems, spending an average of 21 euro for 11 articles. It follows that the turnover per customer and the number of purchased articles per customer are 50% lower with self-checkout systems than with traditional checkouts. It is striking that nearly 40% of the customers of the supermarket in Tostedt use the self-checkouts. In contrast to the other stores, this store, in addition to the possibility of paying by credit card, also offered its customers the option of paying in cash, which was in fact preferred by many customers. Furthermore, this supermarket had approximately the same number of traditional checkouts as of the new self-checkout systems in operation. The core results of the receipt analysis are shown in the following illustration:

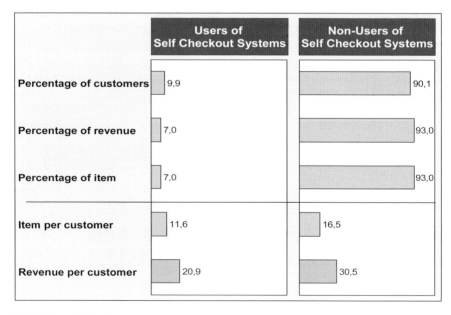

Fig. 6. Receipt Analysis

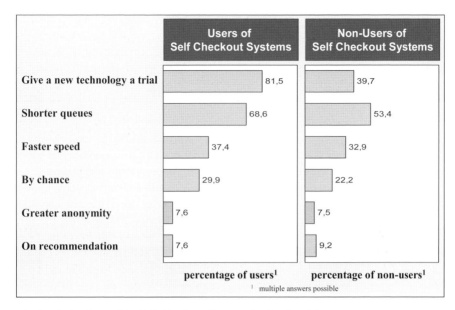

Fig. 7. Motivation to Use Self-Checkout Systems for the First Time

Survey Results

In essence, the results of the receipt analyses are confirmed by the results of the customer interviews. It is seen that there are comparable shares of users and nonusers of self-checkout systems. The users of the new checkouts differ from those who do not use these systems in that they buy fewer items, the worth of their purchases is lower, and they complete their purchases more quickly. Almost 40% of the users often or always use the new checkout systems, and a growing number of customers want to use the self-checkout systems in the future. The positive response of the users to this innovation is also shown by the high satisfaction rate of 80% and the 70% of customers who would recommend this system to others. These high rates of satisfaction are also a result of the low number of problems encountered during scanning and paying for purchases. As can be seen from Figure 7, more than 80% of users state that their reason for testing the self-checkout system stems from their wish to give new technologies a chance. Other important reasons for the first use are shorter queues and a faster checkout process. Reasons such as greater privacy or recommendation by others are of minor importance to present users. All nonusers attach less importance to the above-mentioned reasons for testing the new systems, with the exception of recommendation by friends. They prefer to adopt a "wait-and-see" attitude and tend to follow opinion leaders. Moreover, the new checkout systems were unknown to about one third of the group who had not yet used them prior to the survey.

In the present users' view, flexible payment modes (cash, credit/ debit card payment), ease of use, and shorter waiting lines are points in favor of the new checkout systems. The aspects of faster checkout processes and better control over purchases are of less importance to present users. The checkout process at the self-checkout systems takes the same length of time as that with traditional checkouts, so that time savings cannot be anticipated from an objective point of view. It must, however, be mentioned that the sense of time is different. In one case the con-sumer has to wait while the checkout process is carried out by the cashier, and in the other the consumer is active as cashier him- or herself. The possibility of better protection of privacy with the new checkout systems is deemed insignificant. All in all, present nonusers evaluate the advantages of self-checkout systems as less important. In particular, they are skeptical about the ease of use of the new checkout systems and doubtful about whether the queues are shorter. Furthermore, the per-centage of nonusers paying by bank card/credit card is considerably lower than that of users. It is also striking that present nonusers have a similar opinion to present users on aspects relating to control and privacy. As can be seen from Figure 8, the main differences are found in the assessment, in particular, of ease of use and shorter queues.

Both users and nonusers assume that the new checkout systems will destroy jobs and judge this unfavorably. The present nonusers especially consider it a disadvantage if self-checkout systems allow payment by credit card only. This explains why the rate of use for self-checkout systems is 8 times as high in the

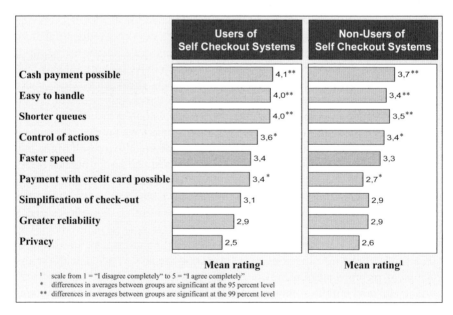

Fig. 8. Perceived Advantages of Self-Checkout Systems

store offering the option of paying in cash at the self-checkouts as in the other two shops, where this is not possible. Consequently, the additional offer of the option of paying in cash could contribute greatly to a higher rate of use of the new checkouts. All consumers considered the checkout process as more impersonal, and the present nonusers attach more importance to this disadvantage than users do. The same is true for the evaluation of the complexity degree in relation to the operation and the concern that problems may be caused by wrong use of the new checkouts. In this context, the nonusers attach greater – albeit still not very high – importance to these potential disadvantages. The main reasons for not using the new systems are inadequate knowledge about self-checkouts (32 %[2]) and lacking interest (26 %), followed by uncertainty, complexity, and unknown mode of operation (10–%). Further reasons are of secondary importance.

In summary, we can say that the principal results of the IDC study by Boone (2003) and those of the BCG study (2003) are confirmed by the present research with German consumers. (Boone 2003; Boston Consulting Group 2003). The German consumers, too, see shorter queues and shorter checkout processes as the main relative advantages of self-checkout systems. In addition, they want to have greater flexibility with the payment modes. They too see better control possibilities and better privacy protection as less important aspects of the new checkout systems. In contrast to this, German nonusers regard low complexity, i.e., ease of use as particularly important. This requirement is regarded as fulfilled, as least by the consumers who use these new systems. The research also showed that sufficient support, e.g. by means of easily remembered operating instructions or personnel assistance would result in a reduction of risk and thus to the testing of the new checkouts. The results of the survey support the hypothesis that the likeliness of

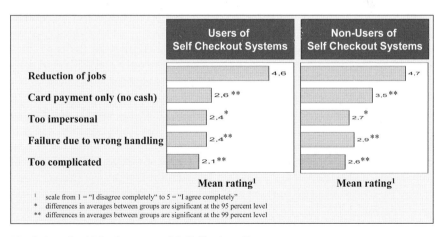

Fig. 9. Perceived Disadvantages of Self-Checkout Systems

---

[2] The percentages do not sum up to 100 because this question allowed multiple replies.

accepting an innovation is high if this is compatible with personal requirements, values, and habits. In a weakened form this also applies to the importance of recommendation by friends. This confirms the essential hypotheses of the adoption/ acceptance theory explained in chapter 3.

Implications: Measures to Increase Customer Acceptance

When compared at international level (see also the chapters on Global Trends in European, U.S., and East Asian Retailing in this book), German consumers are less open minded than others vis-à-vis self-checkout systems, yet the survey results described above and the receipt analyses indicate a growing acceptance of this innovation in Germany. This development is supported by the growing penetration and acceptance of other self-service systems. However, the new checkouts cannot entirely replace the traditional checkouts with cashiers, because the self-checkout systems are mainly used for purchases of a few items only and because a certain group of consumers persistently rejects using them. Therefore, the self-checkout systems can only serve as a supplement to or partial replacement for traditional checkouts. Even so, the results anticipated by the retailers, such as improved customer service, improved handling of the checkout process, and reduction of labor costs may still be achieved (NCR 2004).

For the successful introduction of self-checkout systems it is essential that the adoption/acceptance factors be taken into account. The first priority is to emphasize the advantages of shorter queues and the perceived faster checkout process. A high degree of flexibility in payment modes should be offered in any case. While exclusion of the option of paying in cash may perhaps be the technically simpler solution, it is contrary to customers' wishes. Easy operation is one of the crucial factors in the success of the new checkout systems. During the introductory phase in a shop, the complexity of the system and the uncertainty of the consumers should be reduced by appropriate measures. One conceivable solution would be to detail assistants to answer customers' questions, if required, or help them during the checkout process. This has been successfully practiced by METRO Group since the introduction of its self-checkout system. Operating instructions that are easy to read and understand should be available at the new checkouts. Furthermore, it is important that consumers become better informed about these new checkout systems, because lacking information and knowledge will prevent them from using the new technology. This has been shown both by the present study and by the IDC study. This problem will gradually be solved by positive word-of-mouth publicity. The use of the self-checkouts can be increased by the strategic integration of these systems into existing checkout systems. As the new checkouts are mainly used for purchases with few articles, a logical solution would be to locate them near express checkouts, or to replace the express checkouts by self-checkout systems. This would ensure that the flow of customers is led directly to the new checkout systems.

canned food. These routines and habitual behaviors are highly important to consumers, but also to retailers in that they provide a basis for loyal/repeat patronage.

Occasionally there are significant changes: a consumer gives birth to a first child, moves to a different city, or takes up paragliding. These changes in the way a person lives give rise to a re-evaluation of consumer lifestyle, generating new needs and wants, with consequences for consumer choice. The first-time parent finds him-/herself asking whether to buy cloth or disposable diapers, whether to buy them in a drugstore or a supermarket, which aisle they are in, whether it is better to buy a 20-pack or a 40-pack, and so forth. A process of orientation and learning goes on. This need not be a protracted process. The first-time parent soon has answers to his/her questions about diapers, and the second-time parent hardly needs to ask the questions.

It is evident that consumer lifestyle is an amalgam of routine and habit, punctuated by significant changes, all of which shape needs, wants, and desires. Underlying drivers are both external to the consumer (culture, demographics, etc.) and internal (motives, personality, etc.). The impact of happenstance cannot be overlooked either. In particular, retail situation and consumer mood often have a powerful, if unplanned, influence on needs, choices, and experiences. Thus, the purchasing of a different brand of coffee is as likely to reflect a temporary stock-out situation as a change in consumer lifestyle or a change in needs and wants. Equally ephemeral are consumer mood swings (e.g., pleasure/displeasure, arousal/nonarousal), which have the potential to mediate other effects and which might give rise to quite idiosyncratic or out-of-character purchasing behavior. Where stock-outs occur frequently or where certain moods are associated with particular shopping circumstances, these happenstance factors may come to have longer lasting effects on behavior.

Achievements on the Report Card

The generic framework in Figure 1 summarizes our understanding of retail customers. Quite a positive story can be told of our current state of knowledge when we drill down into the framework. First, much is known about the specific components. Consider the "consumer choices" box: this has been comprehensively studied, giving insights into patterns of shopping trip incidence (in terms of time–of–day, day–of–week, season–of–year), shopping frequency and inter-purchase intervals (e.g., the regular 1-week cycle for main grocery purchases, supplemented by three or so top-up trips), store choice (for brands/private labels, product categories and product clusters), multi-item purchasing and basket-of-goods effects, and mode of travel and associated activities before/after visiting a store or mall.

Second, many of these observed patterns are predictable, using either descriptive (pattern-based) models or decision (response-based) models. Examples include gravity and spatial interaction models to capture flows of consumers from homes to shopping malls (Wilson, 2000) and stochastic models of shopping trip incidence and store choice (Ehrenberg et al., 2004). Both these examples work with aggregated data and focus on finding patterns in revealed behavior. Different, but no less successful, are models that make use of stated preference data (e.g., to predict choice of travel mode on shopping trips, Louviere et al., 2000). Other approaches are broader in scope, such as the attitude-intention-behavior models of Ajzen and Fishbein (specifically, the theory of reasoned action and the theory of planned behavior). These theories relate attitudes to behavior through intentions, in ways that recognize that other factors may prevent consumers from engaging in behavior that is consistent with their attitude (e.g., disposable income and available credit will impose limits on purchasing and other people will exert influence on a consumer's choices, as will the consumer's own perceptions of his or her freedom to choose) (East, 1997).

Third, there are considerable quantities of data to draw upon, enabling the calibration of models of consumer choice. Some retailers (e.g., Tesco in the UK) have internal databases that are extremely comprehensive [a by-product of massive investment in technology, automation, and customer relationship management (CRM) initiatives including customer demographic and transactional data from loyalty/rewards programs]. As a result, individual-level information can be captured about the basket of goods bought, the frequency of shopping, responsiveness to price and promotion, etc. Radio frequency identification (RFID) technology promises to offer further insights into the behavior of shoppers in store, supplementing existing observational techniques (notably video surveillance) and store-atmospheric studies. These internal sources are complemented by external sources, such as consumer panels (operated by TNS, AC Nielsen, GfK, etc.), and census, GIS and spatial interaction data (such as that provided by GMAP Consulting), and considerable amounts of ad hoc and qualitative research. All in all, there is a great deal of data that can be used to validate or disprove our ideas about the behavior of retail customers.

Deficiencies on the Report Card

Counterbalancing these positives are several shortcomings. First, many retail customer studies are extremely ad hoc and context specific (e.g., a one-off market research study might be undertaken of brand choices made by customers at a Madrid-based Continente hypermarket—this would provide information for the store operator in Madrid but it tells us nothing about whether similar choices are to be expected at this store next year, or at other Madrid stores, let alone at stores in Barcelona, or Carrefour hypermarkets in Toulouse). By contrast, more systematic approaches enable norms to be established, which then can be used as reference points or benchmarks when examining specific cases (e.g., how does brand choice at the Madrid store compare with company/industry norms?).

Second, of the systematic analyses that have been undertaken, the vast majority are based on patronage of, and purchasing at, grocery outlets. Undeniably, grocery retailing is important. As consumers we regularly and routinely spend much effort, time, and money on grocery shopping. It accounts for a large proportion of the retail spend of all consumers. Moreover, considerable amounts of data are available. But groceries represent a fraction of what might be described as retailing. In consequence, there is a pressing need for more systematic, analytical studies of the purchasing of non-groceries (everything from laptops and lingerie to Land Cruisers and Lego).

Third, the analytical challenges involved in broader scale research projects cannot be underestimated. Even within the grocery context it is hard to agree on such basic issues as decision sequences and consideration sets (does the consumer choose the store, followed by the brand, and then the SKU, or follow the reverse sequence, or is there a simultaneous choice process?). These specification problems are compounded when the list of decisions is expanded (say, to all the questions listed in the right-hand box in Figure 1) and when the inter-relatedness of decisions is acknowledged (e.g., the purchasing of private labels is in part a simple problem of brand choice, but it is confounded with issues concerning store choice, relative prices, social norms, and so forth). Nor are these decisions made independently of a wider set of decisions (e.g., are we interested in looking at a self-contained trip to a Metro Cash & Carry store, or a multi-purpose trip to a Düsseldorf shopping mall in which METRO Group features alongside visits to Tengelmann and C&A?).

Overall, the report card presents a mixed story. An impressive body of knowledge has developed with regard to our understanding of retail customers. This is of considerable commercial and academic interest. But the record must be tempered with the fact of significant deficiencies. Perhaps this is inevitable—analysis is always an unfinished project. One reason for this is that society evolves. The lives of consumers change, and their needs, wants and desires alter, as do their choices. It is as if the analyst is aiming at a moving target. This is the theme of the second section in this chapter.

Prospects

Looking to the future, consumer choices are being influenced by several forces of change. In the opinion of some commentators these forces of change amount to nothing less than a buyer-centric revolution (Mitchell, 2004; Prahalad, Ramaswamy, 2004). Four such forces are considered here: the rise of technologically savvy customers; the way fad and fashion consciousness have become so pervasive; the importance of experiential shopping; and consumer assertiveness. There are, of course, other changes that are not considered here (e.g., the impact of demographic change, of more open markets, and of migration). The goal is not to be comprehensive, but simply to highlight the impact of a few of the most significant and universal changes.

In terms of Figure 1, each change has an impact on consumer lifestyles, shopping orientations, values, attitudes, and beliefs, which then re-shapes consumers' needs, wants and desires and ultimately influences consumer choices. This presents us with a considerable number of analytical challenges.

Technologically Savvy Customers

There is nothing new about the use of technology in retailing; it is seen in back-room operations [e.g., in freight management systems, automated stock control, electronic purchase-order systems, efficient customer response (ECR) systems, electronic article surveillance (EAS), and eCRM], in front-of-store control [e.g., automated temperature and lighting systems, electronic shelf labeling (ESL) systems, and now RDIT], and also in interactions with final customers (notably through checkout scanning, EFTPOS payments, virtual stores, and on-line sales). Historically, much of this has been hidden from view, but the role of technology is now more evident to customers. At the same time, customers are themselves becoming savvier. Recent developments illustrate the point.

Technology is increasingly involved in almost everything we do as consumers. Electronic gadgetry surrounds us in the form of video, audio, mobile, wireless, and computer devices: from TVs to PCs and notebooks, from mobile and cell phones to smart phones, from Palm Pilots to PDAs, from digital cameras to GPS navigation devices and satellite radio. In most developed countries household ownership and usage rates are very high for established technologies, and as a consequence consumers are ready to allow technology into any aspect of their lives. When it comes to new technologies, consumers are willing to adapt and innovate. They fit these new technologies into their lives even if this requires attitudinal and behavioral change. The phenomenal uptake of iPod in the year of its launch shows how rapidly a particular new-technology can diffuse through consumer markets. More generally, we have seen the growth of on-line information gathering (e.g., Froogle, the product search engine and shopping directory spun-off from Google), on-line shopping (for browsing, purchasing, and delivery), and on-line auctions (e.g., eBay) across sectors as diverse as grocery retailing and memorabilia collecting. This is a remarkable shift in behavior; just ten years ago no ordinary consumer did any of these things on-line.

We see that consumers are able to make effective use of technology. They are quick to master new technologies, because of refined problem-solving skills and the ability to acquire procedural knowledge (we know how to operate things—usually without reference to user manuals and with minimal instruction). Some consumers will have declarative knowledge too, but a defining feature of the technologically savvy is not that they have facts at their fingertips, but that they can deduce how things operate, know where to go for further advice, know what questions to ask when making a purchase, and know how to get the most from technology.

Consumers are empowered by the information that technology makes available. They are no longer dependent on salespersons and promotions, but can obtain the latest facts from authoritative sources simply by searching Google or Yahoo!. "Best-buy" information and product specifications are at their fingertips. So too are competing offers and cross-buying opportunities ("if you liked that, why not try this"). And for categories such as music they have the option of buying only what is required on a pay-per-item or pay-per-view basis.

It is also evident that consumers want to exert more control in relation to their use of technology. This is seen in the acceptance of "user-directed" technologies, which give consumers the flexibility to make as much use of a technology as they wish. The Web is a prime example: consumers browse from site to site at their discretion, and navigate through sites in ways that best meet their personal needs. In-store, user-direction means a readiness to access touch-screen information kiosks and ATMs, and to make use of self-service U-Scan checkout systems and smart trolleys. These features come together in the Personal Shopping Assistant (PSA)—a central element of the METRO Group's Future Store Initiative (for more detail on this initiative, see chapters by Litfin, Wolfram and Kalyanam, Lal, Wolfram in this book). There are parallels here with the introduction of self-service grocery retailing, which was readily accepted by consumers in the 1960s; however, consumer expectations have risen in the intervening years. Today, consumers want the control and flexibility offered by user-directed technology, but also expect to be informed (e.g., regarding special offers and aisle layouts) and provided with service benefits (e.g., using the interactive touch-screen of a PSA to order delicatessen items and be advised when the order is ready to collect).

A wide range of analytical questions arises from this growth in the number of technologically-savvy customers. In-store, what adoption rates are to be expected for PSA-type services? Are there impediments to adoption? How easy is it for customers to acquire the appropriate procedural knowledge, and must they be trained? Does the customer's ability to gather more information (from PSAs, information kiosks, electronic advertising displays, ESLs, etc.) impact on his or her final behavior? And, if so, what aspects of behavior are most affected: store and brand choice, or the weighting given to product and service attributes, or the amount of time spent shopping?

On-line, are there patterns in the way customers patronize Web sites (in terms of visitation and repeat-visitation rates, frequency of visitation, inter-visit intervals)? Are there new habits and routines—different from those in the past, but now every bit as consolidated and engrained? How do these patterns differ from those associated with physical stores? Have new patterns of cross-buying emerged, and do these contrast sharply with established patterns based on the co-location of merchandise in-store? (Weitz' chapter on Electronic Retailing in this book sheds light on some of these issues.)

Also, how do answers to these questions vary for different consumers? Are some consumers technologically savvy across the board—always innovators, always informed, always at ease with new technologies? Or is there more fragmentation than this? Perhaps a consumer is innovative with respect to some technologies (on-line shopping say), but not others (not, for example, PSAs).

Fad and Fashion Consciousness

Fashion has become a defining feature of contemporary culture. It is not simply a matter of which shoes, gloves, and hats to choose when browsing through Sears, Printemps, or Takashimaya (in the traditional sense of 'fashion retailing'), but whether the restaurant, automobile, movie, album, artist, TV show, soap star, etc. is in vogue. Consumers have a heightened-sense of what is 'in' ("so now") and what is 'out' ("so passé"). This applies to the length of pants, to the color of handbags, to the popularity of a neighborhood restaurant. Even the language we use to describe fashion is governed by what is in fashion ("so now" is already sounding passé).

It is through fashion that consumers are able to maintain their identity, express who they are, and create and re-create their self-image (relating to the left-hand box of Figure 1). To an AbFab generation versed in marketing and media speak this comes easily and naturally. The process is reinforced by the media-rich society in which we live—from images writ large on brash billboards through Lagerfeld fashion shots in Vogue to portrayals on popular lifestyle TV programs. In these various ways we have ample opportunity to refine and hone our skills as creators of self-image and to assess whether we are buying into the right fashions, styles and merchandise. Sadly, this does not necessarily mean we feel more confident about our choices; shopping-related anxiety appears to be on the rise.

Associated with these developments is the seemingly insatiable appetite for ephemeral purchases. Children's fad merchandise is an extreme form of this, such as card-collecting crazes (Pokemon, Dragon Ball Z, Tamagotchi, etc.), or successive generations of "must-have" electronic games (PS1, PS2, Xbox, etc.) or the bursts of enthusiasm associated with roller-blading, skate-boarding, scooting, or the latest Hollywood movie. Tie-in merchandising gives extra saliency to these fads: the McDonald's Happy Meal that ties in with Shrek movie merchandise, the KZone magazine article that promotes a computer game that is itself a spin-off from the latest Harry Potter novel. Any pestered parent is only too aware of the pressure to buy these items. Significantly, they are dropped as quickly as last year's dress styles once they go out of fashion, becoming fodder for seasonal sales and markdowns.

Fads and fashion have always posed analytical problems because they necessarily imply change (last year's color is never the same as this year's). It is no coincidence that most analytical modeling focuses on groceries, the purchasing of which is comparatively stable. Really new fashion-dependent or innovation-dependent products pose particular problems. Some of these products come and go like shooting stars, with highly condensed product life cycles (e.g., psychedelic neckties and the IBM PC Jr.); others become widely accepted, with impressive household penetration rates. It is a challenge to determine how consumers in these really new markets are to be understood, and even to know whether previous experiences in related markets offer useful analogies.

There is also the problem of predicting changes within established or evolving markets. Over a ten-year period CDs have not changed much from a technological viewpoint, but that cannot be said of the popular artists appearing on the discs (notwithstanding the staying power of pop-stars like Cliff Richard and Kylie Minogue, most artists have quickly come and gone). It is the cast of brands and sub-brands—or varieties, models and SKUs—to which consumers respond. If these elements within markets are always changing because of the vagaries of fads and fashions, the task of predicting sales is a perilous one.

There are, however, countervailing factors. Arguably, few fashions or innovations are truly new. Any consumer who has experience of CDs and TVs quickly appreciates the concept of DVDs. Any one who has ever used a floppy disk has a basic idea of what a USB can do. Moreover, even fashion-dependent and innovation-dependent markets can settle down and present consumers with a set of familiar competitive offerings (cosmetics, perfumes, and fragrances illustrate the point—the names L'Oreal, Chanel, Clinique, and Estee Lauder are very familiar to consumers, even though specific subbrands and varieties come and go). These markets cannot be described as stationary, but nor are they unfathomable.

Experiential Shopping

London retailer Fortnum & Mason is a purveyor of fine teas, game pies, and luxury hampers; one reason for its success since being established in 1707 is its aura and the customer experience it creates. As this example shows, "experiential shopping" is not new. However, for several reasons, it has now become a norm—as the following examples show.

Nowadays it is difficult to distinguish retail from nonretail activities. There is some fuzziness in the way activities are defined. The shopping mall is enlivened by buskers, children's entertainers, in-store fashion shows, and multiplex cinemas, making it into a venue for public performance and entertainment, as much as a place for conventional shopping. Likewise, the distinction between shopping and eating out has become blurred. Food halls in shopping centers and coffee kiosks in bookshops are de rigueur (not content with selling books, Barnes & Noble offers a place in which to relax, drink coffee, listen to stories, join a book group and meet writers).

A further characteristic of contemporary retailing is that so often we shop when we are on the move—shopping has become an integral part of the travel experience. What started as a convenience at transport nodes (e.g., news stands at railway stations) has become a retail industry in its own right (e.g., duty-free outlets at airport hubs from Frankfurt to Singapore). By extension, tourism and retail experiences have become intertwined: the traveler now sees the coast of New England as a lengthy antiques and craft mall; tourist quarters from Rome to Sydney offer the traveler luxury branded products (usually with the same cast: Prada, YSL, Christian Dior, Donna Karan, Bvlgari, Ralph Lauren, etc.); merchandise sales help sustain experiential theme parks, such as Euro Disney in Paris, Lego-land in Billund, and Movie World on the Australian Gold Coast; international visitors are more likely to be drawn to oil-rich Dubai for its shopping festivals than for its undoubted natural attractions.

We see that in affluent societies the balance between utilitarian and hedonistic motives for shopping has shifted. Customers still weigh up the functional value of products in terms of the ability to satisfy basic needs and wants, and they continue to have regard for prices, promotions, discounts, lines of credit, interest payments, etc. Nevertheless, affluent customers seek more than this. They want pleasure from the activity of shopping, which means the atmosphere and ambience must be appropriate and certain standards of service must be met (for more discussion of shopper experience management in retail settings, see chapter by Burke in this book). Attention turns to the emotions of customers: are they pleased, satisfied, contented, and hopeful, and are they aroused, stimulated, excited, and frenzied? What is more, the social influences that have such an impact on fashion con-sciousness also impact on shopping experiences. Who you are with, and to whom you refer, will influence the way browsing, choice, purchasing, and con-sumption are experienced (e.g., gift-buying with an older friend compared with gift-buying with a child). Arguably, the influence of social norms in these con-texts is becoming greater.

The overall impact of these characteristics is to suggest a symbiotic relationship between retail and nonretail activities, offering consumers opportunities to fulfill utilitarian and hedonistic motives. For customers, activities are blurred into an unfolding set of interrelated experiences: a cinema visit is also an opportunity to purchase the theme music on CD and buy popcorn with movie tie-in merchandise; no international flight is complete without duty-free purchases of Absolut Vodka, Dolce & Gabbana shoes, or L'Oreal body lotions and a pre-flight Pepsi, Evian, or Sunkist.

Conceptually, this fuzziness between retail and nonretail highlights the problem of defining retailing as a distinct activity. In turn, this begs the question: how do consumers view retailing, and does a degree of fuzziness concern them? Fur-thermore, the relevance of studying bundled activities now becomes only too apparent—we buy brands, not in isolation but in the context of multi-purpose trips and in combination with varied activities. Analysts must address new sets of questions. What implications are there for the way consideration sets and choice sets are defined? Which brands are in direct competition and in what ways? How do consumers respond to co-branding, tie-ins and cross-selling? Do they see strong complementarities between brands in different sectors even when there is no formal co-branding?

Also, from an analytical viewpoint, a spotlight is cast on the spatial and envi-ronmental aspects of retailing. Some of the richest experiences demand the co-location of activities, implying agglomeration in certain locations. But does this mean CBD locations or off-center locations? And how does this sit with the cen-

in Helsinki, but how the citizens of that city and other cities are distributed across what might be seen as a savviness spectrum and whether those who are savvy on one scale are generally that way inclined, and whether this correlates with other factors (e.g., are they more or less likely to be fashion-conscious or buyer-centric?). At this scale, a greater sense of order is likely to be observed. With this in mind, a meaningful way forward—if we are to continue to understand retail customers as effectively as in the past—is to extend and enhance proven analytical approaches (such as those described in the first section) to take full account of the buyer-centric revolution that is having a profound impact on contemporary retailing (as described in the second section).

Acknowledgments

The support of the METRO Group is acknowledged, as is partial funding from Australian Research Council Grant DP0344446.

References

Christaller, W. (1933): Die zentralen Orte in Süddeutschland: Eine ökonomisch-geographische Untersuchung über die Gesetzmässigkeit der Verbreitung und Entwicklung der Siedlungen mit städtischen Funktionen. Jena.

East, R. (1997): Consumer Behaviour. Prentice Hall, London.

Ehrenberg, A.S.C., Uncles, M.D. and Goodhardt, G.J. (2004) Understanding brand performance measures: Using Dirichlet benchmarks. Journal of Business Research, 57 (12), 1307-1325.

Kozinets, R.V. and Handelman, J.M. (2004): Adversaries of consumption: Consumer movements, activism, and ideology. Journal of Consumer Research, 31 (3), December, 691-704.

Lösch, A. (1940): Die räumliche Ordnung der Wirtschaft. Jena.

Louviere, J.J., Hensher, D.A. and Swait, J.D. (2000) Stated choice models – Analysis and application. Cambridge University Press, Cambridge UK

Mitchell, A. (2004): The buyer-centric revolution: The rise of reverse direct marketing. Interactive Marketing, 5 (4), 345-358.

Prahalad, C.K. and Ramaswamy, V. (2004): Co-creation experiences: The next practice in value creation. Journal of Interactive Marketing, 18 (3), Summer, 5-11.

Sheth, J. N. and Sisodia, R.S. (1999): Revisiting marketing's lawlike generalisations. Journal of the Academy of Marketing Science, 27 (1), 71-87.

Wilson, A. (2000): Complex spatial systems. Prentice Hall, Harlow.

Future Trends in Multi-channel Retailing

Peter Sonneck and Cirk Sören Ott

TNS Infratest, Bielefeld, Germany

Introduction

Commercial retailers find themselves in an increasingly complex environment. On one hand, this complexity is shaped by establishment of new channels and store formats, while there is also moderation of the earlier "store-specific offered goods" targeted at the consumer. On the other hand, consumers also demonstrate multi-optional behaviour and needs structure.

This chapter will outline the status quo currently prevailing in the retail world. In the first part, we intend to show the characteristics of consumer needs and behavioural patterns set against the background of immensely diverse channels and store formats. The second part will deal with the question of how retailers are able to react within the existing framework of multi-channel strategies, and provide some basic guidelines.

Characterizing Consumer Behaviour

The term "multi-channel retailing" is a new way of referring to an "old" theme (cf. Schramm-Klein, 2003). The food retail store has been using the stationary store format parallels for some time now. However, over recent decades, non-food retailers have combined the stationary store format with catalogue sales. The concept of multi-channel used today refers to the Internet and e-commerce. This may either be a new contact perspective, offering potential for new sales by dispatcher/sender; it can be used simply as an advertising medium (information platform on the Internet, picking up any goods at a stationary retailer); or it can be used as a sole distribution channel (e.g. Amazon).

The various channels can complement each other (i.e. the dispatch retailer) or they can be used to gain a new customer segment that had hitherto been unavailable for reasons of positioning. This is now possible with multi-channel (i.e. placing a store brand in the food area segment as opposed to simply being positioned

M. Krafft and M.K. Mantrala (eds.), *Retailing in the 21st Century: Current and Future Trends*, 221
DOI 10.1007/978-3-540-72003-4_14, © Springer-Verlag Berlin Heidelberg 2010

in the brand-name retailer segment). When we refer to multi-channel, we interpret this concept as including all ways in which the consumer can contact a retailer or a retailer can contact the consumer. This includes all stationary and non-stationary formats and channels. Products and/or services sold can appear under on the same brand name. This is not an absolute condition, although it may well be the deliberate intention of the retailer.

Consumers have a wide choice of store formats and channels from which to make purchases. Consumers are continually making new choices on purchasing sources, and their choice is directed by different occasions, diverse situations and what they actually need. In selecting the source for a purchase, the consumer follows an individual decision-making pattern that is not obvious. In other words, segmentation of consumers is increasingly subject (exclusively or primarily) to socio-demographic determination. There are other factors that are of prime importance in the selection of a retailer. Many other factors impact on this choice, and they can exert a lasting effect on the choice of retail outlet (see, e.g., chapter by Uncles in this book).

The lack of exclusivity or clarity is a decisive factor resulting in generalization of consumer behaviour. The principle of "the more the merrier" is at work here. Different outlets, store formats and channels are used either simultaneously or in succession. Analysis carried out by TNS shows that this behaviour is an expression of a basic trend directed towards satisfying consumer need: consumers expect more and more convenience in making their purchases. They want to spend less and less time on making them. Consequently, they will seek out and use the shopping outlet that best fits their particular situation on the basis of their needs.

The concrete motives of consumers may one day favour a discount store over a shopping mall; they might place an order on e-Bay before going on to a speciality store. They'll order a new outfit from a mail-order catalogue today before buying a fashionable outfit from a store in the city. Consumers are highly individual and independent of the sector.

Table 1 illustrates significant retail branches and the overlapping of various store formats and channels which result in specific consumer behaviour. Consumers are able to purchase food and other products for their daily needs through various store formats, while also being able to purchase almost every product available through a range of different channels. A DVD is available in a large supermarket, as well as in a speciality store or at a service station. A drill can be found in a specialist store, but also in a discount store or in a conventional mail-order company's catalogue.

The consumer is well aware of which retailers have specialized in a particular product line and which offer particular items for a limited period only. The drill or the notebook in the discount store or the large supermarket is usually available as a special sales promotion for a limited period only.

Table 1. Overlapping Usage of Various Store Formats and Retail Channels

Store formats/ channels	Main branches of retail:							
	Food	Cloth-ing	Multi-media	Entertain-ment electronics/ appliances	Household goods/ Home textiles	Watches/ Jewellery	Cosmetics/ Drugstore products	DIY
Discounter	X	X	X	X	X		X	X
Supermarket	X	X	X				X	
Shopping mall	X	X	X	X	X	X	X	X
Department store		X	X	X	X	X	X	X
Branch specialist store		X	X	X	X	X	X	X
Specialist trade store	X	X	X	X	X	X	X	X
Mail order		X	X	X	X	X	X	X
Newspaper stand	X		X					
Service station	X		X				X	
Tele-shopping		X	X	X	X	X	X	X
Internet shops		X	X	X	X	X	X	X
Internet auctions		X	X	X	X	X	X	X

The criteria of price, quality and range are only three of a large number of complex determining factors. Depending on the channel or store format, these criteria can exert an individual impact on the consumer. One set of channels may be used to meet a need, while another set of channels is used to generate the need. If you want to purchase a drill, you go to a DIY store. The drill available from the discounter at a low price motivates the consumer to buy it there. The parallel usage of store formats and channels is becoming increasingly multi-layered and blurred. As retailers present their products in more and more widely differing ways, consumers' behaviour also becomes more diverse in terms of their use of the range of channels on offer.

Consumers have a wide spectrum of intentions they can draw on in order to celebrate shopping as an event. They make their purchases secure in the belief that they have taken independent decisions and acted of their own free will. In addition to these motives, and depending on the context, the consumer becomes a multi-channel buyer: the impulse buyer, smart shopper, the good deal (only discount) buyer, the event buyer or the needs-only buyer. But since motives are the decisive point in consumer behaviour – dependent on the situation, intention or product – it is difficult to place such any consumer in a specific channel.

Individual Consumer Benefits from Different Store Formats and Channels

Consumers perceive an individual benefit in the different store formats and channels. The situation determines what is useful. The store-format and channel choice is closely associated with the decision on situation. The unconscious decision-making process undertaken by the consumer checks the available shopping resources. Which shopping alternatives are available to the consumer? How much time am I willing to invest in gathering the information and the actual purchasing? What basic quality am I looking for in my purchasing need? How much am I willing to invest? How well informed am I? What further advantages or services do the different retailers provide? Another factor that comes into play is whether the customer needs a "fun" or "event" element in that day's shopping Where will I be inspired and get new ideas? What kind of atmosphere awaits me? What concrete experience I already have with one channel tells me that I can meet my actual purchasing need through another channel as well?

Stationary Retail

The direct benefit of a stationary retailer is provided by the local access to the retailer in addition to its ability to supply the products. Whatever products are offered at a stationary retailer can immediately be registered by all the senses. The purchased products are available for immediate use by the consumer.

The consumer gets products from all sectors in a stationary retail store. Brand-specific stores have been differentiated into various store formats as a result of global commercial trade:

When we address the issue of daily shopping for food and non-food products, consumers are confronted with a diversified variety of (large) supermarkets, shopping malls, department stores, discount stores and specialist stores. Each of these types of store offers a particular benefit to the consumer. Large supermarkets offer a diverse range of products in a large shopping area (department stores do the same, but in a smaller space). The supermarket provides for the needs for the consumer in its neighbourhood with a wide range, but has a rather shallow product range. The discount store offers a limited range of products with prices much lower than the normal price range. The specialist store is characterized by a limited range of products but extremely good service and excellent advice.

The individual benefits can also be transferred to other sectors. The specialist store always represents good advice and personal service. The department store stands for a large range of products that are immediately available to the consumer at reasonable prices, and the discount store provides a contrast, with a limited range of (sometimes no-name) products at the lowest possible prices.

Specialist stores, department stores and discount stores – but also drug stores – are in first place when it comes to food and other products being bought for our daily needs. Local proximity is the decisive factor determining the choice of

- Retail has to give consumers what they want.

- Basic insights into today's and tomorrow's multi-optional consumer are required. To put it clearly: "one" consumer no longer exists; the consumer wants one thing today and something else tomorrow.

- Retailers have to embrace and attract consumers wherever they happen to be. In the shopping mall, at the discount Store, at the computer or at the newspaper stand round the corner.

- Success in retail requires innovation, flexibility and customer orientation – these are "must-haves". This applies to communication and to policies on lines of distribution, location, product range and personnel.

- Retail is not simply judged on the products it offers but also on what the company concerned represents.

Analyses have demonstrated that an attractive product selection – even when products are also attractive in terms of price and service – can never balance out a negative image that has become attached to a retailer. The retailer itself is seen as a brand, and the brand equities communicated by a retailer have to be balanced against the apparent needs and the continuing requirements of the consumer. A store brand must be seen to involve not only rational but also emotional benefit to the consumer, as well as continually polishing the retailer's own image (see, e.g., chapter by Grewal et al in this book for more on retail success factors in today's world).

Strategies for Multi-channel Initiatives

Today's multi-channel systems already have a high empirical value: the retailer segment concentrating on only one store format or on selling to a specific consumer channel is gradually dwindling. On the other hand, important retailers with worldwide sales activities are implementing multi-channel Strategies and planning to augment their portfolios with more channels and/or store formats.

The conclusion reached forms the key initial focus for further strategic discussion. Retailers have to be where consumers need them. Retailers have numerous options for building up further channels in order to achieve this goal.

It is necessary to make decisions on three levels if retail business is to find the right strategy:

1. Store format and channel segmentation: the first step involves identifying the segments that have not been covered, or only partially, by the present store formats or channels. If sufficiently relevant, one or more segments, or a new restructuring of existing market segments, can be used to implement a new store format or a new channel, which can then be included in the portfolio.

2. Market positioning: unique positioning of store formats and channels within the market, with the goal of achieving a distinctive profile for consumers and the competition. Aside from the core profile strategies relating to quality and price leadership, it is crucially important to improve image. Examples of this could be "event shopping" or "supply".

3. Portfolio implementation: implementation of multi-channel strategies follows a basic development of growth and expansion, reduction or dwindling, or retaining the same formats or channels.

   a. For example: expansion of a store format can be attained by an increase in outlets.

   b. A retaining strategy is followed when an existing store format is used to realize and attain the highest possible margin.

   c. Elimination of store formats.

   d. New development of store formats

   e. Integration of existing store formats within the portfolio.

Guiding Principles for Successful Multi-channel Retailing

The Retailer as an Observer and Participant in the Market

This understanding is a basic prerequisite for successful multi-channel marketing. Retailers focusing solely on market observation and reacting to actual trends along the lines of "me-too" strategies are missing the opportunity for directional participation and action initiated by themselves. The innovative approach and the courage to launch something new on the market are also recognized and respected by consumers. This is an intrinsically invaluable competitive asset and should definitely be used.

Innovative Exploration of New Store Format Combinations

Willingness to try something new also entails identifying latent trends, pursuing these trends and testing them for relevance. There is a tendency for future trends to be on the streets. Consumers are the best judges of what inspires them and what and where their needs are. Explorative research techniques are able to provide answers on these issues. They are also able to assist in making what has been learnt operational and implementing the insights gained using a further stage of quantitative assessment.

Segmentation of Existing Customers

A continuing "must-do" for retailers relates to precise knowledge of existing customers and far-reaching consumer potential. This information is imperative for conversion to a successful Multi-Channel Strategy and cannot be over-emphasized. Aside from the hard economic facts – such as turnover, average sales slip, customer frequencies etc. – precise analytical, demographic and psychographic segmentation of customers reveals the potential opportunities and risks entailed in expansion of the store-format portfolio. Which customers use which store formats? How can cross-selling behaviour be characterized? Which customer segments are moving towards the store formats used by the competition or even to other channels? What are the reasons and intentions behind this behaviour? What commercial relevance does this behaviour have?

Channel Fit: Not Everything Can Be Had Everywhere

It is important to coordinate the channel, the products and target consumers in a sensible manner.

For example: standardized goods are basically a positive development, because they allow consumers to form their own opinions without the help of a salesperson. Products requiring a great deal of consultation and advice are not necessarily ideal for online sales. Before establishing a new channel it is important to consider what the level of acceptance will be among customers for the new product or service being offered in the new channel. If a new channel is added to an existing one it is important that the same service is offered through both.

New Store Formats and Channels Must Be Pretested for Acceptance

Implementing a new store format or channel usually involves substantial investment. This is the main reason why many innovative ideas never come to pass. It does not matter if the new initiative is a line extension – the addition of a new selling line in an existing retail brand – or relates to establishing a new channel under a new brand. In both cases it is important to examine and possibly fine-tune the core benefits and service, in addition to presentation and image. This is best be done with a suitable test.

Continuous Examination of Store Formats and Channels

Existing and new channels and store formats must undergo continuous observation and evaluation to allow recognition of future trends under a retailer's own roof and appropriate reactions:

What relevance does the channel have for the company overall? How adequate is the acceptance of the store formats for existing and potential customers? What is the motivation or reason behind nonacceptance? Where do customers see the outstanding added values? Is the image presented mirrored in the consumer? What potential is there for customer loyalty and winning new customers?

Creative Elements of Identity – Cultivation of the Image

A company presenting itself to consumers under one brand name through a range of channels is well aware of the importance of maintaining and caring for presentation, communication, the core benefits and the services on offer.

In cases where consumers are able to communicate with the same company by different routes, the creative elements of the corporate identity have to be unique and unambiguous. This involves a phenomenal balancing act. On the one hand, it is important to emphasize the specific details of the individual store formats and channels. On the other hand, however, consumers have to be convinced that they are receiving the same quality and customer service whether they go to the stationary store or make their purchases online by way of the Internet. Consumers cannot be allowed to perceive any disadvantages for any of the channels they are able to access. If a consumer has a negative experience with any one of the channels the image of the entire company can be irreversibly compromised. Don't's include different prices or availability of certain items only by one of the channels.

Where different store formats and channels do not appear under a common brand name, it is important to differentiate the different aspects of service. Every retail channel with its own label needs a dedicated and unique brand profile. If this is achieved, corporate design elements may even be adopted from the channel. This may be deliberate or unintentional, and the independent brand profiles of the store formats and channels might be watered down. For example, if a discounter appears as a *hidden spin-off* right beside an existing self-service warehouse and the discount store adopts the brand name elements of the warehouse chain, this would impact negatively on the Discounter, because its authenticity would no longer be credible for the customer. There is also potential for the self-service warehouse to be infected by the discounter's negative image (since the discounter's image correlates negatively with its own image).

Joint Venture: Synergy Potential Beyond Business Borders – Recognition and Implementation

Top players in the international retail landscape have store format and channel know-how in addition to sector expertise when it comes to product range and procurement. They have acquired this knowledge through many years of experience. Retail companies often break new ground if they want to establish more channels. (For example when a DIY branch store expands its sales range on the Internet or via dispatch). In the other direction, a dispatcher may want to expand its DIY business in a professional way.

Channel experts can derive benefit from each other if they set up a joint venture with the channels (such as DIY stores, catalogues and Internet) are linked under a common brand label.

- Know-how on operating type comes together and builds synergy advantages.

- Multi-channel marketing exerts a customer loyalty effect and counteracts the behavioural changes of the customer.

- There is better customer acquisition and customer potential is better addressed through the use of different media and sales.

- Sales are maximized by addressing full customer potential.

Multi-channel marketing offers the following benefits for consumers:

- A wide choice of times, locations and methods of shopping with this DIY retailer.

- Determination of provision for gathering information, transactions and possible returns by consumers.

- Possibility of correlating the advantages of each channel with avoidance of disadvantages (e.g. shopping 24 hours a day, viewing the product at the location and customer service).

Implementation of multi-channel management involving strong sales channels and control at the level of the multi-channel are requirements for a successful joint venture.

Differentiation: As Global as Possible, as Regional as Required

Regional and cultural characteristics exert a definite influence on the opportunities and risks relating to whether the different channels are accepted. As far as global retailers are concerned, it is particularly important to determine what global relevance specific multi-channel strategies have for the company. Only one principle is applicable here: as global as possible and as regional as required (e.g., see chapter by Mierdorf, Mantrala, Krafft in this book on METRO Group's international growth strategy). It is therefore essential to assess the efficiency of training and best practice in using of a Channel for a specific country or region.

Management Tools and Application in Market Research

As we have seen, it is more important than ever to understand the needs of the consumer. We need to know how consumers view the different formats and channels and why consumers use the ones they have chosen. Retailers needs an answer to the issue of how these two factors – basic need and perception – relate to each other, in order to be in a position to come up with statements on the action that needs to be taken:

- What general possibilities are available in multi-channel proposals?

- How can I improve and expand my established store format position in the market?

- Where are the dangers inherent in the competitive store formats and/or channels?

- How can I attack the competition?

Segmentation

The retail trade is endeavouring to understand the needs of its customers and its customer potential better. Most research is based on rational determining factors, such as quality, price and product choice. If the retail trade initiates consumer segmentation of this nature, the actual and target relationship structures between consumers and their (own) store format or channel are derived on this basis.

However, changes in purchasing behaviour make it essential to apply segmentation procedures. This approach identifies more in-depth – often emotional – needs structures inherent in consumers. Different formats radiating personality and symbolism also have to be considered.

If both are known, it is much easier to achieve a format-specific offer that meets customers' requirements.

There is sound evidence to support the advisability of viewing consumer needs and the perception of formats, differentiated into three needs levels:

- Functional, rational needs (e.g. price, availability, convenience) that are easily accessible.
- Identity needs (affiliation with certain groups, e.g. social classes) that are difficult to quantify.
- Emotional/psychological needs (e.g. control, activity, security) that cannot be quantified directly.

In Germany, "more affluent" customers also buy at Aldi because it is "chic", while in the UK nobody is likely to stress openly that they cannot afford to shop at other outlets than those they actually use. Knowledge of these aspects is important for optimum communication with target groups and for successful management of portfolios.

Perception of Store Formats and Channels

- Store formats/channel characteristics (e.g. price, quality, selection, accessibility) that are obvious.
- Social values (e.g. in general only, male, female, young, old) aimed at social identity.
- Symbolism/personality (e.g. strong, determined, passive) affecting the emotional/psychological level.

In the same way as customers, the format also radiates its own "identity". For example, in many countries the tele-shopping format still has a less favourable image with many potential customers. Use of the levels of need described above allow more in-depth identification of inhibitions or obstacles than simply "bad offer" or "too expensive." These are probably some of the true reasons and represent key barriers to effective marketing.

Furthermore, emotional needs and perceptions cannot be adequately assessed in verbal form. Market research offers qualitative and quantifiable assessment procedures using nonverbal techniques to avoid the issue of rationalization.

Combining both levels – consumers and formats – allows both levels to be set in context, and the congruence between provider and needs can then be highlighted. The ultimate goal is to derive workable measures for an optimum fit between the two.

Customer Loyalty

Competitors are fighting for market shares within the wide range of online, offline and mail-order trade and deploying a variety of the communications mix available. A special significance is attributed to the structure of customer loyalty. Only those retailers who have created a genuine structure for customer loyalty will succeed in protecting themselves against the situation where their customers visit another outlet at the next available opportunity. Only customers with an emotional bond to "their" retailer are resistant to other infiltrating influences. Customers with a definite emotional bond do not need to be convinced of the desirability of returning. They are immune to the activities of the competition. They exhibit less price sensitivity and prefer to leave a larger proportion of the contents of their wallet with "their" retailer rather than with another.

A company that practises multi-channel retailing can be in a position create a better bond with customers more effectively than one with only one format. Naturally, the requirement here is that customers recognize that they are shopping at "one" company, which in turn means that the connection must be clearly visible and desirable.

En route to successful multi-channel retailing, companies need to conduct a separate examination of the status of customer commitment. Investigation of the formats implemented followed by a cumulative assessment can lead to an improved overall strategy.

Actual studies have shown that customers using both a stationary store and the same retailer's online shop, for example, have a far better bond with their retailer than other customers who only use one channel. This confirms that it makes sense to draw customers' attention to this multi-offer.

It is not sufficient to determine the favourite store mainly used for shopping if the aim is to measure customer loyalty for a particular format. For example, a certain store may be frequented because there are too few alternatives available, or even none at all. The actual quality of customer loyalty can only be assessed if relative factors within an overall psychological model are evaluated. TNS has identified three main components for measuring the strength and intensity of the relationship between consumers and format. These components are satisfaction with this format, the consumer commitment to this format (how important it is for consumers to shop at this precise venue) and the level of ambivalence consumers have towards other formats or retailers.

Depending on the intention, assessing these factors allows consumers to be bundled or clustered according to the intensity of their loyalty within the store format and channel. The levels of intensity are as follows: from embedded to ready to change, or on the noncustomer side from attainable to completely unattainable.

This collective data allows retailers to make an adequate judgement of the situation. It can be viewed as a sort of early warning system: how many of my customers am I at risk of losing to the Internet? or How many of my customers are attainable? This information is extremely useful for the development of existing formats and for establishing new formats.

Linking Segmentation and Customer Loyalty

How successful are attempts at bonding various customer segments by means of dedicated store formats and channels? Which segments are by contrast loyal to the competition? The answers to these questions are provided if the segments determined are brought together and referred to the provider-specific bonding groups or clusters. This offers extensive possibilities. On the basis of the market-research data outlined, channel fit can be strategically optimized.

In this context, rational and emotional needs have been successfully evaluated, as have image and communication (in each case from the consumer's perspective), for relevant retailers and their portfolios. These dimensions represent and highlight precise strategic points at which retailers need to make adjustments to suit consumers in order to optimize their own portfolios.

Outlook

The future of retailing will be influenced by further expansion of store formats and channels. An important issue here is whether a single-channel or a multi-channel strategy is the right objective for the future. It is therefore imperative to create a channel mix that is recognized as such by consumers and from which consumers derive genuine emotional added value.

One of the leading forces in the future will be the massive role played by technology in breaking down the barrier between the "real" and "virtual" worlds. E-Commerce will be redefined, if it succeeds in offering alternative Internet-based channels. E-Commerce needs to interconnect these channels actively in the perception of consumers, and consumers have to use them proactively.

The "store with connectivity" is a reality and exists in Seattle, Washington (USA). Customers in the outdoor chain store, REI, have access to an area arranged according to the principles of an event shopping experience. Using a laser scanner, customers can call up information on all the products they are interested in. The "secret" of this concept is that all this information is stored in a central database and is accessible to everyone online. At REI, the lists are updated automatically and continuously as soon as a scanner records a request or a product is automatically taken off the list because it has been purchased by mail, over the phone, on the Internet or in one of the 77 stores throughout the country. The database is therefore automatically up to date. The same products are available at all the stores and by all channels: each product offered online can also be purchased offline, and each product available in the stores can be purchased online.

This mixed concept will be the driving force for future retail. Data mining and web analyses give insight into what customers have purchased, while also offering information on which products customers have looked at. This will helps retailers to coordinate their advertising campaigns.

Products purchased online and then picked up offline increase offline turnover. When purchases are ordered offline, customers tend to buy other products as well. This trend has also been identified by Tesco in England. Tesco in England delivers Internet orders through the branches. All purchase data is stored on the consumers' customer cards. Customers have access to this information through their home computers or even on pocket computers. At present, Tesco uses this giant database for personalized mail distribution of promotional material and discount coupons or for selection of bargain offers. Tesco distributes customer magazines for five different target groups every three months.

OTTO – one of the largest mail-order company in the world – has just started to expand its stationary retail store business. Mail order is no longer enough in today's competitive retail business. Today's customers have a huge choice. The future belongs to the multi-channel companies, since single-channel companies (e.g. OTTO in its original form) have reached the limit of their growth potential.

As outlined above, multi-channel trading also means total linkage or networking of the retailer's dedicated distribution portfolio. This makes economic sense and is also desirable from the customers' perspective, because this is the most successful choice.

The authors believe that the future of the retail trade does not lie in a "parallel configuration", but rather in a network of channels and store formats that is transparent for consumers. The retailers of the future will identify this trend and adapt their portfolios accordingly.

References

Dach, C. (2002): Sind Multi-Channel-Anbieter wirklich überlegen? Handelsjournal, (1), 24-25.

Dach, C. (2002): Vorteile einer Multi-Channel-Strategie: Eine nüchterne Betrachtung; Synergien zwischen Ladengeschäften und Online-Shops aus Konsumentensicht. Institut für Handelsforschung an der Universität, Cologne.

Feldmann, L., Schögel, M. and Staib, D. (2004): Blackbox Kunde – Warum Kunden wo und was einkaufen. Rüschlikon.

Nunes, P., Cespedes, F. (2003): The customer has escaped. Harvard Business Review (11), 96-104.

Ott, C S. (2005): Controlling und Monitoring einer Betriebstypen-Marke; wie der Handel die Wirkung seiner Marketingaktivitäten effektiv überprüft, TNS Infratest Papers, Bielefeld.

Pooler, J. (2003): Why we shop. Emotional rewards and retail strategies. Westport.

Schögel, M. (2001): Alternative Vertriebswege: Neue Absatzkanäle – neue Herausforderungen, Symposium Publishing, Düsseldorf.

Schramm-Klein, H. (2003): Multi-Channel-Retailing: verhaltenswissenschaftliche Analyse der Wirkung von Mehrkanalsystemen im Handel. Wiesbaden.

Schramm-Klein, H. (2003): Zwölf Grundsätze zur Gestaltung von Multi-Channel-Systemen. Science Factory, (1), 10-14.

Retail Competition

Edward J. Fox and Raj Sethuraman

Cox School of Business, Southern Methodist University, Dallas, USA

Introduction

Forty years ago, a consumer who wanted to buy prescription medicine in the US or many other western countries would have visited a local independent drugstore. Today, a US customer can fill prescriptions at any number of drugstore chains (e.g., Walgreens or CVS), supermarkets (e.g., Kroger or Albertson's), mass merchandisers, or supercenters (e.g., Wal-Mart or Target) in town, not to mention mail-order providers (e.g., AmeriCan Meds 1-800-469-0955) and online pharmacies (e.g., www.Drugstores-Online.com). The increased number of options for purchasing pharmaceuticals illustrates the high intensity of retail competition in today's consumer goods marketplace, driven by discerning consumers with heightened expectations and varying tastes, along with technological advances that facilitate efficient distribution of products and provision of retail services.

As the above example shows, most product categories can now be purchased in several different retail formats. A *retail format* is comprised of stores that offer the same, or a very nearly the same, variety of product categories.[1] Formats that have emerged in recent years, mass merchandisers, supercenters (supercenters include both a mass merchandise store and supermarket under one roof), warehouse clubs, and dollar stores, are collectively known as *nontraditional formats*. Formats with a longer history, such as grocery, drug, and department stores, are more *traditional formats* (see also chapters by Ahlert, Blut, Evanschitzky; Weitz, Whitfield; Dawson in this book).

Perhaps the most important trend in retail competition is the increasing competition between retailers of traditional and nontraditional formats in the product categories that they offer in common. We refer to this type of competition as

---

[1] Stores of a given retail format offer generally similar promotion, pricing, assortment, store location, and merchandising strategies. However, differences in those strategies are important factors in within-format retail competition.

M. Krafft and M.K. Mantrala (eds.), *Retailing in the 21st Century: Current and Future Trends*, 239
DOI 10.1007/978-3-540-72003-4_15, © Springer-Verlag Berlin Heidelberg 2010

between-format competition and will devote considerable discussion to this emerging trend. Of course, retailers of the same format also compete with each other for market share and consumers' "share of wallet," a phenomenon that we term *within-format competition*. As noted, stores of the same format offer very similar varieties of merchandise. For example, all department stores sell primarily apparel and goods for the home; all supermarkets sell perishable and dry grocery products along with health and beauty items; and all warehouse club stores sell a wide variety of products, including food, packaged goods, apparel, and durable goods. Though the variety of products is very similar within one format, retailer prices, assortment, and store location strategies can differ substantially.

The objective of this chapter is to investigate the two types of retail competition – within- and between-format – by identifying key trends, offering insights and predictions about the future, discussing open issues, and highlighting topics for future research. Our discussion of retail competition will focus primarily on retailers of packaged goods products, such as grocery stores and mass merchandisers. The discussion is organized around four key dimensions of retail competition.

- *Price* – Prices of items within and across categories, which may vary from week to week as a result of promotions

- *Variety* – Breadth, or number of categories typically carried by the outlet

- *Assortment* – Depth, or number of items within a category

- *Store location* – Where the retail store is located and how this affects cost of shopping to consumers

The next section discusses the impact of nontraditional formats on retail competition. Then, for each dimension of competition, we draw on the available research to assess its effect on consumer shopping behavior and highlight trends in competition within and between retail formats, making predictions about the future and identifying questions that are as yet unresolved.

The Impact of Nontraditional Formats

Open Issue: Are Traditional Formats in Decline?

The catalyst of competition between formats has been the emergence of hyper-efficient mass merchandisers, in particular Wal-Mart, which carry an exceptionally wide range of products. Mass merchandisers (and the supercenter format they pioneered) offer packaged goods categories in common with supermarkets and drugstores and apparel and home categories in common with department stores, and overlap with the offerings of most category specialty stores (also known as "category killers"). As a result, mass merchandisers and supercenters are in competition with supermarkets, drugstores, department stores, and category killers for many purchases. Because of Wal-Mart's well-publicized cost advantage (which is also enjoyed, to a lesser extent, by other nontraditional format retailers), competition for these categories has prompted many to sound the death knell of traditional formats. Although predicting the demise of these formats is premature, there is evidence to support this concern. This evidence includes (1) the dramatic inroads that Wal-Mart's supercenters have made in grocery sales in the last decade – Wal-Mart now sells more grocery products than any other retailer in the world, and 28% of US shoppers now claim to shop for groceries regularly at mass merchandisers or supercenters (Food Marketing Institute 2002, p. 23); (2) recent high-profile bankruptcies of category killers such as K-B Toys and Toys 'R' Us; and (3) the general malaise among department store retailers.

Trend: Traditional and nontraditional formats are competing for store visits rather than for customers. A recent study found that a supercenter opening cost a nearby supermarket 17% of its business, primarily because customers made fewer visits to the supermarket (Singh, Hansen, Blattberg 2004). Most of the consumers who patronized the supercenter continued to shop at the supermarket, albeit less frequently. This study highlights the point that competition between retailers of traditional and nontraditional formats is competition for store visits, not for customers. Another study shows that the more mass merchandisers a household visits, the more grocery stores it also visits (Fox, Montgomery, Lodish 2004). This suggests that a visit to a mass merchandiser is not necessarily a substitute for a grocery store visit; rather, consumers use both formats as part of their shopping strategies. Traditional format retailers must therefore focus on defending the "share of wallet" of their customer base in order to remain viable.

Trend: Greater consolidation across retail sectors. In response to the growing competitive threat from nontraditional formats, traditional formats are consolidating. This consolidation is due more to mergers and acquisitions than to organic growth. A few recent examples are the sale of much of the Eckerd drugstore chain to CVS, the sale of May department stores to Federated, and the purchase of Kmart by Sears. The underlying rationale is that larger retailers will have the scale necessary to reduce costs so that they can compete with Wal-Mart and other low-cost mass merchandisers. As a result, retail concentration has increased significantly, with Kroger, Safeway, and Albertsons now comprising 53.4% of supermarket sales; Walgreen's, CVS and Rite Aid representing 73.2% of drugstore sales; and Costco and Sam's Club making up 89.5% of warehouse club sales (shares of various retail sectors in 2003 are computed from Troy 2004 and the Top 150 Annual Industry Report 2004).

For consolidation to be successful, however, the larger firms that remain must exploit their scale to reduce costs. This requires eliminating overhead and redundant functions, centralizing operations, and negotiating concessions from their suppliers. Without such changes, consolidation results in retailers that are bigger, but still do not have lower cost structures.

Retail Price Competition

Consumers Emphasize Value

In recent years, the proliferation of nontraditional retail formats, a weaker global economy (especially since the 9/11 terrorist attack), and the availability of price information on the Internet have all resulted in greater consumer price consciousness. Consumers exhibit price consciousness by purchasing items on special promotions, shopping across stores and formats in search of bargains, patronizing discounters, and purchasing more low-priced private-label products (Sethuraman 2003). The phenomenal growth of Wal-Mart is a testament to the increasing emphasis on value.

At the aggregate market level, consumers' emphasis on value can also be understood from the household income distribution. The distribution of US household incomes in the year 2000 is shown in Figure 1. The distribution is highly skewed – although the average income is $55,409, the median household makes only $41,486, and over 58 % of US households earn less than $50,000 per year. Because the majority of households have limited disposable income, they are likely to be price sensitive. Moreover, high-income households buy no more in most packaged-goods categories (e.g., toilet tissue, detergent, salty snacks) than low-income households of the same size. In fact, because high-income households spend more on money eating out, they may actually buy fewer grocery items. As income levels continue to polarize because of the growth of low-paid service jobs, price sensitivity is likely to increase, at least for frequently purchased consumer goods. In order to serve the mass market of consumers in coming years, retailers must therefore price their goods so as to offer the value these consumers seek.

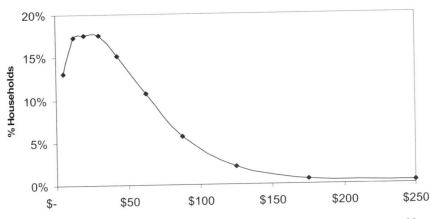

Fig. 1. US Household Income Distribution for Year 2000* Within-Format Price Competition

Open Issue: Promotional or everyday low pricing? To offer value to customers, retailers generally use one of two pricing strategies: (1) frequent promotional discounts, known as HiLo pricing, or (2) everyday low prices, commonly abbreviated as EDLP. On average, EDLP stores offer lower prices than HiLo stores, but discounting by HiLo stores allows opportunistic shoppers to pay lower prices there than in EDLP stores. The interplay between these two pricing strategies can be illustrated in the context of competition between supermarkets. By offering temporary price promotions each week, HiLo supermarkets price discriminate between opportunistic shoppers, who are willing to invest time and effort searching for bargains, and those who are not. Consumers whose costs in terms of time are low and/or enjoy greater benefits from searching for low prices will gather information from different supermarkets, and may even shop at multiple stores. They gather information about weekly price deals by studying the feature advertisements of competing retailers and may even be willing to visit multiple stores to take advantage of price deals at each store, a practice known as cherry-picking. In fact, a recent industry study finds that one-third of US households shop at multiple grocery stores in an average week (Food Marketing Institute 2002).

We can shed some light on price competition between EDLP and HiLo stores by understanding who shops at EDLP stores and why. EDLP retailers require scale economies to make it possible for them to offer low prices, so they operate fewer stores in a geographic market (to draw customers from a larger trade area) than do HiLo retailers, though their stores are larger (to gain scale economies and accommodate the traffic). As a result, for most shoppers, visiting EDLP stores requires more travel than visiting less distant HiLo stores. EDLP stores are also more time consuming to shop, because of their larger size. Shoppers who are loyal to EDLP supermarkets have one or more of the following characteristics: (1) low opportunity costs of time – these shoppers are willing to spend more time shopping, perhaps because they have lower wage rates or fewer time constraints; (2) greater benefits from shopping at low-priced EDLP stores – the lower prices found at EDLP stores can be applied to the needs of a larger family (Bell, Ho, Tang 1998; Briesch, Chintagunta, Fox 2005); (3) big-basket shoppers – infrequent shoppers buy a large basket of goods when they visit a supermarket (Bell, Lattin 1998), so that the lower prices available at EDLP stores are effectively magnified by the big basket[2] ; and (4) brand loyalty – brand-loyal shoppers are unwilling to buy whatever brand a HiLo retailer offers at a discount as a substitute for their preferred brand, which limits their ability to be opportunistic.

A substantial segment of shoppers switch between EDLP and HiLo supermarkets, depending on the purpose of their shopping trip (Fox, Metters, Semple 2003). These shoppers sometimes stock up and sometimes simply fill in between major trips. When stocking up they will be willing to travel to a less convenient EDLP

---

[2] Big basket shoppers also have less flexibility to delay purchases, which prevents them from changing the timing of their purchases to accommodate the deal schedules of HiLo retailers.

store. However, if they intend to purchase only a small amount, these shoppers will choose a more convenient HiLo store (Bell, Ho, and Tang 1998). Thus, the more often consumers shop, the more likely they are to choose HiLo stores; the less often they shop, the more likely they are to select EDLP stores. EDLP supermarkets can influence consumers' shopping frequency by providing incentives for big-basket shopping, which are basically volume discounts, frequent shopper programs, and other, less narrowly targeted, means.

In summary, consumers shop most often at HiLo stores, because they value the convenience of HiLo stores and/or because they can take advantage of the price discounts. In the grocery sector, those who shop at EDLP stores do so because they have low opportunity costs of time (e.g., low wage rates), and/or they can apply EDLP stores' low prices to larger shopping baskets. Still others switch between EDLP and HiLo supermarkets, depending on whether the purpose of their shopping trip is to stock up or to fill in supplies between major purchases.

Between-Format Price Competition

Trend: Increased price competition between formats. The consumer trend toward price consciousness, together with the implementation of information and supply-chain technologies by retailers, suggests that price competition between retail formats has increased. The industry has recently witnessed the implementation of several retail technologies that reduce operating costs, allowing retailers to lower prices to consumers (Sethuraman, Parasuraman 2005). For example, customer-operated check-out registers reduce front-end labor costs; cross-docking reduces inventory and storage costs; collaborative planning, forecasting and replenishment (CPFR) reduces supply costs; and radio frequency identification (RFID) technology offers the promise of reducing product tracking and inventory costs. According to one Sainsbury (UK) manager, RFID tags have reduced their receiving-function time from two and a half hours to 15 minutes.

Prediction: Mass merchandisers will keep prices low and enjoy a widening price advantage. Mass merchandisers, though they do not all use an EDLP strategy, offer significantly lower average prices than other formats for a given basket of goods. Because they are less reliant on promotions, mass merchandisers sell fewer discounted items than supermarkets or drugstores do. The only available study with a bearing on price competition between formats shows that mass merchandisers could increase short-term revenues by raising their overall price levels, while supermarkets and drugstores would lose revenues by raising prices (Fox, Montgomery, Lodish 2004). Interestingly, the study also finds that mass merchandisers could increase short-term revenues by offering more promotions. Why do mass merchandisers keep their prices low, despite the revenue they could gain by raising prices and the already substantial gap between their prices and those of other formats? The mass merchandiser business model depends heavily on scale and its associated cost advantage – the greater the scale, the greater the cost ad-

Open Issue: Will nontraditional formats successfully penetrate urban markets?
The low-cost business model of nontraditional formats benefits from the low real
estate and labor costs in rural and some suburban areas. It is therefore not surprising that mass merchandisers and supercenters have experienced nearly all of their
growth in such areas. However, the limited populations of rural markets mean that
they can support relatively few large stores, and nontraditional retailers are ap-
proaching saturation level in many of these markets. This raises the question of
whether urban markets represent a growth opportunity for these formats, particularly in light of the rapid growth of dollar stores in these markets.

From the retailer's perspective, the concentration of consumers in urban markets is attractive, and the density of these markets offers some benefits in transportation and distribution efficiency. However, real estate costs are high, and there is
very limited availability of sites with 100,000 square feet of space or more. Most
potential sites require stores to occupy multiple floors, which causes operational
problems for most nontraditional retailers. These real estate issues, along with
higher labor costs and taxes, represent major hurdles for low-cost operators. In
addition, consumers in urban areas have a stronger preference for spatial convenience because of traffic congestion and the availability of many other shopping
outlets. Urban consumers are therefore less likely to prefer the widely dispersed
"big box" stores offered by most nontraditional retailers. Together, issues about
compatibility with their existing business model and consumer acceptance of their
formats call into question the opportunities for success of nontraditional retailers
in urban markets.

*Prediction: Wal-Mart will continue to grow by expanding its grocery offerings,
and then ...?* Wal-Mart's remarkable size – roughly 8 % of all US retail purchases
are made at Wal-Mart stores, and 82 % of US households shop there at least once a
year (Information Resources, Inc 2002) – and phenomenal history of growth
make its future decisions relevant for a wide range of retail competitors and
potential competitors. In the short term, its growth strategy is clear. In the US,
Wal-Mart's capital expenditures will be focused on supercenters for the next
few years, after which it will roll out the Neighborhood Market format more
widely.[4] Though the few Neighborhood Market stores currently in operation
have failed to generate supercenter-sized returns, the smaller store format continues to be prominent in Wal-Mart's future plans. Rolling out a second format
with a full range of grocery items offers Wal-Mart two important benefits: (1)
the convenience of Neighborhood Markets enables Wal-Mart to attract quick
convenience trips from shoppers who stock up at supercenters, thus getting a
greater "share of wallet" from those customers; (2) another grocery format allows
Wal-Mart to exploit its already extensive food distribution infrastructure and
negotiating clout with suppliers.

---

[4] Assumes no major legislation or regulatory constraints that limit Wal-Mart's strategic
options.

If the Neighborhood Market format is successful, Wal-Mart will achieve a dominant share of the US grocery sector in the next decade. As growth in the grocery sector slows and saturation is approached, can Wal-Mart's growth rate remain in double figures? Any strategy aimed at achieving this would have to take advantage of the company's scale and operational expertise while targeting a sector that was sufficiently substantial to allow for meaningful growth. Within the US, the most attractive opportunity might be the sale of automobiles. Despite Wal-Mart's less-than-successful pilot program of selling used cars in Houston, automobile retail nevertheless represents a compelling opportunity for the world's largest retailer. With over a trillion dollars in sales, it is the largest retail sector in the US. It is also highly fragmented, with powerful suppliers (automobile manufacturers) administering a relatively inefficient channel. On the other hand, it is uncertain whether Wal-Mart can adapt to the high-service selling environment that predominates in automobile sales and also whether local and state regulators will allow Wal-Mart entry into this sector. Yet if Wal-Mart could exploit its scale and bring efficiencies to automobile retail, it could fuel the company's growth for another decade, both literally and figuratively.

Open Issue: How can major US retailers best expand internationally? Increased local competition, limited domestic expansion opportunities, and the availability of large, relatively under-served retail markets in developing counties are prompting US and European retailers to seek growth abroad. Asia, Russia, and Eastern Europe appear to be the most promising markets for the next decade. European retailers, in particular Ahold and Carrefour, have been at the forefront of international expansion, at least in terms of the percentage of sales generated from international markets. For example, 85 % of Ahold's sales in 2004 were international, compared to 16-18 % for leading US retailers Wal-Mart and Costco (A.T. Kearney, Inc. 2004). Wal-Mart is committed to increasing international sales, with a target of 33 % of its revenue in the next few years, and Costco is planning further expansion in Asia. Because of global demand for their services and operational models that can, at least to some extent, be exported, we expect US retailers to focus on international markets in the next decade.

The question, then, is not whether major US retailers will expand internationally, but how they can do so most successfully. Specifically, we ask:

- What format(s) should they export?
- When should they enter these markets, as first mover or later entrant?
- What pricing strategies should they use?

The answers are not obvious. We would expect that low-price formats such as hypermarkets and discount stores, with their associated cost advantages, should be successful in price-sensitive developing markets. However, A.T. Kearney's research shows no correlation between the type of retail format and international success (A.T. Kearney, Inc. 2004). Being an early entrant in an emerging market is advantageous because the most attractive retail locations go first – locations are particularly important in emerging markets because of inadequate transportation and infrastructure. However, being a first mover is inherently more hazardous, because of uncertainties in these markets. In addition, prices offered by new entrants, may need to be lower than those of local competitors (for products of like quality) initially in order to gain acceptance in the market. Yet such a penetration pricing strategy could result in early losses, testing the resolve of retailers attempting to expand internationally.

In summary, in order to succeed in emerging international markets, retailers have to be flexible in terms of format, time of entry, and pricing strategy. They must also be able to keep costs low and possibly withstand initial losses. A few major global retailers, notably Wal-Mart, Carrefour, and METRO AG, are well positioned for international success because of their diversity of store formats, deep pockets, and efficient cost management systems (see, for example, the chapter by Mierdorf, Mantrala, Krafft in this book).

References

A.T.Kearney, Inc. (2004): Emerging Priorities for Global Retailers, Chicago: A.T.Kearney, Inc. Marketing and Communications.

Bell, David R., Teck Hua Ho and Christopher S. Tang (1998): Determining Where to Shop: Fixed and Variable Costs of Shopping, Journal of Marketing Research, 35 (August), 352-69.

Bell, David R., and James M. Lattin (1998): Grocery Shopping Behavior and Consumer Response to Retailer Price Format: Why "Large Basket" Shoppers Prefer EDLP, Marketing Science, 17 (1), 66-88.

Briesch, Richard A., Pradeep K. Chintagunta, Edward J. Fox (2005): Assortment, Price, and Convenience: Modeling the Determinants of Grocery Store Choice, Working paper. Dallas, TX: Southern Methodist University

Food Marketing Institute (2002): Trends – Consumer Attitudes and the Supermarket, Washington DC: Food Marketing Institute.

Fox, Edward J., Richard Metters, and John Semple (2003): Every House a Warehouse: An Inventory Model of Retail Shopping Behavior, Working paper, Dallas, TX: Southern Methodist University.

Fox, Edward J., Alan L. Montgomery and Leonard M. Lodish (2004): Consumer Shopping and Spending Across Retail Formats, Journal of Business, 77 (2), S25-S60.

Information Resources, Inc. (2002): IRI Insights on Channel Differentiation, Chicago: Information Resources, Inc.

Metters, Richard, Michael Ketzenberg and George Gillen (2000): Welcome Back Mom and Pop: Big Retailers Are Starting to Think Small Again, Harvard Business Review, 78 (3), 24-26.

Sethuraman, Raj (2003): Measuring National Brands' Equity over Store Brands, Review of Marketing Science, 1 (2), 1-26.

Sethuraman, Raj and A. Parasuraman (2005): Succeeding in the Big Middle through Technology, Journal of Retailing, 81(2), 107-111.

Singh, Vishal P., Karsten T. Hansen, and Robert C. Blattberg (2004): Impact of Wal-Mart Supercenter on a Traditional Supermarket: An Empirical Investigation, Working paper, Pittsburgh, PA: Carnegie Mellon University.

Top 150 Annual Industry Report (2004): DSN Retailing Today, 43 (13) 30-38.

Troy, Mike (2004): Sales Rise 6.5%, Lending Credibility to Rebound, DSN Retailing Today, 43 (13) 15.

PART III:

Trends in Retail Management

PEOPLE

New Challenges in Retail Human Resource Management

Julia Merkel[1], Paul Jackson[2], and Doreén Pick[3]

[1] University of Coventry, UK
[2] METRO AG, Duesseldorf, Germany
[3] University of Muenster, Germany

Why Do We Need Professional Human Resource Management in Retailing?

Such terms as globalization, process management, and value-based management dominate the current discussion of management in retail companies. There has been an increasing realization that people are one of a company's key assets. Retail means working and serving customers in a direct, personal way. This calls for special actions from retail companies to fulfill the demands of an increasing number of well-informed and sophisticated consumers. In view of all the changes in both national and international contexts, it is absolutely essential to get the right people if a business is to be successful and sustainable.

Retailing is a major labor-intensive industry sector. Therefore, companies are continually challenged to re-organize and adapt their structures to become more efficient. The necessity for part-time workers, because of long store opening hours and peaks in the trading day/week, requires a flexible framework to optimize labor processes. Emotionally, the workforce needs orientation and vision in changing times. Human resource management (HRM) has to provide a "coach," not only to organize, but also to support employees and management mentally and professionally in fulfilling their tasks in terms of future company goals. People are the driving force behind all transactions that occur in retailing outlets. In the future world of retailing, there will be an increasing need to adapt and change towards a more formative and proactive style of HRM.

M. Krafft and M.K. Mantrala (eds.), *Retailing in the 21st Century: Current and Future Trends*, 257
DOI 10.1007/978-3-540-72003-4_16, © Springer-Verlag Berlin Heidelberg 2010

Changes

Changes in Retail

The formats of retailing have been evolving continuously over the last 100 years, and individual retailers have changed tremendously in the products they sell and in the manner in which they operate. Retailing of lifestyle products impacts directly on the changing culture of our societies—one has only to think of the introduction of the Sony Walkman or the Apple I-Pod to grasp the international range of consumer needs. In order to provide an expanding product and service range, retail has had to alter and amend its approaches to satisfy ever more voracious and increasingly sophisticated consumers. For several years, retailers have had a prominent role in today's society in their capacity as employers: the retail industry employs one in nine of the UK workforce, for example (Gilbert 2003). Nearly two thirds of employees are female. Therefore, special concepts in HRM are required to allow for the compatibility of work and family. Gilbert (2003) also points out that: "[T]he retail sector has had a reputation for not supporting its employees and for having lower pay and longer hours than other sectors." Future HRM has to find a practical approach that will lead to the right balance of companies' and employees' needs in terms of payment and hours for the workforce, and service guarantees for their customers. The developments in many European countries show the changing attitudes of young university graduates for whom retailing now provides modern and attractive career prospects. However, retailing is still far from the first choice for top graduates and this needs to change.

Environmental factors such as economic, social, political, cultural, and demographic developments are driving the rapid changes in the retail business. Retail management and HRM departments have to be aware of all these changes. Some of the environmental factors are described below.

New Forms of Trading

New trading formats have been the lifeline allowing businesses to gain and sustain competitive advantage. New trading formats are constantly appearing at both ends of the spectrum. Higher margin goods, sometimes even with designer labels, have coexisted with the increasing demand for more aggressive pricing such as that applied by hypermarkets, off-price retailers, and hard discounters. Often, consumers switch from smaller local stores to supermarkets, and increasing numbers of consumers are using new channels for Internet and TV shopping. The international press reports the continuing success of new forms of online retailing (e-tailing) in Europe and the USA, as well as rapid changes in Eastern Europe and Asia in use of the Internet. Within these trading formats, new professions, working careers, and functions are developing very fast. To succeed, HRM has to recognize and manage these changes in retailing human resource requirements. Exchange of knowledge is one of the basic prerequisites: For ex-

HR Challenges	• Company Strategy • Added Value Management • Change Management • Recruitment and Retention • Employability and Lifelong Learning

General Conditions	• Corporate Governance • Technology / IT Infrastructure

Fig. 1. Challenges and General Conditions for HRM

- The critical resource of most businesses is no longer financial capital, but rather their employees (Barber, Strack 2005). Consequently, identifying and gathering the data for human capital valuation and assessment of the return on human resource investments is an important task for HR managers.

- HRM itself must develop, moving from being a 'personnel' department to its new role as a strategic business partner and building the basic structural foundation that will enable companies to organize and optimize their return on human resources.

The emerging trends that persistently need HR attention currently include some of the areas discussed below. We make a distinction between HR challenges and general conditions (Figure 1). In the case of HR challenges HRM has direct influence, while general conditions are contingencies within which HRM has to operate. This list is not exhaustive, but looks at some selected current trends and needs.

Current HR Challenges

- *Company Strategy.* HRM has to adapt its entire program to the company's overall vision and strategy. It is known that organizations with good human capital management generally create substantially more shareholder value than other companies. The significance of human capital is especially visible in the case of a merger. The success of a merger depends much more on the competencies of the staff and management than on other aspects, such as finance, IT, and production. Hax and Majluf (1991) feel that it is therefore essential for well-planned practices and highly efficient HR functions to be aligned with the business of the company concerned. An HR strategy must be 'comprehensive' in the sense of addressing all the different personnel and HR activities central to the long-term development of the firm's businesses. HRM departments have to conceptualize and structure business plans with detailed operations extending from the current to the future state of strategy, organization, and action. These must be based on the organization's mission and common values.

- *Added Value Management.* This confronts HRM with the critical question of what actions add measurable value to the business. There is less certainty about the central direction and more about committed management setting the right tone within the organization for defined values to flourish. Commitment in the form of personal engagement and belief in the organization and its concepts is important. HRM has to support this by elaborating concepts and criteria for their evaluation, some of which should be revised annually. The following behavioral aspects of the workforce should be included in the HRM concept:

  - *Personal Honesty and Integrity*
  - *Self-Motivation and Entrepreneurial Style*
  - *Ability to Communicate the Values and Benefits*
  - *Encouraging Others to Want to Work with the Company and Share its Values; Pride in the Company*
  - *Training and Developing, Coaching, and Mentoring*

- *Change Management.* The most important drivers for change are globalization, technology, and a workforce that is increasingly knowledge-based. Ulrich has stated that there is a need to redefine firms' performance less in terms of cutting cost and more in terms of profitable growth (Ulrich 1997). Managers have to be able to make changes happen of their own volition and also to support the company in its drive for sustained success. Managers have to be able to empower their own staff. Moss Kanter (1989) states that it is only through true empowerment that staff will really contribute to the changing needs of a business, since they will then be doing things because they understand them and for the right reasons, thinking and reflecting on the changes and their likely impact, and above all feeling at ease with the implementation of change. Change management recognizes the need to reflect on the manager's role in the management of change, the identification of problems, and the ability to make changes in either a programmed or a nonprogrammed manner. HRM has to take account of the risks required for the achievement of change in the company.

- *Recruitment and Retention.* Employee recruitment and selection is one the most vital HR functions. However, the retail industry is faced with difficulties in attracting highly educated people. Nonetheless there is a positive trend for change. The challenge for HRM is to show the attractiveness of the retail sector and ensure that appropriate training and careers are available, so that this sector can take a leading place in the competition for available talent. Retail has recently been promoting opening up access to its workforce by declared rejection of discrimination on the grounds of gender or race, and, lately, also by employing more elderly persons. It is also necessary to build up programs for part-time workers. The ability to value diversity within the workforce is a strength, provided that this is backed up by continuous training and correctness. Many organizations run courses on this aspect, usually under the title of 'Increasing Self-awareness,' as the ability to understand one's impact on others is a powerful skill. Next, retention focuses on the goal of keep well-performing staff in the company. This depends not only on interesting work, fair compensation, and a motivating climate and management culture, but also on transparent and achievable career paths combined with a supportive management that provides guidance.

- *Employability and Continuing Education.* This is a major area of challenge to most employers, but especially those who employ large numbers of staff, as retailers do. Staff have to take retraining in order to adapt to a constantly changing external environment. It is a question of mind-set, working environment, and attitude towards self-responsibility. The future will be characterized by the following needs, amongst others:

  – *The need to handle increasing complexity.*

  – *The need for continual enhancement of the management skill sets known as 'Life-Long Learning,'* i.e. the ability to adapt to changing environments, challenges and technology.

  – *The need for a positive attitude to newly emerging opportunities:* Managers themselves have to become life-long learners. This is of particular importance to the changing generations. The process can be aimed, for example, at obtaining further business qualifications, such as an MBA, a marketing diploma, or HRM qualifications, or attending training courses on key skills, such as leadership, or personal development workshops. Some universities are now offering master's degree courses on work-based learning in which projects are directly related to the learning environment of the individual student's workplace. Analysis of actual workproblems can be counted as a credit toward an MA or an MSc. Classroom training fostering positive acceptance of new structures, topics, and technologies is necessary.

  – *The need to communicate regularly and precisely, and transmit meaning and values:* While the company will provide support, it will be the individual managers who have to 'drive' their own learning and that of others in periods of intense change, often using technology such as video conferencing or E-learning/blended learning to pursue their studies. HRM needs to consult with managers on how best to use modern methods.

  – *The need for creative management:* This can be the way to bring new insights into common view or to introduce new issues as an area for the HRM specialist to develop. Many managers are locked into their own reality or their own version of their world, allowing themselves to be trapped into a mind-set of either success or self-perpetuating failure. One of the keys to successful business growth is for managers not to allow themselves to be trapped in a 'psychic prison' (Morgan 2001) of their own making, causing them always to see retail in one dimension only.

Current General Conditions

- *Corporate Governance.* The recent case of Enron and the difficulties faced by retailers such as Sainsbury suggest that the governance of these organizations was grossly at fault in permitting the excessive amounts of power vested in their chief executive officers (CEOs). The nonexecutive directors seem to have abdicated their duties in not restraining the CEOs in their riskier schemes. Expansion, absolute power, soaring costs, and misinterpretation of facts and figures appear to have gone unchecked and a tacit acquiescence to have been entered into, presumably with the goal of presenting stakeholders with a picture that was more positive than the reality. As the impact of the backlash is always difficult to predict, it is likely that HR directors will become more closely involved in the careful examination of candidates' integrity and suitability for high office. It is likely that this will slow the decision-making process within the board environment, but it might be a small price to pay for a more responsible environment acting in the best interests of all parties. HRM needs to motivate the entire staff of their company, to observe and evaluate the 'political' situation within the company, and to react in an appropriate way that can influence the retailer's level of success. HRM has the opportunity, and therefore the duty, to influence national and international codes of corporate governance.

- *Technology/IT Infrastructure.* In some of the new and emerging markets management has to decide whether to implement a total system with all branches totally aligned with the parent company. It can be prohibitively expensive for a branch at the periphery of the organization to lock into a global IT infrastructure that is geared to operations in Western countries where labor costs are very much higher. Retailers operating internationally rely on common platforms and IT structures; the decision to be made is when is the time right for investments?

  A major change in retailing in the future will be the worldwide use of RFID technologies. The success of the METRO Group in developing and running their "Future Store" in Rheinberg as a tightly controlled experiment has had a strong impact on the application of new technologies in 'real business,' since METRO Group has shared the results with industry and with its wholesalers, as well as its IT and logistics providers (see, e.g., chapter by Kalyanam, Lal and Wolfram in this book). The scientific research involves customers' reactions to the new shopping methods, and possibly also staff training in the use of intelligent technologies and introductions to available information and changing processes for customers.

In conclusion, there has been, and continues to be, a great deal of activity surrounding staff appraisal. The management of progression, or performance monitoring, continues to exercise HRM professionals, who wish it to be as fair as possible to individuals, but also want the company to obtain maximum benefit from the exercise. While the strategy should be systematic, it also needs to be continuous, with a fully implemented set of key metrics. A full look at each individual's future, which can be a position as well as a set of personal goals, should be carried out at regular intervals. HRM professionals must ensure that line managers can perform this function.

Next, we discuss approaches that address current HR challenges in retailing.

Fig. 2. Approaches to Challenges and General Conditions for HRM

Approaches to HR Challenges in Retailing Practice

Building up and Keeping Motivation

As indicated in Figure 2, HRM has to ensure that the workforce is motivated and trained to satisfy consumers' needs. Retailers have to develop the employee value proposition. This means an attractive position with the fulfillment of employee needs and expectations and achievement of a good, unique image in terms of recruiting and keeping human capital. We list below some approaches to retaining an adequate sales force. HR quality cannot be assured without investment. Such investment has to be justified in economic terms and must therefore be constantly monitored:

- Planning the HR costs and expenditures for the annual business budget and forecasts

- Supplying key data needed for planning the workforce at all levels and providing benchmark data on key performance indicators, such as average working hours per store opening hour, turnover per working hour, profit per working hour

- Elaboration of systems to measure the work involved in and results of HRM (training investment per employee, rate of internal job placements, etc.)

- Providing common and communicated values of the company to give the workforce a strategic framework and common mind-set

- Creating a transparent internal job market

- Offering the staff a perspective for the future and clear career paths

- Flexible models of working times, such as part-time working concepts, annualized hours contracts, and balancing of profession and family with the aid of sabbaticals

- Ensuring adequate processes, tools, and budget to allow for members of the workforce to achieve their objectives and ambitions

- Continuing education of executives and employees within actual training programs and a corporate university

- Training the workforce in soft skills and mentoring to ensure proper alignment of their values with the company's values and beliefs

- Initiation of an employee suggestion/inquiry system to improve the process of cooperation

- Recruitment of talented graduates from exchange programs with universities worldwide

- International education within internal exchange programs, with participants from different countries

- Apprenticeships and educations in new professions to build up the best workforce

- Sharing company success with employees (incentive systems at all staff levels, based on parameters that are accessible to employees)

- Offering fringe benefits, such as discounts for shopping at the employer's stores, company cars, equity programs, retirement arrangements, company nursery/kindergarten, and other social benefits.

The Future of HRM and Final Remarks

Most employees spend a substantial amount of time at work. Some people therefore consider their job decisions on joining a retail company or some other industry in the context of social environment. HRM has to keep an eye on such constraints, as the retail trade is anxious to attract the best employees. Future HRM will concentrate on supporting management and workforce and outsource administrative tasks to contractors. In future, there will be more intensive collaboration and networking with external parties. New professions in retail, such as that of IT specialist, are developing. HRM must also place greater emphasis on ethical working conditions, safer working environments, and equal-opportunity policies (ending sex/age discrimination, inclusion of minorities, etc.). In any company, HRM has to build up trust and commitment among all persons working in that organization. Continued reliance on traditional processes is definitely no longer a recipe that promises much success. HR management has to assure fast and market-oriented actions that are appropriate to complex market situations.

HRM will have to set priorities on the HR strategy and its realization, but will be viewed on the operational side more in the role of a service center. In future, the issue of management development will gain even greater importance.

To sum up, HRM has to be aligned with the business strategy of the company, to work in keeping with all of its corporate objectives, and to be prepared not only to help in implementing all changes necessary but also to instigate and be at the vanguard of change programs. Further, HRM should be aware of employee interests within the organization yet conscious of its place as the 'power house' when controversial business decisions, such as downsizing, have to be implemented. Lastly, it plays a key role in ensuring that constant retooling and retraining takes place in the operation to meet ever-evolving challenges. Life-long learning should be an integral part of any business, to enable it to respond to its rivals' activities with fresh initiatives within the company.

HRM specialists have to ensure the long-term performance of "their" retail organizations. It is a big challenge for HRM to meet the future needs, and the task is wide ranging. How well HR managers perform their function will determine whether a retailer registers a sustainable success in the future. We have tried to show in this chapter the comprehensive and central role of HRM in retailing. Retail has been and will continue to be an exciting field of business throughout the world. The main function of the retail sector is to work with and for people all over the world, so that retail has the chance to give people interesting and fulfilling workplaces.

References

Barber, F. and Strack, R. (2005): The Surprising Economics of a "People Business", in: Harvard Business Review June 2005, pp 81-90.

Davies, G. (1999): The Evolution of Marks and Spencer. Service Industries Journal. 19, 3, 60-73.

Dawson J.A. (2001): Strategy and opportunism in European retail internationalisation British Journal of Management, 12, 253-266.

Dawson, J.A. (2000): Retailing at Century End: some challenges for management and research. International Review of Retail, Distribution and Consumer Research, 10, 119-148.

Gilbert, D. (2003): Retail Marketing Management, 2nd edition, Prentice Hall.

Hax, A. and Majluf, N. (1991): The Strategy Concept & Process. A pragmatic Approach, Prentice Hall.

Mellahi, K., Jackson T.P. and Sparks, L. (2002): An exploratory study into failure of a successful organisations: the case of Marks and Spencer, British Journal of Management, 13, 15-29.

Morgan G. (2001): Images of Organisation Sage, London

Moss Kanter R. (1989): When giants Learn to Dance Simon & Schuster, London

Seth, A. and Randall, G. (1999): The Grocers: the rise and rise of the supermarket chains, London: Kogan Page, Social Science Research, 24, 28-62.

Ulrich, D., Losey, M.R, Lake G. editors (1997): Tomorrow's HR Management New York, John Wiley & Sons, Inc.

Ulrich, D. (1997): Human Resources of the Future: Conclusions and Observations, in: Tomorrow's HR Management, edited by Dave Ulrich, Michael R. Losey et al., 354-360, John Wiley & Sons.

PRODUCT

Retail Assortment: More ≠ Better

Susan M. Broniarczyk and Wayne D. Hoyer

University of Texas at Austin, USA

Product assortment strategy is a central yet complex issue for retailers. Retail product assortments have undergone drastic changes in the past decade from unparalleled large assortments in the early 1990s to the current emphasis on streamlined, efficient assortments. The purpose of this chapter is to provide guidance to retailers making these important assortment strategy decisions.

Consumer assortment perceptions have been shown to be one of the top three criteria, along with location and price, in determining retail patronage. In the 1980s and early 1990s, retailers assumed that larger product assortments better met consumer needs. Broad assortments should increase the probability that consumers will find their ideal product and offer flexibility for variety seekers. Thus, in an effort to serve the customer, the number of products offered in supermarkets escalated from 6000 stockkeeping units (SKUs) in the 1980s to over 30,000 SKUs in the early 1990s. However, the Food Marketing Institute issued two imperative reports that called this increasing assortment into question. First, these broad assortments resulted in higher inventory costs and more out-of-stocks for retailers (see Verhoef & Sloot chapter in this book for further information on out-of-stocks). Second, these higher costs made it difficult for conventional supermarkets to compete against the growing retail formats of discount stores, warehouse clubs, and supercenters.

As part of its 1993 report, the Food Marketing Institute conducted a field study in which it reduced SKUs in six product categories (cereal, pet food, salad dressing, spaghetti sauce, toilet tissue, and toothpaste) at 24 test stores. Redundant SKUs were eliminated and shelf space was held constant, with more space now allocated to high-market-share items. Importantly, the results showed no significant negative impact of SKU reduction on sales. In other words, this initial evidence suggested that efficient assortment might result in cost savings without loss of sales. However, it was difficult to draw definite conclusions as the magnitude of SKU reduction in these categories was vague.

In another series of in-store studies, Dreze, Hoch, and Purk (1994) examined a 10 % reduction of low-volume SKUs in eight test categories over a 4-month period.

Their shelf-reset procedure was similar to that in the Food Marketing Institute study, with shelf space held constant and freed-up shelf space reallocated to high-volume SKUs. Across eight categories, they found that sales increased by 4% for 30 test stores compared with 30 control stores. These results began to indicate the possibility that smaller assortments might even have a positive effect on sales.

In the remainder of this chapter, we review recent research that further questions the conventional wisdom on assortment and shows that more product assortment does not necessarily lead to a better shopping experience. The chapter is organized around four research questions: (1) How do consumers perceive assortment? (2) How should assortments be organized? (3) How does assortment affect consumer product choice? and (4) How do marketing mix variables interact with assortment?

How Do Consumers Perceive Assortment?

Assortment is traditionally defined as the number of SKUs offered within a single product category. However, consumer perceptions often differ from objective reality. Although the aforementioned studies examined the impact of SKU reduction on sales, they did not provide any insight into how consumers actually perceived assortment. In a seminal paper, Broniarczyk, Hoyer, and McAlister (1998) reported that assortment perceptions were influenced by three factors: (1) the number of unique SKUs offered, (2) the heuristic of the total space devoted to the category, and (3) the availability of a consumer's favorite SKU.

Assortment Dimensions. In keeping with the traditional definition of assortment, the number of unique items offered was directly correlated to consumer assortment perceptions. However, consumer assortment perceptions were found not be a one-to-one function of the number of items offered, as consumers do not process assortment information in a great amount of detail. Instead, their laboratory studies conducted by Broniarczyk et al. (1998) showed that consumers were not sensitive to a SKU reduction by 25-50% in the popcorn category if the size of the shelf space was held constant and their favorite item was still available. In fact, consumer perceptions actually *increased* following a 25% SKU reduction if shelf space was held constant. This increase in assortment perception was due to popular SKUs being duplicated, which made it easier for consumers to find their favorite products. This finding leads Broniarczyk et al. (1998) to suggest that consumer assortment perceptions have both a cognitive dimension (total number of SKUs offered, size of category space) and an affective dimension (availability of favorite, ease of shopping).

Broniarczyk et al. (1998) confirmed this multi-dimensional view of assortment perceptions in a convenience store field study. The leading five product categories (accounting for 80% of sales) were subjected to a 54% SKU reduction at two test stores, and assortment perceptions in the test stores were compared against those in two control stores. In-store intercepts with customers revealed no change in assortment perceptions, but customers did report that it was now easier to shop. In addition, overall sales increased by 8 % in one of the test stores and by 2 % in the other. Thus, substantial SKU reduction was shown to have positive affective consequences without negatively affecting consumers' cognitive perceptions of assortment.

Product Dissimilarity and Attribute Dispersion. Two follow-up papers further developed our insight into how consumers perceive assortment by specifying mathematical models of consumers' cognitive assortment perceptions. Hoch, Bradlow and Wansink (1999) modeled the assortment of a product category as the dissimilarity of product pairs (i.e., product-based approach). In an experimental test of hypothetical products, attribute differences between SKUs were found to have a substantial impact on assortment perceptions. Uniqueness of product pairs was found to be critical, with assortments containing duplicates severely penalized. However, it is important to point out that there are diminishing returns to increased uniqueness. Adding a unique feature to one of two products will have more of an effect on pair similarity if the products are currently identical than if they already differ in multiple attributes. That is to say that beyond a certain point, adding further attribute differences between product pairs has no additional assortment benefit.

Van Herpen and Pieters (2002) use an attribute-based approach to model the assortment of a product category as a function of the dispersion of attribute levels across all products in the category and the correlation between product attributes. An assortment is varied to the extent that attribute levels are dispersed and a low level of association exists between attribute pairs. For instance, the four products black cotton sock, black nylon sock, white cotton sock, and white nylon sock offer greater assortment than the four products two black nylon socks and two white cotton socks. In the latter set, the attributes of color and fabric material are perfectly correlated, thereby reducing assortment. The model of Hoch et al.(1999) would make a similar prediction, as the latter set also increases the number of product duplicates. Although different conceptually, the product pair dissimilarity model of Hoch et al. (1999) and the attribute-based model of Van Herpen and Pieters (2002) have been shown to be mathematically similar when accounting for assortment size. Both models have received empirical support in laboratory experiments, but would benefit from further validation in the field.

Brand-Size Effects. Boatwright and Nunes (2001) did examine SKU reductions in the field, in an on-line grocer's assortment. Specifically, they found that an average of 56 % SKU reduction in 42 product categories did not affect sales (Boatwright, Nunes 2001). They found that retailers could trim brand-size combinations while maintaining the total number of brands and sizes offered in the assortment. Consider an assortment of six products: brand A in size X, size Y, and size Z and brand B in the same three sizes. This assortment could be reduced to four products with all attribute levels maintained by brand A offering sizes X and Y and brand B offering sizes Y and Z. This reduced number of items would be predicted to have null or positive effects on consumer assortment perceptions as the dispersion of attribute levels across products remains constant (Van Herpen, Pieters 2002) and the dissimilarity between product pairs is increased (Hoch et al. 1999). However, a note of caution: 60 % of customers whose favorite SKU was eliminated reduced or stopped their category purchases.

Summary and Implications. Retailers and manufacturers need to understand that consumer assortment perceptions are not simply a function of the number of items offered in the product category. A key principle is that consumer perceptions of assortment are also a function of the similarity of the items in the assortment, the size of the shelf display, and the availability of their favorite products.

The multi-dimensional nature of assortment perceptions implies that retailers may be able to reduce the number of items offered without decreasing consumers' perceptions of assortment. The threshold for reducing SKUs without adversely affecting consumer assortment perceptions is likely to be dependent on several factors. Key implications are: (1) There is an inverse relation between the initial size of the assortment and the magnitude of SKU reduction on assortment perceptions (Van Herpen, Pieters 2002). This means that large SKU reductions are more likely to decrease assortment perceptions when the initial assortment size is small rather than large. (2) There is a link between distribution of SKU sales and magnitude of SKU reduction on assortment perceptions. If sales are uniformly distributed across products in the category a significant reduction in SKUs is likely to make the favorite product unavailable for a large proportion of customers. However, if the majority of sales are driven by a few products (e.g., 80 % sales are driven by 20 % of products), a reduction of low-selling SKUs will have minimal adverse impact on the availability of customer favorites. For instance, in the convenience store field study, few customers reported that their favorite was unavailable following the ≥50 % SKU reduction because the majority of products accounted for a negligible portion of sales (Broniarczyk et al. 1998). (3) Mathematical models offer guidance on strategic SKU reduction by identifying products offering the lowest unique value to the assortment, such as redundant brand-size combinations.

How Should Assortments Be Organized?

In addition to assortment perceptions, it has also been recognized that the manner in which assortments are *organized* can have a significant impact on how consumers process information. Prior research has clearly highlighted the fact that the manner in which information is presented greatly influences the way consumers process information about the brands. In particular, consumers tend to be constructive processors who adapt their decision-making style to the information display format. Thus, if information is organized by brand, consumers tend to process by brand. If information is organized by attribute, consumers are more likely to make comparisons across attributes. Researchers in marketing and consumer behavior have identified various key aspects of assortment organization that can influence how consumers process assortment information.

Nature of the Display. A series of studies by Itamar Simonson and Stephen Nowlis has examined how the nature of the display influences consumer processing. Side-by-side displays favor brands with a lower price or with superior features because the display makes it easy to compare the brands. Brands with high prices are better served by separate displays that inhibit comparison (such as an end-of-aisle or perimeter display). In fact, Dreze et. al. (1994) found that location in the display is far more critical than the number of facings. Brands in the middle of a display are more likely to be compared and to influence perceptions of variety.

Organize by Brand or Model? Another way to organize assortments is by brand or by model. For example, a retailer could either group all the models of a particular brand together (e.g., Sony, Magnavox, etc.) or group all different types of models together (e.g., all low-priced models together, mid-range models together, and high-end models together). When options are organized by model or tier, consumers are more likely to select the mid-line and top-of-the line brands (owing to a tendency to avoid the cheapest brand). A study of yogurt found that organizing the display by brand encouraged consumers to buy the same brand in different flavors. However, organizing by flavor caused consumers to think about flavor first and then buy different brands. Thus, a brand display encourages more brand loyalty, while an attribute-based display encourages brand switching and variety seeking.

Ordering of Brands. Retailers can also determine the order in which brands and information are processed. This is very easily accomplished in on-line environments, by controlling which brands are presented first. In store this can be accomplished by the position of the brands in the display (right-to-left and left-to-right, as well as shelf level). Consumers can also develop internal ordering of products. Research has shown that such ordering of information can have a big impact on consumer evaluations.

For example, when consumers engage in limited information search, a declining order (best to worst) leads to the most positive evaluations. This occurs because consumers tend to see only the brands that are rated most positively. When a search is extensive, however, evaluations are more positive for an increasing order (worst to best). Exhaustive searching ensures that all the brands are processed (especially the most positive ones at the end). Thus, it is clear the retailers should consider the likely search patterns of their consumers in determining how the brands are ordered.

How Well the Display is Organized. At the extremes, assortments can be either well organized or rather disorganized. When the assortment is large, actual variety is easier to recognize when assortments are organized. With small assortments, however, organized assortments can actually make the lack of choice more salient.

Further, if actual variety is increased in a disorganized manner, the disruptive impact on consumers will be less than if it was increased in an organized manner.

Symmetrical vs. Asymmetrical Assortments. When assortments are asymmetrical (i.e., some items appear more or less frequently than others) it is easier for consumers to appreciate the variety in them than it is in a symmetrical assortment (where all items are presented equally – Kahn, Wansink 2004). This occurs because low-frequency items carry more information and are rare compared with those that are high in frequency and are therefore more redundant. This notion is consistent with Hoch et al.'s statement (1999) that uniqueness of items in an assortment is critical.

Comparability with Consumer Knowledge Structures. Assortment displays (either in physical stores or on line) have the potential to be very complex as they contain vast amounts of information. Consumers deal with this complexity by developing an "internal structure," which involves categorizing brands and information into knowledge structures called "schemas." For instance, when categorizing the product category of popcorn, consumer A may organize the options around different brands (Orville Redenbacher, Pop Secret, Jolly Time) whereas consumer B organizes the options around different flavors (butter, low fat, cheddar). In a series of studies, Morales et al. (2005) show that when a consumer's internal structure for the category matches the external structure of the shelf display the consumer is more likely to perceive greater variety and be more satisfied with his/her choice.

Product schemas become more established in memory and play a stronger role in information processing as consumers gain experience with a product category. Thus, if consumers are very familiar with the product category, the internal schema structure is likely to be strong and it is critical that the assortment organization be congruent with their prior knowledge. However, when familiarity with the product category is low, consumers will not have well-developed schemas and it is more important for the assortment structure to be congruent with their situational shopping goals (e.g., foods for a snack, foods to take to the beach).

Summary and Implications. Not only do retailers and manufacturers need to determine the size of their assortments; it is also critical to evaluate carefully how these assortments are organized. Our summary of research on this topic identifies a number of key principles: (1) Side-by-side displays facilitate brand comparisons, while separate displays are better for high priced brands. (2) Organizing by brand encourages consumers to buy by brand, while organizing by model stimulates the use of other attributes such as price. (3) Evaluations tend to be more positive when brands are in worst-to-best order. (4) Organized displays are better for large assortments, but for small assortments they make the lack of choice more apparent. (5) Asymmetrical assortments make it easier for consumers to see the variety in an assortment. (6) It is important to align assortments with consumers' internal knowledge structures if consumers are familiar with the product category.

How Does Assortment Affect Product Choice?

The previous section discussed how assortment organization affects consumers' assortment perceptions and product choice. This section reviews recent research in consumer behavior and psychology to further extend our understanding of how assortment affects product choice. Across a wide range of products and service, consumers report a desire for large assortments. Yet, the consumer decision-making literature suggests that larger assortments may have negative consequences.

Decision Difficulty. The information overload literature has shown that increasing the number of product alternatives increases the cognitive load, thereby increasing consumers' decision difficulty. A large number of product alternatives also leads to consumer confusion and lower consumer satisfaction with the decision process. Increased cognitive effort further results in task-induced negative affect, with consumers preferring to choose alternatives that are easy to evaluate. The decision difficulty, confusion, and negative affect associated with large assortments may lead consumers to walk away from the shelf display without purchasing.

Likelihood of Purchase. Iyengar and Lepper (2000) recently examined this dual attraction/difficulty characteristic of large assortments. They found that large assortments initially attracted consumers to the shelf display, but the decision difficulty they encountered on trying to make a choice was demotivating, increasing regret and leading consumers to walk away without making a purchase.

Specifically, in a series of studies, Iyengar and Lepper (2000) compared consumer reaction to six options (small assortment) versus 24 options (large assortment). In a field study in an upscale grocery store, they showed that consumers were more attracted to a sampling station when it offered 24 varieties of jam (60 % of shoppers sampling) than when 6 varieties of jam were offered (40 % of shoppers sampling) even though extent of sampling was comparable in both situations (average of 1 or 2 jams). Consumers who sampled were then given a coupon that was redeemable if they purchased a jam from the regular shelf display. Purchase likelihood exhibited a strikingly different pattern, with consumers more likely to purchase after sampling from the small (30 % purchase) than from the large (3 % purchase) assortment. That is, although consumers were initially more attracted to the larger than to the smaller assortment, they were actually less inclined to buy. As the number of options increased, consumers were less certain that they could select the best option. Thus, most consumers did not make a purchase from the large assortment.

Even when consumers do choose to make a purchase from a large assortment, there are still negative consequences from a broad product selection. In follow-up laboratory studies, Iyengar and Lepper (2000) found that when consumers chose a product from a large assortment they were less satisfied with their product choice. These consumers experienced higher levels of regret over the idea that other, foregone, options might have been more preferable.

Moderating Factor of Consumer Expertise. Additional research suggests that large assortments may cause more difficulties for some consumers than for others. In particular, choosing from large assortments is likely to be more difficult for those who do not possess well-defined product preferences (Chernev 2003). For these consumers, choice is a two-stage process of first deciding their ideal attribute combination and then locating the product in the assortment that best matches this ideal. Deciding the ideal attribute combination is more overwhelming when faced with a large than with a small assortment. Thus, consumers without well-defined preferences fare better with smaller assortments.

Conversely, for consumers who have well-defined preferences, product choice is a single-stage process of locating the product that matches their established ideal. For these consumers, a large assortment increases the probability of finding a match with their ideal. Thus, in a series of laboratory studies, Chernev (2003) has shown that consumers with well-defined preferences in a product category prefer large to small assortments.

Moderating Factor of Assortment Alignability. In addition to consumer individual differences, the type of assortment may also affect consumer choice. The models of both Hoch et al. (1999) and Van Herpen and Pieters (2002) showed that attribute dissimilarity increased assortment perceptions. This attribute dissimilarity can be further specified as either an alignable or a nonalignable attribute difference. Alignable attributes are defined as different levels of the same attribute, so that consumers are making tradeoffs within an attribute. Nonalignable attributes, on the other hand, involve comparisons among different attributes, so that consumers are making tradeoffs between attributes. For instance, in computers, an alignable attribute would be processor speed, which might vary from 1.60 GHz through 2.40 GHz and 2.80 GHz to 3.00 GHz. A nonalignable attribute would be computer peripherals, which might range from monitor through printer and fax to speakers.

Nonalignable attributes are more likely to increase perceived assortment than alignable attributes. However, Gourville and Soman (2005) show that increasing brand assortments of nonalignable attributes can have a negative impact on brand choice. They compared choice between two brands, one brand (brand A) offering a single product option and the second brand (brand B) offering either a single product option or five product options. When brand B increased its product assortment from one to five options and the attribute differences were nonalignable, its market share relative to brand A *decreased* from 53 % to 40 %. However, when the attribute differences were alignable, the opposite pattern emerged. When brand B increased its product assortment from one to five options and the attribute differences were alignable, its market share relative to brand A *increased* from 53 % to 73 %.

There are several causal mechanisms underlying this differential effect of assortment type on product choice. First, nonalignable assortments place a heavier cognitive load on consumers than alignable assortments, as comparisons between attributes are more difficult than comparisons across levels within an attribute. Thus, consumers may choose to simplify their decision by selecting the brand offering fewer options.

Second, nonalignable assortments have been shown to lead to higher levels of regret than alignable assortments. When choosing between nonalignable attributes, consumers with budget constraints must make a tradeoff between attributes. These consumers are likely to experience a sense of regret about the options foregone: a computer peripheral choice of a monitor, for example, means completely foregoing a printer, fax, or speakers. When choosing among alignable attributes, however, regret is minimized as the choice between levels of a common attribute (e.g., 1.6GHz versus 2.0Ghz) still results in the consumer obtaining an item with that attribute (e.g., a computer processor). Third, nonalignable assortments increase consumer expectations more than alignable assortments. Even if only one peripheral is within a consumer's budget, his/her ideal computer package may now include multiple peripherals (e.g., both a monitor and a printer). If this increased ideal point is unrealistic (given the consumer's budget constraints), it may deter consumer purchase or, if consumers do purchase a single peripheral option, increase purchase dissatisfaction.

Summary and Implications. Large assortments have several negative effects on product choice. (1) Large assortments increase choice difficulty, increase negative affect, increase regret, and decrease product purchase. (2) These negative consequences have been shown to be more likely in consumers without well-defined preferences. (3) These negative consequences are more likely for nonalignable than for alignable assortments. Thus, if consumers do not have well-defined preferences they are more likely to make a purchase from a smaller display offering alignable differences between options. If consumers possess well-defined product preferences they prefer a large assortment, as it increases their ability to find their ideal. However, even for these consumers, a large assortment of nonalignable attributes may increase expectations regarding the ideal product to a level that is simply unattainable – leading to purchase deferral.

How Do Marketing Mix Variables Interact with Assortment?

Assortment perceptions and decisions do not operate in isolation; rather, the influence of assortments on consumer information processing and decision making may interact with other key marketing mix variables, such as price, store environment, region, and competitive considerations. Thus, it is important to examine the interactive nature of these different variables. Unfortunately, however, the academic research attention devoted to this important topic has been rather sparse.

Assortment and Price. Some studies have examined the joint effects of assortment and pricing. Since a key goal of product category management is to maximize profit for the category, assortment and pricing decisions are inseparable. In fact, according to McIntyre and Miller (1999, p. 296): "this joint decision is believed to be one of the most central problems in retailing." Furthermore, pricing variables often dominate assortment considerations. In one field experiment, assortment manipulations had approximately a 5-6 % impact on category profits, while in another study (Dreze et al. 1994), price manipulations had a 32 % impact on category profit. Thus, it is clear that the pricing must be considered when making assortment decisions (see also chapters by Simon, Gathen, Daus, and Bolton, Shankar, Montoya in this book).

McIntyre and Miller (1999) propose an empirical approach for improving optimal assortment/pricing decision combinations. With this approach, retail shoppers are asked to provide information about their reservation prices for brands in their consideration set. Then, a simple choice rule is developed to model and forecast the sales of each item in the set given the stated prices. In an empirical test of this model, this approach resulted in significantly more profitable assortments than a constant markup rule or a regression approach. Note, however, that this model is more applicable to high-involvement product categories. Research is still needed to develop a model for common, frequently purchased product categories.

Assortment and Other Marketing Variables. A study by Koelmeijer and Oppewal (1999) increased our understanding of assortment composition by modeling item and store choice as a function of assortment, store ambience, price, and competing store characteristics. Some key findings were that an increase in assortment size generated additional purchases relative to the attractiveness of the items added and reduced the likelihood that customers would go to another store. Further, having a competing store nearby and poor store ambience will hurt a store's drawing power above and beyond assortment effects. While, the study examined only one product category, its real contribution is that it provides a powerful tool for optimizing retail assortments. Using this approach, retail managers can manipulate various marketing mix variables and assortment options to determine the overall effect on consumer choice as well as sales.

It is also important to note that both of the previously mentioned studies were conducted in an experimental context. In the context of actual grocery store data, studies have focused on how assortment overlap, price differentiation, and interstore distance impact on the sharing of customers between stores. A key finding is that assortment overlap and interstore distance are the key determinants of customer overlap. The more similar the assortments of two stores, the more likely they are to have the same customers. Not surprisingly, proximity of the stores increases customer overlap. In addition, stores are more likely to be differentiated on the basis of assortments and match their competitors' prices on identical items. Thus, based on this study, assortment decisions rather than price are critical in differentiating a particular store and giving customers a reason to shop there.

Assortment and Regional Differences. Retailers have long recognized that assortments must be adjusted by region to better meet customer needs. Clearly, having distinctive assortments that appeal to specific customer groups is a key way to achieve competitive advantage. However, because retailers have traditionally relied on aggregate performance measures (i.e., gross margin, sales per square foot, etc.) to evaluate performance of individual stores, regional differences may complicate the assortment planning process. Retailers need to be able to measure merchandise performance accurately at the individual store level.

To address this problem, Grewal et al. (1999) employ data envelopment analysis (DEA) which enables retailers to plan and evaluate the performance of similar stores. Essentially, the performance of individual stores is compared to "best practice" stores, which are similar in terms of certain characteristics (e.g., region, categories). Thus, similar best practice stores can be examined to determine which assortments and practices make their stores successful. Mediocre stores can also be examined in order to identify key ways to improve.

Assortment and Sales Promotion. Finally, a series of experimental studies have highlighted the important interaction between assortment and sales promotion. For example, the likelihood of switching from a low-quality, low-price brand to a promoted high-quality high-price brand tends to be significantly greater than the likelihood of switching from a high-quality brand to a promoted low-quality brand. However, by manipulating assortment and adding another price tier (i.e., a generic brand), retailers can eliminate this effect. Also, the number of items purchased on a particular shopping trip can be increased by offering bundles of preferred items or encouraging the purchase of multiple items in a category through the use of various promotions (see Gedenk, Neslin, Ailawadi in this book for more information on retailer sales promotions).

Summary and Implications. Taking all these studies together it is clear that assortment decisions must be viewed in the context of other marketing mix variables, such as price, interstore distance, store ambience, and region. Considering this, marketing mix variables need to be decided jointly to maximize profit for the product category and the store. The key conclusions are: (1) assortment decisions must be made in the context of pricing decisions; (2) having a nearby competitor and poor ambience will have a negative impact above and beyond assortment effects; (3) similar assortments and close proximity increase customer overlap between two stores; and (4) retailers need to evaluate assortments by region and individual stores.

Summary and Conclusion

The purpose of this chapter was to review the main research findings and knowledge on retail assortments. Table 1 summarizes these key findings. For years there has been a strong belief among retailers that having more assortment is always better. However, a key conclusion that can be drawn from this review is that this is often not the case. Rather, having an *optimal* amount of assortment (which may not be the largest) is more critical. Furthermore, our review demonstrates that through selective reduction and proper organization, retailers can shrink the number of products offered without lowering consumer perceptions of assortment. This is

Table 1. Summary of Findings

How do consumers perceive assortment?
1. In addition to number of total items, assortment perception is a function of similarity of items, shelf display size, and availability of favorites.
2. Large SKU reductions will decrease assortment perceptions more when initial assortment is small than large.
3. If majority of sales are driven be a few SKUs, reduction of low selling SKUs will have minimal impact on assortment perceptions.
4. Mathematical models offer guidance on the unique value of each item in assortment and strategic SKU reduction such as redundant brand-size combinations.
How should assortments be organized?
1. Side-by-side displays facilitate brand comparisons whereas separate displays are better for higher price brands.
2. Organizing by brand encourages consumers to buy by brand while organizing by model stimulates other attributes such as price.
3. Evaluations tend to be more positive when brands are ordered from worst to best.
4. Organized displays are better for large assortments but for small assortments, make the lack of choice apparent.
5. Asymmetrical assortments make it easier for consumers to see variety.
6. Aligning assortment organization with consumer mental representation is important.
How does assortment affect product choice?
1. Large assortments have negative consequences of increasing choice difficulty, negative affect, and product regret.
2. Large assortments decrease purchase likelihood, especially for consumers without well-defined preferences.
3. Negative consequences are more likely for nonalignable than alignable assortments.
How do marketing mix variables interact with assortment?
1. Assortment decisions must be made in context of pricing decisions.
2. Having a nearby competitor and poor ambience will have negative effect beyond assortment.
3. Similar assortments and close proximity increase customer overlap between stores.
4. Retailers need to evaluate assortments by region and individual stores.

particularly the case when assortments for a category tend to be large and when the majority of sales are driven by a few brands. Moreover, the positive benefits of reduced assortments include a higher level of shopper satisfaction with their shopping experience and a higher likelihood that customers will make a purchase from small than from large product assortments.

In addition, we learned that the organization of product assortments is also very critical. Retailers must carefully make a variety of important decisions, including whether to place brands side – by side or in separate displays, whether to organize by brand or model/flavor, how to order brands in the display (well-organized vs. random displays, symmetrical vs. asymmetrical displays) and how to align displays with consumer knowledge structures.

We also found that large assortments increased choice difficulty, increase negative affect and regret, and decrease the likelihood of product purchase. This is particularly the case when consumers do not have well-formed prior preferences and when assortments are more nonalignable than alignable. Finally, we showed that assortment decisions cannot be made independent of other marketing mix variables, such as price, interstore distance, store ambience, and region.

Taking all this together, it is clear that there are a number of key decisions which must be made in relation to product assortments. However, by carefully analyzing each category and optimizing decisions in terms of the factors mentioned, retailers can significantly improve both category and overall store profit. Technology such as RFID tags (see Verhoef and Sloot chapter in this book) will facilitate such assortment management.

References

Boatwright, Peter and Joseph C. Nunes (2001): Reducing Assortment: An Attribute-Based Approach, Journal of Marketing, 65 (July), 50-63; Correction July 2004.

Broniarczyk, Susan M., Wayne D. Hoyer, and Leigh McAlister (1998): "Consumers' Perceptions of the Assortment Offered in a Grocery Category: The Impact of Item Reduction," Journal of Marketing Research, 35 (May), 166-176.

Chernev, Alexander (2003): When More is Less and Less is More: The Role of Ideal Point Availability and Assortment in Consumer Choice, Journal of Consumer Research, 30 (September), 170-183.

Dreze, Xavier, Stephen J. Hoch, and Mary E. Purk (1994): Shelf Management and Space Elasticity, Journal of Retailing, 70 (Winter), 301-326.

Gourville, J. & Soman, D. (2005): Overchoice and Assortment Type: When and why variety backfires, Marketing Science, forthcoming.

Grewal, Dhruv, Michael Levy, Anuj Mehrotra, and Arun Sharma (1999): Planning Merchandising Decisions to Account for Regional and Product Assortment Differences, Journal of Retailing, 75 (Fall), 405-424.

Hoch, Stephen, Eric T. Bradlow, and Brian Wansink (1999): The Variety of an Assortment, Marketing Science 18 (4), 527-546.

Iyengar, S. and M. Lepper (2000): When Choice is Demotivating: Can One desire Too Much of a Good Thing?, Journal of Personality and Social Psychology, No. 6, 995-1006.

Kahn, Barbara E. and Brian Wansink (2004): Assortment Structure on Perceived Variety, Journal of Consumer Research, 30 (March), 519-533.

Koelemeijer, Kitty and Harmen Oppewal (1999): Assessing the Effects of Assortment and Ambience: A Choice Experimental Approach, Journal of Retailing, 75 (Fall), 319-346.

McIntyre, Shelby H. and Christopher M. Miller (1999): The Selection and Pricing of Retail Assortments: An Empirical Approach, Journal of Retailing, 75 (Fall), 289-294.

Morales, Andrea, Barbara E. Kahn, Leigh McAlister, and Susan M. Broniarczyk (2005): Perceptions of Assortment Variety: The Effects of Congruency Between Consumers' Internal and Retailers' External Organization, Journal of Retailing, forthcoming.

van Herpen, Erica and Rik Pieters (2002): The Variety of an Assortment: An Extension to the Attribute-Based Approach, Marketing Science, 21 (3), 331-341.

Out-of-Stock: Reactions, Antecedents, Management Solutions, and a Future Perspective

Peter C. Verhoef[1] and Laurens M. Sloot[2]

[1] University of Groningen, The Netherlands
[2] Erasmus Food Management Institute, Erasmus University Rotterdam, The Netherlands

Introduction

In today's competitive environment, service-oriented retailers are faced with one important question: How can we deliver good service levels to our customers, while becoming more cost efficient at the same time? Superior levels of service to customers are necessary to differentiate these retailers from the strongly price-oriented chains, such as Aldi, Lidl, ASDA, Wal-Mart, and Colruyt. One key differentiator of service retailers is their assortment. In general, service retailers offer more national brands than discounters, and also a wider variety of products. However, offering more variety in products and brands has two important consequences. First, retailers are confronted with more costs in the supply chain, due to higher inventory, procurement, handling, and warehouse costs. Second, more variety also increases the probability that out-of-stocks (OOS) may occur, which may lead to customer dissatisfaction and (temporary) store disloyalty. As service retailers strive to compete with discounters on service, OOS can severely jeopardize their competitive position in the consumers' mind.

It is therefore important for retail managers to manage their assortments in a professional manner (see, e.g., Broniarczyk, Hoyer in this book). In managing the assortment they must strive for an optimal assortment, which at the same time creates customer satisfaction by offering the customers' required products, reduces supply chain costs, and minimizes OOS levels. The minimization of OOS levels is not an easy task for retailers. However, it is very important, as gross margin losses due to OOS are estimated at between $7 and $ 12 billion in the United States (Andersen Consulting 1996). Moreover, the aforementioned dissatisfaction that can result may decrease retailers' overall satisfaction scores, which are now regarded as important indicators for future retailer profitability.

In this chapter we will focus on OOS. We will first discuss the OOS phenomenon. Subsequently, we will focus on consumer reactions to OOS and the antecedents of these reactions. This is followed by discussion of some empirical findings

M. Krafft and M.K. Mantrala (eds.), *Retailing in the 21st Century: Current and Future Trends*, 285
DOI 10.1007/978-3-540-72003-4_18, © Springer-Verlag Berlin Heidelberg 2010

recorded in a study on OOS reactions in eight product categories. After that, we provide some implications for retailers, and discuss methods of reducing OOS levels and negative consequences of OOS. We will also discuss our ideas on the future of OOS. In this future, the introduction and role of Radio Frequency Identification (RFID) is especially interesting.

Out-of-Stock, Out of Business?

Out-of-Stock. Out-of-stocks of SKUs occur rather often in supermarkets. For instance, AC Nielsen reports that in the Netherlands, 7 % of the offered products are OOS on the important shopping days Friday and Saturday. Corresponding OOS percentages for other countries are 7 % for France and 8 % for the US (Roland Berger Strategy Consultants 2002). OOS percentages in the US seem not to be significantly lower than in other countries, even though such techniques as electronic data interchange have been more widely implemented in the US than in other countries. It is therefore not surprising that OOS is one of the most irritating aspects of shopping for consumers. For example, EFMI calculated that the expected loss of revenues due to OOS in the Netherlands is 175 million Euros, or 0.7 % of the yearly turnover of that country's retailers. In Germany, revenue losses due to OOS are estimated at 1 billion euros per year in the food retail channel.

An OOS may occur for several reasons. For instance, it can happen that the demand for a product is unexpectedly high or a store employee has ordered too few products. Generally, OOS leads to a temporary unavailability of the product concerned for the consumer. Thus, when the consumer is confronted with an OOS, s/he would be aware that the product is unavailable for only a limited time period. This contrasts with a brand- or item de-listing, for instance, in which case the brand or item will never be available again.

Consequences of OOS. As already noted, OOS can have severe consequences for retailers. These severe consequences arise because consumers may exhibit a negative response to OOS. OOS reactions can be classified into two clusters: (a) buying a substitute and (b) not buying a substitute during the store visit. From a retailer perspective this classification is very interesting. When a substitute is purchased the retailer will lose almost no sales. However, when a consumer decides not to buy a substitute in the same store, sales are lost. Within these two general reaction clusters six specific reactions can be considered:

a) Substitute purchased

1. *Item switch*: switching to another format or variety of the same brand;

2. *Category switch*: buying a substitute product from another product category; and

3. *Brand switch*: buying another brand within the same product category.

b) No substitute purchased

    4. *Store switch*: going to another store on the same day to buy the item that is OOS;

    5. *Postponement*: postponing the intended buy until the next regular trip to the store;

    6. *Cancellation*: dropping the intended purchase completely or postponing it for a longer period of time.

Brand, item, and category switch should have no negative consequences for the retailer. In fact, a brand switch from a national brand to a private label may have positive profit consequences owing to higher private label margins. Of the "no-substitute" purchase reactions, store switch in particular is a rather negative consequence for retailers. In the case of store switching, consumers visit another store to buy the product that is OOS. In this competing store, consumers can also purchase products in other categories which they would normally have purchased in the store where the OOS occurred. Cancellation is also rather negative, as the planned product is definitely not purchased in the store. The negative consequences of postponement are less clear, as the postponed purchase may occur at a later time. However, postponement may also imply cancellation. Moreover, postponing the purchase may also imply that the postponed purchase is finally actuated in a competing store.

For a retailer, it is important to know the frequency of each of these reactions relative to the others. In an OOS study in eight categories we found that the OOS response of brand switching was the most common among our respondents (34%), followed in declining order by postponement (23%), store switching (19%), and item switching (18%) (for an extensive discussion see Sloot, Verhoef, Franses, 2005). In this study respondents mentioned the specific OOS reactions of canceling their purchase (3%) and switching categories (2%) less frequently. Thus, 45% of the responses (postponement, store switching, and cancellation) imply not purchasing a substitute. Moreover, 22% of the responses have direct negative sales consequences for the retailer. This last figure re-emphasizes the importance of minimizing OOS levels. Overall, brand switching is the most likely response, postponement is the second most likely, while cancellation and category switching are very rare reactions.

Differences in OOS Responses. In the past, several researchers have investigated OOS responses. For an overview of these studies we refer to Sloot, Verhoef, Franses (2005). A more detailed analysis of these studies reveals some interesting exploratory results:

- cancellations and category switch are rare reactions to an OOS in all studies;
- consumers appear to be more likely to purchase a substitute in the cases of nonfood products, such as detergents and tissues, than in the cases of food products such as coffee and soft drinks; and

288   Peter C. Verhoef and Laurens M. Sloot

- in the case of an item OOS, brand switch occurs less frequently than when the brand itself is OOS. That is, in the case of an item OOS, other items of the (preferred) brand are still available. Thus, consumers still can switch within the brand and purchase another item with the same brand name.

It is also important to note that the reported occurrence of the different OOS responses depends on the type of research design. Researchers have used natural experiments with actual out-of-stocks, and survey studies, where consumers reported what they would do in the case of a hypothetical OOS. Our analysis of all these studies shows that "buying a substitute" is more often reported as a reaction when the item is truly OOS than when the consumer is confronted with a hypothetical OOS. This discrepancy in results can be attributed to the difference in what people say (intend to do) and what they actually do.

These results seem to suggest that retailers should concentrate on reducing OOS in food categories. It also suggests that retailers should select the research design carefully when measuring potential OOS responses.

Antecedents of Consumer Reactions to OOS

In the retailing literature, several studies have investigated the antecedents of reactions to OOS. Based on a review of this literature, we developed the general model below which includes five clusters of variables that explain reactions to OOS (see Figure 1):

- Brand-related antecedents;

- Product-related antecedents;

- Store-related antecedents;

- Situation-related antecedents; and

- Consumer-related antecedents.

Brand-Related Antecedents

An important brand-related antecedent is *brand equity or brand strength*. A brand has high customer-based brand equity when consumers react more favorably to a product with the brand identified than to one whose brand is not (Keller 2002). In general, consumers value high-equity brands more than low-equity brands. Hence, reactions that are negative for the brand, such as brand switching, occur less often for high-equity than for low-equity brands. In hedonic product categories the effect of brand equity may even be stronger, as in these categories brands have opportunities for building brand equity (Sloot, Verhoef, Franses 2005). Fast-moving consumer goods retailers can use several measures for brand equity. For instance, one can use market share or price premium as a proxy for brand equity. The advantage of using market share as a measure is that it has easily adopted implications for the retailer, e.g., try to minimize OOS for brands with high market shares.

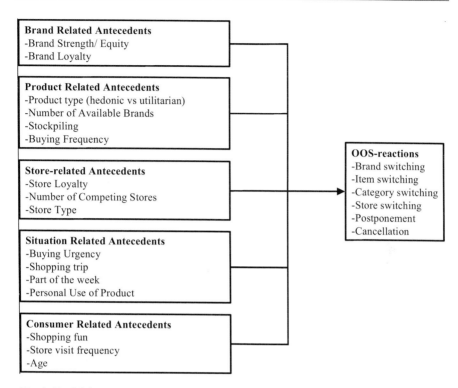

Fig. 1. Explaining OOS Reactions

A second important brand-related antecedent is *brand loyalty*. Whereas brand equity can be considered as a brand characteristic (that distinguishes between weak and strong brands), brand loyalty can be seen as brand strength at the consumer level. Many studies show that brand-loyal consumers are more likely to switch to another item of the desired brand or switch stores to buy the preferred item of the brand. Thus, retailers should aim to avoid OOS for brands with many brand-loyal consumers. Note, however, that brand loyalty correlates with brand strength measures, such as market share.

Product-Related Antecedents

Important product-related antecedents are the *hedonic level* of the product category and the *number of available brands* in the category. In *hedonic* categories, such as chips, beer, cola, and cigarettes, brands are more highly valued than in utilitarian categories, such as detergents and margarine. Therefore, negative consequences for the retailer of a brand being OOS occur more often in these categories. Similarly, the negative consequences of an OOS brand are greater in categories with *many available (differentiated) brands* because each brand typically fulfills a specific need of a consumer segment which cannot be satisfied by any of the available alternatives.

Conversely, the negative consequences for the retailer are reduced as the *number of available acceptable alternatives* increases, that is, if the OOS brand can easily be replaced by another competing brand available in the same store.

Another product-related antecedent of reactions to OOS is the *stockpile ability* of a product. In the cases of those products that can be and are easily stockpiled at home, e.g., coffee, detergents, and tissues, the most likely consumer reaction to an OOS is postponement or cancellation of the purchase as the consumer can continue to consume his/her inventory of the product.

Lastly, OOS responses can also depend on the *purchase frequency* of products. For products with a high purchase frequency, the purchase of an alternative, less preferred item is not so unattractive for consumers. In these categories, they will have to use or consume the less preferred item only for a short time period. However, for categories with a low purchase frequency the purchase of a different and less preferred item will have more enduring consequences. As a consequence, substitutes will be bought less often in categories with a low purchase frequency than in categories with a high purchase frequency.

Store-Related Antecedents

In the literature, several store-related variables have been introduced as antecedents of OOS responses. For instance, *store-loyal* customers are more likely to switch to another brand or item, rather than switch to another store to buy the preferred item or brand. Brand or item switching can also be expected to occur more often when the *number of available stores* in the neighborhood of the store with an OOS is low. The third variable is *store type*. In service supermarkets, consumers face more extensive assortments offering them more alternatives. Hence, substitutes are more likely to be purchased in these service supermarkets. However, we might also reason that service supermarkets' customers expect more service from a supermarket. Hence, they will be more dissatisfied in the case of an OOS, which might create more store switching.

Situation-Related Antecedents

Situation-related variables are those that relate to the consumer's purchase situation. One such antecedent variable is *purchase urgency*. Consumers are more likely to switch brands or items when the purchase is urgent. Also, the *type of shopping trip* is relevant. We distinguish between trips for weekly purchases and trips for daily purchases. Weekly purchases are rather time consuming. Hence, consumers are less likely to extend this time by switching stores. Not only the type of shopping trip, but also the *part of the week* when this trip is made is also important. When the shopping trip is at the end of the week, consumers are less likely to cancel the purchase of an OOS item than if it was at the beginning of the week (which still leaves an opportunity to make the purchase at the end of the week). Thus, retailers should attempt to minimize end-of-the-week OOS as otherwise they might lead to permanent purchase cancellation rather than just purchase postponement by a few days. A third situation-related antecedent of importance is whether or not the product is purchased for *personal use*. If it is purchased for someone else or for a specific situation (i.e., party), consumers are less likely to switch to a less preferred item or brand. For instance, if a consumer knows that visitors coming to a party prefer a specific brand of beer, such as Heineken, Warsteiner or Budweiser, s/he will not be inclined to switch to another brand.

Consumer-Related Antecedents

Consumer-related antecedents of OOS reactions include consumer psychographics and socio-demographic characteristics. For instance, researchers have reported more store-switching among consumers seeking more *shopping fun*. Consumers who like shopping do not mind visiting other stores as this has some value for them. Another characteristic is *store visit frequency*. Consumers who often visit stores will find it less difficult to postpone a purchase until their next visit, which will probably occur the next day. Finally, OOS responses are affected by *age*. Older consumers tend to have more time available than younger consumers. Hence, older consumers are generally more inclined to switch to another store than younger consumers.

Some Empirical Findings

We studied the appearance of OOS reactions in eight product categories [for an extensive discussion see Sloot, Verhoef, Franses (2005) and Sloot et al. (2004)]. We examined the general cross-category reactions as well the occurrence of reactions broken down by product category. These results are displayed in Table 1 and provide some interesting insights.

Table 1. OOS Reactions in Eight Product Categories

Product category	Substitute purchased			No substitute purchased		
	Brand switch	Item switch	Category switch	Store switch	Post-ponement	Cancella-tion
Crisps (*n*=91)	41%	21%	4%	9%	18%	8%
Cola (*n*=98)	26%	16%	4%	22%	31%	1%
Eggs (*n*=97)	58%	14%	3%	5%	19%	1%
Margarine (*n*=102)	20%	26%	0%	15%	36%	4%
Milk (*n*=94)	51%	14%	4%	15%	14%	2%
Beer (*n*=102)	43%	5%	0%	22%	27%	4%
Cigarettes (*n*=91)	11%	30%	0%	51%	8%	1%
Detergents (*n*=74)	24%	23%	0%	15%	31%	7%

The results in Table 1 clearly show that OOS responses vary with product category. For instance, for cigarettes, the majority of consumers state that they visit another store when their brand is OOS. However, for eggs, only 5 % would do this. Postponement occurs relatively more frequently for margarine, cola, detergents, and beer. All these categories can be stockpiled. Hence, customers might have some quantity of the item in stock at home at the time of the planned purchase.

Using the data reported in Table 1 and data on the antecedents as discussed in the preceding section, we set out to explain the OOS responses. In our analysis we focused on the most common responses: brand switching, store switching, item switching, and cancellation/postponement. Cancellation and postponement were combined as one reaction, as both mean no purchase. The results of this study are displayed in Table 2 and provide several interesting insights.

Table 2. Overview of Significant Antecedents of OOS Reactions in Study of Eight Product Groups

Antecedent	Brand switch	Store switch	Item switch	Cancel/ postpone
Brand related				
Brand strength	–	+	+	
Brand loyalty	–			
Product related				
Hedonic nature of product		+		
Number of alternatives	–	+	+	
Stockpiling		–	–	+
Purchase frequency				
Store related				
Store loyalty				
Number of stores				
Store type				
Situation related				
Buying urgency		+		–
Shopping trip				
Part of week			+	–
Personal use				
Consumer related				
Shopping fun				
Store visit frequency				
Age	–	+		

First, the most significant antecedents are brand- or product-related antecedents. Surprisingly, there are no significant store-related antecedents; also, the importance of situation-related and consumer-related antecedents is not very high. Theoretically, this is very interesting. This implies that consumers base their OOS reaction mainly on brand and product category characteristics, and store characteristics are not that important. That is, *brand- and product-related antecedents are much more important than store antecedents.* This also has important practical implications. Further, OOS responses vary between product categories and brands. Thus, for some brands and/or product categories, the consequences of OOS responses are less severe for the retailer than for other brands and/or categories. Hence, retailers may decide to focus their OOS minimization policies on particular product categories and/or brands. Second, the study reveals a rather important role for brand strength, which has a negative impact in terms of brand switching and exerts a positive effect in terms of store switching and item switching. Thus, strong brands still have such a strong consumer franchise that consumers stick with the brand even when it is OOS. This implies that brand manufacturers with strong brands still have negotiation power with their brands, as consumers are willing to switch stores even when the brand is only temporarily unavailable. For retailers, this implies that OOS is most problematic when it occurs for strong brands. Having brand-loyal customers does not help in this situation. Thus, retailers should try to minimize OOS for strong brands.

Implications for Retailers

Reduction of OOS. In general, retailers should be fully aware of the negative consequences of OOS, as these occur in approximately 45% of OOS occurrences. Thus, retailers should aim to minimize, if not avoid OOS. Theoretically, however, the negative impact of OOS may differ between products, brands, stores, situations, and consumers. Empirically, variations in OOS responses across product categories and brands are especially important. Therefore, retailers should consider their OOS reduction policies carefully. Retailers should determine for which categories and which brands minimizing OOS is especially important. Figure 2 displays an easy-to-use two-by-two matrix which indicates which strategies should be employed for different brand equity-product type combinations. In utilitarian categories, reduction of OOS of low-equity brands should not be a priority as these OOS have only a small negative impact for retailers. In fact, retailers may decide to simplify their assortment of low-equity brands in these categories. OOS should be reduced for high-equity brands in utilitarian categories. However, offering a large number of high-equity brands in these categories may create more inventorying problems, leading to more OOS. In order to reduce OOS, and the consumer annoyance that can result from this, retailers may decide to simplify the assortment of high-equity brands in these categories by de-listing a few brands. This may have some negative consequences which, however, may be mitigated by offering more alternatives under the remaining brand names. Note that this recommendation holds only for retailers with very extensive assortments. Retailers with limited assortments made up of only a few high-equity brands should be very careful about de-listing any of these brands. Next, low-equity or weak brands in hedonic categories require less attention while reducing OOS of high-equity brands in hedonic categories should always be a top priority.

OOS also requires more attention in categories with many brands and in categories with a high buying urgency such as cigarettes. Finally, retailers should also aim to reduce OOS at the end of the week, as OOS in this part of the week may more often result in cancellation of purchases.

In general, however, our key message is that retailers should aim to eliminate OOS completely, as it has strong negative sales consequences. This, however, might prove to be difficult. Despite the adoption of efficient consumer response (ECR) by many retailers, OOS is still a common phenomenon. New technology may perhaps be used in the future to completely avoid OOS. However, in many instances, OOS does not necessarily imply that the retailer is "out-of-business" for the consumer.

Table 3. Different OOS Strategies for Brands and Product Categories

	Utilitarian products	**Hedonic products**
Low-equity brands	• Low priority in reducing OOS occurrences • Simplify assortment of low-equity brands	• Medium priority in reducing OOS • Stock the main items of a wide variety of low-equity brands
High-equity brands	• High priority in reducing OOS • Simplify assortment by gradually reducing the number of listed high-equity brands • Extend the number of items of "surviving" high-equity brands	• Top priority in reducing OOS • Seek cooperation with main brand manufacturers to reduce OOS levels • Use caution in reducing allocated space and listed items for high-equity brands

(Source: Sloot, Verhoef, Franses 2005)

Policies to Mitigate Effects of OOS

Although several policies can be applied to reduce OOS levels, OOS will remain a common phenomenon in the next few years. There are several actions retailers can implement to mitigate negative OOS effects: One important action is the use of shelf announcements in which the retailer communicates to the customer that the product is OOS. A shelf announcement can be seen as an additional service to consumers. One might expect that such an announcement might rather exacerbate the negative effects of OOS. We interviewed some store managers on the use of announcements. They questioned their effectiveness. One disadvantage of them is that the OOS becomes more obvious to consumers, especially as it draws it to the attention of consumers who were not actually planning to purchase the product or brand that is OOS.

OOS announcements can provide different messages on the OOS:

- they can suggest other products, to increase item or brand switching;
- they can inform the customer of the approximate or exact time when the product or brand will be available again;
- they can apologize for the OOS;
- they can provide information on the reasons why the product or brand is OOS; and/or
- they can provide information on additional services or a promotion to compensate consumers for the inconvenience of the OOS. For instance, customers could be offered a coupon entitling them to a 50 % reduction on the item that is OOS when they next purchase it.

We investigated the use of OOS announcements in the "Cola" product category (for an extensive discussion see EFMI 2000). We interviewed 599 consumers on the use of these announcements. Approximately 50 % of the consumers believed that the announcement provided useful information. We also asked what information should be provided in the announcement? More than 50 % of the consumers preferred the expected time of availability and/or apologies for the inconvenience of the OOS. Almost half of the interviewed consumers also valued information on the reasons for the OOS. Approximately 30 % of the consumers preferred suggestions for an alternative product.

We also tested four announcements. It appeared that the majority of consumers did not notice the announcement. However, this clearly depends on the color of the announcements. Orange announcements worked pretty well, while white announcements were observed to have a much lesser effect. Our test also revealed that consumers appreciated OOS announcements that offered consumers coupons or an additional service, such as home delivery of the product that is OOS. We also investigated whether an OOS announcement created more satisfaction. Our results show, however, that categories without OOS announcements are rated significantly higher than categories in which OOS announcements are used. Thus, the effectiveness of OOS announcements might indeed be questioned. OOS announcements heighten awareness of the OOS among consumers, making it more obvious and probably creating more dissatisfaction. At least our results show that it is perhaps wiser not to inform the consumer; rather, the OOS should be corrected as soon as possible.

Policies to Reduce OOS Levels. As already noted, many retailers could benefit greatly from reducing OOS levels. In an extensive research project on OOS, the Coca Cola Retailing Research Council (1996) found that the majority of OOS occurrences were due to mistakes in stores, 70% of the OOSs having occurred because store employees had not ordered the product in the last order round. A more recent study by Roland Berger Consultants also reveals that buyer mistakes are the number one cause of high OOS levels. Frequent mistakes are:

- order size too small, faulty estimation of sales potential;
- assigned shelf space too small for the product/brand;
- "Gaps" on the shelf filled with other SKUs, so that the (potential) OOS situation has not been observed during visual inspection of the shelf by the store's staff and therefore no order was placed; and
- missing shelf tags, which causes store personnel to overlook the OOS situation.

The Coca Cola Retailing Research Council suggests several practical solutions for these mistakes:

- Do not leave gaps on the shelf. Store personnel can then see clearly when ordering of the product is necessary.
- Tell store personnel in which categories and instances OOS risks are very high (i.e., sales promotions, fast-moving items).
- Check regularly whether category plans have been correctly implemented and whether shelf tags are present.
- Create a database on sales of SKUs during the week and use past sales data to forecast sales. This is especially important during promotions. The famous SCANPRO model is one that might be used for this purpose.

As discussed, many mistakes are made when store personnel are responsible for ordering products and brands. An automated ordering system may overcome some of the problems. Pilot studies have shown that OOS levels can be substantially reduced by the use of such systems. Roland Berger Consultants (2002) claim that the OOS level can be reduced by 50% when manufacturers and retailers work closely together and retailers use an automated ordering system. A pilot study for the Dutch EDLP chain Jumbo has also yielded good results: In this study OOS levels decreased substantially, to levels below 2%.

There are also other supply chain-oriented techniques that may substantially decrease OOS levels (see, e.g., chapter by Huchzermeier, Iyer in this book). These techniques include:

- application of electronic data interchange (EDI) between retailers and suppliers. In a study in the US, when 31 retailers used EDI, this substantially lowered their OOS levels;

- use of continuous replenishment planning (CRP). Again in studies in the US, OOS levels were reduced for 55 % of the retailers applying CRP, while at the same time the inventory level of products was decreased by 32 %; and

- application of a cross-docking program; this appeared to reduce OOS substantially at ShopKo.

Future of OOS: 10 Years From Now. Given that pilot studies of several supply chain techniques have given positive results, we have expect that OOS can be reduced to a very low level in the future. With the increasing availability and quality of store level data, many retailers will adopt automatic store ordering systems which will result in substantial reductions in OOS.

An important new development in the context of OOS reduction is the use of RFID by manufacturers and retailers. It is important, however, that RFID tags are used for all individual products. RFID tags send electronic signals, which can be recognized by specialized systems. When RFID tags are available for each individual product, the inventory level of each product per store can be observed constantly throughout the day. This sounds very easy, but in practice it is difficult to establish. For instance, even traditionally unpackaged products, such as vegetables and meat, should have RFID tags when a customer has made his/her choice and has added the product to the basket. This is rather difficult to achieve. Note, however, that more and more products are packaged. Furthermore, it is important that there should be a perfect system that observes all products with RFID tags. This means there should be no products that can pass an RFID scanner unobserved. Another important issue is the placement of RFID tags in the package. In urban areas and large cities, thieves may try to get rid of the RFID tag in order not to be caught, especially when stealing expensive products such as razor blades, cigarettes, and personal care products. Thus, it is important that the RFID tags are attached to the product in such a way that it is almost impossible to get rid of the tags. Small RFID tags can be installed in the tops of bottles, for instance. Note that an important consequence of good use of RFID tags is that inventory losses due to theft should be eliminated. Theft is an important reason for OOS, as theft can cause brands to become OOS without being noticed by the retailer in the inventory system, leading to fewer orders than required. When retailers succeed in implementing a perfect system, the retailer has information on its inventory at both store and warehouse levels. This information is available in real time and, in order to reduce OOS even further, should be available to all parties in the supply chain. Suppliers can also use the real-time information to keep their inventories at a sufficient level to supply orders from the retailer on a just-in-time basis. When a smart automatic ordering system is used in the supply chain, fast-moving products can than be ordered on time and with the required order size.

The use of RFID tags combined with automatic ordering systems can thus substantially reduce OOS levels in the future. We are inclined to think that 10 years from now, OOS will hardly occur in modern retailing. However, this view is probably too optimistic. Although retailers should be able to reduce OOS substantially, there are still economic and practical issues that may function as a barrier. First, delivery of products to the stores will be fixed in time, to keep supply costs low. Thus, although the new system observes and/or predicts OOS perfectly, delivery of the required products may take some time. Second, retailers will keep optimizing their shelf space. An improved ordering system will probably cause retailers to reduce the number of facings of a product so as to create space for additional items in their assortment. As a consequence, shelf inventory decreases and the probability of an OOS situation increases. Keeping these caveats in mind, we still expect that the use of RFID by retailers in Western Europe and the use of automatic ordering systems will substantially reduce OOS levels in the future. On the basis of the pilot studies reported, we expect that the current level of approximately 7% will be reduced to approximately 3% to 4% by 2015.

Conclusion

This chapter has discussed an important topic in today's retailing: OOS. We have also briefly discussed the closely related topic of permanent assortment unavailability because of brand de-listings. Both discussions provide useful guidelines for retailers. It important for retailers to aim at reducing OOS, as it severely impacts store profitability. However, although OOS reduction is currently a top priority of retailers, future technological developments, such as the use of RFID, may reduce OOS levels substantially. As a consequence, it will become a less important issue in retailing in the next 10 years, at least insofar as our expectations become reality.

Note, finally, that the OOS literature also provides interesting insights into the consequences of brand de-listings by retailers. Brand de-listings mean permanent unavailability of a brand. These de-listings have become an important issue for many retailers, which are forced to increase ROI and to save costs as they are in competition with very cost-efficient discount chains. Our discussion shows that even temporary unavailability of a product can have severe negative consequences for the retailers. Permanent unavailability of brands can perhaps lead to permanent negative consequences, such as permanent losses in category and/or store sales. However, the scale of these negative consequences clearly depends on a number of factors, such as brand equity, remaining assortment size, and the assortment composition. The findings reported in the OOS literature can provide retailers with helpful suggestions on de-listing brands without consequences being too negative.

References

Campo, Kathia, Els Gijsbrechts and Patricia Nisol (2000): Towards Understanding Consumer Response to Stock Outs, Journal of Retailing, 76 (2), 219-242

Erasmus Food Management Institute (2000): Out-of-Stock, Out-of-Business?, Rotterdam: EFMI.

Keller, Kevin Lane (2002): Building, Measuring, and Managing Brand Equity, New Jersey, Pearson Education

Roland Berger Strategy Consultants (2002): Optimal Shelf Availability, presentation held at ECR Europe conference, Barcelona

Sloot, Laurens M., Peter C. Verhoef, Rocco Kellevink, Harry Commandeur, Ed Peelen (2004): "Het Verklaren van Consumentenreacties bij Out-of-Stock", Jaaboek van Marktonderzoek, Vrieseborgh, Haarlem, 101-118

Sloot, Laurens M., Peter C. Verhoef and Philip Hans Franses (2005): The Impact of Brand Equity and the Hedonic Level of Products on Consumer Stock-Out Reactions, Journal of Retailing, 81 (1), 15-34

Vergin, Roger C. and Kevin Barr (1999): Building Competitiveness in Grocery Supply Through Continuous Replenishment Planning: Insights from the Field, Industrial Marketing Management, 28 (2), 145-153.

Recent Trends and Emerging Practices in Retailer Pricing

Ruth N. Bolton[1], Venkatesh Shankar[2], and Detra Y. Montoya[3]

[1] W. P. Carey School of Business, Arizona State University, Tempe, USA
[2] Mays Business School, Texas A&M University, USA
[3] W. P. Carey School of Business, Arizona State University, Tempe, USA

Changing Retail Environment

Profitability in retailer pricing has become a paramount concern. Retailers, especially, grocery retailers, are operating on razor-thin margins. On average, a supermarket's margin is about one percent of net sales. A typical supermarket today is bigger than ever before, with several thousands of items – and, due to mergers and acquisitions, it is part of an even larger retail chain. Prices are set weekly on these items, so supermarkets are challenged to develop a coherent and profitable pricing strategy. Moreover, retailers receive trade allowances from manufacturers for promotional pricing. Pressured by competition and by consumers who have come to expect frequent price discounts, retailers have fallen into a price-promotion trap. Although only about 20 % of retail sales come from promotions, supermarkets devote about 80 % of their week managing them. The same retail pricing battle is being waged across department stores, convenience stores, and stores in other traditional retailing categories.

The current focus on profitable pricing strategies is also due to a changing retail landscape. Cross-channel consumer shopping is becoming increasingly common and is altering the pricing practices of many retailers. Competition across retail channels and formats such as grocery (e.g., Kroger), drug (e.g., Walgreens), mass merchandise (e.g., Wal-Mart), convenience and gas (e.g., 7 Eleven), club (e.g., Costco), and dollar (e.g., Dollar General) appears to be much more intense than ever before. Ongoing expansion by Wal-Mart's Supercenters, plus recent growth in club and dollar stores, has lowered the price floor in many markets and categories. Concurrently, the growth of dollar stores is challenging the dominance of the giant low-cost mass merchandiser, Wal-Mart. This phenomenon parallels the rise of low-cost competitors in other industries. For example, competition in the airline

M. Krafft and M.K. Mantrala (eds.), *Retailing in the 21st Century: Current and Future Trends*, 301
DOI 10.1007/978-3-540-72003-4_19, © Springer-Verlag Berlin Heidelberg 2010

industry has intensified with point-to-point airlines, such as Southwest Airlines and Jet Blue, stealing market share from the long standing hub-and-spoke airlines, such as United Airlines and Delta Airlines.

The goal of this chapter is to outline the trends in the retailers' macro-environment, discuss current retailer pricing, and derive implications for emerging pricing practices. The chapter is organized in the following way. First, we describe four environmental trends: retail consolidation, changing manufacturer practices, advances in technology and innovation, and the emergence and growth of e-tailing. We discuss how each of these environmental factors has influenced current retailer pricing practices. Second, with regard to current retailer pricing, we address two key questions: How prevalent are discount prices or "every day low price" strategies? What retailer pricing strategies are successful in today's competitive markets? Our investigation of these questions yields a typology of current pricing practices. Third, we argue that our analysis of current pricing practices suggest that retailers are moving toward an approach we call "customized pricing." This approach requires each retailer to build a coherent strategy for its products based on its strategic position in the marketplace. Last, we close by predicting the widespread adoption of customized pricing as marketplace trends make it increasingly profitable.

Retail Consolidation and Its Effects on Retailer Pricing

Consolidation and Retail Formats. Mergers and acquisitions (M&A) have resulted in the consolidation of retail chains, thereby substantially altering the retail competitive arena. Driven by Wal-Mart's dominance as the top grocery retailer in the US, acquisitions have continued to define the retail industry. The recent sale of Albertsons and their Sav-on/Osco stores (now owned by Supervalu and CVS, respectively) is just another example of the ongoing grocery industry consolidation trend. Consequently, the effects of consolidation on retail formats have varied substantially. In some cases, mergers involving retailers with the same format have resulted in retailers with a single dominant format and brand name. For example, CVS drugstore chain has renamed and reformatted all the stores acquired from Eckerd drugstore chain as CVS stores with a CVS format. In some other cases, different retail brand names and formats have been preserved. For example, Safeway has retained the Randalls retail brand name and style after acquiring all the Randalls stores.

Why Consolidation? The financial rationale for consolidation is that retailers can maintain or strengthen their competitive positions in the marketplace by increasing their size, thereby lowering costs (by improving their bargaining position vis-a-vis manufacturers), expanding revenues from consumers and markets, and gaining market share across channels and formats. For example, the newly merged Kmart-Sears retailer may be able to compete more effectively against the retailing behemoth, Wal-Mart on costs by improving the bargaining position with manufacturers through scale economies.

Consolidation facilitates retailers' efforts to streamline their offerings and extend their reach. The replacement of the Eckerd brand by the CVS brand in drugstores enables CVS to leverage its more popular brand name and efficient store format in expanded markets, and thus compete more aggressively against Walgreens, its leading drugstore competitor chain.

A third reason for consolidation is to become more attractive to customers by offering a wider assortment than competing retailers. For example, Federated's merger with May Department stores has increased its selection and broadened its customer base.

Last, consolidation helps improve the profitability of retailers by increasing the distribution of retailers' higher margin private label offerings vis-à-vis national brands. For example, in Switzerland, five retailers account for 88% of the grocery market after consolidation. Consequently, Switzerland also has the highest share of private labels (38%) in the grocery industry among all developed nations.

The Effect of Consolidation on Retailer Pricing Practices. How does consolidation affect retailers' pricing strategies? Retailers span more markets and channels, but their increased span of control challenges them to manage multiple formats or integrate (or even eliminate) multiple systems. As a result, consolidated retailers' decision making is more centralized, whereby strategic distribution, pricing, and merchandising decisions are set at corporate headquarters and handed down to each division.

At the same time, however, consolidation is forcing retailers to address the unique challenges of market-specific competition and clientele for each retail division or format in their pricing strategy. Retail divisions and formats must concurrently manage their business within corporate guidelines and remain competitive in their respective markets. Within each division and format, individual stores are faced with the challenge of simultaneously complying with corporate mandates and being competitive within their trade areas. Successful retailers appear to be delicately balancing these apparently conflicting needs of local versus corporate pricing, division versus store level pricing autonomy, chain versus store level pricing and promotional tools to remain competitive.

How Changing Manufacturer Practices Influence Retailer Pricing

How Manufacturers' Account Management Practices Influence Retailer Prices. Post-retailer consolidation, manufacturers have treated retailer pricing as a chainwide coordinated strategic variable. By focusing on a single buyer for an entire chain, they are able to sell more efficiently with fewer account managers. The end result is that manufacturers direct their selling efforts at the corporate headquarters level, rather than at the market or store level. Retailers typically appoint a specific manufacturer as "captain" for each major category. They rely on the consumer behavior analysis and pricing recommendations of the category captain. Since category captains are likely to make pricing recommendations at the corporate headquarters level, retailers frequently develop chain-wide pricing guidelines for the category. Retailers expect manufacturers' representatives to possess the skills and resources to deliver business-building information and share category goals and objectives. However, manufacturers may not be knowledgeable about multiple retail formats, market and store differences that are relevant to the development of a coherent pricing strategy for the retailer.

Consequences of Trade Promotions on Retailer Prices. The grocery industry relies heavily on manufacturer's trade allowances or promotional funds, which account for about 54 % of the marketing dollars. Trade allowances have traditionally been used to adjust pricing and support promotions at the retail level. Manufacturers provide trade funds to the retailers in the form of either scan-back allowances, wherein reimbursement is based on units sold by the retailer, or as off-invoice allowances, whereby reimbursement is based on units purchased by the retailer. Manufacturers typically dislike off-invoice allowances because they may lead to forward buying or diverting, rather than supporting their brands. In fact, retailers are not required to pass along trade discounts to the consumer, and studies have shown that retailers pass through only a fraction of their trade allowances, typically discounting leading brands to draw store traffic.

Promotion inefficiencies, combined with the conflicting objectives of manufacturers and retailers, make it likely that trade allowances will be decreased, or regulated or eliminated. Wal-Mart already forgoes all allowances and negotiates a lower total price or "dead net cost". However, its aggressive tactics have been difficult for other retailers to imitate, fueling their disenchantment with trade allowances. For example, Safeway attempted to use "dead net cost" with a few manufacturers, but encountered great resistance from them. Federated has opted to dramatically reduce the number of coupons distributed in order to focus on "everyday value."

Supermarkets' heavy reliance on trade allowances has also made it difficult for them to calculate their true SKU costs, making price wars an unattractive option in the current environment. Hence, the use of promotional dollars can be disadvantageous for grocery retailers wishing to compete on price. However, promotions do allow retailers to highlight their strengths vis-à-vis their competitors.

Given the conflicting objectives of manufacturers and retailers and the differences in trade allowances across retailers, the development of an effective pricing strategy has eluded retailers in many categories and with different formats. Consider the situation in toy retailing. Toy retailers include specialty retailers, who carry a variety of toys, and discounters, who carry a smaller assortment at very low prices. Toys 'R' Us is the leading toy specialty retailer and Wal-Mart is the leading toy discounter (as well as the leading toy seller). In 2004, two major specialty retailers, FAO Schwartz, a small chain selling premium toys and KB Toys, a national chain with over 750 stores, declared bankruptcy. More recently, the profitability of Toys 'R' Us has faltered. Thus, specialty toy retailers have not been able to effectively compete on price with mass merchandiser or discounters.

How Advances in Technology and Innovation Influence Retail Pricing

Adoption of Price Optimization Software. Information management and supply chain management helped by technological advances, have driven retailers' costs down. In the 1990's, supply chain tools helped improve efficiencies in the flow of goods, but did not always ensure that retailers have the right merchandise, in the right stores, at the right price, at the right time. Retailers traditionally relied on rules-based pricing decisions, such as a percentage markup or seasonal pricing. More recently, retailers have embraced optimization methods such as retail merchandise optimization, price optimization, retail revenue management. Price optimization software predicts demand for individual products based on historical price and sales data, competitive pricing, local demographics, inventory, and promotional data.

Today, retailers are challenging traditional "rules" of pricing with prices generated from statistical modeling and data mining. The use of price optimization software has increased gross margin dollars on markdown items for many retailers. Price-optimization software can also help retailers manage non-negotiated prices on seasonal items, recommending when to reduce prices and when to sell products at full price. For example, Whole Foods Market has recently deployed a price-optimization tool across its Southern division.

Pricing Implications for Different Retail Formats and Stores. The shift toward data and technology driven pricing approach, vis-à-vis approaches based on "experience" or "hunch" has been a cultural change for many retailers. Retailers may feel they are losing control when prices are set by computer software. Some retailers are still relying on a blended centralized, rules-based pricing strategy. One argument against price optimization is the potential negative effect on market share. Many retailers fear that the differences in prices across items within a product line (i.e., flavors) may confuse the consumers and possibly drive down sales.

How the Emergence of E-Tailers Is Influencing Retailer Pricing

The explosive growth in Internet usage has led to the rapid emergence of e-tailing. In addition to many "pure" e-tailers, many traditional or bricks-and-mortar retailers now use the Internet as an important channel. For example, Nordstrom's is expecting a 25% increase in direct, mostly online, sales for 2006. Multi-channel shopping is also emerging as a key phenomenon in consumer shopping behavior. These changes have spawned stream of research on relative prices of the online and offline channels and on online price dispersion, defined as the distribution of prices (such as range and standard deviation) of an item with the same measured characteristics across sellers of the item at a given point in time (See Pan, Ratchford, and Shankar 2004 for a review). Higher price dispersion within and across retail channels, including the Internet, reflects market inefficiency and greater perception of differences among retailers by consumers.

Many studies show that online price dispersion is at least as high as offline price dispersion (e.g., Ancarani and Shankar 2004). Numerous factors contribute to online price dispersion, including variability in e-tailer service attributes (e.g., shopping convenience, product information, shipping and handling), e-tailer visibility and reputation, market characteristics (e.g., number of competitors, time of online market entry), and category characteristics. Interestingly, e-tailer service quality attributes explain only a portion of online price dispersion and market characteristics are important drivers of price dispersion (Pan Shankar and Ratchford 2003). Price dispersion has remained persistent online, narrowing over time (Pan, Shankar, and Ratchford 2003; Ratchford, Pan and Shankar 2003). Despite the introduction and growth in use of online shopbots, prices have not converged and online markets remain inefficient.

Multi-channel shoppers constitute an important segment of shoppers for the retailers. They tend to buy more often, buy more items, and spend more than shoppers using only one channel. They are also typically younger, more educated and affluent. There is mixed evidence on the relative prices of the same item at pure e-tailers, traditional stores and multi-channel retailers. Ancarani and Shankar (2004) found that although listed prices were lower online, prices adjusted for shipping costs were higher online. Multi-channel retailers have higher average prices than pure play e-tailers, regardless whether the price is posted price or full price, including shipping costs.

Overall, it appears that there are sufficient differences across channels and by price type (list or full price) that retailers can differentiate themselves and price effectively across channels. This is evident when we consider how retailers operating in traditional channels have responded to competitive pressures by creating consumer-friendly, in-store experiences through customized product assortments, an emphasis on customer service and attractive atmospherics. Both Wegmans, a 77-store eastern *U.S. supermarket* chain, and Trade Joe's, a specialty grocery chain with 271 stores located most densely in Southern California, have been very successful in differentiating themselves and pricing effectively. Many of Wegmans' newer stores offer a large square footage, an extensive variety of foods aimed at an upscale clientele and a Market Cafe with in-store dining areas. Trader Joe's sells *gourmet* foods, *organic foods*, *vegetarian food*, unusual *frozen foods*, imported foods, domestic and imported *wine*, and "alternative" food items – as well as basics like bread, cereal, and eggs – and features a South Seas decor. (Interestingly, it is currently owned by a family *trust* set up by German *billionaire Theo Albrecht*, one of the two brothers behind *ALDI*.)

How Channel Blurring Is Affecting Retailer Pricing

Channel Blurring: What and Why?

Channel blurring is the phenomenon in which the distinctions between retail channels or formats are getting blurred due to changes in both the supply and demand conditions (Luchs, Inman and Shankar 2006). On the supply side, many retailers are moving beyond their traditional product assortments to stocking and selling newer product categories. On the demand side, more customers are patronizing alternative channels than before.

Channel blurring is occurring due to several reasons. From the supply standpoint, retailers that are successful in one format are transferring their competencies to another format.

For example, Wal-Mart has moved from a sole mass merchandiser format to include a grocery format through its Neighborhood stores. Furthermore, some retailers have expanded their stores, creating supercenters. Increases in store size lead to shelf space opportunities, enabling them to stock and sell more products. Finally, competitive pressure is forcing retailers to change to a broader, more profitable or traffic-inducing product mix.

From the demand perspective, for a given category, consumers are shopping at more channels, including the dollar and club channels more than before. Segments of consumers are also engaging in cherry-picking behavior across retail channels. Time pressure is causing more consumers to "shop-at-sight" and use shopping lists less often. Therefore, retailers are carrying broader product assortments.

Effects of Channel Blurring on Retailer Pricing

Channel blurring has important effects on the prices and pricing practices of retailers. Individuals and households are increasingly using multiple channels to buy the same product. There is greater opportunity for consumers to compare prices across channels and consumers use prices at different channels as reference prices for a product in a particular channel. As a result, in a product category like facial tissues, the share of grocery stores is declining at the expense of mass merchandise and warehouse club, and dollar stores (Luchs et al. 2006). There is increased price competition among retail channels. The average grocery store manager now bases prices in his store on the prices prevailing at nearby drug club, and dollar stores, in addition to those at the closest grocery stores.

Because of channel blurring, a store in one retail format or channel can now use a particular product associated with another channel as a traffic builder, offering rock-bottom prices on that product. This practice is creating pricing pressure for retailers across all channels. However, such a practice is also creating pricing premium opportunities for non-promoted products that might now be more available across all the channels due to channel blurring. A retailer needs to do a careful

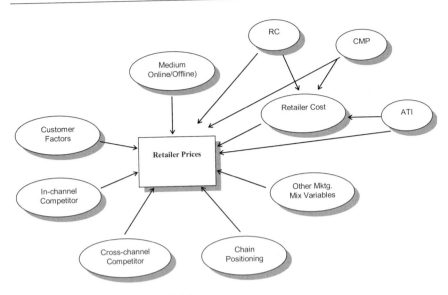

Fig. 1. A Framework of Retailer Pricing

RC = Retail Consolidation; CMP = Changing Manufacturer Practices; ATI = Advances in Technology and Innovation

analysis of channel blurring and the shopping patterns in its market to come up with sound pricing policy for all its products.

The different influences on retailer pricing can be captured by a framework shown in Figure 1. As discussed before, retail consolidation, changing manufacture practices, advances in technology directly affect both retailer cost and prices. In addition, the medium or channel (Internet vs. offline), other marketing mix variables such as advertising and promotion, customer factors, positioning of the retailer, and competition within and across channels or store formats influence retailer prices.

Current Pricing Practices

The preceding discussion of the changes in the retailing landscape leads to two key questions about current pricing practices:

1. How prevalent are discount pricing or "every day low price" strategies?

2. What retailer pricing strategies are successful in today's competitive markets?

Conventional wisdom is that most retailers use one of two store-wide pricing strategies: "EDLP or "HiLo". An EDLP policy involves offering consistently low prices on many brands and categories and is often perceived to be practiced by some supermarket chains (e.g., Food Lion and Lucky), as well as by Wal-Mart (Shankar and Krishnamurthi 1996). A HiLo policy is characterized by steep temporary price discounts with higher "regular" prices for many brands and categories, and is typically perceived to be practiced by supermarkets such as Kroger and Safeway. However, retailers are being forced to reexamine their traditional pricing strategies to survive in the new retail landscape. Innovations in information technology and supply chain management and centralized buying have significantly reduced retailer costs, and lower costs enable retailers to offer consistently lower prices than before. These trends suggest a movement toward an EDLP policy. However, many retailers seem to be following a Hi-Lo pricing policy, offering price discounts in response to competitive price pressure – even when lower prices don't reflect lower costs.

It is also widely believed that retailers' pricing decisions are primarily driven by the principles of category management. Category management, identified as one of the four strategies of the efficient consumer response (ECR) initiative in the early 1990s, has evolved over time in different retail chains. Under category management, a retailer first identifies the roles of the different categories, such as destination, support, and ideal roles. For each category, the retailer decides its pricing policy based on its role. Further, the retailer decides prices and promotions for the brands in the category to maximize the profits for the category, given the pricing policy for the category. While category management principles are still in vogue, retailer pricing has become more complex and increasingly customized. Surprisingly, successful retailers use an arsenal of different strategies, such as exclusive pricing, moderately promotional pricing, and aggressive pricing strategies, that are customized to fit brand, category, and market conditions, according to a large-scale empirical study of US supermarkets (Bolton and Shankar 2003; Shankar and Bolton 2004).

Conventional wisdom also suggests that retailers should customize their pricing to the store clientele's price sensitivity, and researchers have studied the determinants of consumer price sensitivity (Bolton 1989a, 1989b; Shankar and Krishnamurthi 1996). However, research by Bolton and Shankar (2003) and by Shankar and Bolton (2004) also reveals that successful retailers customize prices by many other factors, including competitor prices and deals, brand strength, and category storability. The remainder of this section summarizes the findings from their two studies (hereafter called "S&B"). The trends in the retailing environment have accelerated this movement toward customized pricing.

Five Retailer Pricing Strategies

S&B analyzed data from over 200 grocery stores in 17 chains, including Lucky, Dominicks, Jewel Osco, Safeway and Food Lion, in five markets in the United States of America (USA), as well as interviewed product managers and store managers. Data were collected from three large cities (New York City, Los Angeles, Chicago) because they represent a diverse sample of chains and stores (both large and small), and two moderate-sized cities (Pittsfield, Massachusetts and Marion, Indiana) because they are demographically representative of the population of the USA. The product categories studied – spaghetti sauce, bathroom tissue, liquid bleach, ketchup, mouthwash and frozen waffles – represent a diverse range of product categories. Altogether, 1364 brand-store combinations from six categories of consumer packaged goods in five U.S. markets over a two year time period were studied.

Unlike prior research, S&B developed measures of retailers' pricing strategies specific to the brand-store combination rather than chain-wide or store-wide measures. They also measured retailer pricing decisions for a given brand and store combination using continuous measures rather than viewing pricing policy as a dichotomous decision (EDLP or HiLo). Moreover, they considered promotion or deal intensity (i.e., frequency of displays or newspaper features) and the coordination of promotions with price are important aspects of retailer pricing decisions. Thus, S&B characterized store-level pricing decisions for brands along four independent dimensions: price consistency, promotion or deal intensity, price-promotion coordination or support, and relative brand price within the category.

Retailer pricing strategies can be characterized as combinations of the four independent pricing dimensions, where each dimension is a separate continuum. They discovered that, although chains and stores may use EDLP and HiLo as positioning or signaling strategies, retailers actually practice five different pricing strategies at the brand-store level: Exclusive, Moderately Promotional, HiLo, EDLP, and Aggressive pricing strategies. Table 1, adapted from Bolton and Shankar (2003), shows a description of each strategy as a combination of the four underlying pricing dimensions. It also shows the distribution of brand-store combinations across the five clusters on each of the pricing dimensions. Each of the brand/store combinations were classified as high, medium (average) or low on each of the four pricing dimensions based on their median scores.

HiLo and EDLP Strategies Are Practiced at the Brand-Store Level, Not the Chain Level. Pricing strategies that are roughly equivalent to HiLo Pricing and EDLP Pricing are used by about half (56 %) the brand-store combinations in our database. A HiLo Pricing strategy (11 %) is characterized by average relative price, high price variation, high deal intensity, and high deal support. This strategy is comparable to a storewide HiLo pricing strategy, albeit at the brand-store level, with a combination of dimensions and levels that seems intended to make a retailer competitive with its rivals through promotions. An EDLP pricing strategy (45 %) consists of average relative price, low price variation, moderate deal intensity, and moderate deal support. This strategy is comparable to a storewide EDLP strategy, albeit at the brand-store level. This combination of dimensions seems intended to offer value to customers.

Table 1. Pricing Strategies and Mean Scores on Dimensions (Clustering by Brand-Store)

Pricing dimensions / Pricing strategy (% prevalent)	*Relative price*	*Price variation*	*Deal intensity*	*Deal support*
Exclusive pricing (8%)	High	Medium	Low	Low
Moderately promotional pricing (14%)	Average	Medium	Medium	Medium
HiLo pricing (11%)	Average	High	High	High
EDLP (45%)	Average	Low	Medium	Medium
Aggressive pricing (22%)	Low	High	Low	Medium

(Source: Bolton and Shankar 2003, "An Empirically Derived Taxonomy of Retailer Pricing Strategy," Journal of Retailing)

An Aggressive Pricing Strategy is Commonly Adopted. Aggressive pricing is not reported in the business press – but it is utilized by nearly one fourth (22%) of all brand store combinations. It entails offering low prices and medium deal support, accompanied by high price variation and low-medium deal intensity. In other words, price, rather than deals (i.e., features or displays) is the key weapon used for competing. This previously unknown strategy can explain apparently "inconsistent" behavior observed in the market place, such as when a chain that claims to practice an EDLP strategy offers less stable prices (for some categories) than a chain that is considered to practice a HiLo strategy for brands in the same category. Chains that are positioned as EDLP chains may appear (superficially) inconsistent for some brands and categories – but they have simply tailored their overall strategy to recognize differences in consumer demand and competition within and across categories.

EDLP pricing and Aggressive pricing are the most commonly adopted pricing strategies at a brand-store level. This finding reflects the competitive nature of the retailing landscape.

Moderately Promotional and Exclusive Pricing Strategies are Practiced. Moderately promotional pricing – corresponding to an undifferentiated strategy – is also fairly common (14%). In contrast, Exclusive pricing is the least adopted strategy (8%). Since it is characterized by low deal intensity, low deal support and a high brand premium, this strategy can only be profitable for a small number of brands. It may be only appropriate for brands with high brand equity and manufacturer advertising.

How Retailers Should Approach Pricing

Retailers require new pricing practices to create and sustain a competitive advantage in the marketplace. After studying successful retailers' pricing practices, Bolton, Shankar and Montoya (2005) claim that a new approach has emerged, which they call "customized pricing." This approach requires retailers to build a coherent strategy for its products based on its strategic position in the marketplace, just as a house is built by following an architectural plan that has been customized to a particular geographic site (See Figure 2 from Bolton, Shankar, and Montoya 2005). The rest of this section is a reproduction and adaptation of their work.

Successful retailers have developed many different pricing practices that are neither chain nor store-wide, such as EDLP or HiLo (See Table 2). Instead, their strategies are customized to take into account additional factors such as competitive activity, brand strength, and category storability. The implementation of customized pricing is based on the following steps: (1) Understand key drivers of store pricing; (2) Segment market by store format and channel; (3) Neutralize price as a competitive weapon; (4) Manage promotion intensity to avoid head-to-head competition; (5) Create distinctive categories; and (6) Tailor prices by market, category, customer, competitor, and brand.

Understand the Key Drivers of Retail Pricing

The first step is to identify the key determinants of pricing relevant to a particular retailer. These determinants can be classified under several broad classes of factors: market, chain, store, category, manufacturer/brand, customer and competitive retailer. Under each factor, a number of variables could potentially influence retailer pricing. For example, among chain factors, chain positioning and chain size could be important determinants for a retailer. Similarly, under competitor factors, the deal frequency and price level of competitive retailers in the same channel, those of retailers from other channels in the geographic neighborhood could be driving retailer prices for a retailer. A retailer could use point of sale store level scanner data over the past several weeks to determine the key factors that drive prices at its store and other stores.

Segment by Store Format and Store Cluster

After competitor factors, category and chain factors are the factors that most influence retailer pricing strategy. A retailer tends to coordinate price and promotion when the store is located in metropolitan cities (as opposed to smaller cities), and when it is part of a large chain or a chain that is positioned as having a HiLo strategy. Price promotion coordination is greater for brands in large stores and with large category assortments. Price promotion coordination is likely to yield greater

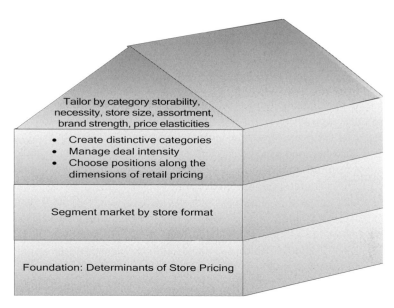

Fig. 2. The Architecture of Retail Pricing

(Bolton, Shankar, and Montoya "Building a Profitable Retailer Pricing Strategy – From the Ground-Up," Working Paper, 2005)

Table 2. Customized vs. Conventional Retailer Pricing

	Conventional Retailer Pricing	Customized Retailer Pricing
Types	•EDLP, and HiLo pricing	•Includes Exclusive, Moderately promotional, Aggressive pricing in addition to EDLP and HiLo
Key Determinants	•Market price sensitivity •Costs	•Competitor prices, deals •Brand strength •Category storability •Customer price sensitivity •Store size and assortment......
Key Steps	•Determine category role •Price destination categories low •Decide on discounts for each category, brand	•Identify key determinants of pricing in the market •Segment market by store format •Choose strategies along four key dimensions •Manage deal intensity •Create distinctive categories •Tailor by brand......
Advantages/Limitations	•Spend most time in deciding and executing promotions •Unprofitable when competitors discount	•Based on a balanced set of factors •Not overly dependent on discounts
Focus	•Discounts, promotions and final prices on myriads of brands every week	•Overall store profitability •A coherent pricing policy •Non-price attributes
Time Horizon	•Short and Medium-term •Tactical orientation	•Long-term •Strategic orientation

(Source: Bolton, Shankar, and Montoya, 2005, "Building a Profitable Retailer Pricing Strategy – From the Ground-Up," Working Paper)

benefits in such situations due to the large scale of retail operations. These observations suggest that a successful retailer segments its stores by format (e.g., Kroger, Dillon, Fry's and Ralph's are four store formats operated by the same retailer) and by store cluster (e.g., upscale, ethnic). Variable pricing can then be applied to each format and cluster by varying markups on items and/or categories to attract targeted customers to their stores. At the same time, retailers should take into account chain size and store size. Larger chains and stores have scale economies and cost efficiencies that enable them to price and promote more aggressively.

Position Along Key Pricing Dimensions and Neutralize Price as a Competitive Issue

Retail competition comes from multiple channels (supermarkets, mass-markets stores, club stores, convenience stores, online stores, etc) and it has a pervasive influence on retailers' pricing decisions. However, although competition has a dominant influence, retailer pricing decisions are also influenced by category characteristics (e.g., storability and necessity), chain positioning and size, store size and assortment, brand preference and advertising and customer factors (e.g., price sensitivity). When these factors come into play, retailers have some pricing latitude – and they should exploit them by positioning along these factors! The key to neutralizing price is to set competitive price points on "known value items" (that have high household penetration, large annual purchases and high purchase frequency) and feature or display them. On other items, it may be possible to obtain a small (say, five to nine) percent premium over mass-market prices and still maintain share.

Manage the Intensity of Promotions to Avoid Head-to-Head Competition

The intensity of retailer promotions and the extent of price-promotion coordination depends on the market type, chain size, chain positioning, store size, category assortment, storability, necessity, brand preference, relative brand advertising own deal elasticity, cross price elasticity, and cross deal elasticity. Retailer pricing and promotion strategies were less coordinated for storable categories and more coordinated for necessity categories. In contrast, price promotion coordination is also higher when consumers are less own-price and own-deal inelastic yet still willing to switch.

Retailers need not match competitors' price and deal decisions if a product is not a known value item. Instead, they should look for categories and brands that present opportunities to build store traffic and loyalty, etc. For example, retailers seem to use higher price-promotion intensity and coordination for necessity categories, for brands with high preferences, and in markets where consumers are price insensitive, but can still be enticed to switch. Trade promotion management software may help monitor promotion effectiveness (Kontzer 2004).

Create Distinctive Categories

Retailers must differentiate their categories from competing retailers through distinctive product assortments. A large category assortment is associated with price inconsistency and less intensive promotion – but high levels of coordination of price with promotions and low relative prices. Retailers targeting price sensitive shoppers typically carry a greater assortment of brands in a given category and promotional elasticities are lower for categories with more brands, so a retailer with a large assortment can more effectively utilize its resources by reducing promotions, but closely coordinating price and promotion activities. Highly storable and necessary categories such as bathroom tissue have high price-promotion intensity. Thus, they can serve as a "traffic builders," which tend to be promoted more intensely. In contrast, perishable categories such as ketchup and spaghetti sauce may require a more consistent pricing strategy to steadily rotate the inventory. Household necessities have lower price consistency and higher price-promotion intensity than non-essential categories.

Tailor Prices to Customers, Brands, and Stores

Retailers charge lower prices when consumers are more own-price elastic and less own-deal elastic. This observation may explain why pricing decisions differ across stores in the same chain – individual outlets may have different clienteles. Which brands should be promoted together? Which brands does your clientele respond to? Prices are typically lower when brand preference and relative brand advertising are lower, and when chains position themselves as EDLP rather than HiLo stores. At the same time, retailers seem to be flexible. For example, they may choose to be less price consistent for brands in discretionary (non-storable, non-essential) categories where it is possible for price changes to stimulate increases in primary demand (rather than simply stockpiling).

Pricing Strategies in the Future

In the preceding section, we described how current pricing practices seem to reflect a fundamental change in retailers' approach to pricing, namely the emergence of customized pricing. We believe that customized pricing will be increasingly adopted by retailers in the coming years. However, we also predict that customized pricing will become increasingly profitable due to the following four trends.

Evolution Away from Traditional Trade Allowances

Both manufacturers and retailers realize the undesirability of current trade allowance practices. Retailers are interested in shifting away from trade deals and towards dead net costs, so that they can assess the effectiveness of price and promotions. However, this shift won't lead to a wide scale adoption of EDLP pricing practices. Instead, pricing strategies that reflect different competitive positions – accompanied by unique differential advantages – are likely to emerge in the marketplace. For example, recent research examined 48 announcements of retailer customer service strategies and their relationship to shareholder wealth (Wiles 2007). It found that there were significant financial returns (i.e., abnormal returns of 1.09 percent, on average) arising from credible announcements of a shift in a retailer's customer service strategy. This value is sufficiently high (compared to studies of other strategies) to suggest that service is one of the more profitable competitive positioning strategies available to retailers.

Retailers will develop a better understanding of their unique features (scale, product assortment, service, and so forth) for which customers are willing to pay, and alter their pricing practices accordingly. The conversion to dead net cost – required to implement more sophisticated pricing practices – may not be easy for traditional retailers. However, software systems offered by outside suppliers may be particularly useful during the transition period.

Increased Adoption of Pricing Customized to Local Market Conditions

Retailer pricing software tends to ignore the pricing activities of competing retailers and clientele characteristics. We predict that retailers will eventually adopt customized or variable pricing – albeit relying on sophisticated pricing software, rather than intuition and pricing heuristics – to respond to market conditions. We predict that future pricing practices will reflect a better balance between the cost efficiencies obtained over the past decade and the revenue benefits that can be derived from increased flexibility to respond to local market conditions. Further, we expect grocery retailers to continue testing "personalized pricing" within the context of their loyalty programs.

Greater Pricing Flexibility

In the future, retailers will be less price consistent for brands in "discretionary" (non-storable, non-essential) categories where it is possible for price changes to stimulate increases in primary demand (rather than simply encourage stockpiling). We expect that, as pricing software allows more sophisticated strategies, retailers will exhibit increasing flexibility across brands, categories and stores – as well as over time. The use of electronic shelf labels (ESL) is sometimes offered as an example of how retailers are trying to improve customer service. However, they also enable retailers to change prices on any item at anytime – based on the time of day, week, season, competition or even current weather conditions. Although the implementation of ESL has been slow based on costs, electronic labels may be a glimpse into the future of the execution of in-store pricing.

More Multi-channel Price Consistency

Retailers are interested in optimizing prices on each item across channels: Internet, bricks-and-mortar stores, and catalogs (or through direct mail). A few studies have examined retailer pricing practices across multiple channels (e.g., Ancarani and Shankar 2004; Pan, Ratchford, and Shankar 2005). They indicate that there are ample opportunities for retailers to differentiate themselves from one another and compete on non-price attributes. Hence, despite price dispersion across retailers within a channel and across channels, we believe that the same retailer will price consistently across its different channels.

Summary

The retail landscape is being significantly altered by retail consolidations, changes in manufacturer practices, advances in technology, the emergence of e-tailing, and channel blurring. In this new retailing environment, there is a renewed emphasis on profitable pricing strategies. We have described the effects of these trends on retailer pricing and analyzed successful pricing strategies, which point to the increasing use of customized pricing practice. A customized retailer pricing strategy based on a six-step pricing architecture might be useful for retailers. In the future, we anticipate a movement away from heavy trade allowances, increased customization to local conditions, greater pricing flexibility, and more multi-channel consistency of retailer pricing.

References

Ancarani, Fabio and Venkatesh Shankar (2004): Price Levels and Price Dispersion Within and Across Multiple Retailer Types: Further Evidence and Extension, Journal of Academy of Marketing Science, 32 (2), 176-187.

Bolton, Ruth N. (1989a): Relationship between Market Characteristics and Promotional Price Elasticities, Marketing Science, 10 (1), 24-39.

Bolton, Ruth N. (1989b): The Robustness of Retail-Level Price Elasticity Estimates, Journal of Retailing, 65 (2), 193-218.

Bolton, Ruth N. and Venkatesh Shankar (2003): An Empirically Driven Taxonomy of Retailer Pricing and Promotion Strategies, Journal of Retailing, 79 (4), 213-224.

Bolton, Ruth N. and Venkatesh Shankar and Detra Montoya (2005): Building a Profitable Retailer Pricing Strategy – From the Ground-Up, Working Paper, Arizona State University, Tempe, AZ.

Luchs, Ryan, J. Jeffrey Inman, and Venkatesh Shankar (2006): Channel Blurring: An Analysis of Retail Marketing Structure, Presentation at the Marketing Science Conference, Pittsburgh.

Pan, Xing, Brian T. Ratchford and Venkatesh Shankar (2002). Can Price Dispersion in Online Markets be Explained by Differences in e-tailer Service Quality? Journal of the Academy of Marketing Science, 30 (4): 443-456.

Pan, Xing, Brian T. Ratchford and Venkatesh Shankar (2004): Price Dispersion on the Internet: A Review and Directions for Future Research, Special Issue on Online Pricing, Journal of Interactive Marketing, 18 (4).

Pan, Xing, Venkatesh Shankar, and Brian T. Ratchford (2002): Price Competition Between Pure Play vs. Bricks-and-Clicks E-Tailers: Analytical Model and Empirical Analysis, Advances in Microeconomics: Economics of the Internet and e-Commerce, 11, 29-62.

Pan, Xing, Venkatesh Shankar, and Brian T. Ratchford (2003): The Evolution of Price Dispersion in Internet Retail Markets, Advances in Applied Microeconomics: Organizing the New Industrial Economy, 12, 85-105.

Ratchford, Brian T., Xing Pan, Venkatesh Shankar (2003): On the Efficiency of Internet Markets for Consumer Goods, Journal of Public Policy and Marketing, 22 (1), 4-16.

Shankar, Venkatesh and Ruth N. Bolton (2004): An Empirical Analysis of Determinants of Retailer Pricing Strategy, Marketing Science, 23 (1), 28-49.

Shankar, Venkatesh and Lakshman Krishnamurthi (1996): Relating Price Sensitivity to Retailer Promotional Variables and Pricing Policy, Journal of Retailing, 72 (3), 249-73.

Wiles, Michael A. (2007), The Effect of Customer Service on Retailers' Shareholder Wealth: The Role of Availability and Reputation Cues, Journal of Retailing, 83 (1).

Retail Pricing – Higher Profits Through Improved Pricing Processes

Hermann Simon, Andreas von der Gathen, and Philip W. Daus

Simon ◆ Kucher & Partners, Strategy and Marketing Consultants Bonn, Germany

The Retailing Industry Crisis and How to Get Out of It

The average profit margin of European retailers is a mere 0.7%. Most companies blame the difficult economic environment for this low profitability. Yet the disastrous situation is largely self-inflicted, as is indicated by two facts.

First, for years growth has been slower in the retailing industry than in private consumption, indicating a structural problem within the industry. In Germany, for instance, while private consumption grew by some 3.2% p.a. from 1994 to 2003, revenue growth in the retailing industry stagnated during the same period and even decreased, by 2.8% in 2002 and 1.0% in 2003 (see Figure 1). Traditional retailers were hit particularly hard, and their profits were depleted by massive price wars induced by competition for customers and market shares.

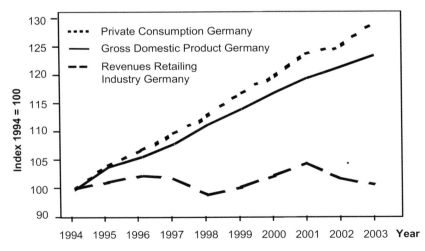

Fig. 1. Revenues in the German Retailing Industry Relative to GDP and Consumption Growth

(Source: M+M Eurodata)

M. Krafft and M.K. Mantrala (eds.), *Retailing in the 21st Century: Current and Future Trends*,   319
DOI 10.1007/978-3-540-72003-4_20, © Springer-Verlag Berlin Heidelberg 2010

Secondly, some companies have been able to grow despite the trend. Hypermarkets and discounters such as METRO Group, Carrefour and Aldi, and also focused retailers such as IKEA, Zara, and Hennes & Mauritz have grown. These retailers have continued to increase their revenues and profits year after year. They prove that a difficult economic environment is not necessarily an obstacle to growth.

Large price decreases and structural changes in the market cause severe problems for traditional forms of retailing. But how can retailers escape the crisis and improve their profit situation? In the fundamental profit formula there are only three profit drivers: price, volume, and costs.

- In the area of *costs*, many advances have been made. In fact, cost cutting has so far been the principal instrument used to improve profits in the retailing industry. Retailers were able to reduce general expenses and capital costs. Furthermore, they reduced purchase costs directly and indirectly, e.g. by pushing manufacturers to increase allowances for advertising. However, most gains in cost reductions were immediately passed on to the consumers via lower prices. Consequently, profit margins did not improve. At the same time, the potential for further cost reductions decreased. Further cost cuts are now no longer possible without large prior investments in technology.

- In saturated markets, an increase in *volume* is only possible through a gain in market share. In an effort to increase their market share, many discounters applied aggressive expansion strategies. This eventually led to an over proportional area expansion relative to revenue growth. Huge excess capacities were created in the market. To compensate for the decrease in area productivity, most competitors tried to increase revenues via aggressive pricing. However, the possibilities of boosting profits through increases in volume are limited for most retailers.

- *Price* is the third profit driver. Price has a more pronounced leverage in profit than does volume (assuming marginal costs greater than zero), because a price increase directly affects profits, whereas an increase in volume raises profits only by the additional revenue minus marginal costs.[1] Figure 2 (see next page) shows how dramatically a price increase of only 1 % (with constant volume) would improve the profit situation of selected retailers. A company such as METRO Group, for instance, could improve profitability by 66 % through a price increase of 1 %. The figure also indicates that even the market leaders are earning profit margins of only 1 % or 2 %, despite massive cost-cutting efforts over the last few years.

---

[1] An example: Assuming a profit margin of 5% and constant volume, a 2% increase in price would lead to a 40% increase in profit. In contrast, an increase in volume by 2% would lead to a profit increase of only 20%, assuming constant price and marginal costs of 50% of the price. In both cases, revenue increases by 2% but the effect is very different.

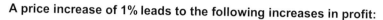

A price increase of 1% leads to the following increases in profit:

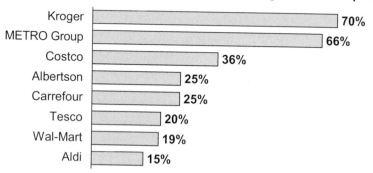

Fig. 2. Profit Improvement from a 1 % Price Increase – No Volume Reaction Assumed[2] *(Source: Annual Reports of 2003, for Aldi Data from F.A.Z. 2004)*

In summary, it can be said that price is the biggest profit driver in the retailing industry. Hence, for most retailers improvement of their pricing process offers the best way out of the disastrous profit situation. In the following sections we will first discuss exactly what a pricing process is and how improving such a process is different from price optimization in general. We will then give a short overview of current pricing practices and pricing trends in the retailing industry. Finally, based on the analysis of current pricing practices, we will indicate some starting points for improving each phase of the pricing process within a company, from the definition of strategic guidelines via price determination to controlling and monitoring.

The Paradigm Shift: From Price Optimization to Pricing Process Improvement

Past pricing research has focused on *price optimization*. Economists designed models to find the optimal profit-maximizing price for a specific product. In these models, concepts for determining prices were traditionally adapted from microeconomic pricing theory ("classic pricing theory"). The objective of microeconomic pricing, however, is to explain the behavior of market participants and to draw conclusions about the efficiency of markets or economies. Therefore, many price optimization models have only limited relevance for business practice (Wiltinger 1998). Furthermore, most models cannot be applied, or only with difficulty, in situations in which companies need to price not just one but thousands of products within a short period.

---

[2] The profit increase due to a 1% price increase with constant volume is calculated as the ratio of the price increase to the company's actual profit margin.

For instance, at Galeria Kaufhof GmbH, a major German retail chain, almost half a million products have to be priced every season, and some managers are individually responsible for pricing more than 15,000 products. Obviously, in such an environment it is not feasible to calculate price elasticities and price-response functions for all products.

As a result, companies that offer many products or have highly standardized prices should not focus their attention solely on price optimization at individual product level ("*What* is the correct price for Product X?"). Instead, they must broaden their view of pricing and take the entire *pricing process* into account, including all preliminary and subsequent activities ("*How* are prices determined and implemented?"). Only by taking a holistic approach towards pricing can such companies tap their full profit potential.

Wiltinger (1998) defined the term "pricing process" as a decision-making process within a company taking account of one or more price components. Price components can be list prices, discounts, rebates, bonuses, etc. The entirety of price components is considered in determination of the transaction price ("pocket price"), which is the final price of a product that the customer actually pays. Hence, according to Wiltinger, the results of a pricing process are the *components of a transaction price*. We suggest that this definition should be enlarged. The result of a pricing process is not just the components of a price, but both the *entire transaction price* and its *implementation in the market*; that is to say *that a pricing process is a set of rules and procedures that helps a company to determine and implement (transaction) prices*.

Although the structure of pricing processes is industry specific and might differ even from company to company, we suggest dividing pricing processes into five phases (Figure 3): (1) strategy development, (2) review of internal processes, (3) determination of prices, (4) implementation, and (5) controlling and monitoring.

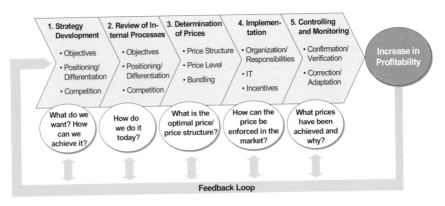

Fig. 3. Phases of the Pricing Process

(Source: Simon ◆ Kucher & Partners, Strategy & Marketing Consultants)

Phase 1 is the start of the pricing process, where strategic requirements are defined and targets set with respect to profit, volume, general price level, market share, and positioning. Within Phase 2, a thorough review of the status quo and of existing processes is performed. Prior to any reorganization of the pricing process, issues such as current practice, internal competencies, price structures, and price differentiation must be carefully analyzed. Phase 3 consists of determining price levels through developing clear sub-processes relating to price structure, price level, and price differentiation. This will also determine what information and what decision models are needed to support pricing decisions. Implementation, Phase 4, is often neglected by organizations. Key success factors to be aware of are clear definitions of responsibility, application of target-oriented incentives, and development of supporting IT tools. Finally, controlling and monitoring processes are developed in Phase 5 for the purpose of sustaining the pricing process implemented.

From experience we can say that, in most retail companies, money is wasted because there are inefficiencies and malfunctions in all phases. Consequently, there is potential for profit improvement in all phases. The sum of improvements usually leads to profit increases of one to two percentage points (not percent) – an enormous effect for any retailer!

If we look at what happens in each phase it becomes apparent that the improvement of pricing processes covers a wide range of topics, such as:

- IT-supported data sourcing, processing and data analysis with models, methodologies, and rules. Data used for analysis can have subjective components (e.g., estimates and experience) as well as objective components (e.g., market and competitor data).

- The involvement and training of personnel, the development of competencies, the definition of responsibilities, and the creation of suitable incentive structures within the company.

- Internal and external negotiations and the development of decision-making guidelines and success standards, and also the introduction of controlling and monitoring systems.

Despite its complexity, however, the improvement of pricing processes is an extremely attractive alternative to cost-cutting measures, because – in contrast to cost cutting – it leads to quick (but long-lasting) improvements in profits. These quick gains result from three effects (see Figure 4). First, an *investment advantage* is created because no costly severance payments or store closures are necessary. A *time advantage* is created because price has an immediate impact on profit and cash flow, whereas the profit effects of cost cutting are often do not become noticeable until several three-month periods have passed. Third, improving pricing processes has a *profit advantage* over cost cutting. As already pointed out, our experience shows that a professional reorganization of pricing processes increases the rate of return by one to two percentage points. The impact of pricing process improvement is therefore often much more far reaching than that of cost cutting.

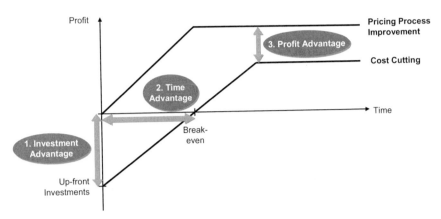

Fig. 4. Quick Gains Through Pricing Process Improvement Relative to Cost Cutting
(Source: Simon ◆ Kucher & Partners, Strategy & Marketing Consultants)

Despite their great importance for managers, pricing processes have so far very rarely been examined in academic studies. (The only investigations of pricing processes within companies were conducted by Wiltinger 1998 and Dutta, Bergen, Zbaracki 2002.) This is partly because marketing research has traditionally had a microeconomic perspective on pricing, as discussed above. Furthermore, in most companies pricing processes are regarded as highly sensitive executive management issues and it is extremely difficult to gain access to adequate information. Our model of the pricing process therefore represents an important step forward in the direction of an integrative and holistic view on pricing and may serve as a framework for future pricing research.

Current Pricing Practices in Retailing

Before discussing concrete approaches to improving retailers' pricing processes in the next section, we will first focus on current pricing practices and characteristics of the retailing industry (see also the chapter by Bolton, Shankar, Montoya in this book).

Most retailers are organized by product categories. Buyers have the operative responsibility for these product categories, which often comprise hundreds or even thousands of items. These buyers (as opposed to sales people or executive managers in other industries) also set the final product prices. Often the manufacturers of consumer goods aggressively enforce recommended retail prices for their brand labels and leave no room for price decisions to be made by retailers.[3] Therefore, most buy-

---

[3] Although resale price maintenance is officially not allowed by Fair Trade Acts in Europe and the USA, de facto powerful consumer goods manufacturers succeed in imposing their prices on retailers.

ers make price decisions primarily for private label brands. Store managers, in contrast, have no price-setting power in most retailing companies – only at the end of a season or during promotions are they allowed to alter prices within certain predetermined ranges. For example, at the German-based discounter Aldi, price decisions are centralized, but regional managers are allowed to lower prices for a limited number of promotional products, for instance if their turnover rate is low.

In most retail companies, strategic pricing decisions are made by the executive management of the company. In a top-down approach, the chief executive and heads of the purchasing department develop general pricing guidelines and adopt overall target revenues and target profits for the company. These general targets are then broken down into revenue and profit targets as well as target price levels for each purchasing department, product category, and product group (see Figure 5).

During this process many factors are taken into account, such as competition, shifts in consumer demand for each product group, price image aspects of the company, etc. Often the price positioning is differentiated along channel lines (e.g., retail outlets, catalog, Internet) and regions. For instance SportScheck, a leading retailer of sports goods, differentiates catalog prices according to product sizes (the same tee-shirt costs more in size XXL than in size L), whereas store prices for tee-shirts do not vary with size.

The purchasing departments then develop operative targets for a certain period based on the strategic targets for each product group. To accomplish this, product groups are differentiated into price segments, e.g., high-, medium-, and low-price products. For each of these price segments, the range of prices is predetermined. Quantities for each price segment are determined on the basis of previous years/seasons and estimates of market development.

On the basis of the targets for volumes, profits and final price levels for each price segment, buyers determine the range (e.g., the proportion of private brand products, the number and kind of products within each price category, etc.) and

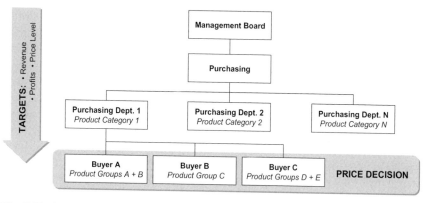

Fig. 5. Typical Organizational Structure and Pricing Responsibilities in Retail Companies

start sourcing the products from regional or global markets. Therefore, since prices are practically determined *before* products are selected and sourced/bought, this process can also be described as *price-led target costing* (Swenson et al. 2003). This target-costing approach – and all pricing practices that result from it – is very typical for the retail industry in general. It explains why most retailers adjust volumes rather than prices. For example, during a soccer world championship, virtually all retailers purchase and sell larger volumes of soccer balls to meet the higher demand, rather than increasing prices.

Retailers see their biggest challenge in determining volumes and reducing purchase costs to a minimum. They do not yet see the challenge in optimizing retail prices or, least of all, in improving pricing processes. When will they finally recognize that price is the biggest profit driver? Up to now, most retailers have passed up chances of improving their profit situation at virtually every phase of the pricing process. In the following section we will show retail companies the starting points for analyzing and eventually improving their pricing process within the company.

Reorganizing the Pricing Process in Retailing

Pricing processes are complex and company specific. Although many retailers have common characteristics – large ranges, a purchase-driven product-category organization, volume adjustments rather than price adjustments, etc. – their starting points for the reorganization of pricing processes might be entirely different. Following the structure of the pricing process shown in Figure 3, the following paragraphs illustrate where and how pricing processes can be improved.

Phase 1: Strategic Guidelines

As shown in Figure 3, in the first phase both the strategy and the positioning of the company and its products (price policy, price level, price sequence, etc.) must be defined. A well-formulated strategy and clear positioning are crucial parts of an effective pricing process. In practice, however, many companies have no clear strategy and pursue several objectives at once though these might be at odds with each other (e.g., market share, profitability, revenues). For instance, there are typically conflicts between volume and profit targets. Figure 6 indicates that price increases lead to increases in profit and volume only in very specific circumstances (Quadrant I). More often, trade-offs between volume and profit growth have to be made (Quadrants II and III).

This simple lesson seems to be ignored by many retailers. When discounters such as Wal-Mart, METRO Group or Aldi enter the stage with aggressive everyday low price (EDLP) strategies, established retailers mostly react by reducing their own prices (cf. Shankar,Bolton 2004; Bolton, Shankar 2002). Instead of accepting

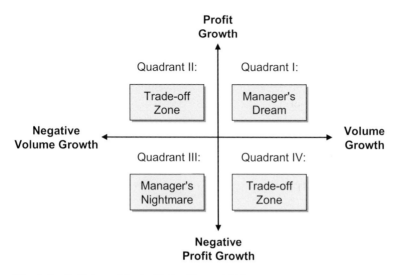

Fig. 6. Profit-Volume Matrix (Dolan/Simon 1996)

small falls in market share and relatively moderate decreases in profits, they engage in price wars leading to drastic profit losses.

Discounters, in contrast, are in a good position to compete by way of prices owing to their smaller ranges. German discounters Aldi and Lidl, for example, sell
the most profitable products in each product category (mostly products with high
turnover rates) and have only about 670 items on offer. Items with unattractive or
even negative margins are not kept in their ranges, whereas traditional retailers
offer several thousand articles, including highly unprofitable, image-building
products (Huchzermeier, Iyer, Freiheit 2002). Discounters with small ranges not
only have larger margins; in addition, their purchasing costs are lower because of
their lower number of suppliers (increased purchasing power), lower logistics
costs and lower merchandising expenditures. Consequently, traditional retailers,
which cannot ever enjoy the same cost advantages as the discounters, simply
should not try to compete via price, because they will eventually lose any price
war. This is also illustrated by the breakeven analysis in Figure 7 (see next page).
It shows that retailers must reduce costs drastically in order to adopt an EDLP
pricing strategy successfully.

When designing a price strategy, retailers must keep in mind that lower prices
are not the only way to differentiate. They should highlight other attributes that are
of value to the customer and cannot be easily imitated by competitors, such as superior product quality, additional services (e.g., home delivery, a nursery for small
children), a unique shopping environment, additional marketing activities (e.g., loyalty programs (e.g., see chapter by Reinartz in this book), non-price promotions, and
so on (Shankar, Bolton 2004; Shankar, Krishnamurthi 1996). British grocery retailers have answered the discount challenge successfully in recent years by offering
well-targeted economy/value ranges and intelligent services and loyalty programs.

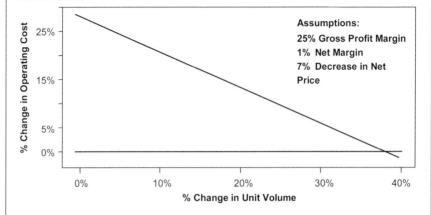

Why EDLP Pricing Strategies Are Bound to Fail for Normal Retailers

Hoch/Drèze/Purk (1994) calculated the needed change in operating costs for a food retailer as a function of changes in unit volume. They assumed an initial gross margin of 25% and operating costs of 24% (as a percentage of the original price). The graph shows the results for a price decrease of 7%:

A volume increase of 39% is required for an EDLP strategy to deliver break even-profits without having to decrease operating costs. Costs must be reduced dramatically if volume increases resulting from price reductions are lower: for a 20% increase in volume, operating costs have to be reduced by more than 14%. If the volume increase is merely 3% – a realistic amount for most competitive retail markets – operating costs have to be decreased by as much as 27%! Hence, for most retailers, price wars are bound to end in disaster.

Fig. 7. Breakeven Cost Reduction Analysis for an EDLP Pricing Strategy
(Source: Hoch, Drèze, Purk 1994)

Phase 2: Review of Internal Processes

As Figure 3 shows, Phase 2 consists of a review of the existing pricing process within the company. There is no doubt that this phase is very important. However, it often proves to be unexpectedly complex and time-consuming. The reason for this is that most companies do not understand pricing as a closed-loop process. Hence, different pieces of information and data about pricing activities have to be collected meticulously from many departments, which can be a tedious process. For example, data might come from the accounting department, the purchasing department, and marketing, and others besides. And it then often has to be disaggregated into customer, region or product category units. There may be several areas in which information that is crucial for making sound price decisions is not available in the right quantity within the company, is not present at the right locations, or is even completely lacking.

Table 1. Starting Points for Pricing Process Improvements and Resulting Profit Increases

Industry	Revenue	Starting Points for Process Improvement	Increase in Return on Sales in Percentage Points
Wholesaler	$1-5 bn.	- Classifying customer and product groups based on price elasticities - Anti-discount incentives for the sales force	2.0
Software solutions	$100-500 m.	- Reconfiguration of the selling process and guidelines - Stronger centralization	8.0* *from -3.0 to +5.0
Engineering	$5-10 bn.	- Systematic quantification of value-to-customer - More comprehensive and reliable competitive intelligence	1.0
Bank	$1-5 bn.	- Far-reaching extraction of brand value - Raising the pricing competence of the customer representatives	1.6
Tourism	$5-10 bn.	- More strongly differentiated price structure - Indicator-supported identification of opportunities with profit potential	1.6
Supplier	$5-10 bn.	- Use of value-pricing instead of cost-plus for innovations - Better forecasting of cost developments for long-term contracts	1.2
Express service	$5-10 bn.	- Systematic recognition and elimination of loss-making business - International price discipline, controlling, and monitoring	1.5
Chemical specialties	$0.5-1.0 bn.	- More thorough analysis of multi-stage customer value chain - New price-decision hierarchy and use of key account management	1.1
Machinery	$100-500 m.	- Reduction in overengineering through target valuing/target costing - Standardization of processes, especially for limited/small-run series	1.5

(Source: Simon ◆ Kucher & Partner, Strategy & Marketing Consultants)

In most cases, merely reviewing existing pricing processes shows flaws and weak spots within the company and highlights a wide scope for improvement. It comes as no surprise that the starting points for pricing process improvements discovered during this review phase differ very widely from industry to industry and even from company to company. Table 1 shows different starting points for pricing process improvements for selected projects in different industries. As discussed above, in most cases increases in return on sales resulting from such improvements differ by one to two percentage points.

In summary, it can be said that the improvement of pricing processes cannot be seen as a standard procedure. Instead, the unique situation of each company has to be analyzed individually. A thorough review of the internal processes shows starting points for efforts to improve pricing processes.

Phase 3: Determination of Prices

Phase 3, the determination of prices, is definitely the most complex and difficult phase of the pricing process. When pricing their products, most retailers already take into account that customers are more price sensitive in certain product categories and regions than in others. However, most retailers do not *quantify* how a variation in prices affects customer demand or profit margins. Instead of this, they apply simple decision rules (see Figure 8) or base their price decisions on intuition (Simon 1989). To optimize prices, however, price elasticities, profit margins, cross-product effects, and the intensity of competition have to be taken into account.

---

1. **The lower the price in absolute terms, the higher the mark-up.**

2. **The higher the turnover rate, the lower the mark-up.**

3. **For products with a high price perception ("political" products such as bread, milk, butter) the mark-ups should be very low.**

4. **Mark-ups should be lower for commodities than for specialities.**

5. **Mark-ups should be geared towards the competition ("shop-window calculation")**

Fig. 8. Rules of Thumb in Retailer Pricing (Simon 1989)

When reorganizing pricing processes, first *price elasticities* (i.e., the effects of prices on volumes) should be quantified. They should only be measured *per product category* and per region. Only for the most important products in terms of revenue might it be worthwhile to measure price elasticities at product level. Furthermore, the most important drivers of price elasticity per product category should be identified.

Historical scanner data might yield the required information. Scanner technology is an excellent tool to support quantitative analysis, because every purchase is registered by date, article, and price. Prices can be changed without major effort by means of a computer command and a change to the pricing tags on the shelves. These are ideal preconditions for conducting price tests and an analysis of price-quantity effects. Prices can be changed systematically, and the effects on sales volume can be measured.

Alternatively, price elasticities can be deduced by looking at price variations over time or for different points of revenue (Simon 1992). Figure 9 (see next page) gives an example of a price analysis for a coffee brand. If no data is available or if no trained personnel is available for analysis and interpretation of the data, it is permissible to substitute expert interviews with store managers, as these also yield useful information on price effects.

Price elasticity is influenced to a large extent by the price image. The price image is defined as each customer's individual perception of a retailer with regard to the price level (Simon 1992). A study conducted by Ahlert, Kenning, Vogel (2003) revealed that only about 40% of all consumers have an idea of the real prices of items that they buy regularly, and a mere 20% (16%) of all consumers could name the lowest (highest) price of 1 out of 91 articles. Throughout all item and product groups, prices were overestimated by as much as 15% on average. Since customers usually remember very few prices, usually only a few products have very high price elasticity, while most products do not. Consequently, when consumers choose the retailer with the best price image for their shopping this retailer is not necessarily the cheapest one.

Ultimately, constant quantitative monitoring of the pricing process is indispensable to the identification of starting points for improvement and exploitation of full profit potential. Starting points for price process improvement can also be detected by carrying out so-called lost-order analysis. Why did customers not purchase certain products? Is price really the reason, or are there other more important factors, such as long waiting times, shopping environment, arrangement of racks?

Conclusion

In the face of the overall low profitability in the retailing industry we strongly encourage retailers to devote more attention and energy to pricing. Among the three profit drivers volume, costs, and price, price is by far the most effective one. Price increases without a loss in volume lead to much greater profit improvement than volume increases without price reductions. Compared with cost, price has an investment advantage because no upfront investment is required. It also has a time advantage, since the profit effects of a better price are seen without a time lag. And price offers an overall profit advantage since, after the cost-cutting spree of recent years, the potential for profit improvement is higher on the price side than on the cost side.

The textbook paradigm of price optimization is not applicable to retailers, with their typically large ranges, frequent price changes, and price promotions. Rather, we suggest the adoption of a process view of pricing. The pricing process includes all aspects of the determination of the final transaction price. It starts with the strategy, which comprises objectives related to profit, volume, market share, positioning, general price level, etc. The reorganization of pricing processes requires careful and critical examination of current practices and understanding of the existing price structures, price differentiation, the competition, and the internal competencies. Phase 3 of the pricing process addresses the determination of prices: what rules are applied, what information is used, and how price levels, price structures, discounts, or bundle prices are determined. These rules are followed by the organizational aspects of Phase 4: responsibilities, incentives, and information technology. Last but not least, a continuous process for monitoring and controlling prices and margins has to be set up.

Our experience as pricing consultants has proved many times that profits can be greatly increased through a reorganization of pricing processes. Considering the state of actual price decision-making, this is not too astonishing. Retail pricing in practice is rather far from what we call a "Six Sigma Approach" to pricing, i.e. a process during which price determination and implementation are comprehensively and unequivocally organized. With regard to pricing processes, retailers can learn a lot from other industries, e.g. pharmaceuticals, airlines, telecommunications, and hotels and tourism. An increasing number of companies in these industries are reorganizing their pricing processes and are surprised by the positive effects on profits. This is the way retailers should go to achieve higher profitability.

We are convinced that after the eras of cost reduction, supply chain improvement and information technology upgrading pricing will become the predominant area for profit improvement. The tools and processes are here. Retailers only have to use them. Quick wins and sustainable higher returns are almost certain.

References

Ahlert, D./Kenning, P./Vogel, V. (2003): Grundlagen des Preismanagements – dargestellt am Beispiel des deutschen Lebensmitteleinzelhandels, Lehrstuhl für Betriebswirtschaftslehre, insb. Distribution und Handel, Muenster.

Basuroy, S./ Mantrala, M.K./Walters, R.G. (2001): The Impact of Category Management on Retailer Prices and Performance: Theory and Evidence, Journal of Marketing, 65 (October), 16-32.

Bolton, R. N./Shankar, V. (2002): An Empirically Driven Taxonomy of Retailer Pricing and Promotion Strategies, Journal of Retailing, 79 (4), 213-224.

Dolan, R. J./Simon, H. (1996): Power Pricing – How Managing Price Transforms the Bottom Line, New York, The Free Press.

Dutta, S./Bergen, M./Zbaracki, M. (2002): Pricing Process as a Capability: A Case Study, Marketing Science Institute Report No. 01-117, Cambridge, Mass.

Hoch, S.J./Drèze, X./Purk, M.E. (1994): EDLP, Hi-Lo, and Margin Arithmetic, Journal of Marketing, Vol. 58 (October), 116-27.

Huchzermeier, A./Iyer, A./Freiheit, J. (2002): The Supply Chain Impact of Smart Customers in a Promotional Environment, Manufacturing & Service Operations Management, Vol. 4, No. 3, 228-240.

Shankar, V./Bolton, R. N. (2004): An Empirical Analysis of Determinants of Retailer Pricing Strategy, Marketing Science, 23 (1), 28-49.

Shankar, V./ Krishnamurthi, L. (1996): Relating Price Sensitivity to Retailer Promotional Variables and Pricing Policy, Journal of Retailing, 72 (3), 249-73.

Simon, H. (1992): Preismanagement: Analyse, Strategie, Umsetzung, 2nd Edition, Wiesbaden, Gabler.

Simon, H. (1989): Price Management, North-Holland.

Swenson, D./Ansari, S./Bell, J./Kim, I.-W. (2003): Management Accounting Quarterly, Vol. 4, No. 2.

University of Essen/Mercer Management Consulting (2003): Retail-Studie – Preis- und Sortimentsmanagement als Erfolgshebel im Einzelhandel, Universität Essen.

Wiltinger, K. (1998): Preismanagement in der unternehmerischen Praxis, Wiesbaden, Gabler.

Current Status and Future Evolution of Retail Formats

Dieter Ahlert, Markus Blut, and Heiner Evanschitzky

University of Muenster, Germany

Introduction

Present-day consumers are faced with an ever-growing variety of retail formats to satisfy their needs and want. The emergence of new retail formats can be explained in at least three ways: First, it can be argued that the changing demand patterns of consumers may lead to different formats. For example, there are value-oriented shoppers, price-oriented shoppers and convenience shoppers. Each type of consumer may cause the retail industry to consider new retail formats. Secondly, retailers themselves may decide to develop a certain format that best fits their internal strength. By so doing, they hope to obtain a competitive advantage. A third explanation for the emergence of new retail formats may be the changing role of the manufacturing industry. Excess product supply can force prices down, which in turn may lead retailers to purchase opportunistically.

Whatever the reason for the emergence of new retail formats, it is certain that new formats offer opportunities for both traditional and new retailers to increase their market share and their profitability. On the other hand, it may also cause erosion in the retail landscape. Those players who are unable to take the chances that come with a change in the market may lose market share or even disappear (see chapter by Fox, Sethuraman in this book for more insights into between-format versus within-format retail competition).

One way for retailers to evaluate the chances for certain retail formats is to take an international perspective. While most developed countries share the same basic retail formats, their importance and dissemination vary substantially across different countries.

This chapter attempts to provide an overview of the dissemination of retail formats in the "G8" countries. A classification of retail formats provides the terminological basis used to describe the evolution of these formats between the year 1999 and today. A closer look at an individual country gives an indication of what

M. Krafft and M.K. Mantrala (eds.), *Retailing in the 21st Century: Current and Future Trends*, 337
DOI 10.1007/978-3-540-72003-4_21, © Springer-Verlag Berlin Heidelberg 2010

particular format is dominant in that country. This in turn offers retailers in other countries the opportunity to identify gaps in their own national retail landscape and suggests possible ways of identifying best practices for certain retail formats. Without attempting to be comprehensive, this paper concludes by identifying some future trends in retailing.

Classification of Retail Formats

In order to explain the existence and the dynamics of retail formats, we first attempt a classification of such formats. On the basis of how their marketing instruments have developed, five formats can be distinguished (M+M planetretail 2004):

- Cash & carry stores and warehouse clubs
- Convenience and forecourt stores
- Discount stores
- Hypermarket and superstore operators
- Supermarket and neighborhood store operators

Cash & carry stores and warehouse clubs. Cash & carry is a membership-based type of wholesale trade level, which depends on retailers and commercial customers. In the area of food, the proprietors of independent businesses are especially likely to use this concept. It is usually based on self-service, resembling a supermarket in this, with cash payment of goods at the checkout (a point of difference from a wholesale supplier). In some countries, particularly some eastern European countries, this type of outlet also sells to private customers. Therefore, this article analyzes the development of this format, although it is mainly a wholesale concept (see, e.g., description of Metro Cash & Carry stores in the chapter by Mierdorf, Mantrala, Krafft elsewhere in this book). The format of *warehouse clubs* is also extensively organized and depends on both business customers and private customers on a membership basis. Normally an annual contribution has to be paid, which gives the customer the right to purchase.

Convenience and forecourt stores. The *convenience store* is a small self-service-based format sited in highly frequented locations and has long opening times. The focus is on convenience products such as ready-to-serve food and fast food, but in most cases a small selection of regular food and nonfood products is also offered. A *forecourt store* is also a convenience business; it is often tied to petrol stations and sometimes run in association with petrol companies. It depends on customers who have forgotten things during their regular weekly shopping trips.

Discount stores. Discount stores are characterized by efficient background systems enabling them to offer their customers only a limited breadth of assortment, but this efficiently at a high turnover speed. Consequently these businesses are often run in less than 1,000 square meters. This concept has its origins in Germany and for this reason has become most widespread in Europe. It appears to take one of two forms. The hard discounter sells his own brands exclusively and concentrates on the price, whereas soft discounters offer a mix of manufacturer's and own brands in their ranges.

Hypermarket and superstore operator hypermarkets. These retail outlets are self-service shops with a selling area exceeding 5,000 square meters and a correspondingly high turnover. As a rule, they offer a comprehensive range of nonfood items in addition to a complete food range. Depending on the individual design, the nonfood area can be equivalent to that of a department store. The *superstore* is a self-service store with a selling area of between 2,500 and 5,000 square meters. Superstores are similar to hypermarkets in that they offer a comprehensive range of food, but the nonfood range is limited owing to the smaller area. The *discount superstore* is an extensive format occupying an area exceeding 2,500 square meters and offering a selection of nonfood items, such as household goods and health and toiletry products, but also food. This format typically has a strong focus on low prices, and it is mainly found in North America.

Supermarket and Neighborhood Store Operators. The supermarket is a self-service store with a food range; it occupies an average of between 400 and 2,500 square meters, in which the particular size determines whether nonfood products are on offer and in what quantities. The *neighborhood store* is a small food store with less than 400 square meters of floor space. In principle, this format is similar to that of a supermarket; nevertheless there are also still many full-service neighborhood stores. The food department is a separate food area in a department store, often occupying a complete floor of the building. It can either be rented to a supermarket operator or run by the department store itself. Apart from a mass market-orientated version, operators are also found in the premium area.

Analysis of Retail Formats in G8 Countries

National Market Share of Different Retail Formats

Canada

Up to 2002, Canada was able to show constant economic growth at an average rate of 6 %, which is the strongest since 1999 (M+M planetretail 2004). This development was promoted in particular by the sound domestic economic data, and also by growing domestic investments and consumer spending. The leading retail businesses in Canada are the two Canadian companies Loblaw and Sobeys, which have at their disposal comprehensive portfolios with various distribution outlets ranging from hypermarkets (1999: 48 %; 2003: 51 %) to small neighborhood stores (1999: 32 %; 2003: 28 %).

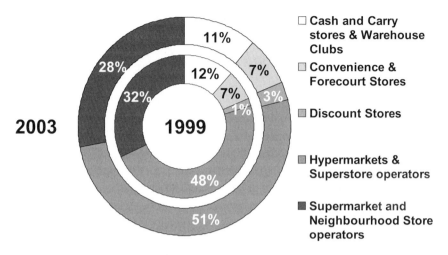

Fig. 1. Canada: Evolution of Retail Structures
(Source: M+M planetretail 2004)

Despite the growth of numerous companies the Canadian food trade remains fragmented (M+M planetretail 2004). One of the facts responsible for this is that the mostly small Canadian communities are spread all over the country. The largest Group in the country, Loblaw, ranks merely second compared with the independent retailers. This is also due to the large area in which it occurs in international comparison, because of the dense distribution of cash & carry markets as well as warehouse clubs (1999: 12 %, 2003: 11 %). This is why most smaller, independent retailers organize their buying mainly via wholesalers, which enables them to stand their ground in the market. In addition to this, large-scale formats have a long tradition in North America.

Wal-Mart entered the Canadian market by taking over the Woolco chain. Safeway, in contrast with the extensive Wal-Mart markets, runs mainly a supermarket chain designed to meet luxury, up-market requirements. The German company Tengelmann is also represented by its A&P line. The trend towards discounters seen in the European countries seems to be beginning in Canada, albeit at a very low level so far (1999: 1 %; 2003: 3 %). If the growth of the discounter sector does continue, this will be mainly at the expense of the classic supermarkets. The other operators represented in Canada originate mainly from the American market. For the time being, the most important are still Loblaw, A&P (Tengelmann), Sobeys, Wal-Mart, Metro-Richelieu, Costco, and Safeway (world of retail 2004).

France

The French economy has received a boost in recent years from an increasing number of tax cuts, which have caused a rise in consumer spending. The household goods area is the one that has profited most from this development, however (M+M planetretail 2004). In European comparison, France has been ensured one of the leading positions, helped by a moderate rise in inflation. Only the rising unemployment has had a negative effect on growth, as it puts pressure on consumer spending.

In the recent past the French government has introduced tighter legislation concerning the construction of large-area hypermarkets, so that the financially strongest French retailers have switched increasingly to convenience (1999: 6%, 2003: 7%) and discount concepts (number of outlets in 1999: 8,259; in 2003: 12,375) (Bordier 2004). Nevertheless, France is the home of the classic hypermarkets and the country of origin of numerous successful operators who, apart from a high market share (1999: 48%; 2003: 46%), also show high area productivities (Myers 2003).

The French food trade is determined decisively by the company Carrefour. This strong position of Carrefour was reached in 1999 when it merged with Promodès in response to the increasing presence of Wal-Mart in the European market (Myers 2003). This further speeded up the concentration process in the country (Colla 2004). The next two places in the ranking are occupied by Alliances Leclerc and Intermaché, both of which were formed by mergers of independent retailers. Although France is the home of several companies that have achieved worldwide success, foreign companies, especially the German discounters Aldi and Lidl, are endeavoring to gain a share of the market by opening numerous markets, at the expense of supermarkets and traditional retailers. In the same way, the German company METRO Group successfully has entered the market with its cash & carry concept (number of stores in 1999: 3,558; in 2003: 4,450). The own-brand-name share has been able to grow owing to the progressive concentration in the trade, this growth has further increased METRO Group's gain in power. Despite the increasing pressure of competition from foreign operators, the most important companies in the French market at present are Carrefour, Intermarché, Leclerc, Auchan, and Casino (*World of Retail* 2004).

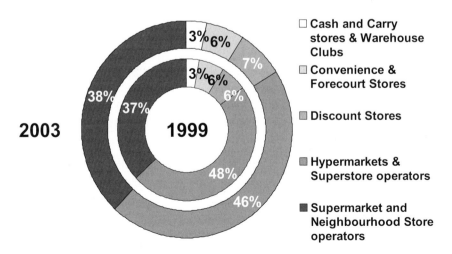

Fig. 2. France: Evolution of Retail Structures
(Source: M+M planetretail 2004)

Germany

During the past few years the German economy has been characterized by low growth rates and rising unemployment, resulting in a negative consumer climate. This negative development has already been forced numerous trading companies out of business (M+M planetretail 2004). Therefore, the already high degree of concentration in the German market has intensified further. Despite this, the German market remains the largest in Europe and at the same time the one with the highest share of discounters (1999: 30%, 2003: 38%). The worldwide leading discounters Aldi and Lidl originated in Germany (Colla 2004). Forced by this tense situation, smaller independent retailers have often had no option but to merge with larger groups, such as Rewe or Edeka. The large trading groups followed a strategy of excessive diversification for a long time, which is why they now have numerous outlets in the form of hypermarkets (1999: 25%, 2003: 25%) through supermarkets (1999: 33%, 2003: 25%) and discount stores (Myers 2003 and Bell 2001).

After many years of clearing up the market and rationalization, the German food trade is in the hands of just a few large companies, although a small number of independent operators also remain in the market (M+M planetretail 2004). METRO Group, Germany's largest trading company, also owns a comprehensive portfolio of outlets, among which the cash & carry format in particular has proved very successful, due to the technological advantage enjoyed by the group. For all these reasons, the German market is the most difficult market in Europe.

Not only Wal-Mart from the USA, but also the French company Intermarché and Marks and Spencer from the UK, have already attempted to gain access to the market in Germany, but failed owing to the extremely difficult competitive conditions.

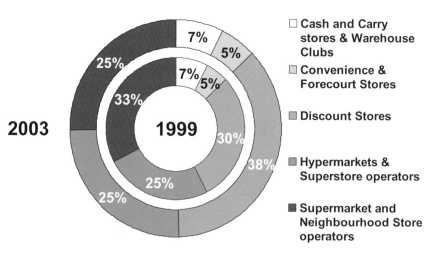

Fig. 3. Germany: Evolution of Retail Structures
(Source: M+M planetretail 2004)

Both companies are still showing losses, which should scare off further retailers from attempting to enter the market. At present, the leading trading companies are METRO Group, Rewe, Edeka, Aldi, Lidl, and Tengelmann (World of Retail 2004).

Italy

Since the 1990s, growth rates had remained stagnant in Italy. From 2000 onward, an improvement can be noted (M+M planetretail 2004). Within the country there are still considerable differences between the industrialized North and the rural South. The differing regional subsidies to companies still remain a political issue contributing to distortion of the retail landscape. Inflation used to be one of the main problems in Italy but is now under control following introduction of the Euro. Not only consumer spending, but also retail turnover have undergone moderate development.

The yields in the retail trade, however, have been stable since new outlets were opened, and economies of scale may have been secured by this means (M+M planetretail 2004). This trend toward increasing professionalism in the Italian retail landscape has met with strong fragmentation of the market (Bordier 2002). Apart from the high number of independent retailers, which is typical for the Italian market, particularly in the rural areas, modern trading formats have been implemented mainly in the North of the country, not least due to the massive influence of French hypermarkets (1999: 28 %; 2003: 30 %) and German discounters (1999: 6 %; 2003: 7 %) with high levels of ability in logistics, in the management of product ranges, and also in offering better private labels than the traditionalists (Myers 2003). For these reasons, established companies are trying to defend their position by exploiting their knowledge of Italian customers and their regional origins (Colla 2004).

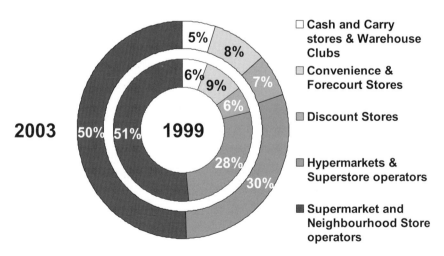

Fig. 4. Italy: Evolution of Retail Structures
(Source: M+M planetretail 2004)

Despite the massive influx of the French companies Carrefour and Auchan, the Italian cooperative alliance Coop Italia still dominates the food trade at present. Therefore, the concentration in the market is lower than the European average. With intensified concentration, the Italian retail landscape will, however, catch up with those in the other European countries (Bordier 2002). The most important operators in the Italian market to date are Coop Italia, Carrefour, Auchan, Esselunga, and METRO Group (World of Retail 2004).

Japan

Japan was once the world's booming economic center, but it now bears the hallmark of deflationary tendencies, which have forced numerous weaker trading companies out of business (M+M planetretail 2004). The Japanese consumer attaches great importance to quality and convenience. Despite the very low interest rate, Japanese consumer spending is stagnating. The strong convenience orientation of Japanese consumers (1999: 35 %; 2003: 38 %) makes it difficult for more traditional retail concepts to grow. Moreover, consumers are highly demanding with respect to new trading concepts. For instance, French hypermarkets did not do well in Japan because the consumers were prejudiced against low prices. They assumed that it would not be possible to offer good quality at these prices being asked. The cash & carry area is relatively underdeveloped and does not even have a market share of 1 %. The rather small land mass area of Japan is one factor responsible for this development, as is the exceedingly high population density. The cost of land for development, especially in the mega-cities, is very high, so that in many cases retailers cooperate to create networks of small convenience stores and

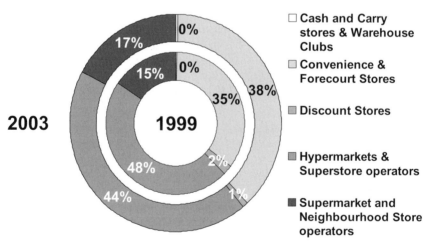

Fig. 5. Japan: Evolution of Retail Structures
(Source: M+M planetretail 2004)

supermarkets (1999: 15 %; 2003: 17 %). For this reason, Japan is the home of the most stores based on modern convenience concepts. Extensive formats, such as hypermarkets and superstores, on the other hand, are beset with problems. Despite the volume they turn over, established hypermarkets and superstores are rather few in number and are rather small and limited to the larger cities. Correspondingly, hypermarkets accounted for only 12 % of the total number of outlets, but for 44 % of the total turnover in 2003.

Even though the general merchandise superstores with floor areas of over 5,000 square meters in the large towns have an important role in the Japanese retail landscape, the overly expensive locations are a hurdle for foreign operators wishing to gain access to the Japanese food retailing market (M+M planetretail 2004). This explains why this market is still in the hands of the established Japanese trading companies: Ito-Yokado, Aeon, Uny, Daiei, and Lawson. In the past these companies were able to build and defend a complex network of outlets and differing retailing chains (World of Retail 2004). However, both Costco and the French operator Carrefour have been able to build up a steady presence in Japan.

Russia

Despite Russian politicians' declared intention of liberalizing and privatizing the Russian economy, there are still considerable structural problems in the trade market (M+M planetretail 2004). The Russian retail landscape is still under pressure from the weak economy, which is itself due to the immense financial burdens of the late 1990s, which led to a collapse of domestic demand (outside of the black market). The present high inflation is also a problem for retailing turnovers. As in Canada, the rural areas are particularly thinly populated, so that turnover there is low.

The larger domestic and foreign trading companies still aim their concepts at the more densely populated areas of Russia, such as Moscow, in order to appeal to wealthier consumers. If one compares the trading structures of 1999 and 2003 a radical change becomes visible. While the retailing trade in 1999 was characterized first and foremost by networks of small independent retailers and kiosks, these formats were steadily losing ground by 2003 (1999: 83 %; 2003: 57 %). Modern formats such as hypermarkets are expanding, mostly in the cities (1999: 7 %; 2003: 20 %), while discounters do not yet have a substantial share of the market (1999: 7 %, 2003: 1 %). The large portion of cash & carry markets can be attributed to the existence of the numerous independent retailers, who organize their procurement via this format

In the future, operators of the newer formats can expect substantial growth rates in Russia. Auchan is already present in Russia, and other companies, such as Cora, Leclerc, and Carrefour, are considering taking this step. Edeka, METRO Group (with the cash & carry area), and Tesco are also expected to increase their presence. The most important companies at present are Ramstore Hyper, Obi Diplomat, Perekryostok, Sam Holding, and Sadko (World of Retail 2004).

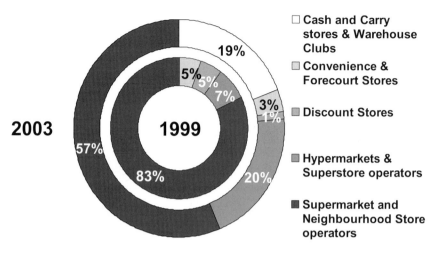

□ Cash and Carry
stores & Warehouse
Clubs

□ Convenience &
Forecourt Stores

■ Discount Stores

■ Hypermarkets &
Superstore operators

■ Supermarket and
Neighbourhood Store
operators

Fig. 6. Russia: Evolution of Retail Structures
(Source: M+M planetretail 2004)

United Kingdom

The British market is growing steadily, and the companies operating there are achieving considerable growth in turnover (M+M planetretail 2004). In particular, the segments electronics, household goods, and DIY are enjoying above-average growth. This positive development began in the early 1990s and has continued to the present time. Only the rising real estate prices can slow down further growth.

The British retail landscape has always been characterized by restrictive construction regulations, which is why the extensive superstores have a long tradition of having a high-quality range of products (1999: 65%; 2003: 64%) (Myers 2003). Owing to the high concentration of operators and the resulting adaptation of the formats, the established companies have been able to claim a high proportion of total turnover. This situation has led the traditional formats also to stock a wide range of high-grade products, which is reserved in the other European countries for specialized superstores. At present there is a comprehensive network of markets in the suburbs, as well as superstores and hypermarkets on green-field sites. This is why the leading operators in the past have limited themselves to the expansion and conversion of existing markets rather than opening new ones (M+M planetretail 2004).

At present the British retail landscape is experiencing increasing differentiation of trading formats. Therefore, new concepts such as convenience stores (1999: 8%; 2003: 10%) are concentrated especially in the suburbs in addition to the high streets (Bordier 2004). Although the soft discounter has so far not been able to register noticeable gains in market share, the hard discount format will slowly conquer market shares (Colla 2004).

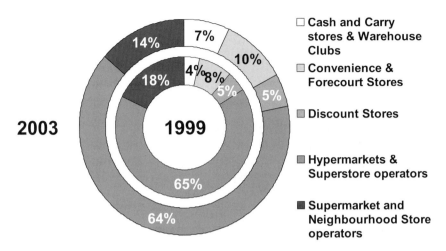

Fig. 7. United Kingdom: Evolution of Retail Structures
(Source: M+M planetretail 2004)

Since Carrefour pulled out of the UK, there have been no further attempts by French operators to enter the market. Apart from this the market is strikingly cosmopolitan, with the German discounters Aldi and Lidl accompanied by the Danish chain Netto, and also Dunnes from Ireland. The largest foreign operator with the highest growth potential is Wal-Mart (Colla 2004). The most important companies remain Tesco, Asda, Sainsbury, Morrisons/Safeway, and Somerfield (World of Retail 2004).

USA

The US economy is one of the richest and most influential in the world. While it has recently been through a weaker period, it is meanwhile well on the way to recovery (Murray 2004). The important indicators, such as inflation, real wages, productivity, interest rates, and business profits, reveal a return to positive trends. This development is also reflected in retail trade turnover. By virtue of this, the American retail trade has been able to increase turnover further in recent years (M+M planetretail 2004).

    The retail trade sector in the USA, with its immense network of superstores and hypermarkets (1999: 80%; 2003: 76%), department stores and large-scale consumer markets, large-floor-area discount stores, warehouse clubs (1999: 10%; 2003: 12%), and convenience stores (1999: 6%, 2003; 8%), is virtually immeasurable in terms of both number and diversity (see also Weitz, Whitfield, in this book). The leading companies in the American market are characterized by diverse innovation and high standards. For this reason, it is not surprising that many of the formats developed in the USA have since been successful in other parts of the world. It is also no surprise that the leading retailer in the USA is also the largest worldwide: Wal-Mart. The

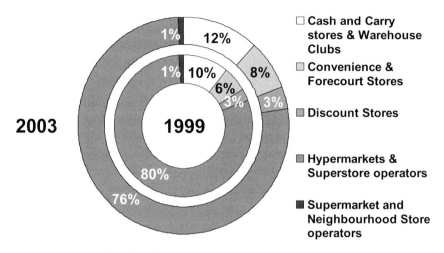

Fig. 8. USA: Evolution of Retail Structures

(Source: M+M planetretail 2004)

only foreign companies worth mentioning are Ahold, Delhaize, and Sainsbury. The American market is clearly dominated by Wal-Mart, Safeway Inc., Kmart, Albertsons, and Costco (world of retail 2004). In future, the question to ask is whether the other operators can continue to compete against Wal-Mart.

Evolution of Retail Formats

Cash and Carry Stores & Warehouse Clubs

Those tracking the distribution of cash & carry stores and warehouse clubs across the "G8" nations between 1999 and 2003 will discover that their percentage increased by 3 % during this period. Among other things, this change has been triggered by the rapid growth of this format in the Russian market.

In North America, stores with large floor areas, in particular those taking the form of membership-based warehouses, have a long-standing tradition. The strong increase in the number of cash & carry stores in Russia and in some areas of Canada can be explained by the large number of independent retailers organizing their sales activities by way of this format. If the current trends for concentration in the various trade environments continue in the future, the market share of independent retailers can be expected to decline, which will also result in reducing the market share of cash & carry stores. In addition, wider distribution in other countries is difficult, since this concept requires large shop floor areas. How quickly this concept will spread in the individual regions will depend on the legal framework in the country considered and on the availability of attractive locations. The legal conditions and the availability of suitable premises in Japan, for example, are unfavorable for this concept and for other large-area formats.

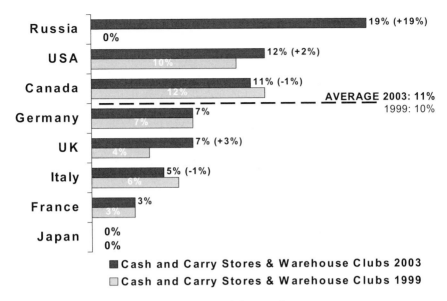

Fig. 9. Cash and Carry Stores & Warehouse Clubs: Development

(Source: M+M planetretail 2004)

Convenience and Forecourt Stores

The concept of convenience stores originated in Japan, and such stores have increased their market share by 1 % over the past five years. In Japan, in particular, where this concept has always been widespread, it has experienced additional growth. In addition, it has continued to expand in the UK and in the US. In countries where a strong focus on price has always prevailed and supported the spread of discounters, or where consumers have relatively little spending power, however, it has not yet become very popular.

The widespread presence of this trading format in Japan and in the United Kingdom is attributable mainly to the availability of adequate areas (Bordier 2004). In addition, both the US and the UK are countries where there has always been a high degree of quality and service orientation, a situation that favored the spread of convenience stores. It is therefore realistic to assume that along with any growing economic focus on the third sector, convenience stores will become increasingly widespread.

Discount Stores

Whereas convenience stores are widespread mostly in countries where consumers place little focus on price, the situation is exactly the reverse for discounters. Although the latter have increased their market shares in almost every country, resulting in a total increase of 2 % over the past 5 years, they have begun to spread mainly in European countries, and in Germany in particular (Bell 2001).

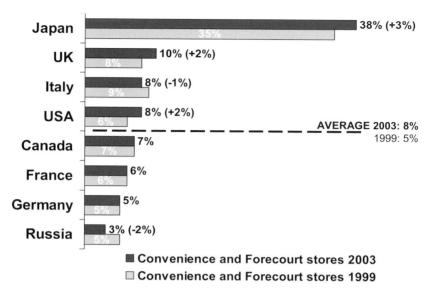

Fig. 10. Convenience and Forecourt Stores: Development

(Source: M+M planetretail 2004)

In addition, owing to their insignificant space requirements, discount stores have no reason to worry about any major restrictions based on the legislation in the respective countries. The growth of discounters usually proceeds at the expense of supermarkets. However, consumers who are not prepared to satisfy their basic consumption by restricting their purchases to a limited number of products might slow the growth of discounters.

The increasing price competition that has become apparent in all countries, reinforced by the market entry of international trade systems, favors discounters. Discounters also continue to flourish in countries facing a relatively tense economic situation.

Hypermarket and Superstore Operators

Hypermarkets and superstores stagnated in the years 1999 through 2003. Only the recent developments in Russia, where the percentage of hypermarkets has increased from 7 % to 20 %, have made it possible for this format to boost its market share to 45 %.

These concepts have always been present more in the Anglo-American countries, in which Wal-Mart operates. Thanks to its strong local market position in the UK, Tesco has been able to make progress in these areas and has begun to restructure its formats in the face of increasing competition. The same applies to Carrefour in France and the spread of its formats. All competitors make use of knowledge about their customer base in order to customize their product ranges and services (Murray 2004).

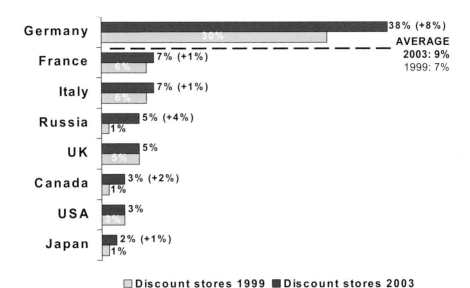

Fig. 11. Discount Stores: Development
(Source: M+M planetretail 2004)

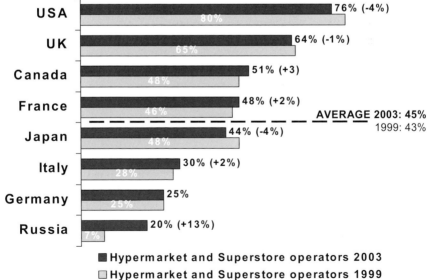

Fig. 12. Hypermarket and Superstore Operators: Development
(Source: M+M planetretail 2004)

In the future, competing discounters will be a vitally important factor. Both formats use low prices to distinguish themselves from their competitors. In Germany, for example, discounters are more widespread, whereas Wal-Mart has not yet been very successful. In the US and France, however, the opposite holds true.

Supermarket and Neighborhood Store Operators

The market share held by supermarkets and neighborhood stores has declined to 29% over the past five years. Even without the marked decline in Russia, this trend would still have been negative, albeit not as marked.

Supermarkets are typical for countries that continue to boast a large number of independent shops. As a result of increasing competition, these enterprises feel the need to join cooperative groups. It might be worth mentioning, however, that trading companies with more than one subsidiary tend to experience accelerated growth, whereas the formation of cooperative systems frequently results in deficiencies in efficiency and effectiveness arising from problems involved in achieving conformity in the management of independent enterprises. Consequently, supermarkets have little image-creation potential.

Restrictive legal requirements restrain the growth of large-floor-area systems and support supermarkets. These general trends will not necessarily lead to a total disappearance of this format in the future, provided that the current deficits are eliminated in the years to come.

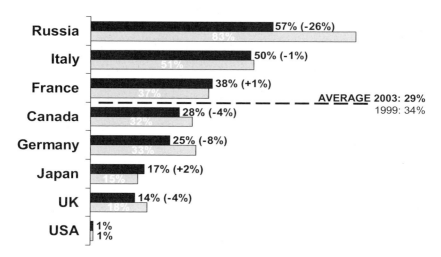

Fig. 13. Supermarket and Neighborhood Store Operators: Development

(Source: M+M planetretail 2004)

Future Trends in Retailing

The retail landscape is different now from how it looked ten years ago, and it will most likely look different again ten years from now. Making long-term predictions is a hazardous endeavor. Therefore, we will just outline some possible future trends on the basis of our observations of the current status of the retail landscape, without trying to be comprehensive (see also chapters by Dawson and Larke elsewhere in this book). We do not consider the impact of demographic change, which may lead to more convenience-orientated formats, or the role of emerging economies (e.g., China as the world's upcoming "workbench") in the global division of labor. Neither trend is yet fully understood, and hence predicting future scenarios would be like looking in a crystal ball. Therefore, we take an evolutionary approach to explaining the emergence of the trends in new retail formats. In particular, three related trends can be anticipated:

1. Retailers striving for success may consider filling gaps in the national retail landscape.

2. The quest for differentiation may lead to retail branding strategies.

3. New technologies may induce changes in distribution channels.

Gaps in the National Retail Landscape

A closer look at the dissemination of retail formats in the G8 countries leads to two major conclusions: the dissemination of convenience stores and of discount stores is unevenly, across nations and there may therefore be opportunity for competitive advantages.

Convenience stores have enjoyed steady growth in Japan over the years. It can be anticipated that convenience stores will gain market shares especially in countries that have a tradition in higher service orientation in retailing, such as the United States and the United Kingdom. The format "convenience store" may turn into a profitable niche in less service-oriented countries, especially Germany. There is a gap between discounter and supermarket. Legal restrictions in some countries (e.g. operating hours in Germany) may encourage cooperation between filling stations and convenience stores.

The next striking observation involves discount stores. It seems that Germany in particular is leading this trend in retailing, with a market share of 38 % for this format. The average proportion in G8 countries is less than 10 %. It can be anticipated that discount stores will gain market shares from supermarkets – as has been the case in Germany – especially in Russia and Italy. Russia is still searching for a national retail landscape. It is the fastest changing G8 market. Hard and soft discounters based in Germany may have a good chance of entering the market successfully. Italy, on the other hand, is not changing dramatically. Nevertheless, the slow economic growth and the unfavorable situation in southern Italy may also mean an opening for discount stores.

On the basis of these observations, it can be anticipated that German discounters are likely to export their retail formats to other countries, especially in the food retail market. A decline in the number of neighborhood stores, in Russia in particular, makes room for expansion of discounters. Also, it is likely that the popularity of convenience stores seen in Japan will spread to other G8 countries, and especially to Germany. In Germany, neighborhood stores are losing market share, and since discount stores are already very well represented there may be a comfortable niche for convenience stores. The relaxation of regulations governing store operating hours will also intensify this trend.

Retail Branding

A large proportion of a retailers' revenues come from selling (national) brands. Since most of any retailer's competitors also sell the same brands, finding a way of differentiating itself from the competition is particularly challenging. One possible response to this challenge is the introduction of private labels. Yet another answer is retail brand equity, meaning that the retailer's own brand is accepted as one to which consumers respond more favorably than to those offered by competing retailers. In retail practice, both options can be found: mainly large retailers have developed strong private-label merchandise (particularly in the UK), while others have such a strong brand name that the average consumer does not make a distinction between store and brand (e.g., the discounter Aldi from Germany).

The rise of the retailer as a brand is one of the most important trends in retailing. Understanding the image of a retailer as a brand and an appreciation of how brands impact on its image and ultimately on customer loyalty and profitability are important issues both for retailers and for the manufacturers of branded products, who rely on them to sell their own branded merchandise. Therefore, it can be anticipated that the market share for private labels will increase and larger retailers will position themselves as retail brands.

Trends Emerging from New Technology

It is generally believed that Internet technology will redefine the role of retailing. It will open up the way for new retail formats and new retail strategies. While, for instance, the share of US Internet retail sales is still less than 4% of total US retail sales (US Census Bureau 2004), the share of e-commerce sales is steadily growing throughout the world. According to Taylor Nelson Sofres Interactive's "Global e-Commerce Report," the world-wide increase in e-commerce activity is most evident for certain product categories, such as books, music CDs, videos, electrical and electronic goods, sports equipment, and toys, and for services such as consumer banking and finance and health information. The global growth in Internet activity has been attributed to the rapidly increasing number of computer users and the progressive development of Internet infrastructure in most countries, and especially the G8 countries.

Internet retailing is most likely to influence consumers' shopping behavior. E-Satisfaction, E-loyalty, and E-patronage are not only emerging fields of research in retailing, but also bring challenges to retailers with them. It can be anticipated that the "hybrid customer" will play an ever more dominant role. Retailers in particular must adapt to the buying behavior of "channel-hoppers," who use multiple channels to satisfy their needs and wants (see, e.g., Weitz chapter on electronic retailing in this book). This is a challenge especially for solitary retailers, since they are not embedded in a larger network of outlets operating a common database. A trend to more horizontal cooperation, as exemplified by franchising, can be anticipated.

RFID (radio frequency identification), a method of remote storage and retrieval of data using devices called RFID tags will also have a technology-induced influence on the evolution of retail formats. An RFID tag is a small object that can be placed on a product. It contains antennas to enable them to receive and respond to data from an RFID transceiver. Therefore, RFID tags allow a product to be tracked individually as it moves from location to location, even up to the point where it is in the consumer's hands. RFID may help retailers to decrease logistic costs. It may also be used to replace cashiers with an automatic system that needs no barcode scanning. Because of its logistical significance, discounters may profit from this innovation.

On trend rooted in new technologies is the emergence of ever more sophisticated loyalty programs. For instance, Tops, a wholly owned subsidiary of Central Retail Corp., will become the first supermarket chain in Asia to utilize loyalty-card technology that offers personalized benefits – including discounts, financing and personal shopping lists – while at the same time creating a vast database about the shopping patterns of its customers. Such CRM strategies enable retailers to create convert shoppers into loyal customers (for more information on loyalty programs in retail see chapter by Reinartz in this book).

Conclusion

The retail and trade market is one of the most important drivers of national economies. Therefore, it is necessary to develop it, especially in postmodern economies with highly demanding consumers and intense competition. In this paper, the current status quo of the retail landscape in the G8 countries has been shown. It can be noted that retailers are in a seemingly constant state of flux. The dominant player worldwide is clearly still Wal-Mart. When it comes to retailing, however, what works today will very probably not work tomorrow. The challenge is to identify the next development while it is still the next. Therefore, analysis of the current status of the retail landscape offers a good insight into the future shape of this extremely important market.

References

Bell, R. (2001): Grocery Retailing in the Germanic Markets, European Retail Digest, 29, pp. 25-29.

Bordier, A. (2002): Size is not everything in European Retailing, European Retail Digest, 35, pp. 1-3.

Bordier, A. (2004): European convenience retailing: a changing market, European Retail Digest, 42, pp. 66-70.

Colla, E. (2004): The Outlook for European Grocery Retailing: Competition and Format Development, The International Review of Retail, Distribution and Consumer Research, 14, pp. 47-69.

Murray, F. (2004): America, European Retail Digest, 42, pp. 71-73.

Myers, H. (2003): European Food Retailers: Paths for growth, European Retail Digest, 38, pp. 1-5.

M+M planetretail (2004): http://www.planetretail.net/, 22.12.2004.

U.S. Census Bureau (2004), United States Department of Commerce E-Stats, http://www.census.gov/estats.

World of Retail (2004): http://www.kamcity.com/WOR/, 22.12.2004.

Electronic Retailing

Barton A. Weitz

University of Florida, Gainesville, USA

Introduction

Perspectives on electronic retailing have changed dramatically over the past seven years. In 1998, most analysts predicted that a new breed of high-tech, web-savvy entrepreneurs would dominate the retail industry. Everyone would shop over the Internet, stores would close owing to lack of traffic, and paper catalogs would become obsolete. The prospects for electronic retailing were so bright that companies invested, and lost, billions of dollars in Internet retail entrepreneurial ventures such as Webvan, eToys, and Garden.com – companies that are no longer on the retail landscape.

Even though online retail sales continue to grow much faster than retail sales through stores and catalogs, we now realize the Internet is not a revolutionary new format replacing stores and catalogs. Although the Internet continues to provide opportunities for entrepreneurs, in the retail industry it is primarily used by traditional retailers as a tool, complementing their store and catalog offerings, for growing revenues and providing greater value for their customers. For the majority of retailing activity, the Internet is a facilitating rather than a transformational technology (Weitz 2001).

For example, REI's website enables its customers to buy merchandise that is available in its stores online. Orders can be shipped to the customer or be picked up at a store. Besides providing this e-commerce capability, the Web site has more than 45,000 pages of schedules for events and clinics in local stores, extensive product information, comparison charts, and how-to articles on a comprehensive range of outdoor sports and activities. As a result, REI offers online shoppers across the world an experience that complements its stores, where its staff provides personalized assistance in selecting the right outdoor gear, apparel, and accessories.

This chapter first describes the unique benefits and limitations offered by an electronic channel relative to store and catalog channels – factors affecting the potential growth of electronic retail. Then it reviews the approaches electronic

M. Krafft and M.K. Mantrala (eds.), *Retailing in the 21st Century: Current and Future Trends*, 357
DOI 10.1007/978-3-540-72003-4_22, © Springer-Verlag Berlin Heidelberg 2010

retailers are taking to exploit the advantages of an electronic channel and addresses its limitations. The chapter concludes with a discussion of issues associated with electronic retailing, such as the types of merchandise that can effectively be sold online, the potential increase in price competition resulting from the low search costs associated with online shopping, and what firms are best positioned to exploit the potential for an electronic retail channel.

Potential Growth of Electronic Retailing

Even though the annual growth of electronic retail sales is more than 30 %, the electronic channel accounts for slightly less than 3 % of retail sales in the United States and Europe, and an even smaller percentage in Asia. The relative benefits and limitations of Internet shopping as against shopping through traditional channels (stores and catalogs) will affect the future penetration of electronic shopping (Alba et al 1997).

Benefits of Shopping over the Internet

The following, somewhat futuristic, scenario illustrates the potential benefits of shopping online. Laurie Waters wants to buy a present for her son Allan, whose 13th birthday is in a few days. On her home computer, she accesses her personal shopper program called FRED, and has the following dialog:

FRED: Do you wish to browse, go to a specific store, or buy a specific item? [Menu appears and Laurie selects]

LAURIE: Specific item

FRED: Occasion? [Menu appears and Laurie selects]

LAURIE: Gift

FRED: For whom? [Menu appears]

LAURIE: Allan

FRED: Type of gift? [Menu appears]

LAURIE: Toy/Game

FRED: Price range? [Menu appears]

LAURIE: $75–$100

[FRED shops the world electronically, visiting the servers for companies selling toys and games in Europe, Asia, Africa, Australia, and North and South America.]

FRED: 121 items have been identified. How many do you want to review? [Menu appears]

LAURIE: 5

[FRED selects the five best alternatives on the basis of information about Allan's preferences, typical preferences for children Allan's age and Laurie's preference for nonviolent, educational toys. Details of five toys appear on the screen, with the price and brand name of each. The retailers selling the toy are also listed beneath each one, along with the nearest store with the toy in stock. Laurie clicks on each toy to get more information about it, including evaluations by *Consumer Reports* and comments from parents who have bought the toy. With another click, she sees a full-motion video of a child Allan's age playing with the toy. Finally, she selects a toy.

FRED: The nearest stores that have the toy in stock are listed below along with the prices. Do want to pick the toy up at a store, have it shipped to your home, or shipped to your office? [Menu appears]

LAURIE: Pick up at Toys "R" Us store near Perimeter Mall

FRED: Toys "R" Us suggests several books that appeal to children who like the toy you have selected. Do you want to review these books?

LAURIE: Yes

[The books are displayed on the screen. Laurie reviews the books and decides to order one.]

FRED: Would you like this gift wrapped?

LAURIE: Yes

[The different designs for wrapping paper are displayed on the screen and Laurie selects a baseball motif.]

FRED: How would you like to pay for this? [Menu appears]

LAURIE: American Express

More Alternatives. This scenario illustrates that, besides the benefits offered by all nonstore channels (convenience and security of shopping from home or work at any time), the electronic channel has the potential for offering a greater selection of products. However, the benefit of having many more alternatives has diminishing returns for consumers. It is unlikely that anyone would look through all 121 alternatives located by FRED. Having many alternatives is only meaningful if customers have access to intelligent agents such as FRED that can identify consideration sets based on the consumer's preferences.

More Information. The electronic channel also has the potential for providing customers with as much information as they need to make a decision. Customers shopping online can drill down through web pages until they feel comfortable with their choice. Also, the information on the electronic channel database can be frequently updated and is available all day and night. Finally, the electronic channel can format the information so that customers can use it effectively when evaluating products.

Personalization. Perhaps the most significant benefit of the electronic channel is the ability to use the Internet's interactive capabilities to economically personalize information. Service-oriented retailers such as department and specialty stores hope their sales associates will provide this benefit. They would like their sales associates to know or find out what their customers want and then recommend appropriate merchandise. However, an electronic agent such as FRED can be more effective in searching through an extensive range of alternatives, selecting a small set, and providing the information that the customer typically considers when making a purchase. Also, FRED is never in a bad mood, is paid nothing, and is always available – 24/7.

In the future, electronic agents such as FRED may be computer software programs bought by consumers or offered as a service to their customers by retailers or third parties. These agents could learn about a consumer's preferences by asking questions or analyzing past search and purchase behaviors.

Problem Solutions. The electronic channel also offers an opportunity to go beyond the traditional product information offered in stores to provide tools and information for solving customer problems and selling ancillary services. For example, online wedding sites, such as www.weddingchannel.com, offer couples and their families planning guides, tips, and an opportunity to chat with other couples getting married. The site sells wedding dresses, invitations, and flowers. Couples can create gift registries, featuring Federated stores, and broadcast them to their guests by e-mail. They can select potential reception locations by looking at photos. Finally, they can have their personal area on the site, on which they can post their own wedding pictures.

Limitations of Electronic Shopping

Although the electronic channel offers some unique benefits, it also has some limitations relative to stores and catalogs. Some of these limitations are the opportunity or ease with which consumers can: (1) browse through the retail offering, (2) locate information needed to evaluate merchandise, (3) use all five senses – touching, smelling, tasting, seeing, and hearing – when evaluating merchandise, (4) receive personal attention, (5) have their privacy protected, (6) provide a stimulating experience that can be shared with others, (7) purchase merchandise with cash, and (8) get the merchandise when they buy it. These issues do not arise or are less difficult for consumers to deal with when shopping in stores. For example, if a store shopper wants to know whether a store stocks an item that the shopper cannot find, the consumer can simply ask a store employee. However, when shopping online, the consumer has to send an e-mail to the retailer and sometimes wait days for a response.

Factors Affecting the Growth of Electronic Sales

Two important factors affecting the growth of electronic retailing are: (1) the number of people with broadband access and (2) the degree to which electronic retailers exploit the benefits and address the limitation of electronic shopping.

Internet Access

A substantial number of people worldwide have access to the Internet and thus can potentially engage in electronic shopping. According to the Computer Industry Association Factbook, in 2004, 934 million people had Internet access, and it estimated that this figure will increase to 1.35 billion by 2007. The countries with the greatest access are the United States (185.5 million people), China (99.8 million). Japan (78.1 million), Germany (41.5 million), United Kingdom (33.1 million), South Korea (31.7 million), France (25.5 million), Italy (25.5 million), Brazil 22.3 million), Russia (21.2 million), and Canada (20.5 million).

In August 2004 in the US, about 75 % of people with Internet access were classified as active at-home users. Nielson/Net Ratings estimates that, in July 2004, 50 % of the US homes with access had broadband connections. Broadband's prevalence is important, because consumers need such connections to take advantage of many of the innovations in electronic retail offering discussed below. Nielson/Net Rating also reported that the 2004 average monthly usage for member of their US panel was 25 hours in 31 separate sessions visiting 52 domains. However, in the US in 2004, only 26 % of active Internet users (64 million people) bought products and/or services over the Internet. Thus, there is a substantial number of active Internet users who do not shop over the Internet.

Exploiting the Benefits and Addressing the Limitations –
Electronic Retailing Best Practices

Given the significant penetration of Internet usage in industrial counties, the primary factor driving the growth of online retail sales will be the degree to which electronic retailers exploit their benefits and address their limitations (Putnam 2003). This section reviews some of the steps retailers using an electronic channel are taking to make shopping online more appealing.

Security Concerns. Perhaps the biggest challenge for online retailers is establishing and maintaining trust. Spam, fraud, identity theft, and fly-by-night e-retailers threaten consumers' fragile trust in online marketplaces. However, reputable retailers have taken steps to offer secure connections and protect their internal data. Also, as consumers become more accustomed to placing orders over the Internet, their concerns about security are diminishing. Retailers offering customers the option of calling in an order rather than ordering online report that the vast majority of orders are placed online.

Although consumer security concerns are declining, online retailers face increasing losses owing to credit card fraud. It is estimated that credit card fraud will cost online US retailers more than $1 billion in 2004. Online retailers use a variety of fraud management techniques, including using in-house or commercially available screens, requesting card verification numbers, and checking orders with credit card authentication services.

Browsing – Navigation and Search. Before an electronic channel was offered, consumers rarely described their shopping process as searching for a product they needed. They used terms such as browsing and window shopping, behaviors that often lead to unplanned purchases. Such browsing is more difficult for consumers shopping online.

When using an electronic channel, customers have a much more limited visual field than they do in a store. Only a limited number of items can be featured on the first web page and subsequent web pages viewed by shoppers. In contrast, in a store, many other items are in a shopper's sight line beyond the items prominently displayed on an end-cap or on mannequins. Although shoppers in stores do not mind walking a few steps to look more closely at merchandise, there is a substantial reduction in "foot traffic" on secondary Web pages.

Online retailers are addressing this limitation in two ways: (1) customizing the main page to display items of interest to the customer and (2) improving the search function. We shall discuss the customization of the main page in the section below on personalization.

The ease of navigation and quality of the search function facilitate browsing through a web site as well as locating specific merchandise. More than half of online purchasers use the search function to locate products. The search function is typically the second most heavily trafficked page on a retail Web site.

Traditional web site search functions rely on the exact words the shopper has entered in the search box. Many retailers now use "intelligent" search functions that respond to natural language inquiries such as "sweater under $100" and then refine the search by responding to secondary questions such as "ones that are red." These intelligent search functions also interpret the words and grammar to match responses to the retailer's merchandise assortment. For example, when searching the website of an automobile part retailer for an "air filter," a search function will not include coffee filters but may include links to related products, such as "engine cleaners." This search capability enables the retailer to accommodate the shopper's initial inquiry and also cross-sell and up-sell more effectively. Finally, these intelligent search functions get better over time as they learn the terminology used by the retailer and its customers.

However, implementing an intelligent search function can cost millions of dollars, along with an annual maintenance cost. For retailers with less complicated product lines, these costs may not produce an acceptable ROI.

Provision of Sufficient Information and Customer Service. At many points during the shopping process, consumers may need information before making a purchase. Service-oriented store retailers satisfy this customer need through their sales associates. However, providing timely information is more challenging for electronic retailers.

Consumers find the traditional online solution, posting web pages with retailers' policies and FAQs, fails to meet their needs. It is often difficult to comb through a list of FAQs to locate the information needed. Another standard feature addressing this need is the offer of an 0800 number or an e-mail address for asking questions. However, these solutions often fail to provide the timely information customers seek and may not be feasible for the consumer using the house's only telephone-line with a dial-up connection to access the retailer's website. Two new applications for responding to customer information needs in an efficient and timely manner are live, online chat and automated self-service solutions:

Online chat provides customers with the opportunity to click a button at any time and conduct an instant messaging e-mail conversation with a customer-service representative. Other applications allow a consumer to initiate a voice conversation with a customer-service representative. These applications also enable electronic retailers to automatically send a proactive chat invitation to customers on the site. The timing of these invitations can be based on the time the visitor has been on the site, the specific page the customer is viewing, or a product on which the customer clicked.

These *self-service solutions* are economically attractive. The average cost per customer service session for self-service is $1.17, as opposed to $7.80 for live chat, $9.99 for e-mail, and $33 for a telephone customer session.

Electronic retailers vary in how they make the tradeoff between stimulating sales and increasing customer satisfaction with the cost of providing online instant chat. Some online retailers make this service option available and highly visible on their home page and highly trafficked pages, while others deliberately make these services hard to find to encourage customers to use less costly options such as FAQs and self-service applications.

Overcoming the Need for Sensory Information. When evaluating some types of merchandise, information about "look-and-see" attributes, such as grams of fat in a breakfast cereal or color and style of a wool scarf, can be effectively communicated over the Internet. However, "touch-and-feel" attributes are more difficult to communicate online. Owing to the problems of providing "touch-and-feel" information, apparel retailers experience returns rate of more than 20% on purchases made through an electronic channel and only 10% for purchases made in stores.

3-D/Zoom Imaging. Electronic retailers are taking steps to overcome this limitation by converting "touch-and-feel" information into "look-and-see" information. Online customers now expect large, accurate product images. However, electronic retailers are going beyond offering the basic image to giving customers the opportunity to view merchandise from different angles and perspectives using 3-D imaging and/or zoom technology. Although only a limited number of electronic retailers are employing these technologies for a few products, the use of these image-enhancing technologies has increased conversion rates (the percentage of consumers who buy the product after viewing it) and reduced returns.

However, these imaging technologies can frustrate consumers using dial-up connections because of the slow download times. Also, some of the technologies require plug-ins that have to be downloaded and may not work effectively with all browsers. Finally, some retailers initially utilized these imaging technologies but have now removed them because visitors were not using them.

Virtual Models. To overcome the limitations experienced because apparel obviously cannot be tried on, online apparel retailers have started to use virtual models. These virtual models enable consumers to see how selected merchandise looks on an image with similar proportions to themselves and then rotate the model so the "fit" can be evaluated from all angles. The virtual models are either selected from sets of "pre-built" models or constructed on the basis of the shopper's response to questions about their height, weight, and other dimensions.

For example, at Landsend.com, online shoppers choose a model that looks like them. The customer then dresses the model using a "click-and-drag" interface. Items are suggested while the customer "tries on" apparel. Land's End reports that customers using the virtual model feature are 28 % more likely to make a purchase and spend 13 % more on the average purchase. When JCPenney offered this feature on its website, more than 100,000 customers saved their model for future visits.

In a similar way to the imaging technologies discussed previously, the virtual model technology is complex and results in slow download speeds for consumers who have no broadband connections. Also, the present applications are not true fit predictors, but provide some information about how combinations of apparel and accessories look together and what apparel styles might flatter a specific figure. However, these applications are harbingers of future applications in which customers can have a personal, 3D, digitized body scan serve as an actual model rather than a virtual model. Also, the measurements for the body scan could be inputted along with information about the garment to a predictive model advising customers on how well a specific item fits using a five-star rating system and then suggesting the appropriate size.

Personalization. One of the attractive features of Laurie Waters' online shopping experience, previously described, was the personalized service offered by FRED. This personalization assisted Laurie in satisfying her need for a gift. Had FRED's services been offered by a retailer, the personalization would have engendered Laurie's loyalty to the retailer. When a retailer has a thorough understanding of her preferences and uses this it effectively to facilitate Laurie's shopping experience, she has little incentive to switch to other retailers lacking this capability.

Although not achieving the level of personalization offered by FRED, Amazon.com is clearly on the forefront in terms of personalizing its offering. Visitors are greeted by a personalized "store" featuring their name and recommending products based on their past purchases, click-stream data, or expressed preferences. Besides personalizing the websites, customers can elect to receive e-mails announcing the availability of new product in which they might be interested. However, an important issue related to personalization is that of privacy concerns.

Privacy. Although detailed information about individual customers helps retailers to provide more benefits to their better customers, consumers are concerned about retailers violating their privacy when they collect this information. These concerns are particularly acute for online customers, because many of them realize the extensive amount of information that can be collected without their knowledge. Besides collecting transaction data, electronic retailers can collect information by placing cookies on visitors' hard drives.

In the US, legal protection for individual privacy is limited. Existing legislation is limited to the protection of information in a few specific contexts, including government functions and practices in credit reporting, video rentals, and banking. However, the European Union (EU) is much more aggressive in protecting consumer privacy. Some of the provisions of the EU directive on consumer privacy are:

- Businesses can only collect consumer information if they have a clearly defined the purpose, such as completing the transaction.

- The purpose must be disclosed to the consumer from whom the information is being collected.

- The information can only be used for that specific purpose.

- The business can only keep the information for the stated purpose. If the business wants to use the information for another purpose, it must initiate a new collection process.

Businesses operating in Europe can only export information from the 25 EU countries to importing countries with similar privacy policy. Thus, US retailers cannot transfer information from Europe to the US, because the US does not have similar privacy policies. Basically, the EU perspective is that consumers own their personal information. Retailers must get consumers to explicitly "opt in" and agree to share this personal information. On the other hand, personal information in the US is generally viewed as being in the public domain and retailers can use it any way they desire unless consumers explicitly "opt out."

There is a growing consensus that personal information must be fairly collected and the collection must be purposeful. The information should be relevant, maintained as accurate, essential to the business, subject to the rights of the owning individual, kept reasonably secure, and transferred only with the permission of the consumer. To address these concerns, most online retailers that collect customer information have posted privacy policies.

Cash Purchases. The lack of credit cards inhibits teens and tweens, a sizable and fast growing retail segment, from shopping online. However, several Internet service providers let parents establish an account for children using a credit card to set the initial balance. The teenager logs onto the site using a password, browses the site's electronic retailer partners, selects desired merchandise, and puts it in an electronic shopping cart. The shopping site takes care of the payment. Using their own passwords, parents can check up on their teens' buying habits and balance.

Although online retailers are using technology to address the limitations of online shopping, the store channel continues offer superior benefits to an electronic channel, such as providing information about "touch-and-feel" product attributes and ability to get products immediately after purchasing them, and offering a stimulating, social experience. Thus, most analysts project that online retail sales will only be 4-5% of total retail sales by 2010. However, retailer websites play a major influence on retail shopping behavior. A recent survey of a representative sample of Internet users found that more than 40% of consumers shopping for consumer electronics, books, PCs and peripherals, clothing, and CDs visited a retailer's website and then shopped at its store. This synergy between electronic and store channels is one factor leading to the growth of multi-channel retailing that will be discussed briefly at the end of this chapter and in more detail in the chapter by Sonneck and Ott in this book.

Electronic Retailing Issues

What Types of Merchandise Will Be Sold Effectively Through the Electronic Channel?

Presently, the greatest penetration of Internet sales is for travel services, computers and peripherals, and books. In purchasing these products and services, consumers feel the "look-and-see" information provided is sufficient. Other product categories, such as automobiles and houses, have had limited Internet sales, because the information available over the Internet is insufficient to make high-risk purchase decisions. Also, one suspects that products with important "look-and-see" attributes will not be purchased over the Internet (Zeng, Reinartz 2003).

Even though it is limited to providing "look-and-see" information, in some situations the electronic channel might even provide better information than stores. For example, if Laurie Waters went to a store to buy a toy for Allan, she might just see a picture on the side of the box containing the toy. However, by shopping online, she can get superior information from the full-motion video clip showing a child playing with the toy.

The difficulty of providing "touch-and-feel" information online suggests that jewelry, clothing, perfume, flowers, and food, products with important touch-and-feel attributes, will not be sold successfully through an electronic channel. This type of merchandise is presently sold through nonstore channels, such as catalogs and TV home shopping and, as discussed previously, electronic retailers are using technology to convert "touch-and-feel" attributes into "look-and-see" attributes.

Branded Merchandise. Branding, both the branding of the merchandise and the retailer's brand image, overcomes many of the uncertainties in purchasing merchandise without touching and feeling it. Consider branded merchandise such as Nautica perfume or Levi's 501 jeans. It is not possible to smell a sample of the perfume or try on a pair of the jeans before buying, but this need not matter since the brand insures that each bottle smells the same and each size fits the same.

The retailer's brand reputation can also provide information about the consistency and quality of merchandise. For example, consumers might be reluctant to buy produce online because they cannot see fruits and vegetables before purchasing. However, the same consumers would be likely to feel comfortable buying fruit from the Harry and David catalogs or Internet site, because Harry and David has established a reputation for selling only the highest quality fruit (Ba, Pavlou 2002). Branding even provides enough information to facilitate the sales of high-risk products with important "touch-and-feel" attributes, such as high-fashion apparel (bluefly.com and Neimanmarcus.com) and expensive jewelry (bluenile.com).

Gifts. In other situations, "touch-and-feel" information might be important but the information in a store is not much better than the information provided electronically. Since the gift-giver lacks complete information about the recipient's preferences, stores offer little benefit over an electronic channel.

Thus, the critical issue determining what types of merchandise can be sold successfully online is whether the electronic channel can provide enough information to make sure customers will be satisfied with the merchandise once they get it. There are many buying situations in which an electronic channel can provide sufficient information even though the merchandise has important "touch-and-feel" attributes.

Will Offering an Electronic Channel Lead to More Price Competition?

Many store-based retailers offer similar assortments of branded merchandise and thus have difficulty differentiating themselves on the basis of their merchandise offering. However, price competition between these store-based retailers offering the same merchandise is reduced by geographical constraints. When using the Internet, the number of stores that consumers can visit to compare prices is no longer limited by physical distance. Also, the ease of searching for price information is facilitated by shopping bots.

Although consumers shopping online can collect price information with little effort, they can get information about the quality and performance of products at a low cost. The additional information about product quality might lead customers to pay more for high-quality products, thus decreasing the importance of price (Lynch, Ariely 2000). Also, online retailers can differentiate their offering by providing better services and information. Even with the low search cost, research shows that significant price dispersions for online retailers persists (Ancarani, Shankar 2004, see also Bolton, Shankar, Montoya in this book).

What Resources Are Needed for Successful Operation of an Electronic Channel?

A consideration of the critical resources needed to profitably sell merchandise online explains why so many of these retail Internet entrepreneurs have failed and the evolution to multi-channel retailing. The key resources needed, shown in

Table 1. Resources Needed for Selling Merchandise Online

Resources	Internet retail entreprenuer	Catalog retailer	Store-based retailer	Manufacturer
Brand reputation	NO	YES	YES	YES
Retail skills	NO	YES	YES	NO
Customer information	NO	YES	YES	NO
Complementary merchandise	YES	YES	YES	NO
Unique merchandise	NO	YES	YES	YES
Web-Based information systems	YES	NO	NO	NO
Fulfillment systems	NO	YES	NO	NO

Table 1, are (1) well-known brand name and trustworthy image to attract customers to its website and reduce customer uncertainty in purchasing information, (2) retail skills for developing assortments and managing inventory, (3) customer information to personalize merchandise presentations, (4) complementary merchandise and services to provide a one-stop shopping experience, (5) unique merchandise to reduce price competition, (6) information systems for effectively presenting information on web pages and managing the fulfillment process, and (7) a fulfillment system to efficiently ship merchandise to homes and receive and process returns (Levy, Weitz 2004).

As indicated in Table 1, catalog retailers are best positioned to exploit an electronic retail channel. They have efficient systems for taking orders from individual customers, packaging the merchandise ordered for shipping, delivering it to homes, and handling returned merchandise. They also have extensive information about their customers and the database management skills needed to effectively personalize service. Finally, they have the visual merchandising skills used for preparing catalogs that are similar to those needed in setting up an effective website.

Many store-based and catalog retailers have established brand reputations and the capability of developing assortments and efficiently managing merchandise inventories – resources that most manufacturers and pure electronic retailers lack. Also, store-based and catalog retailers typically have more credibility than manufacturers when suggesting merchandise, since they offer an assortment of brands from multiple suppliers. These traditional retailers also have relationships with vendors, purchasing power, and information/distribution systems to manage the supply chain from its vendors to the retailers' warehouses. Finally, some catalog and store-based retailers sell unique merchandise – they have developed private-label merchandise.

However, most store-based retailers and manufacturers lack the appropriate systems for shipping individual orders to households. Their warehouse systems are designed to fill large orders from retail firms or stores and deliver truckloads of goods to retailers' warehouses or stores. To address this problem, store-based retailers such as Target, Borders, and Toys "R" Us outsource their fulfillment for online orders to Amazon.com and third parties. However, store-based retailers can use their stores as convenient places for online shoppers to pick up their merchandise and return unsatisfactory purchases.

Internet retail entrepreneurs were immersed in Internet technology and had considerable skills in the design of Web sites and developing systems to manage transactions. However, they did not have the wealth of past-purchase data that store-based and catalog retailers had. Also, the electronic-only retailers lacked the retailing skills necessary in building merchandise assortments, managing inventory, and fulfilling small orders to households. Finally, they also lacked the brand reputation to attract consumers and reduce their uncertainty.

Manufacturers also lack some of the critical resources needed to sell merchandise online directly to consumers, by-passing retailers. Retailers are more efficient than manufacturers in dealing with customers directly. They have considerably greater experience than manufacturers in distributing merchandise directly to customers, providing complementary assortments, and collecting and using information about customers. Retailers also have an advantage in that they can provide a broader array of product and services to solve customer problems. Finally, manufacturers lack information and distribution systems to fulfill individual consumer orders.

What Motivates Traditional Store-Based Retailers to Evolve in Multi-channel Retailers?

Traditional store-based and catalog retailers are placing more emphasis on their electronic channels and are evolving into multi-channel retailers for five reasons (see also chapter by Weitz, Whitfield in this book). First, the electronic channel gives them an opportunity to reach new markets, expanding their market beyond the locations of their stores. Second, they can gear up their skills and assets to grow revenues and profits. Third, an electronic channel overcomes some limitations of their traditional formats, for example by way of the convenience and security of shopping from home 24/7. Fourth, an electronic channel enables retailers to gain valuable insights into their customers' shopping behavior. Finally, providing a multi-channel builds "share of wallet" and customer loyalty (Hyde 2001).

Adding an electronic channel is particularly attractive to firms with strong brand names but limited locations and distribution. For example, retailers such as Tiffany's, Harrod's, Saks Fifth Avenue, Bloomingdale's, and Neiman Marcus are widely known for offering unique, high-quality merchandise, but, before they launched an Internet channel, customers had to travel to England or major US cities to buy many of the items they carry.

Store-based retailers can exploit their assets to greater effect when they add an electronic channel. For example, traditional retailers can use their existing format to economically create awareness for an electronic channel. For example, they can advertise the URL of their Web sites on in-store signs, shopping bags, credit card billing statements, POS receipts, and print or broadcast advertising used to promote their stores. The physical stores and catalogs also serve as advertisements for all the retailer's channels.

Store-based retailers can also utilize their stores to lower the cost of fulfilling orders and processing returned merchandise. The stores can be used as "warehouses" for gathering merchandise for delivery to customers. They can offer customers the opportunity to pick up and return merchandise at the stores rather than paying shipping charges.

One of the greatest constraints facing store-based retailers is their store size. The amount of merchandise that can be displayed and offered for sale in stores is limited. By blending stores with Internet-enabled kiosks, retailers can dramatically expand the merchandise assortment they offer.

An electronic channel can provide valuable insights into how and why customers shop and are dissatisfied or satisfied with their experiences. For example, information on how customers shop a merchandise category would be useful for designing a store or a website. The store and website layouts need to reflect whether customers shop by brand, size, color, or price point. Customer willingness to substitute one brand for another is valuable information for assortment planning. The task of collecting this information from store or catalog shoppers would be quite difficult. Someone would have to follow the customers around the store or observe them going through catalog pages. However, collecting data as customers navigate through a website is quite easy.

Although offering an electronic channel may lead to some cannibalization, using an electronic channel synergistically with other channels can result in consumers making more purchases from a retailer. The electronic channel drives more purchases from the stores, and the stores drive more purchases from the website. Retailers report that multi-channel customers spend 30 % more than customers who shop only in the retailers' stores (Myers, Pickersgill, Van Metre 2004); however, it is unclear whether this effect is caused by the availability of an Internet channel.

Evolution of Electronic Retailing

Compared with shopping in stores and through catalogs, online shopping has both benefits and limitations. The store channel enables customers to touch and feel merchandise and to use the products shortly after purchasing them. Catalogs enable customers to browse through a retailer's offering at any time and anywhere. A unique benefit offered by the electronic channel is the opportunity for consumers to search across a broad range of alternatives, develop a smaller set of alternatives based on their needs, and get specific information about the alternatives they want.

To some extent, retailers operating an electronic channel are using new technologies to address these limitations. But, the penetration of online sales is expected to be limited owing to the inherent advantages offered by in-store shopping. Although the bubble burst for most Internet retail entrepreneurs, traditional store-based and catalog retailers are adding an electronic channel and evolving into integrated, customer-centric, multi-channel retailers. This evolution toward multi-channel retailing is driven by the increasing desire of customers to communicate with retailers any time, anywhere, from any place.

By offering multiple channels, retailers overcome the limitations of each channel. Retailers can use websites to extend their presence and the assortment offered by the store channel. They can also use websites to update the information they provide in catalogs. Stores can be used to provide a multiple sensory experience and an economical distribution capability supporting the electronic channel.

References

Alba, Joseph., John. Lynch, Barton Weitz, Chris Janiszewski, Richard Lutz, Alan Sawyer, and Stacy Woods (1997): Interactive home shopping: Consumer, retailer, and manufacturers incentives to participate in electronic marketplaces, Journal of Marketing, 61(July), 38-53.

Ancarani, Fabio and Venkatesh Shankar (2004): Price levels and price dispersion within and across multiple retailer types: Further evidence and extension, Journal of the Academy of Marketing Science, 32, 2, 176-187.

Ba, Sulin and Paul (2002): Evidence of the effect of trust building technology in electronic markets: Price premiums and buyer behavior, MIS Quarterly, 26(September), 243-269.

Hyde, Linda (2001): Multi-channel integration: The new battleground. Columbus, OH: Retail Forward

Levy, Michel and Barton Weitz (2004): Retailing management, Chapter 3, Fifth Edition, New York: McGraw-Hill, 2004.

Lynch, John and Dan Ariely (2000): Wine online: Search costs affect competition on price, quality, and distribution, Marketing Science, 19(Winter), 83-104.

Putnam, Mandy (2003): E-Retailing: Levers for success. Columbus, OH: Retail Forward

Myers, Joseph, Andrew Pickersgill, and Evan Van Metre (2004): Steering customers to the right channels, McKinsey Quarterly, Issue 4, 36-48.

Weitz, Barton, Electronic retailing: Market dynamics and entrepreneurial opportunities, in G. Libecap (ed) Entrepreneurship and economic growth in the american economy, Volume 12. Elsevier Science, 2001, 211-234.

Zeng, Ming and Werner Reinartz (2003): Beyond online search: The road to profitability, California Management Review, 45(Winter), 107-131.

OPERATIONS, PROMOTION, AND MARKETING COMMUNICATIONS

Supply Chain Management in a Promotional Environment

Arnd Huchzermeier[1] and Ananth V. Iyer[2]

[1] WHU, Otto-Beisheim Graduate School of Management, Vallendar, Germany
[2] Purdue University, Krannert Graduate School of Management, West Lafayette, Indiana, USA

Introduction

Supply chain management deals with the effective and efficient coordination of flows of inventory, information and cash to lower the total cost of ownership. The supply chain view always starts with the point of purchase or consumption, e.g., at the retail level and follows orders upstream and product flow downstream from wholesalers, distributors, manufacturers and suppliers.

Since 1993, the fast moving consumer goods (FMCG) and the retail industry have formed an alliance to drive out waste out of their supply chains. The initial goal was to reduce the overall supply chain inventory by at least 5 %. This was triggered by the early successes at Procter & Gamble and Wal-Mart in the U.S. in using category management and supply chain collaboration approaches (including information sharing). At the same time, discounters emerged in Germany, i.e., Aldi and Lidl, and challenged big and small stores alike. By 2004, discounters accounted for 37.4 percent of the overall market. Currently, due to a lasting recession, grocery sales are declining and promotion intensity and frequency are steadily increasing across all store formats, including discounters. Retailers that refuse to collaborate with their suppliers but frequently adopt high-low pricing to attract customers to their stores (and lure them away from the every-day-low-pricing (EDLP) stores) are typically suffering from high inventory costs in their supply chains and large forecast error mostly for promotion items (see also chapter by Bolton, Shankar and Montoya in this book).

Influential references in this area consist of two studies conducted in the U.S., one by the Coca Cola Research Council (1993) and the other by the Food Marketing Institute (1993). In the mid 1990s, two cross-industry organizations emerged: Efficient Consumer Response in Europe (ECR Europe) and later the Global Commerce Initiative (GCI) in the U.S. The official ECR slogan is "working to-

M. Krafft and M.K. Mantrala (eds.), *Retailing in the 21st Century: Current and Future Trends*,   373
DOI 10.1007/978-3-540-72003-4_23, © Springer-Verlag Berlin Heidelberg 2010

gether to fulfill consumer wishes better, faster and at less costs." Since then, the 12 of the largest retailers (responsible for the demand side) and the 12 of the largest branded goods manufacturers (responsible for the supply side) are jointly coordinating the various supply chain initiatives. Besides supply and demand side issues, the management of integrators (communication processes) and enablers (technologies and standards) are also being considered (for further information see, e.g., www.globalscorecard.net). There is strong evidence that the initial goal of reducing pipeline inventory by at least 5 % has been reached and surpassed through the reorganization of the supply chains, the build-up of customer and consumer knowledge, management of new product introductions as well as the (electronic) exchange of mostly sales and inventory data and information.

Through the ECR initiative, a number of innovations (and standards) have been proposed and introduced for the management of supply chains: continuous replenishment or vendor managed inventory policies, cross docking, retail warehouses with efficient pickup and/or distribution logistics systems, extended barcodes for tracking and tracing of inventory, joint forecasting practices, advanced dispatch notification, radio-frequency-identification (RFID) tagging of pallets and cases, online retail exchanges, electronic product codes and catalogs, category management (CM), consumer relationship management (CRM), just to name a few new practices. As of January 1, 2005, according to an EU directive, European food manufacturers and grocery retailers must be able to trace their inbound and outbound material flows. Thus, information integration and exchange along the firm's supply chain is even mandated by law to ensure product safety for consumers.

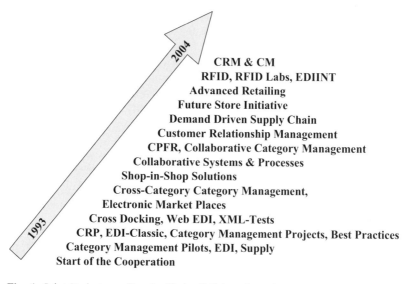

CRM & CM
RFID, RFID Labs, EDIINT
Advanced Retailing
Future Store Initiative
Demand Driven Supply Chain
Customer Relationship Management
CPFR, Collaborative Category Management
Collaborative Systems & Processes
Shop-in-Shop Solutions
Cross-Category Category Management,
Electronic Market Places
Cross Docking, Web EDI, XML-Tests
CRP, EDI-Classic, Category Management Projects, Best Practices
Category Management Pilots, EDI, Supply
Start of the Cooperation

Fig. 1. Joint Projects on Supply Chain Collaboration of METRO Group with Procter & Gamble over a Time Span of 11 Years

One example of successful supply chain collaboration between a retailer and a manufacturer is that between the METRO Group and Procter & Gamble in Germany (Huchzermeier, Burkhardt and van Wickeren 2005). Initially, the retailing company knew very little about its customers. As one METRO Group manager states it: "Ten years ago, we knew nothing about our consumers, the manufacturers told us how to attract customers into the stores. Today this situation has totally changed by us collecting systematically information on inventory and consumers through loyalty cards, purchase and market data." Like most retail companies, METRO Group started with the introduction of category management (see Figure 1). Today, METRO Group's Real hypermarket, for example, utilizes more than 50 category advisorships. A category advisor is responsible for the continuous optimization of the retailer's assortment within a category. In addition, supply chains were reorganized by using central warehouses as central delivery points for suppliers. The then CEO of METRO Group, Dr. Hans-Joachim Koerber, emphasizes that his company will continue to focus on gaining more supply chain benefits to improve its economic value added (EVA) performance. The introduction of RFID tags to track inventory in the supply chain (and consequently monitor out-of-stock situations in retail, e.g., see chapter by Verhoef and Sloot in this book) as well as developing the ability to target marketing activities directly to consumers, e.g., as demonstrated with personal shopping assistants in its Future Store in Rheinberg, are examples of the use of technology to improve retailing performance (see also chapter by Kalyanam, Lal and Wolfram in this book). This new kind of a direct marketing initiative for stores is labeled CRM & CM, since it combines key elements of both customer relationship management and category management.

A recent study in Germany on ECR implementation suggests that so far only large retailers and FMCG companies have been able to reap the benefits of supply

Table 1. Study on ECR

See ECR as a means for process changes only :	77 %
Expect high rewards from new technologies:	60 %
Do not yet exchange their product data files:	40 %
Have not adopted CRM:	50 %
Could not lower their out-of-stock levels at retail significantly:	70 % of manufacturers
Have implemented Collaborative Planning, Forecasting and Replenishment (CPFR) practices successfully:	Only 10 % of retailers and 15 % of manufacturers
Adopted cross-docking:	30 % of FMCG companies and retailers.
View ECR not as a top management issue:	50 %

chain collaboration. The following results have been collected in a survey of industry representatives (the data are presented as percent of total respondents).

Given the above data, it is clear that learning from best practice cases, e.g., the supply chain collaboration of Procter & Gamble with METRO Group, is essential to transition from the current adversarial relationships prevalent in the industry. In this chapter, we suggest that the exchange of information on retail promotions, combined with improved forecasting capabilities, can lead to sustainable win-win situations in the supply chain, i.e., increase sales and market share as well as lower total cost of ownership.

In Section 2, we review the recent literature on collaboration and coordination in a retailer-manufacturer supply chain. Section 3 discusses the potential benefits of information sharing for retail promotions in a competitive environment and collaboration using the CPFR framework as proposed by the Voluntary Interindustry Commerce Standards Association (VICS) in the U.S. Section 4 discusses the channel benefits of information sharing. In particular, we discuss a forecasting model for promotion items called S.M.A.R.T.S. which stands for Supply Management Advances Retail Traffic Strategy. The empirical study utilizes sales data of diapers from Procter & Gamble for a variety of retail stores in Germany. Section 5 concludes with managerial insights.

Supply Chain Coordination

The Bullwhip Effect in Grocery Supply Chains

A key concept that establishes the need for coordination in a retailer's supply chain is the concept of the 'bullwhip effect'. The bullwhip effect describes the situation whereby the demand forecast error increases as we move from the retailer to the wholesaler to the manufacturer and then to the supplier i.e., the demand variance is amplified as we move upstream in the supply chain. The best description of this effect is in a paper by Lee, Padmanabhan and Whang (1997).

Lee et al. (1997) provide four examples of the bullwhip effect, starting with a dataset from Procter & Gamble (P&G) in the U.S. We focus on two examples from that paper – the first example, depicted in Figure 2, shows a fairly steady customer demand for diapers reflected in the retailer's related orders to the wholesaler; with increasing variability in subsequent orders from the wholesaler to the distributor, from the distributor to P&G (greater variability) and finally from P&G to its suppliers (very high variability). Thus, a fairly steady demand stream has been transformed into a highly variable demand upstream. Such variability has significant costs and service level effects.

What is the cause for the bullwhip effect? A supply chain structure with information lags (for order transmission upstream), delivery lags (for physical goods

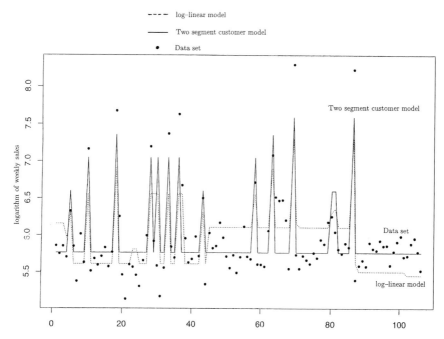

Fig. 6. Predicting Weekly Sales of Canned Tomato Soup in a Store over Two Years Using a Two Segment Customer Model

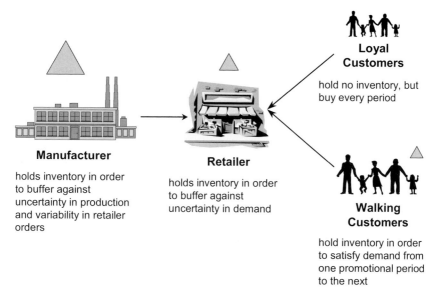

Fig. 7. A Manufacturer-Retailer Supply Chain with Loyal and Unloyal Customers

Consider the set of all customers coming to a store – assume that they can be divided into two segments (we use two as an example, e.g., see Figure 7; more segments may be warranted to model more complex demand environments). One segment purchases at a constant rate and is indifferent to retail prices as long as they are below a certain level. The second segment (non-loyal) will not purchase unless prices are below a certain level (their reservation price) and in addition, will typically stockpile product (when retail prices are low) and thus consume from individual inventory. This is the segment we focus on.

How does this segment of non-loyal customers decide how much to buy? Consider the following calculation that these consumers may carry out. They have a reservation price above which they will not purchase. They have a holding cost they posit to capture the limitations on their storage space (at home or in the car), their liquidity constraint, etc. Now imagine such a customer is being faced with a promoted product whose price is below their reservation price. Intuitively, a breakeven calculation is done by this segment to determine the number of days of consumption to purchase now. Let us use an example to calculate the breakeven number of days of consumption to purchase. For example, if the reservation price is € 1.00, holding cost is € 0.01 and the price during promotion is € 0.90, then the breakeven number of days is (reservation price – promotion price) / holding cost or (€ 1.00 – € 0.90) / € 0.01 = 10 days. Thus, faced with a price of € 0.90, this consumer will buy 10 days worth of consumption today. It is clear that a lower holding cost suggests a greater purchase for the same retail price. It is also clear that a lower promotion price encourages greater purchases from the same customer segment.

Now suppose the promotion price is € 0.90. How should a retailer promote in such an environment? Intuitively, promoting every ten days will get the segment one customers to pay the regular price most of the time and segment two customers to pay the promoted price of € 0.90 every 10 days (the breakeven number of days of consumption). Consequently, it would generate 2-segment purchase patterns similar to Figure 6, offering a rationale for promotion by the retailer.

Given the proposed stockpiling model, we can use statistical approaches to fit its parameters to a given dataset such as that in Figure 6. Observe that the stockpiling model provides a much better fit than a log-linear regression model of prices against actual demand (which is a textbook approach suggested by marketers and economists). The main observation is that the fitted model generates a forecasting model that explains over 74 % of the demand variation using a simple stockpiling model. In simple terms, we can now explain a significant portion of the link between sales and prices. Note, however, that in Figure 6, we still have cases where the observed sales are different from the model suggested sales. This requires us to know the forecast accuracy of the model and thus know the associated forecast error suggested by the model. Once we get that information, we can choose the retail inventory that provides a hedge against this model forecast error, and thus guarantee a relatively high in-stock availability at the store.

Collaborative Planning, Forecasting and Replenishment (CPFR)

What all of the above suggests is that any collaborative initiative between the manufacturer and the retailer has to account for demand swings due to promotions and cannot be content with regular price-based demand forecasts. Collaborative planning, forecasting and replenishment offers an interesting approach to find a way for manufacturers and retailers to manage their affairs through information sharing and collaborative planning. Typically, the focus of CPFR is on regular sales forecast error and not on promotions, as indicated in Figure 8. In this figure, 'Strategy and Planning' refers to a formal agreement to collaborate on joint business plans between a manufacturer and a retailer. 'Demand and Supply Management' imply frequent exchange of sales and order forecasts. 'Execution' deals with accuracy in order generation and fulfillment. Finally, 'Analysis' promotes exception handling and performance assessment on a continuous basis.

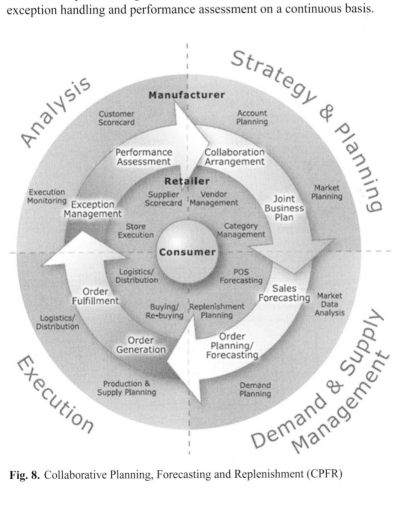

Fig. 8. Collaborative Planning, Forecasting and Replenishment (CPFR)

The European retailer METRO Group, however, decided to focus only on promotions in its pilot CPFR program with Procter & Gamble. (The day-to-day business of managing non-promoted items is performed by the manufacturer. This strategy is termed 'co-managed inventory'). The supply chain collaboration team describes this choice as self-evident as it offered the highest improvement potential and further enhancement of the relations between retailer and manufacturer. The primary objective of this pilot study is to improve efficiency by using the VICS recommended CPFR business model (for further information see www.vics.org). On a weekly basis, METRO Group and Procter & Gamble collaborate on promotion plans and sales forecasts with a twelve-week timeframe. Their rolling horizon planning system includes forecasts by each party, reconciliation daily to update forecasts with observed sales and continuous monitoring. The associated key performance indicators (KPIs) include service level at the warehouse, store and shelf, reduction in depot stock of promotional goods and order accuracy. Today, due to its complexity, the CPFR process has been reduced to only a few steps with a strong focus on frequently exchanging sales and order forecasts as well as continuous performance assessment.

The S.M.A.R.T.S. Model

The Fallacy of Forecasting Single Stock-Keeping-Units

Can one apply a forecasting model of promotion demand such as that of Iyer and Ye (2000) blindly to forecast demand for a single stock keeping unit (SKU)? Consider a retail environment where entering customers are presented the same product in different package sizes with different per-unit prices. Furthermore, suppose the prices vary over time. Customers would then be faced with package sizes whose price difference varies over time. We would then expect to see an environment in which customers switch their preference for package sizes at different points in time, withhold purchases until prices are low enough, stockpile inventory, and monitor price movements (see Huchzermeier, Iyer and Freiheit 2002).

In the following example, we focus on the diaper brand Pampers produced by Procter & Gamble. MADAKOM, a German retailing services firm, provided us with weekly POS data from several grocery retailers located throughout Germany. We selected this particular product since it accounts for 81 % of sales in its category, is an expensive and promotion-intensive item and it triggers store traffic. We plotted price against demand over a period of one year for one stock-keeping-unit (see Figure 9). As can be seen in Figure 9, there does not seem to be a clear relationship between customer demand and price variations for this particular SKU: the points A and B have the same price level but significantly different demand levels and point C shows that when price decreases, the quantity sold decreases as well. These are rather counterintuitive or idiosyncratic observations.

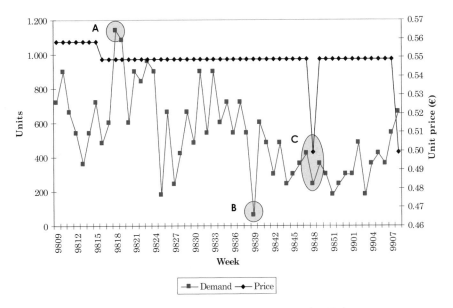

Fig. 9. Idiosyncracies in the POS Data for a Single Stock-Keeping-Unit

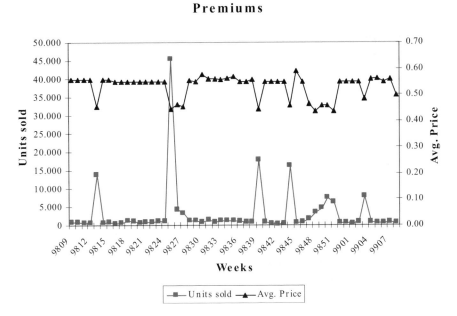

Fig. 10. Aggregated Demand (All Package Sizes) in Units and Price per Unit (in €)

Package Size Switching and Stockpiling Behaviour

These idiosyncracies lead us to believe that one needs to incorporate a consumer choice model where sales are affected by the price differences between package sizes each period. Consequently, we aggregated demand of all packages and determined the average price paid as the demand-weighted price across the various package sizes (see Figure 10). The forecasting model using two customer segments described above can then be applied in a very similar way with two minor modifications. First, we have to solicit consumer reactions to price promotions, e.g., determine their switching behavior across package sizes. (Moreover, it is assumed that customers in segment two do stockpile). Second, the aggregate forecast has to be broken down into forecasts at the individual SKU level.

Figure 11 shows the accuracy of fit of the unit demand forecasting model (based on a two-customer segment model applied to the aggregate demand for a particular diaper type, e.g., Jumbo diapers) relative to actual store sales over one year. It is important to note that the goal of the model is only to determine the fraction of customers who switch during promotions. Figure 11 provides a calibration of the model and simultaneously determines the fraction of customers switching to the larger (most economical) package size.

Accuracy of Forecasts for Single SKUs

Disaggregating the forecasts for the individual SKUs is straightforward. The aggregate demand is multiplied with the fraction of (price-sensitive) customers reacting to promotions. We call this number the "a"-factor where the level of "a" may be very different across retail environments or micro-markets (and certainly across Euro-Land). From the WHU-INSEAD shopper research study, we see that the German, French and Dutch population is far more price-sensitive than the Italian or Spanish. In our data analysis, we observed the following: demand for the large (and promoted) package size(s) can be predicted very accurately. Across all stores, the forecast error for the large package item is around 24 % with 87 % of all cases exhibiting a forecast error of less than 2 % (Huchzermeier, Iyer and Freiheit 2002)! Forecast error for the small package items is around 35 %. This is of little concern, since the fraction of sales during times of promotions is negligible. In both cases, improvements over the current level of forecasting error can be observed which typically varies from 30-140 % with a target of around 50 % which is rarely being achieved.

Information Sharing

How does all this help CPFR and promotions? It is our experience that including the consumer response to promotions through stockpiling and package size switching, the forecast error can be reduced significantly. Thus for CPFR to be

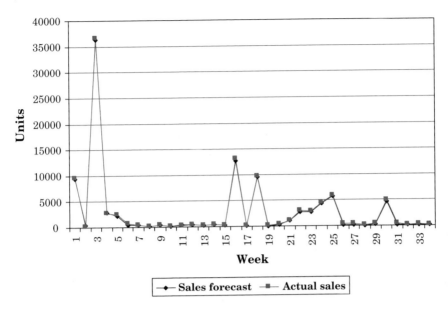

Fig. 11. Forecasts of Demand for the Large Package Item

successful in reducing forecast error and days of supply, a careful consideration of consumer response to promotions is an imperative. As outlined above, we suggest the following approach:

    a. Aggregate the sales data to see unexplainable issues at the SKU level

    b. Model the customer reaction to promotions, i.e., switching across package sizes and stockpiling

    c. Synchronize shipments with demand pull information to make promotions work for both the manufacturer and the retailer

In addition, as suggested by executives from METRO Group and Procter & Gamble at the 2nd ECR Research Symposium at the WHU, the order fulfillment process – which is not part of the standard CPFR framework – must be carefully managed during times of promotion.

Management Summary

Promotion Forecasts and CPFR

Retailer Perspective on CPFR. The retailer has better knowledge on consumer choice to promotions. In addition to market research data, he has access to POS data and information obtained through loyalty programs. The retailer also controls the assortment and merchandising available to the consumer in each store. His input to the collaboration is the understanding how promotions affect consumer choice.

Manufacturer Perspective on CPFR. The manufacturer has a sense of overall market potential. He also controls the product attributes, trade promotions and overall logistics capability. His input to the collaboration is the more accurate read of the market potential over time.

Supply Chain Collaboration. The joint retailer-manufacturer considerations represent the most accurate picture of SKU-level demand in the supply chain. Clearly this suggests the value of collaboration between the manufacturer and the retailer to better understand the consumer response. In other words, a crucial component of CPFR is understanding the "C" as in consumer or even better, Consumer Choice, to succeed in CPFR implementation.

Other Issues in Supply Chain Coordination

Private Labels and Their Effect. A report in 1993 suggested that $ 725 was the premium that a brand loyal family had to pay for a year's worth of supply of products from Procter & Gamble versus private label brands. This caused a significant number of supply chain initiatives to be launched by Procter & Gamble including a focus on smoothing trade promotions. Supply chain management and information sharing offered both Procter & Gamble and retailers opportunities to generate Pareto improving solutions that focused on improving the channel performance for the consumer. Many of the ECR initiatives focus on such efforts.

The Role of Online Exchanges. In the case of METRO Group and Procter & Gamble, the two companies have recently agreed to adopt a co-managed inventory strategy where promotions are being managed jointly. Otherwise, the manufacturer is responsible for the continuous replenishment of products to the retailer's central warehouse(s) or stores. In addition, only the first four steps of the CPFR framework are being practiced, i.e., those related to sharing of demand forecasts. The main reason is that the CPFR process is too complex and too difficult to implement in both organizations. In general, the METRO Group relies on single SKU-based forecasts generated by the SAF software (for further information, see www.saf-ag.com). In case of deviations, e.g., of promotion items, it then utilizes the e-platform GNX to intensify data exchange with its suppliers to synchronize forecasts with replenishments. As pointed out earlier, the forecast error is a function of the stockpiling effect of non-loyal customers and the consumer choice by loyal customers. Consequently, the research related to the S.M.A.R.T.S model as presented above will influence the way the METRO Group will determine promotion forecasts in the future.

RFID Tagging. Today, the capability of tracing and tracking of products is mandated by law in Europe and the U.S. The introduction of RFID tags at the pallet, the case or the item level will increase on-shelf availability and reduce total cost of ownership. The new technology also suggests more integrated manufacturer-retailer communications and promotions in the future (see also chapters by Gedenk, Neslin, Ailawadi and Raman, Naik in this book). For example, in a recent trial, the use of tags for similar promotions has resulted in a sales increase of about 20 per cent at stores using RFID technology (Financial Times 2007). Furthermore, in METRO Group's Future Store in Rheinberg in Germany, Procter & Gamble presents commercials when consumers take certain products from shelves, providing, e.g., information on conditioners for shampoos.

Outlook into the Future

Collaborative Planning and Forecasting In Europe, retail promotions have become a fact of life. While many manufacturers have adopted an every-day-low-costing strategy, few retailers can afford not to promote. In some instances, even EDLP retail chains have been convinced to adopt family packs or resort to price-based promotions. A number of firms have focused on generating supply chain benefits by coordinating replenishments to retailers even in a promotion-intensive environment. In this context, enhancing the retailer's forecasting capability and sharing information about demand and promotion tactics has improved overall supply chain performance. The use of technology for communication and thus information sharing and product tracking will potentially further increase supply chain efficiencies while benefiting the consumer by lowering out-of-stocks.

Risk Management. In markets, where efficient utilization of capital intensive capacity is a key driver of overall supply chain performance, spot markets are complemented by contract markets where options on inventory (or capacity) can be purchased in advance for the exchange of a reservation fee. In case demand exceeds available stocking levels, such options are utilized and the exercise price paid. It can be shown that such arrangements are Pareto-improving for the buyer and the supplier, i.e., more sales are achieved at higher profits for both parties involved (Spinler and Huchzermeier 2003). In the context of promotions, hedging the forecast error through procurement options would almost completely eliminate the need for physical stocks to cover the forecast error, and effectively share the risk between the two supply chain partners. This would lead to the most profitable supply chain design exhibiting the maximum level of performance. This is due to the fact that the overage risk is being shared and thus, the retailer is willing to stock more rather than less units. While improving forecast accuracy, i.e., below 25 % for individual SKUs (according to industry experts), is rather difficult and collaborative planning is becoming standard business practice, introducing contract markets may be the most effective tool for supply chain coordination in a promotional environment in years to come.

References

Cachon, Gérard P./Terwiesch, C. (2006): Matching Supply with Demand: An Introduction to Operations Management. McGraw Hill

Efficient Consumer Response: Enhancing Consumer Value in the Grocery Industry. Food Marketing Institute, 1993

Huchzermeier, Arnd/Burkhardt, Daniela/van Wickeren (2005): METRO Group: Advancing ECR. Case Study, WHU, Otto-Beisheim Graduate School of Management, Vallendar, Germany

Huchzermeier, Arnd/Iyer, Ananth. V./Freiheit, Julia (2002): The Supply Chain Impact of Smart Customers in a Promotional Environment. Manufacturing & Service Operations Management, Summer, pp. 228-240

Huchzermeier, Arnd/Van der Heyden, Ludo (2002): WHU-INSEAD Shopper Research Study. Proceedings of the 2nd ECR Research Symposium. Published by: WHU, Otto-Beisheim Graduate School of Management, Vallendar, Germany, www.whu.edu/prod/ecr

In-store tagging system still in the pipeline. Financial Times, February 22, 2007, p. 21

Iyer, Ananth. V./Ye, Jianming (2000): Assessing the Value of Information Sharing in a Promotional Retail Environment. Manufacturing & Service Operations Management, Spring, pp. 128-143

Lee, Hau L./Padmanabhan, V./Whang, Seungjin (1997): The Bullwhip Effect in Supply Chains. Sloan Management Review, Spring, pp. 93-102

New Ways to Take Costs Out of the Retail Food Pipeline. Coca Cola Retailing Research Council, 1993

Spinler, Stefan/Huchzermeier, Arnd (2003): Risk Hedging via Options Contracts for Physical Delivery. OR Spectrum, August, pp. 379-395

Steckel, Joel H./Gupta, Sunil/Banerji, Anirvan (2004): Supply Chain Decision Making: Will Shorter Cycle Times and Shared Point-of-Sale Information Necessarily Help? Management Science, April, pp. 458-464

Sales Promotion

Karen Gedenk[1], Scott A. Neslin[2], and Kusum L. Ailawadi[3]

[1] University of Cologne, Germany
[2] Tuck School of Business at Dartmouth, Hanover, USA
[3] Tuck School of Business at Dartmouth, Hanover, USA

Introduction

Sales promotions are a marketing tool for manufacturers as well as for retailers. Manufacturers use them to increase sales to retailers (trade promotions) and consumers (consumer promotions). Our focus will be on retailer promotions, which are used by retailers to increase sales to consumers. Typical examples of retailer promotions are temporary price reductions (TPRs), features, and displays.

Sales promotions have an important role in the marketing programs of retailers. A large percentage of retailer sales is made on promotion, as illustrated by the numbers in Figure 1. Also, retailer promotions address consumers at the point of sale. Thus, while advertising in classic media is becoming less effective, communication through promotions reaches the consumer at the place and time where most purchase decisions are made. The Point of Purchase Advertising Institute (POPAI) finds in a study from 1999 that the in-store decision rate of consumers in Germany, for example, is 55%, meaning that more than half of all purchase decisions are made in stores, as opposed to before the shopping trip.

At the same time, the management of retailer promotions is not trivial, for several reasons. First, retailers can use many different forms of price promotions, such as temporary price reductions, coupons, and multi-item promotions, and combine them with nonprice promotions like features, displays, and other POS material. Second, retailer promotions can have many different effects. For example, increases in sales can result from brand switching, store switching, category switching, stockpiling, or increased consumption. In order to evaluate the profitability of a promotion, it is important to disentangle these effects. Third, manufacturers and retailers pursue different goals, and retailers have to take into account the manufacturer's trade promotion policy and its impact on their own margins

M. Krafft and M.K. Mantrala (eds.), *Retailing in the 21st Century: Current and Future Trends*,   393
DOI 10.1007/978-3-540-72003-4_24, © Springer-Verlag Berlin Heidelberg 2010

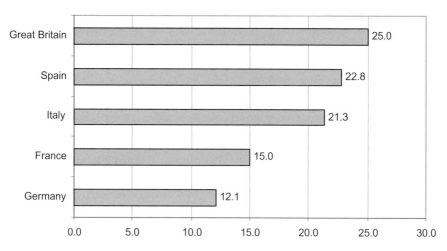

Percentage of Sales (in €) Made on Promotion, January – June 2004

Fig. 1. Percentage of Sales Made on Promotion in Europe (A.C. Nielsen)

when planning their retailer promotions. Such initiatives as efficient consumer response (ECR) and collaborative planning, forecasting, and replenishment (CPFR)
have tried to promote more cooperation between manufacturers and retailers, one
area of cooperation being sales promotions (see, e.g., chapter by Huchzermeier, Iyer
in this book).

Over the last 25 years a large research effort has been spent on studying the effects of promotions. Methods for measuring the success of promotions have been
developed and refined. And many substantive results have been accumulated,
allowing us to make some empirical generalizations.

At the beginning of the 21st century, promotions are facing new opportunities
and challenges as technology plays an increasing part in retailing. Technologies
such as loyalty cards, electronic media at the point of sale, and electronic shopping
assistants are likely to have an impact on how retailers use promotions, e.g. to
allow better targeting of consumers.

The purpose of this chapter is twofold. First, we want to review what we know
about promotions as retailers have used them in the past. Second, we want to discuss the opportunities and challenges for promotions presented by new technologies in retailing.

The chapter is divided up as follows. In the second section, we categorize and
describe promotion instruments that retailers may use. In the third, we give an
overview of the effects of retailer promotions on sales and present empirical results
as to the strength of these effects. We describe new technologies used in retailing
and discuss the resulting opportunities and challenges for promotions in the fourth
section.

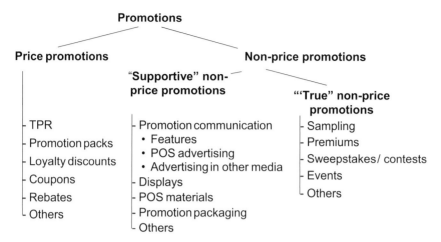

Fig. 2. Instruments for Retailer Promotions

Promotion Instruments

Figure 2 shows different promotion instruments that retailers may use (Gedenk 2002, Neslin 2002).

A first distinction can be made between price and nonprice promotions. The price promotion instrument used most often is a temporary price reduction (TPR). However, other forms of price promotion are possible. Retailers can use promotion packs, i.e., packages with extra content (e.g., "25 % extra"), or multi-item promotions (e.g., "buy three for x" or "buy two get one free"). Loyalty discounts also require the purchase of several units, but the consumer can do this over several purchase occasions. Retailers can also use coupons or rebates. With coupons, consumers have to bring the coupon to the store in order to get a discount. With rebates, consumers pay the full price, but they can then send in their receipt to get a discount.

'Supportive' nonprice promotions are communication instruments used to alert the consumer to the product or to other promotion instruments. Very often they are used to draw attention to price promotions. For example, products on TPR are featured or displayed. Thus, the focus is not so much on the brand as on price. Note that they can also be used without a price promotion. For example, a feature can advertise an everyday low price policy or a new product. Interestingly, there is evidence that consumers may interpret supportive nonprice promotions as a signal for a price cut even if they are not coupled with actual price discounts, since the two are closely linked in many consumers' minds.

Finally, retailers can use 'true' nonprice promotions, where the focus of the promotion is clearly on a brand or store, and not on a price cut. However, instruments such as sampling and premiums are mostly used by manufacturers, and not by retailers. Therefore, our focus in the following will be on price and supportive nonprice promotions.

Effects of Promotions

Overview of Effects

To assess the profitability of retailer promotions, retailers have to take into account their costs, the trade promotion allowances given to them, and the effect of promotions on sales to consumers (for more discussion on this point, see chapter by Bolton, Shankar and Montoya in this book). The biggest challenge for controllers lies in assessing the sales effects. Thus, we will discuss these in this section. Figure 3 shows the effects of a retailer promotion on the sales of the promoted product (Gedenk 2002, Neslin 2002).

In Figure 3, we distinguish between short-term effects, which occur during the promotion, and long-term effects, which involve behavior that takes place after the promotion. Sales for the promoted brand can increase during the promotion by attracting customers from other stores (store switching), inducing customers to switch brands (brand switching), inducing customers to buy from the promoted category rather than another category (category switching), inducing customers who normally do not use the product category to purchase it (new users), or inducing customers to move their purchases forward in time (purchase acceleration). Purchase acceleration can occur because consumers purchase earlier or because they purchase more than they would have done without the promotion. Consumers can either stockpile the extra quantity for future use or consume it at a faster rate. Total category consumption can also increase owing to category switching or if the promotion attracts new users.

While the short-term sales bump will be highest if all these mechanisms are at work, the particular breakdown of the bump into these mechanisms is important for the profitability of the promotion. Therefore, a controller must not stop at measuring

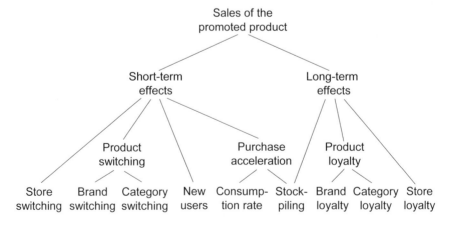

Fig. 3. Effects of Retailer Promotions

the size of the short-term sales bump. Rather, it is important to analyze this bump. An increase in category consumption resulting from new users, category switching, or a higher consumption rate is beneficial for both retailers and manufacturers. If the bump is caused by consumer store switching, this is beneficial only to the retailer. Note there are two types of store switching—direct and indirect. A direct store switch is seen when the consumer visits store A rather than store B. An indirect store switch is when the consumer shops at both stores, but the promotion in store A pre-empts a purchase that would otherwise have occurred at store B. Either form of store switching is beneficial to the retailer.

In contrast, the part of the promotion bump that results from brand switching within the store is good for the manufacturer, but not necessarily for the retailer. The effect on the retailer's profit depends on which product has the higher margin —the product switched to or the product switched from. Accelerated purchases that are stockpiled for future use may or may not be beneficial to the retailer. If retailer profit margin during the promotion period is larger than that during the non-promotion period, it is to the advantage of the retailer to encourage stockpiling. This may be why retailers sometimes use promotion signage such as "stock up and save." If, however, the retailer's promotional margin is smaller than the regular margin stockpiling is unprofitable for the retailer.

In short, measuring the size of the short-term bump in sales actually says very little about whether the promotion is successful from the retailer's point of view. The bump must be broken down as far as possible into the effects shown in Figure 3, and the retailer's regular and promotional margins must be taken into account.

In addition to increases in short-term sales, promotions can have an effect on long-term sales. Consumer stockpiling increases sales during the promotion, but decreases them afterwards. Also, consumer loyalty may change. Manufacturers hope for increased brand loyalty, while retailers would like to increase store loyalty. However, promotions may also have a negative effect on loyalty. Price promotions can decrease consumers' reference prices, thus making the brand/store appear expensive on the next shopping trip. Attribution theory and behavioral learning theory explain how consumers can learn from buying on promotion, but these theories cannot predict whether consumers learn to buy a certain brand/in a certain store, or whether they learn to purchase on promotion.

Finally, a retailer is not only interested in sales of the promoted product, but also in sales of other products in the store. Promotions are very favorable for a retailer if they draw consumers into the store, who then also purchase non-promoted products. This can only occur if store switching is direct and the store-switching consumers are not just cherry picking. If store switching is indirect, consumers shop at both store A and store B, and this is not changed by the promotion in store A. If store switching is direct but the store switchers are cherry pickers, then they only come to the store to buy the promoted product, so that sales of other products do not increase.

What We Know About the Strength of Promotion Effects

Many researchers have developed methods to measure the effects of promotions on sales and applied them to generate substantive results over the last 25 years. Most of these studies are based on scanner data and study fast-moving consumer goods sold in grocery stores. Some studies use store-level scanner data, which have the advantage of being readily available for managers. However, single-source scanner panel data, which combine household and store data, allow a more detailed analysis of promotion effects. With single-source data, researchers can go beyond sales or market share response functions and investigate consumer behavior, such as store choice, category purchase incidence, brand choice, and purchase quantity in more detail. Therefore, many empirical studies are based on this type of data. All these studies, together with laboratory and field experiments, have generated a wealth of results (for reviews see Gedenk 2002, Neslin 2002).

Short-Term Effects

Retailer promotions typically cause a large bump in short-term sales of the promoted brands. Increases in sales by several hundred percent are not unusual. Promotional price elasticities differ across categories and depending on the promotion instruments used. For example, Narasimhan, Neslin, and Sen (1996) find that promotional elasticities are higher for categories with a relatively small number of brands, shorter interpurchase times, and higher consumer propensity to stockpile.

Supportive nonprice promotions can be used to enhance the effects of price promotions by drawing attention to them. For example, Narasimhan, Neslin, and Sen (1996) report on the basis of an Information Resources, Inc., study that a 15% "unsupported" price cut yields an average sales increase of 34% across 108 categories, whereas a 15% price cut supported by a feature generates a 161% increase, and a 15% price cut supported by a display generates a 293% increase. Supportive nonprice promotions can also serve the purpose of framing the deal. After all, a price promotion is like a picture—it looks different depending on which frame you put around it. Possible frames are external reference prices (e.g., "normally 3.99 €— today only 2.99 €") or price cuts expressed in percent ("25% off") rather than in absolute terms ("1 € off"). Sometimes these frames can have strong effects, which result from simply putting up a sign. For example, Wansink, Kent, and Hoch (1998) show in a field experiment that imposing a quantity limit for canned soup ["limit of 4 (12) per person"] increases the average quantity bought per person. Given that consumers who would have bought a very large quantity without the promotion are not allowed to do so, a decrease in average quantity would have been expected. The authors explain their surprising results with an anchoring and adjustment effect. Consumers use the number in the quantity limit as an anchor to adjust their purchase quantity upwards. Another explanation could be that consumers interpret the quantity limit as a signal for a particularly attractive promotion. Finally, supportive nonprice promotions can be used by themselves without a price reduction. Often consumers interpret promotional signs and displays in the stores as a signal for a promotion, resulting in an increase in sales at full margin. In summary, then, not only do price reductions matter, but POS signage, displays, and features can have a large impact on sales and profit contribution.

Many researchers have broken down the short-term sales bump into brand switching and purchase acceleration components. Until recently, empirical analyses seemed to indicate that about three quarters of the sales bump results from brand switching. However, van Heerde, Gupta, and Wittink (2003) have pointed out that these studies, which are based on a breakdown of the elasticity, have been interpreted in an inadequate way. When van Heerde, Gupta, and Wittink performed a unit sales decomposition and look at how much the promoted brand gains and how much competitors lose in sales, they found that two thirds of the sales bump resulted from purchase acceleration and only one third from brand switching. Other authors have shown that purchase acceleration can translate into additional category consumption through a faster use-up rate. For example, Ailawadi and Neslin (1998) find that 13 % of the short-term sales bump for yogurt is due to increased consumption, whereas in the case of ketchup increased consumption accounts for only 5 %. In summary, then, we know that promotions cause substantial purchase acceleration, which, at least in some categories, can result in increased consumption.

The most important promotion effect for a retailer, store switching, has not been studied as much, and the empirical evidence of it that exists is somewhat mixed. A few studies find no effect of promotions on store traffic and store sales, but these studies use store-level data from supermarkets that run promotions every week, so that they can only study differences between the promotion bundles advertised each week. Other studies do indicate that promotions increase store traffic (e.g., Lam et al. 2001) and that a substantial part of the category expansion within the store comes from store switching (e.g., van Heerde, Leeflang and Wittink 2004). The latter study finds that, on average across different types of promotions, store switching accounts for 25 % of the sales bump for tissues and 34 % for peanut butter. The effect is about as strong for unfeatured as for featured promotions, indicating that a lot of the store switching must be indirect. More support for indirect store switching is provided by Bucklin and Lattin (1992), who studied single-source scanner panel data for detergent. They find no evidence for direct store switching from features, but an increase in market share of the store in the promoted category, resulting from indirect store switching.

Even less is known about the extent of category switching that is attributable to promotions. One cross-category effect that has been studied extensively is category complementarity, that is, whether promotions in category A can increase sales in category B if the products are used or purchased together by the consumer. For example, Mulhern and Leone (1991) find sales increases for related products in some grocery categories, but not in others. They also find that if cross-category relationships exist, they are asymmetrical. For example, cakemix prices significantly affect frosting sales, but the reverse is not true. Mulhern and Padgett

(1995) matched actual purchases of consumers with survey data to study the effect of promotions on nonpromoted products. In this study, only 23.2 % of consumers who indicated that they had come to the store because of a promotion bought only the promoted item. This means that cherry picking exists, but not to a very large extent. At the same time, 51.8 % of the consumers who had come to the store because of the promotion bought only nonpromoted items. Mulhern and Padgett found that this is not because the promoted product is out of stock, but because many consumers change their plans once they come to the store, or are disappointed by the promoted item when they inspect it. Note that Mulhern and Padgett find this effect in a home improvement store. In grocery retailing, where products are well known, it seems less likely that many consumers will visit the store because of a promotion but then not buy the promoted product. In summary, then, there is some evidence for positive effects of promotions on nonpromoted products, but it is not very strong. This issue certainly warrants further investigation.

Long-Term Effects

Many researchers have studied the effect of promotions on brand loyalty. They find that temporary price cuts decrease reference prices, increase price sensitivity, and decrease share of category requirements and repurchase probabilities. These findings suggest a negative relationship between promotion and brand loyalty. However, the net effect on brand sales may be positive, at least for some customers. The reason is that consumers show some inertia in their purchase patterns: they tend to repurchase what they purchased last time. A promotion makes it more likely for this inertial effect to occur, because it induces that first purchase. Promotion weakens the inertial effect relative to a non-promotion purchase, but the inertial effect is still positive. As a result, promotions do not necessarily decrease long-term market share (Gedenk and Neslin 1999). In fact, the net impact on share can be positive. Ailawadi, Lehmann, and Neslin (2001) find that, in the long run, decreasing promotion and, as a result, increasing net price had a detrimental effect on customer share of requirements and contributed to a decrease in market share. In addition, Gedenk and Neslin (1999) find that nonprice promotions such as features and sampling have a weaker short-term effect, but are more favorable for brand loyalty than are price promotions, resulting in a stronger positive net effect on brand choice probabilities after the promotion.

Unfortunately, the effect of promotions on store loyalty has not been studied as much. An important measurement issue with regard to store loyalty is whether inherently nonloyal shoppers are self-selected to shop at promotion-oriented stores, or whether promotions in fact erode the loyalty of shoppers over time. Bell and Lattin (1998) provide some evidence of a self-selection effect. They show that consumers who purchase large total market baskets per visit tend to favor stores that feature everyday low pricing (EDLP), whereas shoppers who purchase small market baskets prefer stores that run good promotions. Sirohi, McLaughlin and Wittink (1998) find that perceptions of a store's promotions correlate positively with perceived value and store loyalty. Finally, Taylor, Neslin (2005) provide evidence for a positive effect of a special type of promotion on store loyalty. They studied a loyalty promotion in which consumers could obtain a free turkey product based upon purchases during an 8-week promotion period. They found that this reward program increased sales during the 8 weeks of the promotion ("points pressure effect"). In addition, consumers participating in the promotion purchased more in the store after the promotion. This "rewarded behavior effect" occurs because the goodwill and positive affect created by the reward resulted in the customer having a more favorable view of the retailer and hence purchasing more. In summary, there is some evidence that promotions can have a positive effect on store loyalty, but the issue warrants further investigation.

Future Developments

New Technologies

Retailing is currently facing opportunities from a variety of new technologies. In Germany, METRO Group is currently testing many of these technologies in its "Future Store," a grocery store belonging to the "Extra" chain in Rheinberg. In this paper we will not discuss all of these technologies, but just briefly present those that we expect to have the largest impact on promotions:

- Loyalty cards
- Personal shopping assistants (PSA)
- Electronic shelf labels and advertising displays
- RFID

Loyalty Cards

Loyalty cards have been used by retailers for quite a few years. Nonetheless, they are still included here, since they can be combined with some of the other technologies and they constitute a major basis for targeting promotions. METRO Group in Germany is a participant in the "Payback" loyalty program administered by the company Loyalty Partners. Consumers can collect Payback points in many METRO Group stores, such as Real (grocery), Kaufhof (department store), but also in chains of other retailers, such as Apollo Optik (optician) and Goertz (shoes). Once consumers have collected a certain number of points they can exchange them for a cash payment or a premium. In September 2004, Payback had issued as many as 28.3 million cards to consumers in Germany (the chapter by Reinartz in this book provides more information on the design of loyalty programs).

For METRO Group, Payback provides valuable data for promotion analysis and planning. As in a single-source panel, the retailer has data on consumer purchase behavior at the household level, as well as in-store data on the promotion environment at the time when purchases are made. One disadvantage relative to single-source data is that loyalty card data only concern purchases within the participating chains of stores. Thus, purchases made in a competitor's store cannot be registered. Note also that Payback only provides detailed data for consumers who have acquired their card through a certain chain of stores. Owing to privacy regulations, the rest of the raw Payback data is only available to Loyalty Partners. It can nonetheless be used for targeting consumers, since direct mail promotions, for example, can be sent through Loyalty Partners.

Personal Shopping Assistants

Personal shopping assistants (PSAs) can be attached to customers' shopping carts when they enter a store. At the Future Store, the PSA reads the Payback card of a shopper, so that it can access the purchase history of the customer's household. The PSA display shows an electronic shopping list. It initially proposes a shopping list based on the favorites from previous purchases. The consumer can than modify that list. If the consumer scans the products s/he puts into the shopping car, the PSA calculates total price and indicates savings from products bought at a reduced price (see also chapter by Litfin and Wolfram in this book). In addition, the PSA displays information on promotions in the store. PSAs therefore offer the potential to induce category complementarity and encourage new use, indirect store switching, and purchase acceleration effects.

Electronic Shelf Labels and Advertising Displays

Electronic shelf labels and advertising displays are controlled centrally by WLAN. In the Future Store, electronic shelf labels are directly connected to the price administration system and the checkout system. Thus, prices on the shelves are always identical to prices at the checkout. On LCD displays the labels show the prices of products on the shelf. In addition, special offers may be highlighted by a flashing signal.

Electronic advertising displays are attached to the ceiling in several locations in Future Store. They can display advertising messages or show videos. Messages can be changed within seconds. This type of signage might be very effective at inducing profitable brand switching and indirect store switching as well as new use and purchase acceleration effects (see, e.g., chapter by Kalyanam, Lal, and Wolfram in this book for more detail on technologies being used in Future Store).

Radio Frequency Identification

Finally, an important new technology in retailing is radio frequency identification (RFID). This auto-identification technology uses radio waves to identify individual physical objects. In the US, WalMart is the first to have asked its suppliers to attach RFID tags to pallets and cases of products. In Germany, METRO Group is a pioneer in the usage of RFID. In its Future Store, it is even running tests with tags attached to individual products. So far, this is an expensive exercise, since each tag costs about 30 cents. Also, RFID is still beset with technical problems, such as the receivers' inability to read through liquid and metal. Finally, consumers have strong concerns about privacy. This has induced the Future Store to test deactivating devices, which make sure that RFID tags can no longer be read once the consumer leaves the store. In spite of these current difficulties, many experts expect RFID to develop further and replace identification through UPC/EAN in the future.

So far, tests of RFID have focused on optimizing the supply chain, and reducing costs in logistics. But RFID also offers potential for servicing the customer better, particularly when tags are attached to individual products, and for better analyses of the impact of retailers' in-store merchandising activity.

Opportunities for Sales Promotions

The technologies described above can be expected to affect retailer promotions in several ways, the most important ones of which are related to:

- Better control
- Targeting consumers outside the store
- Targeting consumers in the store
- Cross-selling

We will discuss these aspects in turn.

Better Control

A first effect of the new technologies is increased flexibility with respect to price changes. In particular, electronic shelf labels and electronic displays allow the retailer to adjust prices very quickly. Thus, it becomes possible to run promotions for very short time spans. For example, a retailer could offer a price promotion during the day, when most housewives go shopping, and return to the regular price at night, when many singles shop after their working day is finished. This means that promotions will have an increased potential for price discrimination.

Also, promotions in a traditional retail environment often run into problems with out-of-stocks. Since it is hard to forecast sales bumps caused by a promotion, retailers may not have enough of the promoted product in the shelf or display, and thus not be able to satisfy consumers' demand. RFID technology may help discover out-of-stocks very quickly, so that extra products can be moved to the point-of-sale (see chapter by Verhoef and Sloot in this book for more information on evolving approaches to out-of-stocks reduction).

Targeting Consumers Outside the Store

Price promotions are an important tool in price discrimination. Typically, the price discrimination works through self-selection of the consumers. The promotion is offered to all customers, who then decide whether to use it or not. However, promotions can be an even stronger mechanism for price discrimination if retailers do not offer them to all customers, but target certain consumers. This type of targeting can be an effective way of encouraging profitable store switching, purchase acceleration, category switching, and brand switching.

Targeted promotions can be easily used on the Internet, where customer-specific information is available. Loyalty programs such as Payback can also provide an important database for targeting promotions. Customers can be selected on the basis of demographics and past purchase behavior and addressed individually through direct mail. Tesco, a leading UK retailer, reportedly creates upward of 100,000 separate promotional flyers on a quarterly basis to effectively target its customers with the coupons these customers want. This is also true of CVS, the leading drugstore chain in the US. METRO Group uses Payback data mostly for targeted direct mail coupons. For example, Real frequently sends coupons to households with large shopping baskets.

Targeting can also occur at the category level. For example, loyalty card data can be used to find out which product categories a household does not yet buy in a given retail chain, but might buy there if offered a promotion. Real, for example, has been successful with sending coupons for toys to consumers who have several children but have not yet purchased toys at Real.

A key question, obviously, is which consumers to target. One possible answer would be to address coupon-prone consumers, i.e., those consumers who redeem a relatively large number of coupons. However, coupon proneness in itself does not make a consumer attractive for targeted promotions. It is possible that coupon-prone consumers only use coupons for products that they would have purchased anyway in the store concerned. Thus, it is important to identify consumers who would be induced by coupons to make incremental purchases.

The academic discussion has focused a lot on whether promotions should be offered to loyal consumers or to switchers. At first glance, it seems like a good idea to target switchers. Loyal consumers would buy a given brand in a given store anyway, without creating incremental sales. In contrast, switchers can be prevented from buying a competitor's brand or shopping in a competitor's store. At second glance, however, this strategy can have severe drawbacks. First, as Shaffera and Zhang (1995) point out, targeting switchers may not be profitable in a competitive setting because it results in a prisoners' dilemma. If all competitors target the switchers, the overall price level declines while market shares remain the same, and profits become smaller for all firms. Second, Feinberg, Krishna and Zhang (2002) point out that targeting switchers may cause two negative behavioral effects, which they call betrayal and jealousy effects. A betrayal effect means that consumers' preference for their favored firm will decline if the firm offers a special price to switchers, i.e., to another firm's loyal customers. A jealousy effect means that consumers' preference for their favored firm will decrease if another firm offers a special price to its own loyal customers. In a laboratory experiment, the authors found empirical support for these effects. They show that when firms ignore these behavioral effects they put too much emphasis on targeting switchers. When these effects are taken into account, it may become more profitable to target loyal customers. Overall, then, the question of whether to target switchers or loyal customers is not a trivial one, and it warrants further investigation.

Finally, retailers may consider using customer lifetime value for targeting certain customers with promotions. As in the case of coupon proneness, it is important to note that retailers should not necessarily target the consumers with the highest customer lifetime value. Rather, they should try to identify those consumers for whom promotions will lead to an increase in customer lifetime value.

In summary, targeting consumers outside the store offers potential for more effective price discrimination. However, more research is needed on which consumers to target. Whether retailers' use of targeted promotions will increase in the future will depend on whether attractive target groups can be identified and on whether targeting will lead to a prisoners' dilemma and annoy consumers who are not part of the target group.

Targeting Consumers in the Store

Thus far, targeted promotions have mostly been used on the Internet and via direct mailing, but new technologies also offer the opportunity to target consumers at the point of sale in bricks-and-mortar stores. Customized information on promotion can be presented to the consumer by beaming it on the floor or by displaying it on the PSA or on electronic advertising displays. For example, the information on the PSA may change according to where a consumer is located in the store. The promotion information displayed can be adapted to the individual consumer on the basis of the information read from the loyalty card inserted into the PSA. If products have RFID tags, electronic advertising display can show information about a certain product once the consumer takes it off the shelf.

Cross-Selling

The same technologies offer retailers new opportunities for cross-selling and for exploiting category complementarity. For example, analysis of market basket data together with loyalty card data may suggest that breakfast products and fruits are typically bought together and a particular shopper might currently buy breakfast products in the store but not much fruit. The retailer could therefore create a promotion that offers a price discount on fruit if the customer buys breakfast products. A major question in this type of cross-selling is which should be the promoted brand—the breakfast product or the fruit. Dhar and Raju (1998) show that this depends on the market shares of the two brands and whether they are complements or substitutes. For example, they find that when brands are complements, the promoted brand should be the high-share brand.

In addition, cross-selling may be induced by promotions directly at the point of sale. If individual products have RFID tags, in-store promotions may be based on the products a consumer has already put into his/her shopping cart.

The above discussion has shown that new technologies in retailing offer many opportunities for sales promotions. Promotions are becoming more flexible, can be targeted better at specific consumers, and can be used for cross-selling. Many of the new opportunities occur at the point of sale in bricks-and-mortar stores, where sales promotions can be featured in more prominent and targeted ways. Thus, a general trend expected is that larger parts of the promotion budgets of retailers and manufacturers will be spent on in-store promotions.

References

Ailawadi, Kusum L., Neslin, Scott A. (1998): The Effect of Promotion on Consumption: Buying More and Consuming it Faster, Journal of Marketing Research, Vol. 35 (August), 390 – 398.

Ailawadi, Kusum L., Lehmann, Donald R., Scott A. Neslin (2001): Market Response to a Major Policy Change in the marketing Mix: Learning from Procter & Gamble's Value Pricing Strategy, Journal of Marketing, Vol. 65 (January), 44 – 62.

Bell, David R., Lattin, James M. (1998): Shopping Behavior and Consumer Preference for Store Price Format: Why "Large Basket" Shoppers Prefer EDLP, Marketing Science, Vol. 17 (1), 66 – 88.

Bucklin, Randolph E., Lattin, James M. (1992): A Model of Product Category Competition Among Grocery Retailers, Journal of Retailing, Vol. 68 (Fall), 24 – 39.

Dhar, Sanjay K., Raju, Jagmohan S. (1998): The Effects of Cross-Ruff Coupons on Sales and Profits, Management Science, Vol. 44 (November), 1501 – 1516.

Feinberg, Fred M., Krishna, Aradhna, Zhang, Z. John (2002): Do We Care What Others Get? A Behaviorist Approach to Targeted Promotions, Journal of Marketing Research, Vol. 39 (August), 277 – 291.

Gedenk, Karen (2002): Verkaufsförderung, München.

Gedenk, Karen, Neslin, Scott A. (1999): The Role of Retail Promotion in Determining Future Brand Loyalty: Its Effect on Purchase Event Feedback, Journal of Retailing, Vol. 75 (4), 433 – 459.

Lam, Shun Yin et al. (2001): Evaluating Promotions in Shopping Environments: Decomposing Sales Response into Attraction, Conversion, and Spending Effects, Marketing Science, Vol. 20 (Spring), 194 – 215.

Mulhern, Francis J., Leone, Robert P. (1991): Implicit Price Bundling of Retail Products: A Multiproduct Approach to Maximizing Store Profitability, Journal of Marketing, Vol. 55 (October), 63 – 76.

Mulhern, Francis J., Padgett, Daniel T. (1995): The Relationship Between Retail Price Promotions and Regular Price Purchases, Journal of Marketing, Vol. 59 (October), 83 – 90.

Narasimhan, Chakravarthi, Neslin, Scott A., Sen, Subrata K. (1996): Promotional Elasticities and Category Characteristics, Journal of Marketing, Vol. 60 (April), 17 – 30.

Neslin, Scott A. (2002): Sales Promotion, MSI Monograph.

Point of Purchase Advertising Institute (POPAI) (ed.) (1999): European Consumer Buying Habits Study, Frankfurt.

Shaffer, Greg, Zhang, Z. John (1995): Competitive Coupon Targeting, Marketing Science, Vol. 14 (4), 395 – 416.

Sirohi, Niren, McLaughlin, Edward W., Wittink, Dick R. (1998): A Model of Consumer Perceptions and Store Loyalty Intentions for a Supermarket Retailer, Journal of Retailing, Vol. 74 (2), 223 – 245.

Taylor, Gail A., Neslin, Scott A. (2005): The Current and Future Sales Impact of a Retail Frequency Reward Program, Journal of Retailing, Vol. 81 (4), 293 – 305.

van Heerde, Harald J., Gupta, Sachin, Wittink, Dick R. (2003): Is 75 % of the Sales Promotion Bump Due to Brand Switching? No, Only 33 % Is, Journal of Marketing Research, Vol. 40 (November), 481 – 491.

van Heerde, Harald J., Leeflang, Peter S. H., Wittink, Dick R. (2004): Decomposing the Sales Bump with Store Data, Marketing Science, Vol. 23 (Summer), 317 – 334.

Wansink, Brian, Kent, Robert J., Hoch, Stephen J. (1998): An Anchoring and Adjustment Model of Purchase Quantity Decisions, Journal of Marketing Research, Vol. 35 (February), 71 – 81.

Understanding Customer Loyalty Programs

Werner J. Reinartz

INSEAD, Fontainebleau, France

Introduction

In retailing, loyalty programs (LPs) have been the subject of exploding levels of attention since the late 1990s. Building mainly on the premise that it is less expensive to market to existing customers than to acquire new ones, firms across a multitude of industries have raced to implement one loyalty scheme or another. For example, Internet service provider AOL and American Airlines recently created the world's biggest loyalty program with, respectively, 1.5 million and 38 million members and more than 2000 partners. In Europe, an estimated 350 million loyalty cards were distributed in 1999 for the retailing sector alone.

An LP can be defined as a marketing process that generates rewards for customers on the basis of their repeat purchases. The term "loyalty program" is used here to encompass the many different forms of frequency reward programs. There is not one single definition of an LP because of its considerable overlap with promotional tools. The key characteristics of the term, as it is used herein, are the notions that it pertains to longer-term activity and focuses on supporting or generating repeated customer interactions with a product, store, or brand. Consumers who enter an LP are expected to transact more with the focal company, and in that sense, they voluntarily give up the free choice they would possess otherwise. In exchange for concentrating their purchases with the focal firm, they accumulate assets (e.g., points) that they can exchange for products and services, typically but not necessarily those associated with the focal firm. Therefore, LPs have become an important customer relationship management (CRM) tool used by marketers to identify, reward, and retain their customers.

The degree of growth in LPs has been staggering in the past decade; virtually every retail category now engages into the activity. The most well-known examples of LPs are frequent flyer programs in the airline industry, starting with American Airlines, which established its AAdvantage frequent flyer program in 1981. During the 1990s, many supermarket chains and general merchandise retailers also

M. Krafft and M.K. Mantrala (eds.), *Retailing in the 21st Century: Current and Future Trends*, 409
DOI 10.1007/978-3-540-72003-4_25, © Springer-Verlag Berlin Heidelberg 2010

Fig. 1. European Loyalty Program Penetration

(Source: Mark Kadar and Bernhard Kotanko, (2001) Designing Loyalty Programs to Enhance Value Growth, Mercer Management Consulting. Vol 8 (Spring/Summer))

established loyalty programs, such as the "Carte Iris" program by the French retail chain Champion, the Metro Cash & Carry Card, or the ClubCard of the British retailer Tesco.

According to Forrester Research, 62 % of consumers in the United States belonged to a grocery store LP in 2002. For warehouse clubs, pharmacies, and department stores, this figure was 33 %, 25 %, and 22 %, respectively (Forrester 2003). Similarly, Mercer Management Consulting notes double-digit growth in LPs in Europe in the years just prior to 2001 (Figure 1).

Finally, in a cross-category study of German and Austrian companies, Roland Berger Consultants (2003) found that 61 % of the firms have a LP in place and 64 % plan to accelerate their customer retention activities.

Thus, the prevalence and ubiquity of LPs has remained unchallenged. In many cases, this marketing tool has become a critical component of firms' overall CRM efforts. However, most organizations face LP challenges; though they are conceptually appealing and mostly easy to understand, their implementation is anything but straightforward. In particular, what has become clear to many firms – sometimes painfully – is that loyalty programs do not create loyalty, at least in the vast majority of cases. For example, Roland Berger's (2003) study notes that many firms simply do not feel any strategic impact of LPs. In particular, the participating firms in that study did not achieve their key objectives, such as improvements in customer retention or increased share of customer wallets. Stated differently, for most firms, the factors that make LPs effective and successful remain nebulous. The response to this gap – between desired objectives and current reality – constitutes the basis for this chapter. More specifically, this chapter addresses three critical areas that managers of LPs must think about and answer clearly before their LP can succeed:

- What are some of the key design characteristics of our LPs?
- What are the various conceptual objectives for our LPs?
- What empirical evidence do we have that our LPs achieve their desired objectives?

Although there are, of course, other potentially important aspects of managing LPs, due to space constraints, this chapter concentrates on the answers to these three questions.

A Framework for Organizing the Different Types of Programs

The multitude of LP types that exist attests to the large number of discrete choices within LP design, both within and across different industries. The purpose of this section is to describe and structure the key dimensions of LP design to assist managers who make their LP decision. Generally speaking, there is great discretion with respect to the dimensions to include in LP design and with respect to the level of the offer to choose within each dimension.

Design Characteristics

Loyalty programs can be described along the following dimensions:

A. Reward structure

- Hard vs. soft rewards
- Product proposition support (choice of rewards)
- Hedonic value of rewards
- Rate of rewards
- Tiering of rewards
- Timing of reward redemption

B. Type of sponsorship

- Single vs. multifirm
- Within sector vs. across sector
- Ownership (focal firm vs. other firm)

Reward Structure

The principal motivation for consumers to enroll in LPs is their ability to accrue benefits from the rewards that ensue from their purchase transactions over time. Thus, from a consumer's perspective, the rewards are the key design benefit.

Hard vs. Soft Rewards. One can distinguish financial or tangible rewards (hard rewards) from those that are based on psychological or emotional benefits (soft rewards). Hard rewards comprise the gamut of price reductions, promotions, free products, early check-ins, late check-outs, and so forth. For example, a Flying Blue member of KLM Airlines may receive a free ticket for travel within Europe on KLM after collecting 20,000 miles – a hard reward. In contrast, soft rewards typically are linked to special recognitions of the buyer. They provide the psychological benefit of being treated specially or receiving special status. For example, many frequent travelers who have achieved "Silver" or "Gold" status consider the simple fact that they belong to this category as beneficial (often called the "badge effect"). Naturally, the psychological benefits involved in recognition often comes in a package with tangible benefits such as preferred customer service (e.g., a special service telephone number). When the buyer finds the product or product category important, soft rewards often become more important than hard rewards. For example, members of customer clubs do not receive many hard rewards but enjoy the sense of being a member of a community (e.g., Harley Davidson's owner group HOG).

Product Proposition Support. The rewards entailed in an LP may be directly linked to the company's product offering or be entirely unrelated. For example, the U.S. coffee franchise Starbucks offers an LP that allows participants to redeem their accumulated bonus points for the firm's own products: specialty coffee drinks. This reward clearly and directly supports the firm's product proposition. However, other LPs may allow the member to redeem points for products that are completely unrelated to the focal firm's offering. For example, British Petroleum's LP members may redeem points earned through their fuel-related purchases for merchandise such as first-aid kits, photographic film, coffee mugs, and Barbie dolls.

Ideally, firms would prefer that their LP supports their product proposition, assuming that customers can build up a reasonable amount of assets (i.e., points) through regular purchases. Even better, when they redeem their assets for the company's own products, LP customers may do additional business with the firm (e.g., pay for a companion ticket when redeeming miles for an airline ticket, order room service during a free hotel stay). Roehm, Bolman-Pullins, and Roehm (2002) even find that incentives for packaged goods brands that overlap with the brand (company) associations – and support the product proposition – prompt the accessibility of the brand for customers and thereby help boost loyalty.

Hedonic Value of Reward. Hedonic products are those products whose consumption is associated with pleasure and fun. An interesting result from consumer psychology research shows that consumers prefer hedonic goods to utilitarian goods when it takes them considerable effort to earn it (Kivetz and Simonson 2002). That is, consumers feel better indulging in luxury items when the effort they had to expend to earn that luxury is relatively high, as in the case of an LP reward. For example, a free flight to an exotic destination might be much more attractive to a buyer than vouchers for the local supermarket, even if both had the same face value. Companies therefore have been trying to differentiate their LPs on the basis of the hedonic value of their rewards. For example, the LP connected to PRO7, a German television channel, is the PRO7 Club. One of its most popular rewards is VIP service, which offers rewards from preferred access to becoming a talk show visitor to meeting actors backstage. In the same vein, Mercedes Benz's LP makes it possible for customers to transform their points into a flight in a MiG 29 combat aircraft. Neiman Marcus, the U.S. luxury retail chain, offers an annual list of "wow and cool" rewards, including such items as the services of a world-famous photographer who will come to the customer's home to take a personal portrait.

Rate of Rewards. The rate of rewards refers to the ratio of the reward value to the transaction volume (both in monetary terms). In essence, it answers how much a consumer receives in return for concentrating his or her purchases with the retailer. Needless to say, consumers generally prefer LPs that give them higher reward rates. Likewise, reward redemptions are a key cost factor that firms must consider in the design of their LPs. For example, a McKinsey (2000) study found that the super-market industry functions with a 1% average reward rate (i.e., one cent for every euro or dollar spent), which is a comparatively small loyalty incentive.

Tiering of Rewards. The rate of rewards given to customers may depend on their cumulative spending with the focal firm. The so-called asset accumulation re-sponse function (Figure 2) describes how assets (points) are accumulated as a function of consumers' cumulative spending behavior.

Two principally different response functions exist. In the first case, the buyer receives the same number of assets (per € spent), regardless of his or her cumula-tive spending. In the second case, the buyer receives a greater amount of assets as his or her cumulative spending level increases. Therefore, the second program clearly is relatively more attractive for buyers who spend more. Many airline pro-grams follow the pattern depicted in the second case, which also helps them man-age the size of their LP. If rewards can be accumulated meaningfully only when customers spend large amounts, there will be a corresponding self-selection bias toward high spenders. This trend is of particular interest to those firms that want to concentrate their retention efforts on a small group of high-value customers rather than work with their entire customer base.

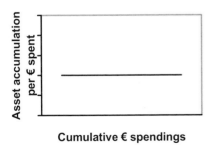
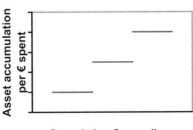

Fig. 2. Asset Accumulation Response Function

Timing of Reward Redemption. The timing of reward redemption represents another important design feature of an LP. Firms prefer to create redemption rules that favor long accumulation periods, which in turn influences customer retention. This effect is also called a "lock-in," because customers build up assets that eventually function as switching costs, locking them in to doing business with the firm. In contrast, customers favor the opposite scenario, with immediate rewards or short accumulation periods. Managers must ask themselves how long it takes to accumulate assets for a representative reward, given a certain buying pattern. The timing of rewards should be determined by minimum redemption rules, the type of reward provided, and the reward rate. If the time to reward redemption becomes too long, customers either lose interest in the program or, even worse, refuse to even join.

Figure 3 shows the time that consumers need to generate a reward worth 50 euro through the LPs of several types of retailers. If the reward rate is too low from a consumers' perspective, LP program adoption will stall, as the Görtz shoe store chain example clearly shows with its unattractive redemption characteristic.

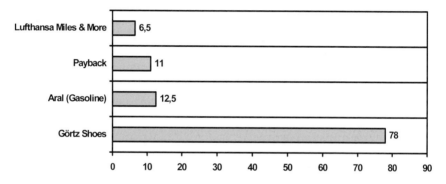

Fig. 3. Waiting Time for Accumulating a € 50 Reward (in Months)

Calculations in Figure 3 are based on the following purchase behavior:
Lufthansa: Business Traveller, 80 % of flights with Miles&More partners
Payback: 70 % of category purchases (grocery, general merchandise, insurance) with Payback partners
Aral: 15.000 km yearly, 80 % with Aral
Görtz: € 300 per year on shoe purchases spent at Görtz
(Source: Roland Berger, 2003)

Type of Sponsorship

The second key design dimensions by which LPs can be described is sponsorship, which refers to the features of the LP's owner and operator.

Single vs. Multifirm. Organizations may establish LPs that reflect only transactions with its own customers, such as that of BP France that includes only the transactions members have made at BP stations in France. Alternatively, organizations might allow LP members to accumulate assets at firms that are associated with the focal firm's LP. For example, members of Tesco's ClubCard can accumulate points through the British utility TXU Energi. The introduction of partners represents one of the major axes of current growth in LP design because it attracts additional LP members through its greater opportunities for asset accumulation. The potential disadvantage of such partnerships is that the LP of the focal company can lose meaning and customer connections if it brings in too many partners. However, a multifirm LP is absolutely necessary when an individual category does not yield enough opportunities for asset accumulation. For example, the German car insurer HDI belongs to the German PayBack LP scheme. Because consumers only buy car insurance once per year, a multifirm scheme overcomes HDI's structural problem of possessing an LP in a low frequency purchase situation.

Within Sector/Across Sector. Another supply-side dimension of multifirm LP design is the degree of across-sector partnering. In other words, to what degree do customers accumulate assets within the same sector or across different sectors? The STAR Alliance – SAS, Lufthansa, United Airlines, Varig, and various others airlines – provides a prime example of an LP structure that remains within the same sector. However, the LP by AOL and American Airlines, with its 2000 or so partners, crosses many different industries.

Ownership. In case of multifirm LPs, the ownership dimension indicates who owns the LP within the network of firms. Is it the focal firm, another firm, or a firm whose sole purpose is to manage the LP? An example of the latter case is the German firm Loyalty Partners, which runs the PayBack scheme and draws together a network of partners across different categories. Its sole purpose is LP management. Whereas joining a network program makes it much easier to establish the firm's critical size, such membership also means that the firm has limited influence on its LP strategy, such as positioning, branding, or member firm selection.

Implications

Today's LP environment shows clearly that the ubiquity and variety of LPs has never been greater. Over time, firms have become more and more experienced with running LPs and more and more creative in deploying various LP design features. What is particularly interesting to notice is that similar loyalty programs across different firms vary tremendously in their effectiveness (Ziliani and Bellini 2004). Likewise, firms in similar industries deploy very differently designed LPs.

The implication that can be derived from this proliferation of LP design in general is straightforward: There is no one default design for LPs. Rather, the design of a specific program must be aligned appropriately on the following issues:

- Is the suggested program design attractive to consumers? Does it sway them to join, stay, and use it?

- Is the program economically viable (for the firm)?

- Does the program achieve its desired strategic objectives (e.g., higher customer retention, better learning about customer behavior)?

A key condition for a successful LP scheme is sufficient consumer adoption and persistent use of the program tools (e.g., loyalty card, member number). Many cases of unsuccessful card schemes were due to a lack of card adoption or lack of commitment to using the card among the target customers (Mauri 2003). These failures could be due to misaligned designs, a lack of appropriate incentives and rewards, or a lack of communication about the LP scheme.

Probably the most common question asked is simply whether loyalty programs work (Dowling and Uncles 1997). Obviously, the answer to this question depends on the design of the LP, because that design directly affects the program's efficiency and effectiveness. For example, features that are highly attractive to consumers, such as high reward rates, are unlikely to be economically viable for the firm.

Therefore, the more important question to ask is whether a specific LP design works for the specific strategic objective. Thus, the answer to the question "Do LPs work?" really depends on the objective that the firm pursues, which may vary tremendously across firms. Commonly cited LP goals include increased customer retention, greater share of wallet, higher sales, more customer information, more positive attitudes toward the company/brand, cross-selling, competitive responses, and so on. Given the variety in these potential objectives and given that companies must make choices with respect to their objective functions, the design of LPs must involve a contingency approach.

Conceptual Objectives of LPs

The moment when they must define the specific objective of a LP provides a key challenge for marketers. The secret is not that the organization needs to generate value at the end of the day; rather, it is how such value comes about – in this case, through the LP instrument. A sobering number of research surveys teach that most LPs fail to achieve their originally stated goals (e.g., Sharp and Sharp 1995; Dowling and Uncles 1997; McKinsey 2000; Leenheer et al. 2002). As evidence, consider that most consumers tend to belong to multiple LPs, even in the same category. For example, in 2002, more than half of the primary grocer shoppers in the United States belonged to two or more grocery loyalty programs, which naturally diminished their specific loyalty to any one grocer (Forrester 2003). Thus, to assess LP program success in the broadest sense, one must be clear about what the dimension of success means. The previous section introduced the notion of an LP objective function; the goal of this section is to outline the following map of the potential objectives that managers might pursue when they implement an LP.

1. *Building True Loyalty.* True loyalty, which combines attitudinal and behavioral customer loyalty, leads to greater commitment to the product or organization. Building such loyalty is not easy to achieve, because consumers are fickle in their purchases in most categories, and economic benefits will always be very important to them.

2. *Efficiency Profits.* Objectives such as higher sales, larger share of wallet, or greater buying frequency compared with the situation without an LP constitute the immediate profit consequences, net the cost of the LP.

3. *Effectiveness Profits.* These profit consequences are realized in the longer term through a better understanding of customer behavior and preferences. Such information enables managers to create sustainable value for customers through, for example, customized products or relevant communications.

4. *Value Alignment.* By aligning the cost to serve a particular customer with the value that customer brings to the firm, the firm can serve its most valuable customers best.

5. *Competitive Parity.* The firm engages in an LP to match competitors who have already done so.

These goals may be pursued individually or collectively. Depending on the LP design, companies focus on one or more of them.

True Loyalty

True loyalty always encompasses both attitudinal and behavioral loyalty, defined as follows: Attitudinal loyalty comprises the favorable, potentially covert beliefs and attitudes a customer holds about the brand or company, whereas behavioral loyalty refers to overt repeat buying behavior. According to this logic, customers may exhibit behavioral loyalty (i.e., purchase a product repeatedly) but do so for various reasons, such as convenience or price. Although behavioral loyalty may be a result of attitudinal loyalty, it can be driven by other factors as well.

Many LPs have been established to "make customers more loyal," a difficult goal to reach simply through programs. Enforcing loyalty by enticing customers with rewards and bonuses is highly unlikely to work in the long run. True loyalty is a function of the true value provided to customers and often involves other factors like the customer's degree of involvement in the product category, the visibility of the product, or the product's value-expressive nature. From the firm perspective, these aspects are hard to control. However, when consumers experience true loyalty, they are more resistant to outside persuasion, less motivated to search for alternatives, and willing to provide greater positive word-of-mouth reports (see, e.g., Uncles discussion of the importance of word-of-mouth influence among retail customers elsewhere in this book).

Building or reinforcing the attitudinal loyalty component is particularly challenging for virtually all low-involvement product categories, such as the grocery industry, a prototypical example. Inducing real loyalty in this category is a tough proposition because purchases are driven principally by tangible considerations, such as value for money.

In contrast, if product involvement is high or the product provides an emotional element, the benefits that LPs offer are better suited to support overall attitudinal loyalty. In the most ideal case, true loyalty finds its expression in community building among customers, which is why the nurturing of attitudinal loyalty is the goal of many customer clubs. Using the brand as a reason to share experiences as a community represents a very powerful expression of loyalty. Therefore, it is not surprising that many companies attempt to build consumer communities around their brands, though such community building works best if the emotional component of the product is high, such as for leisure products (e.g., American Girl dolls, LEGO), or when others' consumption of the brand adds utility to one's own consumption (e.g., Harley-Davidson motorcycles). In many cases, brand communities are linked to special benefits that are unavailable to those outside the community, which creates a distinct in-group/out-group split. For example, Steiff, the venerable maker of teddy bears, has a customer club that offers a limited-edition teddy bear exclusively to its members once a year.

From a managerial perspective, member acquisition typically occurs through self-selection because the customer's degree of involvement and identification with the brand/company is self-driven and therefore outside management's control. Creating customer clubs through which members can identify with and strongly relate to the brand works best for those brands or companies that target relatively small, homogenous markets.

Efficiency Profits

Efficiency profits are the short-term profits that result from a change in customers' buying behavior due to the loyalty program. This change in buying behavior can be measured as, for example,

- Basket size
- Purchase frequency acceleration
- Price sensitivity
- Share-of-category requirements
- Share of wallet
- Retention
- Lifetime duration

Efficiency profits must be calculated net of LP cost, and the most widely used measure of behavioral loyalty is the share of category requirement or share of wallet (e.g., Leenheer et al. 2002). The key idea behind an LP that aims to improve efficiency profits is that customers will build up their switching costs by accumulating assets in the LP. In accumulating these assets, customers forego their free choice because the expected reward seems to make this reduction in free choice worthwhile. Therefore, for a customer to engage in an LP, the overall utility of being in that LP should be higher than any utility the consumer can achieve without the program. As a result, the cost for the firm to entice the customer to change his or her behavior accordingly may be higher than it would be without an LP. For just such reasons, including the high maintenance cost, Safeway, a U.K. grocer, scrapped its ABC loyalty card scheme in 2000, which saved the company £50 million that year (BBC News May 4, 2000), which the firm passed on to consumers by cutting prices. Likewise Leenheer et al. (2002) discovered in their study of seven Dutch supermarket loyalty schemes that four of these LPs gave greater value to members than they earned back in terms of additional revenues.

Another issue inherent in the goal of efficiency profits is the expectation that those customers most likely to join the LP are truly loyal customers who have the most to gain. The problem is that their business would have been guaranteed in the first place, even without an LP. Therefore, the question that arises is whether LPs actually change the buying behavior of previously not-so-loyal customers and whether this incremental business offsets the losses incurred through giving benefits to loyal customers who would have bought anyway (Lal and Bell 2003). Apparently, LPs do not change behavior as much as they reinforce already existing behavior – but at a much higher cost of operation. Several research studies have found that the increase in customer spending due to LPs is surprisingly low. In a study of the Dutch supermarket industry, Leenheer and Bijmolt (2003)) find that LPs yield, on average, € 113 additional revenue per customer per year. McKinsey (2000) also finds that average sales increase 1-3 % among grocery industry LP providers but that these increases tend to erode over time. In the context of general retailing in Australia, Sharp and Sharp (1997) find that LPs have a positive effect on repeat purchase behavior (behavioral loyalty) but that this effect is minimal. Research by Reinartz and Kumar (2003) in the direct response marketing industry shows that LP membership is associated with a longer customer-firm relationship, in line with Bolton, Kannan, and Bramlett's (2000) finding of greater retention among credit card LP members. Finally, Lewis (2004) finds that LPs increase repeat purchase rates in the context of Internet retailing.

In summary, there seems to be a positive, albeit small, effect of LPs on purchase behavior. However, the very quest for short-term profits might be a fallible basis for an LP because (a) profit consequences are questionable due to the high costs of operating the program and (b) this focus does not provide for any competitive differentiation. Despite these concerns, most LPs are built with the short-term goal of selling more to existing and new customers (efficiency profits) in mind.

Effectiveness Profits

Effectiveness profits refer to the medium- to long-term profit consequences realized through better understanding customer preferences and needs. Such an LP is designed to gather cumulative information about individuals, their behavior, and their preferences and then to derive knowledge from this information. This process of learning allows the firm to improve its knowledge about customer preferences continuously and thereby offer an increasingly better value proposition to its various customers through more effective product and communication offerings. Effectiveness profits, more than any other type of LP outcome, are likely to generate sustainable competitive advantage for the firm because the knowledge it gains is hard to copy and the outcomes of well-executed learning are valuable to customers.

Case Study

Achieving effectiveness profits means implementing an information-based strategy that gathers and analyzes information about every transaction. For example, in grocery retailing, data mining generates personalized promotions and recommendations for each customer, so that a vegetarian would not receive a promotion for steak. The store's knowledge that the customer is a vegetarian is derived from either surveys or the customer's buying behavior. If the store's customer intelligence system recognizes that a customer does not buy meat over time, it assumes that customer is a vegetarian, not that he or she simply buys meat elsewhere. Although this assumption could be wrong, a store would rather not bother a customer with costly promotions for categories from which that customer has never bought anything in the first place.

The strategy of using an LP to learn about customer preferences and deploying that learning in the market may result in impressive gains for both customers and organizations. Customers get more of what they truly want, and firms become more efficient because they do not need to engage in costly mass marketing campaigns.

However, the possible downside of a learning strategy is the relative process sophistication required for its implementation. Whereas the collection of massive amounts of data is an all-too-easy step, the analysis of, learning about, and implementation based on these data are far more difficult. Few companies have mastered this strategic capability.

Nevertheless, the strategic sustainability of this approach is uncontested. An example of one of the few companies that seems to have mastered this process is Tesco, the U.K. supermarket chain. Tesco's market share has been rising 52% since the launch of its ClubCard in 1995, while floorspace is up by only 15%.

Value Alignment

Value alignment refers to the goal of aligning the cost to serve a particular customer with the value that customer brings to the firm. Underlying this goal is the understanding that, in any industry, customers have differential economic values to the firm and typically are differentially expensive to serve. For example, if a provider of wireless services were to arrange its customers from highest to lowest value to the firm, it likely would find that business users rack up higher phone bills than do occasional private users. Likewise, if the company arranged the same customers from highest to lowest cost to serve, it would find considerable variance. Some customers are easy to satisfy, whereas others cost the firm significant amounts through their constant use of the customer service function.

If a firm pursues value alignment, it simply attempts to align the profits it receives from a given customer with the cost that the firm incurs to serve that same customer. This goal therefore means that not every customer is treated equally, a notion that some managers find discomforting. However, it permits firms to ensure their best customers are getting the best service. When is this function important? The goal of value alignment is particularly critical when there is great heterogeneity in the customers' value and cost to serve, such as in the airline business, hospitality industry, and financial services industry.

The chart in Figure 4 gives an example of a financial services firm with a highly heterogeneous customer base and the profitability of three very different customer profiles. Tier A represents 31 % of the customer base, Tier B comprises 42 %, and Tier C represents the remaining 27 %. In this fictional example, Tier C customers – more than one-quarter of the firm's total customers – are unprofitable and must be subsidized by the highly profitable ones. This condition is not uncommon to find in banks.

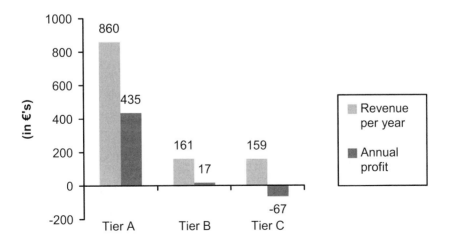

Fig. 4. Value Heterogeneity of Customer Segments

While information about transaction frequencies, dates, amounts, and so forth is collected routinely by banks, other industries typically do not regularly engage in such collections. In general merchandise retailing, for example, it is the LPs that assume this function. Thus, the primary goal of introducing a LP may be to systematically collect customer behavior information, which then can be translated into customer-level profit and loss statements. This information enables the organization to distinguish customer segments according to their economic value to the company and then allocate its resources differentially. Leenheer and Bijmolt (2003) provide empirical evidence that the degree to which customers are heterogeneous in their value to the company is a key driver of LP initiation.

Competitive Parity

In a significant number of cases, pure competitive pressure leads companies to deploy an LP. Dowling and Uncles (1997) find that in practice, despite claims to the contrary, firms often launch LPs to differentiate their brand, preempt the entry of a brand, or preempt a competitor that plans to launch a similar program. Unlike the reasons discussed in the sections above, this objective is driven purely by external forces. In a multi-industry study, Leenheer and Bijmolt (2003) find that the introduction of LPs is driven strongly by the general competitiveness of the environment, as well as by existing competitor programs. For example, markets like grocery or gasoline retail suffer from the condition in which most or all major competitors have an LP, which means they all operate on a higher cost level but market shares eventually return to preprogram levels. This aspect has been investigated in a study by Singh and Jain (2004), who find that firms enter a "prisoner's dilemma" when all of them offer loyalty programs, which in turn results in lower profits for *all* firms. Therefore, LPs based on competitive pressures are unlikely to lead to sustainable advantage for firms, though it might be hard not to introduce one if LPs become part of the expected offer in that industry.

Implications

On the basis of the various objective functions that firms may pursue through their LPs, normative suggestions about their optimality for various situations become clear. Toward this end, Table 1 outlines the key characteristics of LPs according to the program's objective. In particular, the table summarizes the kind of business situation that is most suitable for the respective objectives, how the cost of LPs might be mitigated, the key challenges for each objective, and the likely degree of competitive advantage that can be generated. The last objective – competitive parity – is not included because it is the only goal conceptualized as a defensive, "me-too" tactic.

Table 1. Comparison of LP Objectives

Goal of LP	True Loyalty	Efficiency Profits	Effectiveness Profits	Value Alignment
Most suited for	All branded products (however, the larger the buyer base, the more difficult it becomes to differentiate the brand and manage customer interactions consistently)	Many industries	Firms with access to large amounts of information about customers and firms that communicate directly with end customers	All industries with a highly skewed customer value distribution (e.g., airlines, hotels, rental cars)
Cost of LP *may* be mitigated by		For retail LPs, contributions from manufacturers (promotions)	For retail LPs, contributions from manufacturers (promotions)	
Key challenges	– Providing *meaningful* value that creates differentiation in consumers' minds – Brand building	– Providing acceptable incentives to customers while controlling cost – Program differentiation	– Capability to handle, analyze, learn from, and deploy knowledge from large databases	– Implementing the customer differentiation scheme (deployment automation) – Having fair and equitable relationships in general and still ensuring that best customers are treated best
Degree of competitive advantage created	High (a truly loyal customer base is hard and costly to replicate because it can only be built over time)	Low (it is easy to replicate hard benefits and program costs create major challenges)	High (capability of learning from customer behavior and using it is very difficult to copy and unique to a company's context)	Low-medium (LPs have become standard industry practice)

Economic Viability

Regardless of the different LP objectives, the eventual goal of any program is that it contributes to higher operating profits for the firm. Therefore, assessments of the economic impact of the program must be made continuously. The more strategic the use of the LP (e.g., effectiveness profits), the more difficult it becomes to make these assessments correctly because (a) the impact arguably can be measured only in the longer term and (b) many intangible benefits, such as improved customer goodwill, are hard to quantify. An exemplary assessment of the economics of a grocery LP appears in Table 2, which outlines the key parameters of such an economic calculation and comments on the derivation of the figures.

The key lesson, based on the assumptions made in this calculation, is that a supermarket could barely make a profit on the program. Rather, the program costs (€ 73m) and benefits (€ 75m) seem approximately equal. However, given such a calculation, the manager can begin to question certain assumptions or seek to improve certain response or decision parameters. For example, in this case, if the retailer could collect contributions from the manufacturers of the products it sells, the economic viability would look different. Needless to say, this exemplary calculation must be customized for any given business context.

There is an interesting historic side note to economics calculations: The specific reason LPs are so widespread and began so early in the airline and hotel industries can be traced back to the underlying program economics. Because these industries operate with perishable products under capacity constraints, they can give away rewards to customers for very low marginal costs. For example, if an airline LP member upgrades to business class and pays with miles that have been accrued over time, the airline incurs a very low actual cost for the reward – the seat would have gone empty otherwise. This structural aspect of such industries caused them to deploy LPs very successfully from a very early point. Of course, these economics differ in industries (say, retailing) that must bear the full cost of the rewards they provide. This short history corroborates the finding that LP economics are much more challenging in retailing than in the hospitality industry.

Summary and Outlook

Many organizations currently are transitioning from a transactional to a relational perspective on exchange. This new view requires that firms attempt to maintain ongoing relationships with most of their customers, and one way to do so is through an LP. These programs enable organizations to identify individual customers, observe their transactions over time, and differentiate among them in terms of the resources allocated to them.

The purpose of this chapter has been to (a) summarize evidence about the prevalence of LPs, (b) describe some of the key design characteristics of LPs, (c) explain the various conceptual objectives for LPs, and (d) provide empirical evidence about whether LPs achieve their desired objectives.

The key findings that emerge from existing research on LPs highlight the following central points:

Table 2. Exemplary LP Economics for a Grocery Retailer

Program Revenues				
1		Total # of customers	5,000,000	
2		Yearly spending per nonmember (€)	2,000	
3		% sales increase due to membership	5	
4		Yearly spending per member (€)	2,100	
5		% customers in program	50	
6	=5 × 1	# of customers in program	2,500,000	
7	=6 × 4	Total revenue from members (€)	5,250,000,000	
8	=(4 – 2) × 6	Additional revenue from members (€)	250,000,000	
Program Cost				
9		Program reward rate	2.0 %	
10	=7 × 9	Potential outstanding rewards (€)	105,000,000	
11		% breakage	40	% of assets that never get redeemed
12 =10 × (1 – breakage)		Breakage-adjusted redemption (€)	63,000,000	
13		Yearly program administration cost (€)	10,000,000	
14 =12 + 13		Total yearly program cost (€)	73,000,000	
15 =14/12		Yearly program cost per member (€)	29	
Program Profits				
16		Additional revenue from members (€)	250,000,000	
17		Variable cost	70 %	available contribution margin = 30 %
18 =16 × (1 – variable cost)		Additional contribution margin (€)	75,000,000	
19 =14		Total yearly program cost	73,000,000	

☐ *fully or partially under managerial control*

- Those LPs introduced to gain short-term profits are mostly built on shaky grounds. Firms that pursue this strategy should seriously rethink their approach. Although LPs influence customer behavior, their impact on the bottom line is much less obvious because of the operational costs of new schemes.

- Those LPs that are introduced to learn about customers and thereby provide better value (though greater utility, more customization, less inappropriate offers) seem to be going in the right direction. However, the economics of this approach are much less quantifiable, and the process capabilities the firm needs are substantial in terms of analytical skills, interpretive skills, and rollout capabilities.

In terms of future research opportunities, consider the following nonexhaustive list: From an organizational perspective,

- The huge variety of LPs begs for a more thorough and grounded typology of different programs.

- When and how do companies achieve better success through their specific LP strategy?

- What relative influence do the various design characteristics have on LP success?

- How does the performance of LPs interact with industry, company, and product characteristics?

- Are there systematic traits of organizations that are able to garner effective profits from their programs?

From a consumer's perspective,

- Currently, virtually no insight exists into the redemption behavior of consumers. Once consumers have accumulated assets, how do they dispose of them?

- How exactly do customer preferences for LP design features differ across product categories?

In terms of the future outlook, businesses will persist in using LPs. The proportion of businesses that use LPs in a strategic sense currently is small, but this proportion likely will grow slowly. However, many firms will realize over time that they have not gotten the benefits they expected out of their LPs because of their tactical approach. These firms will face the painful decision to either abandon the program and existing investments in it or invest even more to build strategic LP management capability. Overall, the good news is that strategic LPs can provide significant benefits to organizations.

References

Bolton, Ruth, P.K. Kannan, and Matthew Bramlett (2000), Implications of Loyalty Program Membership and Service Experiences for Customer Retention and Value, Journal of the Academy of Marketing Science, 28 (1), 95-108.

Dowling, Grahame and Mark Uncles (1997), Do Customer Loyalty Programs Really Work? Sloan Management Review 38 (Summer), 71-82.

Forrester Research (2003), Rebuilding Consumer Loyalty, Consumer Technographics North America.

Kivetz, Ran, and Itamar Simonson (2002), Earning the Right to Indulge: Effort as a Determinant of Customer Preferences Toward Frequency Program Rewards, Journal of Marketing Research, 39 (May), 155-170.

Lal, Rajiv and David E. Bell (2003), The Impact of Frequent Shopper Programs in Grocery Retailing, Quantitative Marketing and Economics, 1 (June), 179-202.

Leenheer, J. and T.H.A. Bijmolt (2003), Adoption and Effectiveness of Loyalty Programs: The Retailer's Perspective, MSI Working Paper Series 03-124.

Leenheer, J., T.H.A. Bijmolt, H.J. van Heerde, and A. Smidts (2002), Do Loyalty Programs Enhance Behavioral Loyalty? An Empirical Analysis Accounting for Program Design and Competitive Effects, CentER Discussion Paper (No. 2002-65), Marketing.

Lewis, Michael (2004), The Influence of Loyalty Programs and Short Term Promotions on Customer Retention Journal of Marketing Research, 41 (August), 281-292.

Mauri, Chiara (2003), Card Loyalty: A New Issue in Grocery Retailing, Journal of Retailing and Consumer Services, 10, 13-25.

McKinsey & Company (2000), The Power of Loyalty: Creating Winning Retail Loyalty Programs, [http://www.mckinsey.com/practices/marketing/ourknowledge/pdf/White-Paper_PowerofLoyalty.pdf].

Reinartz, Werner and V. Kumar (2003), The Impact of Customer Relationship Characteristics on Profitable Lifetime Duration, Journal of Marketing, 67 (January), 77-99.

Roehm, Michelle, Ellen Bolman-Pullins, and Harper A. Roehm Jr. (2002), Designing Loyalty-Building Programs for Packaged Goods Brands, Journal of Marketing Research, 39 (May), 202-213.

Roland Berger Consultants (2003), Kundenbindunsgprogramme in deutschen und östereichischen Unternehmen, München: Wien.

Sharp, Byron and Anne Sharp (1997), Loyalty Programs and Their Impact on Repeat Purchase Loyalty Patterns, International Journal of Research in Marketing, 14, 473-486.

Singh, Siddharth and Dipak Jain (2004), Customer Loyalty Programs: Are they Really Profitable? Working Paper.

Ziliani, Cristiana and Silvia Bellini (2004), From Loyalty Cards to Micro-Marketing Strategies: Where Is Europe's Retail Industry Heading? Journal of Targeting, Measurement and Analysis for Marketing, 12 (3), 281-289.

Integrated Marketing Communications in Retailing

Kalyan Raman[1] and Prasad A. Naik[2]

[1] Loughborough University, Leicestershire, UK
[2] University of California Davis, Davis, USA

Introduction

A computer scientist, Mark Weiser, envisioned over a decade ago that future environments would be saturated with computing and communication capability, but yet gracefully integrated with human users (Weiser 1991). His vision manifests itself in smart environments, where useful technologies disappear and "weave themselves into the fabric of everyday life until they are indistinguishable from it." Retailing environments are poised to become such smart environments with modern technologies such as RFID (Radio Frequency Identification), wireless sensors, the ubiquitous Internet, and mobile computing. Communication is the central part of this smart retailing environment that proactively anticipates the consumer's needs and makes recommendations to assist consumers' decision-making process. The key challenge for retailers is to build strong brands by orchestrating in-store communications (e.g., Personal Shopping Assistant) with the usual out-of-store branding communications (e.g., print advertisement). To achieve this orchestration, retailers will find the concept of Integrated Marketing Communications (IMC) relevant for designing profitable marketing strategies.

We organize this chapter as follows. We first present the genesis and definition of IMC and review the standard multimedia model of communications. We next contrast this standard model with the IMC framework, highlighting how retailers should act *differently* to determine the amount and allocation of budgets in the presence of synergies that emerge within the IMC context. In addition, we discuss the effects of uncertainty on the profitability of IMC programs. Finally, we extend the IMC framework to futuristic retailing and identify new research avenues.

M. Krafft and M.K. Mantrala (eds.), *Retailing in the 21st Century: Current and Future Trends*,   429
DOI 10.1007/978-3-540-72003-4_26, © Springer-Verlag Berlin Heidelberg 2010

Genesis and Definition of IMC

The IMC concept originated at Northwestern University, where Professor Don Schultz introduced and developed it further over the last decade. Many companies embraced this concept in practice not only because of the mergers and acquisitions that led to consolidation of the advertising industry (which resulted in one-stop shopping of communications needs such as media and creative, consumer promotions and direct marketing, PR and product placement), but also because of synergies that emerged when various communications activities were integrated within the IMC framework. Consequently, several academic journals devoted space to investigate the deeper implications of IMC for budgeting and allocation; for example, see the special issues of *Journal of Advertising Research*, *Journal of Marketing Communications*, *Journal of Business Research*, and numerous textbooks (e.g., Schultz, Tannenbaum and Lauterborn 1993). The actual application and use of IMC has now spread from North America to Asia to Europe to the Pacific Rim and South America. A commonly used definition of IMC is as follows: IMC is a concept of marketing communication planning that recognizes the added value of the comprehensive plan that evaluates the strategic roles of a variety of communication disciplines—for example, general advertising, direct response, sales promotion, and public relations—and combines these disciplines to provide clarity, consistency, and public communication impact (Schultz et al. 1993, p. 6). For brevity, we propose a new succinct definition[1]:

An IMC program plans and executes various marketing activities with consistency so that its total impact exceeds the sum of each activity's impact.

Standard Model of Multimedia Communications

Here we review the standard model of communications so that we contrast not only its quintessential difference from the IMC framework, but also the resulting differences in managers' decisions and firm's profitability. In standard advertising models, the various modes of communications, for example, television, radio and newspapers, exert independent effects on consumers. Figure 1 depicts this communication process.

Given the lack of consideration of joint effects and cross-media complementarities, inconsistencies could arise between the messages carried by disparate communications media from the same organization. This potential for inconsistencies raised questions about how media advertising works. In addition, cognitive psychology shed new light on consumer information processing, suggesting that consumers absorb information about goods and services from a number of sources, not all of which are formal promotional messages. So, no longer can marketers

---

[1]   We thank Prof. Scott Neslin for suggesting a variant of this definition.

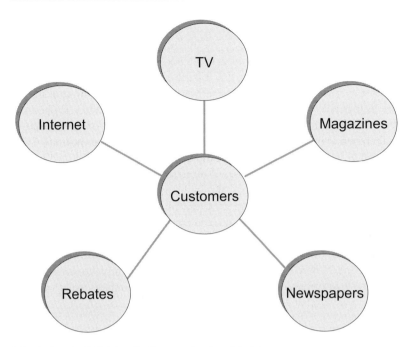

Fig. 1. Standard Multimedia Communications Model

assume that they control the way consumers think about brands via image-building media advertising. Despite these concerns, standard advertising theory offered deep insights by deducing fundamental principles of budgeting and allocation, which we explain in the next two propositions.

Multimedia Budgeting and Allocation

For the sake of clarity, suppose managers expend u_1 and u_2 dollars on two communications activities with effectiveness β_1 and β_2, respectively; then the total budget is $(u_1 + u_2)$, and the budget allocation is u_1/u_2. Based on Naik and Raman (2003), we state the normative result in the following proposition:

PROPOSITION 1: *In multimedia advertising, as the effectiveness of an activity increases, managers should increase the spending on that activity, thus increasing the total media budget. Furthermore, the total budget should be allocated to multiple activities in proportion to their relative effectiveness.*

This proposition informs managers that if an ad agency improves the creative copy, thereby increasing the effectiveness of television advertising (say β_1), then they should *increase* the expenditures on TV advertising (i.e., increase u_1). The force of this proposition lies in cautioning managers against the tempting — but incorrect — intuition: "now that we have a better advertising campaign, we should be able to achieve greater impact with less (or the same) budget."

Another insight from this proposition is revealed by the question[2]: Why should managers spend any dollars at all on the less effective medium? Because they should not continue to invest in the most effective activity after diminishing returns set in. Rather, they should shift the allocation to the less effective medium so as to locate the firm on the steep region of the response curve for the less effective medium rather than stay on its flatter portion for the more effective medium. Consequently, as in proposition 1, the eventual budget allocation results in the optimal proportion β_1/β_2 (and not 100 % to the most effective activity and zero to the less effective ones).

The standard advertising theory also investigated the role of carryover effects, which capture the long-term effects of advertising. Naik and Raman (2003) showed that not only do managers need a larger total budget when carryover effects are large, but that they should increase spending on each of the communications activity proportionately so that the relative allocation remains *invariant* to the magnitude of the carryover effect. We summarize these findings as follows:

PROPOSITION 2: *In multimedia advertising, as the carryover effect increases, the total media budget increases; however, budget allocation does not depend on the carryover effect.*

To develop the intuition for this proposition, we observe that *the carryover effect enhances the long-term effectiveness of communications activities.* Specifically, if λ denotes the carryover effect, then the long-term effectiveness of each activity is given by $\beta_i/(1-\lambda)$, which exceeds the short-term effectiveness β_i (because λ is a positive fraction). Furthermore, the long-term effectiveness of each activity increases *proportionately* by the same factor, $(1-\lambda)^{-1}$. Hence the *relative* proportion β_1/β_2 must necessarily remain unchanged, keeping the budget allocation invariant to changes in the carryover effect.

Integrated Marketing Communications Framework

Managers should recognize that consumers combine the information they receive from various media whether or not the firm itself integrates those messages across media. To prevent consumers from integrating them inconsistently, they should take charge of this process, and this *proactive* view of IMC represents the new approach to media planning (see Schultz and Pilotta 2004 for further details). The overriding purpose of IMC is to manage all marketing activities that impact sales, profits, and brand equity.

---

[2] We thank Prof. Kusum Ailawadi for leading us to this inquiry.

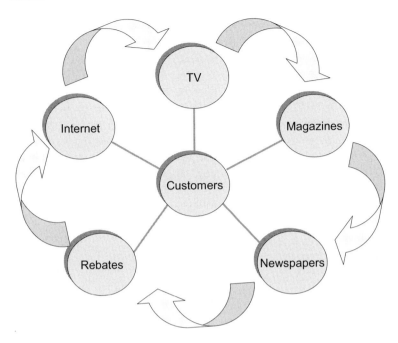

Fig. 2. Integrated Marketing Communications Model

Figure 2 presents the IMC model that emphasizes the role of joint effects or *synergies* (shown by the curved arrows) generated due to the orchestration of multiple activities. In comparison to Figure 1, the concept of IMC is much more than simply using multiple media concurrently as in the standard multimedia model, where the effectiveness of each activity does *not* depend upon any other activity. In contrast, the major difference in the IMC model is that the effectiveness of *each* activity depends upon *all other* communications activities used by the firm.

Another difference between the IMC model and standard models is as follows. Traditional marketing employs a "push" strategy, where communications between a firm and its consumers are designed to promote goods that the firm created and desired to sell. IMC employs both the push and pull approaches. Retailers like Macy's or Nordstrom are examples of companies that attempt to apply the IMC approach by incorporating feedback so that their products and communications can be adjusted to meet consumers' needs. Given this IMC framework, a number of fundamental questions arise:

- Do synergies between media (e.g., television and print advertising) exist in the marketplace?

- How should synergies be estimated using readily available market data?

- How should synergy affect managers' decision about the size of media budget?

- If synergy increases or decreases, how should managers alter the budget allocation?

- How does synergy moderate the effects of advertising carryover on the budget and its allocation?

- Are there catalytic effects of synergy?

- How can managers create synergies and reduce wearout?

- Is there an alternative perspective to investigate the IMC phenomenon?

We address all these issues in turn.

Measurement of Synergy

One of the earliest studies measuring media synergy was conducted by a consortium of radio network companies, who sampled 500 adults, ages 20-44, across 10 locations in the United Kingdom. The main findings indicated that 73% of the participants remembered prime visual elements of TV ads upon hearing radio commercials. In addition, 57% re-lived the TV ads while listening to the radio advertisement. Thus, radio ads reinforced the imagery created by TV commercials, resulting in synergy between television and radio advertising (for further details, see Radio Advertising Bureau at www.rab.co.uk).

Although the estimation of cross-media synergy remained elusive, standard advertising models attempted it by specifying brand sales a *response function* of managers' current actions and past outcomes; for example, $S_t = \beta_0 + \beta_1 u_{1t} + \beta_2 u_{2t} + \lambda S_{t-1} + \varepsilon_t$. Gatignon and Hanssens (1987) pioneered the distinction between a response function and *process functions*, which explain how effectiveness parameters themselves depend on managers' actions. In other words, managerial actions affect not only market outcomes (e.g., sales, share), but also the *effectiveness* of marketing activities. For example, suppose that radio and TV advertising enhance each other's effectiveness. Such effects are captured in the process function (say), $\beta_1 = \beta_1' + \kappa u_2$, which suggests that the spending u_2 increases the effectiveness β_1 in the presence of positive synergy ($\kappa > 0$). When we substitute this process function into the above response function, we obtain the overall model, $S_t = \beta_0 + \beta_1' u_{1t} + \beta_2 u_{2t} + \kappa u_{1t} \times u_{2t} + \lambda S_{t-1} + \varepsilon_t$, thus introducing an interaction term that captures synergy.

We note that this notion of process function is deterministic and static (i.e., without the error terms or lagged βs). Even so, many challenges arise in applying the ordinary least squares (OLS) or related statistical approaches to estimate the parameter for synergy, κ. These challenges arise because OLS and related statistical approaches ignore inter-temporal dependence and non-stationarity in the observed sales process, thereby resulting in biased parameter estimates and incorrect budget determination.

Advanced estimation techniques overcame these challenges and facilitated the *joint* estimation of both response and process functions. Specifically, applying Wiener-Kalman filtering theory, Naik and Raman (2003) developed an appropriate method and demonstrated its application by analyzing the sales and advertising data for Dockers® brand of Khaki trousers in the fashion apparels market. They furnished strong evidence for the presence of synergy between television and print advertising. Furthermore, they generalized this approach to estimate a general nonlinear, non-stationary, dynamic and stochastic process functions (for details, see Naik and Raman 2003, p. 384). Thus, managers can now implement this Kalman filter-based approach to estimate and infer the existence of synergy by using data on retail sales and multimedia advertising (see Schultz 2004).

Multimedia Budgeting in the Presence of Synergy

After managers establish the existence of synergy in their markets, how should they determine the multimedia budget? Applying optimal control theory, Naik and Raman (2003) showed that, in dynamic equilibrium, the total budget should be increased to capitalize media synergies. We present this normative result as,

PROPOSITION 3: *As synergy increases, managers should increase the total media budget.*

This proposition addresses the age-old issue of whether or not managers overspend, i.e., actual expenditure exceeds the optimal budget. Specifically, they show that the literature seems to be over-stating this assertion within the context of IMC. Because previous response models have ignored synergy, the optimal budget is actually understated. Hence, what *appears* to be overspending would represent an appropriate spending level once we account for synergy among multiple media. Thus, overspending is likely to be smaller when the total budget reflects the objectives of orchestrating the communications mix.

It is important to recognize that managers should not simply spend additional money to "do more of the same thing." Rather, the increased budget should be utilized to create synergies between activities (see section 4.6 for a suggestion). The resulting synergies then enhance both short- and long-term effectiveness of marketing activities.

Multimedia Allocation in the Presence of Synergy

Next we note the important finding that budget allocation is *qualitatively* different in the presence of synergy, requiring managers to act *differently* when implementing IMC. Based on Naik and Raman (2003), we state how synergy alters the budget allocation:

PROPOSITION 4: *As synergy increases, managers should decrease (increase) the proportion of media budget allocated to the more (less) effective communications activity. If the various activities are equally effective, managers should allocate the media budget equally among them regardless of the magnitude of synergy.*

The counter-intuitive nature of this result is its striking feature. To understand the gist of this result, suppose that two activities have unequal effectiveness (say, $\beta_1 > \beta_2$). Then, in the absence of synergy ($\kappa = 0$), the optimal spending on an activity depends only on its own effectiveness; hence, a larger amount is allocated to the more effective activity (see proposition 1). However, in the presence of synergy ($\kappa \neq 0$), optimal spending depends not only on its own effectiveness, but also on the spending level for the *other* activity. Consequently, as synergy increases, marginal spending on an activity increases at a rate proportional to the spending level for the other activity. Hence, optimal spending on the more effective activity increases slowly, relative to the increase in the optimal spending on the less effective activity. Thus, the proportion of budget allocated to the *more* effective activity *decreases* as synergy increases.

If the two activities are equally effective, then the optimal spending levels on both of them are equal. Furthermore, as synergy increases, marginal spending on each of them increases at the *same* rate. Hence, the optimal allocation ratio remains constant at fifty percent, regardless of the increase or decrease in synergy.

Advertising Carryover Effect in the Presence of Synergy

We describe how synergy moderates the carryover effect in the next two propositions:

PROPOSITION 5 (BUDGET): *As the carryover effect increases, managers should increase the media budget; the rate of increase in media budget increases as synergy increases.*

PROPOSITION 6 (ALLOCATION): *In contrast to proposition 2, budget allocation depends on the carryover effect in the presence of synergy. Furthermore, as carryover increases (decreases), managers should decrease (increase) the proportion of budget allocated to the more (less) effective activity.*

Based on propositions 2 and 6, managers should act differently: absent synergy, they should allocate the budget to a variety of activities in simple proportion to the relative effectiveness and regardless of the carryover effect; when synergy is present, the allocation should incorporate the information on the magnitude of the carryover effect.

Catalytic Effects of Synergy

Does synergy introduce any fundamentally new advertising effect? Yes, since all media are not alike, managers can capitalize on the "catalytic effects" of ancillary activities. For example, BMW used product placement in James Bond movies, which may not have increased sales of BMW, but made its TV and print advertising more effective. Or Mini Cooper used the real movie, *The Italian Job*, to build its brand image. In other words, managers should use activities such as event sponsorship, free-samples and collaterals, in-transit advertising or merchandising because these ancillary activities enhance the effectiveness of primary activities through synergistic interactions.

This new effect — the *catalytic effect of ancillary activities* — can be defined as follows: a marketing activity is a catalyst if it has negligible direct effect on sales, but exhibits substantial synergies with other activities. For catalytic activities, Raman and Naik (2004) prove the

PROPOSITION 7: *Managers should allocate a non-zero budget to the catalytic activity even if it is completely ineffective.*

We note that, based on proposition 1, managers should allocate the total budget to various media in proportion to their relative effectiveness, and so the completely ineffective activity should not even be considered in the communications mix. In contrast to this traditional way of thinking, managers who seek to orchestrate an IMC program benefit from not only the direct effects, but also the indirect effects of various activities. Therefore, they should *not* eliminate spending on an ineffective activity when it enhances the effectiveness of other activities due to its catalytic properties. Thus, managers should consider the catalytic role of various activities to fully benefit from the synergies generated within IMC contexts.

How Can Managers Create Synergies?

Keller (2003, p. 325) suggests "mixing and matching" communications such that weaknesses in one medium can be compensated by the strengths of another medium. This idea is reinforced by Edell and Keller (1999), who show that a coordinated television and print media strategy led to greater processing and improved memory performance than either television or print media alone. The limited amount of information in TV ads is complemented by the elaboration in a print advertisement, while the limited attention-getting nature of the print medium is complemented via the interest aroused by the television. Thus, by mixing and matching modalities, managers can create synergies among various activities in the communications mix. We encourage further research to discover other mechanisms for building synergies.

Synergy Versus Wearout

The phenomenon of wearout refers to the decline in ad effectiveness (i.e., drop in βs). The marketing literature identifies two types of ad wearout: copy wearout and repetition wearout (see Naik, Mantrala and Sawyer 1998). The former captures the decline in ad effectiveness over time, while the latter describes its decline due to repetitive exposure. Repeated exposure in the same medium produces wearout; to forestall it, an appropriate pulsing strategy needs to be discovered (for details, see Naik, Mantrala and Sawyer 1998). In contrast, *varied* exposures across *different* media can create synergies. A behavioral explanation, based on encoding variability hypothesis, suggests that consumers retrieve brand information more effectively when they encode such information via multiple cues from different media rather than the same cues from a single medium (see Unnava and Burnkrant 1991 for details). We encourage further research to find appropriate "media pulsation" strategies for generating synergies.

Hierarchical IMC?

Another perspective of IMC is that various communication activities move customers through distinct stages of decision process.[3] More specifically, let the decision process be as follows: need recognition ⇒ brand awareness ⇒ brand attitude ⇒ purchase intent ⇒ purchase ⇒ post-purchase evaluation. Then, consumers may be impacted such that activity A enhances need recognition; activity B builds awareness; activity C generates positive attitudes; and so on. The kernel of the idea is to determine whether and which activities facilitate consumers' movement across these hierarchical stages. Note that a "hierarchy" emerges because the later stages require consumers to transit through the earlier stages. To capture consumers' transition across these unobservable (i.e., hidden) stages, we need to apply hidden Markov modeling to formulate, solve, and estimate the resulting hierarchical IMC model. We can incorporate the central essence of this hierarchical notion in a dynamic IMC model by specifying an *upper triangular* transition probability matrix, which ensures the unidirectional flow across stages (e.g., a consumer cannot become "unaware" after having formed brand attitudes). To calibrate such hierarchical IMC models, Smith, Naik and Tsai (2005) have developed a new method that enables the joint estimation of the specific stages to be retained and the specific communications activities that would influence a consumer's transition. We encourage researchers to investigate this perspective of hierarchical IMC empirically.

While the above propositions and discussions advanced our understanding of synergy, we maintained a tacit assumption that the impact of marketing effort on sales is deterministic. When this assumption is untenable, for instance, in turbu-

---

[3] We thank Prof. Scott Neslin for this novel perspective.

lent, volatile markets where uncontrollable factors also may affect sales, we need to incorporate the role of uncertainty in the analyses. To this end, Raman and Naik (2004) generalized the deterministic IMC model by using the Wiener process to represent uncertainty in their continuous-time dynamic model.

Extending IMC to Uncertain Environments

Applying stochastic optimal control theory, Raman and Naik (2004) derived the optimal IMC program for uncertain markets. Below we present their main propositions and discuss the substantive implications.

PROPOSITION 8: *In uncertain markets, the total media budget increases as synergy increases. Furthermore, the proportion of budget allocated to the more (less) effective medium decreases (increases) as synergy increases.*

It is intriguing to find that propositions 3 and 4 in the absence of uncertainty are identical to the above one, seemingly implying that uncertainty plays no role! But jumping to such a conclusion is inaccurate because uncertainty directly affects sales evolution, thereby making the level and growth of sales less predictable in the future. In addition, uncertainty affects the variability in long-term profit, thereby increasing the downside risks of losses and bankruptcies. Thus, uncertainty has serious consequences on both sales and profit.

The proper interpretation of proposition 8, therefore, is that managers should *not alter* their decisions by increasing or decreasing budget in response to the effects of uncertainty on sales and profit. This finding clarifies the conflicting views prevalent in the existing practice. Specifically, advertising agencies advocate that managers should *increase* the media spending in response to demand shocks such as recessions. Whereas an empirical analysis of the national media spending data indicates that managers are likely to *decrease* their media budget during recessions. Resolving these conflicting views, Proposition 8 recommends *neither increasing nor decreasing the media spending, but sticking to the course of action in uncertain times.*

In sum, this proposition highlights the fact that "no action" on budget changes does not imply managerial "inaction," the former requiring knowledge of optimal decision-making under uncertainty, the discipline not to tinker with marketing budgets in the short term, and the commitment to building brands over the long term.

We next describe the effects of uncertainty on the profitability of IMC programs:

PROPOSITION 9: *In uncertain markets, the expected value of long-term profitability of the optimal IMC program increases as synergy increases.*

PROPOSITION 10: *In uncertain markets, the variability of long-term profitability of the optimal IMC program is unaffected by the magnitude of synergy.*

According to these propositions, managers should adopt an IMC perspective to increase the brand's profitability. That is, they should think of marketing communications activities not as a set of independent variables, but rather as a set of interconnected activities with potential synergies. By generating synergies, they not only increase the expected profitability in the long run, but they also keep profit variability unaltered. In other words, synergy imposes no tradeoff between profitability and variability. Thus, an IMC perspective raises profit but leaves its variability unaffected, and so it is prudent to build synergies by orchestrating the communications mix.

IMC and Smart Retailing

Multiplicity of media is a fact of life for modern consumers. They tend to multi-task, to browse the Internet while watching the television, or to read a magazine while listening to the radio. Hence a firm's messages from print, radio, television or the Internet should not conflict mutually. Consistency across multiple media requires managing everything involved in the process of communication, from strategic analysis through database management. However, in the realm of retailing, the role of IMC has received little attention. We believe a better understanding of IMC in the retailing context would benefit both retailers and researchers. To this end, we suggest research avenues to investigate the role of multiple channels of communications to be found in futuristic retailing context.

In existing retailing environments, a consumer visits the retail store to buy a basket of goods and, once inside the selected store, she encounters several competing brands in a product category to choose from. Inside the store, each brand in a product category has limited avenues to provide additional information to consumers to influence their purchase intention or willingness to pay (for more on consumer shopping behaviors see Uncles chapter in this book.). Consequently, branded goods advertise outside the store in mass media via television, print, radio, billboards or in-transit advertising. In such environments, the manufacturer follows the pull strategy (i.e., via mass advertising to build brand image) and the retailer follows the push strategy (e.g., point-of-sale support, coupons, promotions).

In future retailing environments, however, retailers have access to fascinating possibilities for communicating with consumers. For example, consider a personal shopping assistant (PSA), which is a touch-screen Tablet PC mounted on shopping carts. Think of it as "smart carts." It provides information to a consumer *while she shops in the store.* This information includes not just price, promotion, coupon availability, or in-store location of the item, but also inventory at home and preferences for any brands bought on previous shopping occasions. Indeed, the next generation PSA would include an intelligent guidance system for generating recommendation that's personalized for (and by) an individual shopper. If so, what customer-specific messages should the retailer offer to influence a consumer's intention to buy or willingness to pay? Do the retailer's messaging decisions amplify

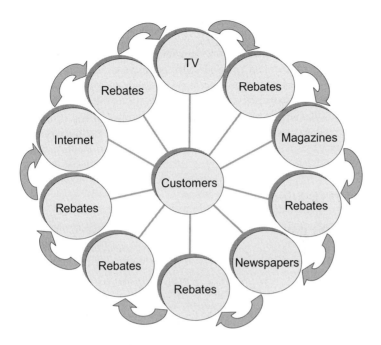

Fig. 3. IMC in Smart Retailing Environments

Legend: *TV = Television advertising*
          PSA = Personal shopping assistant
          EAD = Electronic advertising displays
          IT = Information terminals
          ESL = Electronic shelf labels
          RR = RFID-equipped refrigerators
          Mags = Magazine advertising
          News = Newspaper advertising

or attenuate the effectiveness of in-store individualized promotions (see, e.g., chapter by Gedenk, Neslin and Ailawadi in this book)? (Are there synergies with the out-of-store traffic or brand-building advertising? Does the retailer's ability to provide timely information to consumers inside the store increase brand-switching, thereby increasing the power of retailers relative to manufacturers (who employ out-of-store brand-building strategies)?

To address such issues and related implications for resource allocations, Figure 3 sketches a conceptual model that reveals potential synergies a retailer can build between various in-store communications channels — personal shopping assistant (PSA), electronic advertising displays (EAD), information terminals (IT), electronic shelf labels (ESL), RFID-equipped refrigerators (RR) — for sending messages to its customer franchise (see also Kalyanam, Lal and Wolfram in this book). The activities North-West of the 45° diagonal represent existing communication channels, which essentially build store traffic and mitigate competitive pressure from other retailers in town. In contrast, the activities on the South-East of the 45° diagonal represent new communication channels, which potentially identifies an individual customer and targets personalized communication packets. Thus, synergies can exist at two levels: those between in-store and out-of-store activities, and those within various in-store activities and within various out-of-store activities. We encourage further research to investigate these novel issues.

In conclusion, we predict that retailers of the 21st century will not only embrace emerging technologies like PSA, EAD, IT, ESL and RR, but also employ innovations based on more advanced technologies (e.g., nanotechnology) in the next decade. Such technologies cost substantial investment; the change of technology from the old to the new invokes the well-known biases of sunk costs; the psychological desire to hold on familiar technologies retards the adoption rate; and the painful tradeoffs implicit in replacing part of the workforce with automation is the hardest of all. Yet, every retailer will inevitably adopt new technologies, albeit some sooner than the others. For example, in the United States, the retailing giant Wal-Mart expects every carton and palette it receives to carry a radio identification tag (Feder 2003). Its top hundred suppliers are expected to adopt this technology soon, and the rest of its suppliers to do so by 2005. Indeed, the U.S. Department of Defense now requires its major suppliers to use RFID tags. As large buyers stipulate such requirements, manufacturers will comply, driving the real costs of technology down due to augmented scale and experience effects, thereby inviting additional retailers to embrace such technologies.

This adoption of computing and communications technology marks the dawn of smart retailing environments, thus realizing Weiser's (1991) vision of ubiquitous computing in marketing. A futuristic retailer, such as METRO Group's Future Store, would therefore possess an expanded repertoire of communications modalities for better understanding its consumers. More advanced sensing and recognition devices would fuel an explosive growth of interactive and highly distributed communications. Consequently, retailers' real challenges will be to orchestrate the resulting marketing communications across multiple modalities without overwhelming consumers' limited attention spans. We hope this literature review and the proposed IMC framework provide an impetus for both retailers and researchers to implement managerially relevant experiments and establish the existence of synergies in retail markets.

References

Edell, Julie A. and Kevin L. Keller (1999), Analyzing Media Interactions: The Effects of Coordinated TV-Print Advertising, MSI Report No. 99-120.

Feder, Barnaby J. (2003), Wal-Mart Plan Could Cost Suppliers Millions, New York Times, November 10, 2003.

Gatignon, Hubert and Dominique M. Hanssens (1987), Modeling Marketing Interactions with Application to Salesforce Effectiveness, Journal of Marketing Research, 24 (3), 247-257.

Keller, Kevin L. (2003), Strategic Brand Management, 2nd edition, Prentice Hall: Upper Saddle River, New Jersey.

Naik, Prasad A. and Raman, Kalyan (2003), Understanding the Impact of Synergy in Multimedia Communications, Journal of Marketing Research, Vol. 40 (November), pp. 375-388.

Naik, Prasad A., Murali K. Mantrala, and Alan Sawyer (1998), Planning Pulsing Media Schedules in the Presence of Dynamic Advertising Quality, Marketing Science, 17 (3) 214-235.

Raman, Kalyan and Naik, Prasad A. (2004), Long-Term Profit Impact of Integrated Marketing Communications Program, Review of Marketing Science, Vol. 2, Article 8, http://www.bepress.com/romsjournal/vol2/iss1/art8.

Schultz, Don E. (2004), Two Profs Prove Real Value of Media Integration, Marketing News, Vol. 38, Issue 1, pp. 6-7.

Schultz, Don E. and Pilotta, Joseph J. (2004), Developing the Foundation for a New Approach to Understanding How Media Advertising Works, 3rd Annual ESOMAR/ARF World Audience Measurement Conference, June 13-18, Geneva.

Schultz, Don E., Tannenbaum, Stanley I., and Lauterborn, Robert F. (1993), Integrated Marketing Communications: Putting It Together & Making It Work. NTC Books: Lincolnwood.

Smith, Aaron, Naik, Prasad A., and Tsai, Chih-Ling (2005), Markov-switching model selection using Kullback-Leibler divergence, Journal of Econometrics, forthcoming.

Unnava, H. Rao and R. Burnkrant (1991), Effects of Repeating Varied Ad Executions on Brand Name Memory, Journal of Marketing Research, 28 (4), 406-416.

Weiser, Mark (1991), The Computer for the 21st Century, Scientific American, September, pp. 94-100.

Professor Wayne D. Hoyer, PhD
University of Texas at Austin, USA

Wayne D. Hoyer holds the James L. Bayless/William S. Farish Fund Chair for Free Enterprise in the Department of Marketing at the McCombs School of Business at the University of Texas at Austin. Dr. Hoyer's research interests include consumer decision making, customer insight and customer relationship management, and advertising information processing (including miscomprehension and humor). Dr. Hoyer has published over 60 articles in top marketing journals and other marketing forums. He is co-author with Deborah MacInnis of a textbook on consumer behavior.

Professor Arnd Huchzermeier, PhD
WHU, Germany

Arnd Huchzermeier holds the Chair of Production Management at WHU's Otto-Beisheim Graduate School of Management in Vallendar, Germany. Before this he held an appointment at the University of Chicago after receiving his PhD from the Wharton School. His research focuses on supply chain management. In 2003, he won both the ISMS prize of the Marketing Science Institute and the MSSIP Award from the European Association of Operations Research Societies. In 2002, he received INFORMS' Franz Edelman Finalist Award. He has published in various journals, including *Management Science*, *Manufacturing & Service Operations Management*, *Marketing Science*, and *Operations Research*.

Ananth V. Iyer, PhD
Purdue University, USA

Ananth Iyer holds the Susan Bulkeley Butler Chair in Operations Management and is Director of the Global Supply Chain Management Initiative at the Krannert School of Management, Purdue University. He was on the faculty at the University of Chicago from 1987 to 1996. He received a PhD in Industrial and Systems Engineering from Georgia Tech. His research interests in supply chain management include contracts, customer promotion impact in the grocery industry, quick response in the apparel industry, and spare parts management and procurement issues in the global auto industry. He was the President of the INFORMS MSOM Society from 2002 to 2003.

Professor Paul Jackson, MBA

University of Coventry, UK

Paul Jackson is the Principal Lecturer in Strategy at the University of Coventry, United Kingdom. He is also the manager of the MBA programs for part-time students. Prior to his appointment to the University of Coventry, he worked for Marks and Spencer plc, where he was a senior manager in IT & Logistics. Before this he was a store director for many years and also managed a large distribution center. His primary research interests include failure of organizations, and overseas retail operations. He works as a consultant to a number of differing organizations, mainly in the area of change and logistics management.

Professor Kirthi Kalyanam, PhD

Retail Management Institute, Santa Clara University, USA

Dr. Kalyanam is the J.C. Penney Research Professor, Director of Internet Retailing in the Retail Management Institute at Santa Clara University. He was a visiting Professor at the Graduate School of Business at Stanford University. He also served as Senior Vice President and Chief Marketing Officer of SpinCircuit Inc. Kirthi's PhD is from Purdue University. His areas of expertise include Internet Marketing, eCommerce, and Retailing & Channel Marketing. His most recent article, entitled: "When Is the New What," was featured in the HBR list of Breakthrough Ideas for 2005. Kirthi is the co-author of *Internet Marketing and eCommerce*, forthcoming from ITP Southwestern.

Professor Sanjay Kumar Kar, PhD (Pursuing)

Institute of Petroleum Management, Gandhinagar, India and
Pandit Deendayal University, India

Sanjay Kumar Kar is an assistant professor at the Institute of Petroleum Management in Gandhinagar and an honorary visiting professor at the National Institute of Fashion Technology in Delhi. Previously, he was an academic associate at the Indian Institute of Management in Ahmedabad. He is presently conducting doctoral research at Utkal University, India. He has published articles in Indian Retail Review, Business Perspective, and Pranjana. His current research focuses on category management, retail format mix, and the distribution of natural gas. He also provides training and development programs for executives in the oil and gas industry.

Professor Ram Krishnan, PhD
University of Miami, USA

Professor R. Krishnan (PhD Virginia Tech) is Research Professor of Marketing at the University of Miami. He was previously Director of Graduate Programs and Professor of Marketing at Cal Poly, San Luis Obispo. Professor Krishnan's research has appeared in a number of professional and scholarly journals, including the Journal of Marketing, Sloan Management Review, California Management Review and Journal of Retailing. He has received many distinguished teaching awards, including the UM-EMBA Excellence in Teaching Award, the Δ Σ Π Teacher Award, the College of Business Teacher Award, and the Alumni Award for Best Teaching. Dr. Krishnan is the author of Marketing Research, a college textbook being revised for 2006 release.

Professor Rajiv Lal, PhD
Harvard Business School, USA

Rajiv Lal is the Stanley Roth, Sr. Professor of Retailing at Harvard Business School. He is responsible for the retailing curriculum and co-chairs the Senior Executive Seminar for Retailers and Suppliers. Lal has worked on research and/or consulting projects with a range of companies, such as Staples, Citizens Bank, Nordstrom, Microsoft, Kellogg, Sara Lee D/E, Novartis Pharmaceuticals, Stride Rite Corporation, Oliver Wyman and Company, Fleming Companies, Callaway Golf Company, and Omnitel Italia, on strategy and implementation. Lal's current research highlights building and sustaining customer-centric organizations.

Professor Roy Larke, PhD
ESADE School of Business, Barcelona, Spain, and UMDS Kobe, Japan

Professor Roy Larke is a leading expert on Japanese marketing and consumer behavior. He is the author of numerous articles about Japanese retailing and the distribution system and consumer behavior in Japan, and he is currently editor-in-chief of *Japan Consuming Magazine*. He is the author of *Japanese Retailing*, published by Routledge in 1994, and has written two books about training methodology in Japanese, as well as the Japan Distribution Statistics Handbook. In addition to academic work, he consults for a wide range of companies, particularly those looking to enter the Japanese market. He currently holds posts at the University of Marketing & Distribution Sciences in Kobe and at ESADE in Barcelona.

Professor Michael Levy, PhD
Babson College, Massachusetts, USA

Michael Levy is the Charles Clarke Reynolds Professor of Marketing at Babson College and a co-editor of *Journal of Retailing*. His stream of research includes retailing, business logistics, financial retailing strategy, pricing, and sales management. He has published in such journals as Journal of Retailing, Journal of Marketing, and Journal of Marketing Research and serves on several editorial boards. He is also co-author of 5th edn (McGraw-Hill/Irwin, 2005). Dr. Levy has previously taught at Southern Methodist University and served as Professor and Chair of the Marketing Department at the University of Miami.

Professor Dr. Thorsten Litfin
University of Applied Sciences Osnabrueck, Germany

Thorsten Litfin is Professor of Marketing, Service, and Innovation Management at the University of Applied Sciences of Osnabrueck, Germany. Prior to being appointed to his post at the University of Applied Sciences he worked for three years as a Senior Consultant for Simon Kucher & Partners Strategy & Marketing Consultants. In his projects he has focused on the development of product and pricing strategies for innovative products. Thorsten received his PhD from the University of Kiel. His primary research interests include acceptance of new products, options to enhance the launch of new products, customer loyalty programs, pricing/bundling strategies, and adoption/diffusion models.

Julia Merkel
Head of Corporate Executive Development, METRO AG, Germany

Julia Merkel is Head of Corporate Executive Development at METRO AG, Duesseldorf, Germany. She studied Business Administration at the BA Heidenheim, Germany, and then worked as an Assistant Buyer for Castorama, Lyon, France and held various HR positions at OBI Headquarters, Wermelskirchen, Germany before becoming Managing Director, HR & Administration, at OBI Headquarters. In 1992 and 1993 she was project coordinator for an international cooperation at Mitsukoshi Ltd., Warehouses, Tokyo, Japan.

Zygmunt Mierdorf, MBA
Chief Information Officer METRO AG, Germany

Zygmunt Mierdorf is a member of the Management Board and Chief HR Officer of the METRO Group. Mr. Mierdorf is responsible for the company's IT, e-business, human resources, and real estate divisions. Mr. Mierdorf is also an adviser for several different sales lines. He joined the METRO Group in 1991 and held several different executive positions before becoming a member of the Management Board in 1999. Prior to joining the METRO Group, Mr. Mierdorf had been Administrative Managing Director at Betrix Cosmetics, Group Chief Financial Officer and Chairman of the LRE Inc. Group, and CFO for Black & Decker, Germany. He holds an MBA.

Professor Detra Y. Montoya, PhD
University of Washington, USA

Detra Y. Montoya is an Assistant Professor of Marketing at the University of Washington in Seattle, Washington. Detra received her PhD from Arizona State University. Prior to entering the doctoral program, she spent over five years in Customer Business Development and Multicultural Marketing with Procter & Gamble. Her primary research interests include consumer preferences for product systems, retailer strategies, retail shelf management initiatives, and multicultural consumer behavior. She received the 2003 Center for Services Leadership Doctoral Research Grant and 2004 AMA Valuing Diversity PhD scholarship.

Professor Jeanne Munger, PhD
University of Southern Maine, USA

Professor Jeanne Munger is an Associate Professor at University of Southern Maine, and has held teaching positions at The Ohio State University and Clarkson University. She has won numerous teaching awards and is listed in *Who's Who Among America's Teachers*. Her primary research interests include retailing strategy, customer satisfaction and loyalty in e-tailing, and promotional pricing. She has also worked as a consulting associate for Management Horizons and later as a research associate and strategic planner for F&R Lazarus. She has published articles in journals such as *Psychology & Marketing, Journal of Business-to-Business Marketing,* and *Journal of Product & Brand Management.* She has also developed executive training programs in marketing, retailing, and effective marketing communications and service quality.

Professor Prasad A. Naik, PhD
University of California Davis, USA

Prasad A. Naik is Professor of Marketing and Chancellor's Fellow at the University of California Davis. He develops novel models and methods to improve the practice of marketing. He publishes in top journals such as *Journal of Marketing Research, Marketing Science, Journal of Econometrics, Biometrika, Journal of the Royal Statistical Society,* and *JASA.* He has received an AMS Doctoral Dissertation Award and a Frank M. Bass Award. He was selected for MSI's Young Scholars Program, the AMA's Doctoral Consortium Faculty, and Marquis' *Who's Who in America* and *Who's Who in the World.*

Professor Scott A. Neslin, PhD
Amos Tuck School, Dartmouth College, USA

Scott A. Neslin is the Albert Wesley Fry Professor of Marketing at the Amos Tuck School of Business Administration, Dartmouth College. He has been at the Tuck School since completing his PhD at the Sloan School of Management, MIT in 1978. He has served as a Visiting Scholar at the School of Management, Yale University (1989-1990) and at the Teradata/Duke CRM Center located at the Fuqua School of Management, Duke University (2002). His primary research interests include sales promotion, database marketing, and market response models. He is on the editorial boards of the *Journal of Marketing Research*, the *Journal of Marketing*, and *Marketing Letters* and is an Area Editor for *Marketing Science.*

Cirk Sören Ott
Gruppe Nymphenburg, Germany

Since 2007, Cirk Sören Ott is head of POS and Consumer Research at Gruppe Nymphenburg. Sören has been working with TNS Infratest for 10 years. He was initially responsible for retail research, before moving to the consumer sector. He is now Head of Business Development at TNS Infratest, Germany. He has been concentrating on key clients and key accounts (in the areas of food, beverage, nonfood and retail) and on consulting work over a wide range of market research methods. He has wide experience of working with retailers and on questions of channel and brand management both locally and globally. Sören studied Economies in Bamberg and graduated in 1995.

Dr. Doreén Pick
Free University, Berlin, Germany

Doreén Pick received a PhD in Marketing from the University of Muenster, Germany in 2008. After her apprenticeship in banking from 1993 to 1995, she spent two more years working in public relations and marketing for a bank. She studied in Germany and Italy from 1996 to 2002, and spent more than 2 years working in different positions for a large department store retailer in Essen and a year as a strategy consultant in Berlin. Since May 2009 she is working as an Assistant Professor at the Free University of Berlin. Her special research interests are in the field of service management, customer relationship management, business-to-business marketing and retailing.

Professor Kalyan Raman, PhD
Medill School, Northwestern University, USA

Kalyan Raman is Professor of Marketing at Northwestern University, Medill IMC, Evanston, IL, USA. He was previously at Loughborough University, UK, University of Michigan Flint, University of Florida, AT&T Bell Labs, and Auburn University. He obtained his PhD in Marketing from the University of Texas at Dallas and majored in Statistics at Purdue University. He has published articles in *Marketing Science*, *Management Science*, *Journal of Marketing Research*, *Journal of Consumer Research*, and other scholarly journals. He specializes in optimizing marketing decision making and has expertise in problems with long-term and uncertain consequences. He is currently working on marketing communications and marketing mix problems.

Professor Dr. Werner J. Reinartz
INSEAD, France and University of Cologne, Germany

Professor Werner Reinartz' research focuses are on CRM, retailing, and marketing strategy, and his work has been published in top academic marketing journals such as *Journal of Marketing*, *Journal of Marketing Research*, and *Journal of Consumer Research*, as well as in the applied practitioner literature exemplified by *Harvard Business Review* and *California Management Review*. His research on customer lifetime value has received major academic awards, such as the 2001 Don Lehmann Award and the 2004 MSI/Paul Root Award. He is a member of the editorial boards of *Journal of Marketing* and *Marketing Science*.

Professor Raj Sethuraman, PhD
Southern Methodist University in Dallas, USA

Dr. Raj Sethuraman is an associate professor of marketing at the Edwin L. Cox School of Business at Southern Methodist University in Dallas, USA. He received his PhD in marketing from Northwestern University. Dr. Sethuraman's research focuses on marketing mix, private labels, and channels of distribution. He has won many research awards, including the Davidson Award for the best paper in *Journal of Retailing* (second place) and the Little Award for the best paper in *Management Science*. He serves on multiple editorial boards and consults in the area of marketing research, brand management, and competitive retailing strategy.

Professor Venkatesh Shankar, PhD
Texas A&M University, USA

Venkatesh (Venky) Shankar is Professor of Marketing and Coleman Chair in Marketing at the Texas A&M University. He focuses on Retailing, Pricing, Digital Business, Competitive Strategy, and New Product Development. Venky has a Ph.D. in Marketing from Northwestern University. He is Co-Editor of the Journal of Interactive Marketing and Associate Editor of Management Science. He is a winner of the Direct Marketing Educational Foundation's Robert Clarke Outstanding Educator Award and a three-time winner of the Krowe Award for Teaching. He has consulting or executive training experience with organizations such as Ahold, Allstate Insurance, GlaxoSmithKline, Hewlett Packard, IBM, Intel, Marriott International, PepsiCo, Philips, and Volvo.

Professor Piyush Kumar Sinha, PhD
Indian Institute of Management Ahmedabad (IIMA), India

Piyush Kumar Sinha is a Professor of Marketing at Indian Institute of Management Ahmedabad (IIMA), India. He is also the Chairperson of the Centre for Retailing at IIMA. Before IIMA, he has been faculty at IIM Bangalore, XIMB and Dean at MICA. Piyush holds a Ph.D. in marketing. His current research interests are in the areas of retailing and consumer behaviour, especially in format and store choice, loyalty programmes, petroleum retailing. He is on the editorial board of *International Journal of Applied Decision Sciences* and the Resident Editor for *AMS Review*. Between 1995 and 1999, Piyush worked as marketing manager for a utility and an FMCG company. He lives in Ahmedabad with his wife Jyotsana and daughters, Aakriti and Aparna.

Professor Dr. Hermann Simon
SIMON ◆ KUCHER & PARTNERS Strategy & Marketing Consultants, Germany

Hermann Simon is founder and chairman of SIMON ◆ KUCHER & PARTNERS Strategy & Marketing Consultants. He is a leading strategy, marketing, and pricing expert and the author of more than 30 books, including the world bestsellers *Hidden Champions*, *Power Pricing*, and *Think!*. He is a director of several corporations and serves on the boards of trustees of several foundations. In his "first" life Simon was Professor for Management Science and Marketing at the Universities of Mainz and Bielefeld and Visiting Professor at numerous institutions, including Harvard Business School, Stanford University, INSEAD, and MIT. He is a Past-President of the European Marketing Academy and has been on the editorial boards of various scientific journals.

Professor Dr. Laurens Sloot
University of Groningen, The Netherlands

Dr. Laurens Sloot is an Associate Professor at the Department of Marketing, Faculty of Economics, University of Groningen. He is also founder and director of the EFMI Business School. This business school focusses on emerging topics in the food industry. His primary research interests are retail strategy, assortment management, new product introductions, private labels and shopping behavior. His publications have appeared in many trade journals as well as academic journals such as *Journal of Marketing Research* and *Journal of Retailing*.

Peter Sonneck
TNS Infratest, Germany

Peter Sonneck is Research Consultant at TNS Infratest, Bielefeld. As an expert on international studies he focuses on both national and international surveys within the retail sector, and also advises on international key accounts. Before he joined the company five years ago he gained experience in other market research institutes. Peter studied Sociology in Konstanz and Bielefeld and graduated in 1993. His primary research interests are customer segmentation and shopper research. In his spare time he practices aquatic sports and enjoys being with his family.

Professor Mark D. Uncles, PhD
University of New South Wales, Australia

Mark Uncles, BSc, PhD, is Professor of Marketing, School of Marketing, University of New South Wales (UNSW). His research interests include: buyer behavior, store patronage, loyalty-building initiatives, and cross-country comparisons. Publications have appeared in international journals such as: *Sloan Management Review*; *Marketing Science*; *Journal of Retailing*; *Journal of Advertising Research*; *International Journal of Research in Marketing*; *Journal of Business Research*; and *European Journal of Marketing*. He is on the editorial boards of seven journals, co-editor of the *Australasian Marketing Journal*, and co-author of *The New Penguin Dictionary of Business* (Penguin Books).

Professor Vadlamani Ravi, PhD
IDRBT, Hyderabad, India

Dr. Vadlamani Ravi is an Assistant Professor at the Institute for Development and Research in Banking Technology, Hyderabad. He obtained his PhD from Osmania University, Hyderabad. Prior to joining IDRBT he taught knowledge engineering and was engaged in research on fuzzy systems, neural networks, soft computing, and machine learning at the National University of Singapore. He has published in various international and national journals and is a referee for several international journals, including *Applied Intelligence, Computers and Operations Research, Asia-Pacific Journal of Operational Research,* and *Indian Journal of Engineering and Material Sciences.*

Professor Dr. Peter C. Verhoef
University of Groningen, The Netherlands

Peter Verhoef is Professor of Customer-based Marketing in the Department of Marketing, Faculty of Economics, University of Groningen, The Netherlands. He obtained his PhD at the School of Economics, Erasmus University Rotterdam. His research interests concern customer relationship management, customer loyalty, multi-channel issues, category management, and buying behavior in the specific case of organic products. His publications have appeared (or will appear) in such journals as *Journal of Marketing, Journal of Marketing Research, Marketing Science, Marketing Letters, Journal of Consumer Psychology, Journal of the Academy of Marketing Science,* and *Journal of Retailing.*

Dr. Andreas von der Gathen
SIMON ♦ KUCHER & PARTNERS Strategy & Marketing Consultants, Germany

Dr. Andreas von der Gathen is a Partner with SIMON ♦ KU-CHER & PARTNERS Strategy & Marketing Consultants in Bonn. He is a specialist in the consumer goods industry and retailing, having carried out projects dealing with price and allowance optimization, the development of marketing and brand strategies, and the valuation of brands, for example. Andreas von der Gathen received his PhD from the University of Bochum. He works as a lecturer with IIR, Management Circle, and Management Forum and holds a teaching position in controlling at the University of applied science for Economics and Management (FOM). He is the author of several books and articles.

Professor Barton A. Weitz, PhD
University of Florida, USA

Barton Weitz holds the JCPenney Eminent Scholar Chair and is Executive Director of the Miller Center for Retailing Education and Research at the University of Florida. Professor Weitz was formerly Chair of the American Marketing Association, a member of the Board of the National Retail Federations, and editor of the *Journal of Marketing Research*. He received the AMA/Irwin Distinguished Marketing Educator Award for his lifetime contribution to the discipline of marketing. Professor Weitz is the author of *Retailing Management*, the most widely retailing textbook in this discipline. His research has been honored with two Louis Stern awards and with the Paul Root award for papers making the most significant research contributions.

Mary Brett Whitfield, MBA
Retail Forward, Inc., USA

Mary Brett Whitfield is the director of the Retail Forward Intelligence System™. She oversees the development of more than 50 research publications a year on a variety of topics in the retail industry. Whitfield is a regular contributor to the program, writing about consumer shopping behavior, soft goods retailing and e-retailing. She has more than 12 years of consulting experience with retailers and consumer products companies and four years of experience with retail companies in market research, strategic planning, and sales development roles. Her consulting specialties include industry and company analysis, competitive positioning, and primary consumer research.

Dr. Gerd Wolfram

MGI METRO Group Information Technology GmbH, Germany

Dr. Gerd Wolfram is Head of the CIO-Office of METRO Group. In his last position as Managing Director of MGI METRO Group Information Technology GmbH, he also was Executive Project Manager of the METRO Group Future Store Initiative, a project he is still responsible for today. In the well-known Future Store in Tönisvorst innovative retail technologies and systems are tested in real-live environment. Dr. Gerd Wolfram received a PhD from the University of Cologne. His primary interests are in SW development, networks, and new technologies such as RFID. Furthermore, he is member of national and international committees and working groups (EPCglobal, GCI, GS1 Germany and IKT).